WTO DOMESTIC REGULATION AND SERVICES TRADE

Domestic regulation of services sectors has a significant impact on services trade liberalization, which is why General Agreement on Trade in Services (GATS) disciplines are negotiated in the WTO. With the help of analyses and case studies from academics, regulators and trade experts, this book explores the scope and limits of WTO legal principles to promote domestic regulatory reform. Case studies discuss country-specific challenges and experiences of regulating important service sectors, such as finance, telecommunications, distribution, legal, education, health, postal and logistics services, as well as the role of regulatory impact assessments. The findings will interest trade officials, policy-makers, regulators, think tanks, and businesses concerned with the implications of domestic regulation on access to services markets, and with the opportunities for formulating trade disciplines in this area. It is also a useful resource for academics and students researching regulatory approaches and practices in services sectors.

AIK HOE LIM is a Counsellor in the Trade in Services Division of the WTO Secretariat, where he is Secretary to the body responsible for negotiating domestic regulation disciplines for services.

BART DE MEESTER is an Associate at the Geneva Office of Sidley Austin LLP. He previously worked as a Legal Affairs Officer at the Trade in Services Division of the WTO.

WTO DOMESTIC REGULATION AND SERVICES TRADE

Putting Principles into Practice

Edited by

AIK HOE LIM AND BART DE MEESTER

CAMBRIDGE
UNIVERSITY PRESS

CAMBRIDGE
UNIVERSITY PRESS

University Printing House, Cambridge CB2 8BS, United Kingdom

Published in the United States of America by Cambridge University Press, New York

Cambridge University Press is part of the University of Cambridge.

It furthers the University's mission by disseminating knowledge in the pursuit of education, learning and research at the highest international levels of excellence.

www.cambridge.org
Information on this title: www.cambridge.org/9781107062351

First published 2014

Printed in the United Kingdom by Clays, St Ives plc

A catalogue record for this publication is available from the British Library

Library of Congress Cataloguing in Publication data
WTO domestic regulation and services trade: putting principles into practice / edited by Aik Hoe Lim and Bart de Meester.
pages cm
Includes index.
ISBN 978-1-107-06235-1 (Hardback) – ISBN 978-1-107-63534-0 (Paperback) 1. World Trade Organization. 2. Foreign trade regulation. I. Lim, Aik Hoe, editor of compilation. II. De Meester, Bart, editor of compilation.
HF1385.W78326 2014
382′.92–dc23 2013040418

ISBN 978-1-107-06235-1 Hardback
ISBN 978-1-107-63534-0 Paperback

CONTENTS

CONTRIBUTORS

Editors

AIK HOE LIM is a Counsellor in the Trade in Services Division of the World Trade Organization (WTO) Secretariat, where he is Secretary to the body responsible for negotiating domestic regulation disciplines for services. He was formerly Deputy Head in the Cabinet of WTO Director-General Mike Moore and subsequently Counsellor to WTO Director-General Supachai Panitchpakdi. He was also Secretary/Adviser to the Director General's Consultative Group on the 'Future of the WTO', chaired by Peter Sutherland. He has published in various academic and professional journals on subjects related to services trade, regional trade agreements, education services and human rights. His publications include chapters for several books, such as 'The Future of Trade in Services for Developing Countries' in *Trade and Poverty Reduction in the Asia-Pacific Region* (2009).

BART DE MEESTER is an Associate at the Geneva Office of Sidley Austin LLP. Prior to joining Sidley, he worked as Legal Affairs Officer at the WTO Trade in Services Division. Before joining the WTO, he was researcher at the Institute for International Law of the University of Leuven. He wrote a Ph.D thesis on European and international liberalization of international trade in banking services as Scholar of the Fund for Scientific Research Flanders (FWO Vlaanderen). Bart has published several articles on international economic law, including in *Journal of International Economic Law*, *Journal of World Trade* and *European Business Law Review*. He co-authored a book with Prof. Dr Jan Wouters, providing a legal and institutional analysis of the WTO (2007). He has taught lectures on international economic law and European business law at both undergraduate and graduate level.

Contributors

YUSUF ATIKU ABDALLA is a Ugandan trade expert and senior official at the Bank of Uganda (the central bank of Uganda). He has extensive experience as a trade policy advisor, trade negotiator, economic analyst and researcher, spanning nearly three decades. Over the period, he has provided numerous technical guidance as well as economic and trade policy analyses for policy-makers at high levels in Uganda, including the Ministry of Trade, Industry and Co-operatives, the Bank of Uganda and the Ministry of Finance, Planning and Economic Development. Yusuf completed his undergraduate and graduate studies at Makerere University and the Department of Economics, University of Michigan, respectively. He has also undertaken and completed other postgraduate studies and training in trade policy; quantitative development economics; energy economics and management at the Harvard Kennedy School, the WTO Centre for Training and Technical Cooperation, the University of Warwick and the University of Pennsylvania, respectively. Yusuf's contribution to this book chapter was made when he was an official at the Research Department of the Bank of Uganda. He is currently on assignment as Regional Trade Policy Advisor at the Secretariat of the Common Market for Eastern and Southern Africa (COMESA) in Lusaka, Zambia, on posting by the Commonwealth Secretariat, London.

JOAN APECU works in the Council and Trade Negotiations Committee Division of the WTO. Prior to that (1999–2004), she served in several capacities in the Uganda Law Reform Commission, including as Senior Legal Officer in charge of Law Reform and Research, where she undertook law reform projects in several branches of law. Joan had an academic attachment with the Permanent Mission of Uganda to the United Nations and other International Organizations in Geneva. She has also been an assistant lecturer at the Faculty of Law at the Uganda Christian University Mukono in Uganda. She holds a Ph.D (magna cum laude) in international studies with a specialization in international trade law from the Graduate Institute of International and Development Studies, in Geneva; a Masters of Law (cum laude) in international trade and investment law from the University of Pretoria in collaboration with the Amsterdam Law School; a postgraduate diploma in legal practice from the Law Development Center in Uganda; and a Bachelor of Laws Degree from Makerere University, Uganda. She is an Advocate of the High Court of Uganda.

TOMER BROUDE is the Sylvan M. Cohen Chair in Law, Senior Lecturer at the Hebrew University of Jerusalem in the Faculty of Law and Department of International Relations and the Academic Director of the Minerva Center for Human Rights in Jerusalem. He has taught international law at various law schools in Israel, at the University of Toronto, Georgetown University Law Center, Johns Hopkins University's School of Advanced International Studies, Università Commerciale Luigi Bocconi in Milan, Gujarat National Law University and the Duke University–University of Hong Kong Asia–America Institute in Transnational Law. His fields of research are in international public law, with a focus on international economic law, international trade and the WTO. His publications include *International Governance in the WTO: Judicial Boundaries and Political Capitulation* (2004); *The Shifting Allocation of Authority in International Law: Considering Sovereignty, Supremacy and Subsidiarity* (2008); *The Politics of International Economic Law* (2010), and articles and essays that have appeared in the *Vanderbilt Law Review, Journal of World Trade, World Trade Review, Journal of International Economic Law, Journal of World Intellectual Property Law* and *Columbia Journal of Transnational Law*, among others. In 2007–2009, he served as Co-Chair of the International Economic Law Interest Group of the American Society of International Law; he is one of the founders of the Society of International Economic Law and a member of its Executive Council, and a Member of the International Law Association's Committee on the International Law of Sustainable Development.

RUPA CHANDA is Professor of Economics at the Indian Institute of Management (IIM) Bangalore. She has a Ph.D in economics from Columbia University and a Bachelor's Degree from Harvard University. Prior to joining IIM Bangalore, she was an economist at the International Monetary Fund. She has undertaken research and consulting assignments for many multilateral and Indian organizations. Her research interests include services trade and migration with a focus on information technology and health care, WTO issues and regional trade. She is a member of the Indian Commerce Ministry's Expert Group on Services and was formerly a member of the Indian Planning Commission's High Level Group on Services.

PANAGIOTIS DELIMATSIS is Associate Professor of Law and Co-Director of the Tilburg Law and Economics Center (TILEC) at Tilburg University, the Netherlands. Panagiotis has extensive research and teaching expertise in European and international economic law. His research focuses on regulatory diversity, domestic regulatory reform, good governance and institutional design, and the effects of unduly burdensome domestic regulations on factor mobility. Panagiotis has published extensively on international trade and European law issues in top refereed journals, including the *European Journal of International Law*, *Journal of International Economic Law*, *Common Market Law Review*, *Journal of World Trade* and *World Trade Review*. He is the author of *International Trade in Services and Domestic Regulations: Necessity, Transparency, and Regulatory Diversity* (2007). He also co-edited two collective volumes, the first on *The Prospects of International Trade Regulation* (2011) and the second on *Financial Services at the Crossroads: Implications for Supervision, Institutional Design and Trade* (2011).

HENRY GAO is Associate Professor of Law at Singapore Management University. With law degrees from three continents, he started his career as the first Chinese lawyer at the WTO Secretariat. Before moving to Singapore in late 2007, he taught law at University of Hong Kong, where he was also the Deputy Director of the East Asian International Economic Law and Policy Program. He has taught at the IELPO programme in Barcelona and the Academy of International Trade Law in Macau, and was the Academic Coordinator to the first Asia-Pacific Regional Trade Policy Course officially sponsored by the WTO. Widely published on issues relating to China and WTO, Henry has advised many national governments and the WTO, the World Bank, the Asian Development Bank, the Asia-Pacific Economic Cooperation and the Association of Southeast Asian Nations on trade issues. Henry sits on the Advisory Board of the WTO Chairs Programme, which was established by the WTO Secretariat in 2009 to promote research and teaching on WTO issues in leading universities around the world.

PRALOK GUPTA has a Ph.D in economics and social sciences from Indian Institute of Management (IIM) Bangalore. He is currently working at the Industrial Finance Corporation of India in a managerial position. He has been a visiting and full-time faculty member at various Indian institutions, including the Indo-German Chamber of Commerce. He has also served in the State Audit Services of the Government of Uttar Pradesh. He has been engaged in various consultancy and research projects for corporate bodies, the government and multilateral institutions. His research interests include international trade and related issues concerning poverty and the environment, economics of services trade, regulations, WTO-related issues and international migration.

TINNE HEREMANS holds a Master Degree in Law from the Katholieke Universiteit Leuven (2002) and LLM from Cornell Law School, United States (2004). From 2005 onwards, she pursued a doctoral dissertation at the Institute for European Law, KUL, on the basis of an FWO fellowship. She defended her dissertation on 'Professional Services in the EU Internal Market: Quality Regulation and Self-Regulation' in March 2010. In November 2009, she joined the European Affairs Programme at the Egmont Institute. Her current areas of research include institutional matters and single market policies.

LIOR HERMAN is a Lecturer at the Department of International Relations at the Hebrew University of Jerusalem. His fields of research include international and European political economy, with an emphasis on trade and services, regional integration, governance and international organizations.

KOICHI IWAI is Research Fellow at the Financial Services Agency, Government of Japan. Previously, he held positions at Nomura Securities, Mizuho Corporate Bank, and the Bank of Japan. He has a PhD in international public policy from Osaka University, a Master's Degree in applied finance from Macquarie University, and a Bachelor's Degree from the University of Tokyo.

MASAMICHI KONO is Vice Commissioner for International Affairs, the Financial Services Agency, Government of Japan (JFSA). In his current capacity, he represents the JFSA in various international bodies and meetings, and is responsible for coordinating policies relating to international affairs for the JFSA. He was also Chairman of the IOSCO Technical Committee from April 2011 to May 2012 and is now serving as Chairman of the IOSCO Board. He has had a long career in financial supervision and the regulation of financial services, both in Japan and in the international arena, since joining the public service in 1978. He was Secretary to the WTO Financial Services Committee between 1994 and 1999, and Counsellor of the WTO Trade in Services Division. He has also served for four years at the Organisation for Economic Co-operation and Development (OECD) Secretariat. Since 2005, he is Visiting Professor at

University of Hiroshima, Graduate School of Social Sciences (Finance Program). He is a graduate of Tokyo University.

MARKUS KRAJEWSKI is Professor of Public and International Law at the University of Erlangen-Nuremberg, Germany, and a visiting professor at the World Trade Institute, in Berne. Previously he held positions at the universities of Bremen and Potsdam and at King's College London. His research interests include international and European law, in particular constitutional and institutional issues of WTO law, trade in services, external relations of the European Union and the treatment of public services under European and international law. He is a regular consultant on international trade law for governmental institutions and non-governmental organizations. In the academic year 2009 to 2010 he directed a capacity-building project at the Faculty of Law of Addis Ababa University in support of Ethiopia's accession to the WTO. Since 2011, he has been a member of the Committee on International Trade Law of the International Law Association (ILA). Among his publications are *National Regulation and Trade Liberalization in Services* (2003), *Wirtschaftsvölkerrecht* (2009) and *Grundstrukturen des Rechts öffentlicher Dienstleistungen* (2011), as well as numerous articles in international journals and edited volumes.

NIK AHMAD KAMAL NIK MAHMOD, Ph.D (Aberdeen), is a Professor of Law at the Kulliyyah (Faculty) of Laws, International Islamic University, Malaysia and currently also the Deputy Rector (Student Affairs) of the university. His research interest is in industrial relations and labour law and recently he has ventured into research and publication in international trade law, biotechnology law and access to justice. He is a member of the WTO and Globalization research cluster of the International Islamic University Malaysia. He has served as a consultant for various projects for the Ministry of Higher Education Malaysia and has been actively involved in the promotion of teaching international labour standards in universities in the Asian region under the auspices of the ILO Bangkok office. That project gave birth to the Asian Society of Labour Law and he was the first President of the society from 2008 until 2010. His recent publications include, 'Biosafety Protocol, SPS Agreement and Export and Import Control on LMOs/GMOs', *International Trade Law and Policy* 7(2) (2008) and 'The WTO Rules Versus Multilateral Environmental Agreements: The Search for Reconciliation', *Macquarie Journal of International and Comparative Environmental Law* 5 (2008).

HAMID MAMDOUH is Director of the Trade in Services Division of the WTO. This division is responsible for servicing the WTO Council for Trade in Services, which oversees the implementation of the General Agreement on Trade in Services (GATS). The division is also responsible for providing legal, policy and technical advice to WTO members. Prior to that he was a Senior Counsellor in the Services Division. He had been the Secretary of the WTO Council for Trade in Services since the establishment of the WTO, in 1995. During that time, he was also responsible for all legal affairs in the area of trade in services. During the Uruguay Round negotiations, his responsibilities included legal matters relating to the drafting of GATS. His previous positions in the General Agreement on Tariffs and Trade (GATT) include: Assistant to the GATT Deputy Director-General and legal advisor on GATT dispute settlement. Prior to that he was a member of the diplomatic service of Egypt. As a career diplomat for commercial and economic affairs, his previous posts include: GATT representative of Egypt in Geneva, trade policy advisor to the Minister of Economy and Foreign Trade of Egypt, commercial attaché of the Egyptian Embassy in Canberra (Australia), and Egypt's representative to the United Nations Economic Commission for Africa in Addis Ababa (Ethiopia). As a trained lawyer legal matters have constituted an important part of his work throughout his career.

ANDREW MITCHELL is Professor at Melbourne Law School, Director of the Global Economic Law Network, Assistant Director of Research at the Melbourne School of Government, a member of the Indicative List of Panelists to hear WTO disputes, and a member of the Energy Charter Roster of Panelists. He has previously practised law with Allens Arthur Robinson (now Allens Linklaters) and consults for states, international organizations and the private sector. Andrew has taught law in Australia, Canada and the United States and is the recipient of three major current grants from the Australian Research Council and the Australian National Preventive Health Agency. He has published approximately 100 academic books and journals and is a Series Editor of the Oxford University Press International Economic Law Series, an Editorial Board Member of the *Journal of International Economic Law* and a General Editor on the *Journal of International Dispute Settlement*. He has law degrees from Melbourne, Harvard and Cambridge.

ERICA MOESER has been the President of the National Conference of Bar Examiners since 1994. She is a former chairperson of the

Council of the Section of Legal Education and Admissions to the Bar of the American Bar Association and has served as a law school site evaluator, as a member of the Section's Accreditation Committee, and as the co-chairperson of the Section's Bar Admissions Committee. She worked as the director of the Board of Bar Examiners of the Supreme Court of Wisconsin for seventeen years before joining the National Conference. Erica holds the following degrees: BA (geology), Newcomb College of Tulane University, 1967; MS (curriculum and instruction), University of Wisconsin, 1970; and JD, University of Wisconsin, 1974. She was admitted to practise law in Wisconsin in January 1975. She holds honorary degrees from three law schools. She has taught Professional Responsibility as an adjunct at the University of Wisconsin Law School.

HILDEGUNN KYVIK NORDÅS joined the OECD in 2005 where she works on trade in services. Before the OECD, she worked at the WTO Secretariat, and at the Christian Michelsen Institute and the University of Bergen, both in Norway, where her areas of research and teaching were international trade, economic growth and development. She has published a number of journal articles and book chapters in these fields. She has led a number of projects providing technical assistance and policy advice in developing countries, including developing a macroeconomic model with the Planning Commission of Tanzania. She has been a visiting scholar to the School of Government at the University of Western Cape and to the University of Kwazulu-Natal, both in South Africa, and to Stanford University, United States. She holds a Ph.D in economics.

KRISHNA OOLUN is presently the Executive Director of the Information and Communications Technology (ICT) Authority of Mauritius, the National Regulatory Authority for ICT. He was formerly Senior Lecturer at the University of Mauritius. Krishna is the holder of a Degree in electrical and electronic engineering from the University of Mauritius; MSc in digital instrumentation and imaging systems from UMIST, United Kingdom; Ph.D in communications engineering; and MBA in information technology management, University of Leicester, United Kingdom. He is a Chartered Engineer of the Council of Engineers of the United Kingdom. He is the author of several publications in the field of engineering and ICT regulations. He is the Editor in Chief of the online *Journal of Engineering and Technology Research*. He has also been part of consultancy assignment teams for the SADC and COMESA regions in the field of ICT policy and regulation, and has been involved in the development of various ICT policy and regulatory frameworks for Mauritius.

DARRELL PORTER is the Deputy Executive Director of the Australian Office of Best Practice Regulation. The Office of Best Practice Regulation plays a central role in assisting departments and agencies to meet the Australian Government's best practice regulation requirements and in monitoring and reporting on their performance. It serves a similar role for the Council of Australian Governments in relation to national regulatory proposals.

YOSHITAKA SAKAI is Economist at the Financial Services Agency, Government of Japan. Previously, he served as a technical teaching staff member in the International Monetary Fund. He has a Bachelor's Degree from the University of Tokyo.

IAIN SANDFORD is Counsel in the Geneva office and a member of Sidley Austin's International Trade and Dispute Resolution group. Iain has diverse WTO and international trade experience. He has advised clients on WTO and investment treaty issues, represented companies and governments in various safeguard, anti-dumping and countervailing duty cases, and acted regularly for clients on sensitive export control and sanctions compliance matters. In previous roles, he served as a WTO dispute settlement panellist, headed the international trade practice of a leading Australian law firm, served as a legal officer in the WTO Appellate Body Secretariat, and was a lawyer in the New Zealand Ministry of Foreign Affairs and Trade, where he was involved in a number of New Zealand's WTO cases. Iain is an honorary adjunct Professor of Law at the University of Canberra and is an editorial board member of World Export Control Review.

IRENE KAGGWA SEWANKAMBO is Head of Research and Coordinator at the Office of Executive Director Uganda Communications Commission. Irene heads the research and development function at Uganda's Communications sector regulatory authority, whose mandate covers the broadcasting, postal and telecommunications services. She possesses extensive experience in sector planning, policy development, and implementation of related initiatives such as quality of services regulation, numbering resource management, conducting usage studies, as well as processes for set up of universal fund. In her current role, Irene has enhanced the Commission's collaborations towards enhancement of ICT research and innovation as well as programmes geared to development of ICT for environmental sustainability. In addition to research and development, Irene is the Corporate Coordinator for UCC. She holds an MSc. in communications systems and signal processing from University of Bristol, a Bachelor's Degree in electrical engineering from Makerere University and is completing an MSc. in economic management and policy.

SIVA SOMASUNDRAM is Head of the International Regulatory Affairs department of Australia Post. He is a former senior government official and trade negotiator and has served as Chair of the WTO Working Party on GATS Rules.

LAUREL S. TERRY is Harvey A. Feldman Distinguished Faculty Scholar and Professor of Law at Penn State Dickinson School of Law in Carlisle, Pennsylvania. She writes and teaches about legal ethics and the international and inter-jurisdictional regulation of the legal profession. She is a long-time participant in what is now called the International Bar Association Committee on International Trade in Legal Services and the American Bar Association's Task Force on International Trade in Legal Services. She has written extensively about the GATS and legal services, including in limerick form: 'The GATS and Legal Services in Limerick', *Michigan State Journal of International Law* 15 (2007).

JOEL P. TRACHTMAN is Professor of International Law at the Fletcher School of Law and Diplomacy. Recent books include *The International Law of Economic Migration: Toward the Fourth Freedom* (2009); *Ruling the World: Constitutionalism, International Law, and Global Governance* (2009); *Developing Countries in the WTO Legal System* (2009); *The Economic Structure of International Law* (2008); and *International Law and International Politics* (2008). He has consulted for the United Nations, the OECD, APEC, the World Bank, the Organization of American States, and the US Agency for International Development. Joel has served as a member of the boards of the *American Journal of International Law*, *European Journal of International Law*, *Journal of International Economic Law*, *Cambridge Review of International Affairs* and *Singapore Yearbook of International Law*. He is a member of the bar of the State of New York. From 1998 to 2001, he was Academic

Dean of the Fletcher School, and during 2000 and 2001, he served as Dean ad interim. In 2002, he was Manley O. Hudson Visiting Professor of Law, and in 2004 he was Nomura Visiting Professor of International Financial Systems, at Harvard Law School. He graduated in 1980 from Harvard Law School, where he served as Editor in Chief of the *Harvard International Law Journal*. His undergraduate education was at the London School of Economics and Columbia College.

TANIA VOON is Professor and Associate Dean (Research) at Melbourne Law School, University of Melbourne. She is a former Legal Officer of the WTO Appellate Body Secretariat and has previously practised law with Mallesons Stephen Jaques and the Australian Government Solicitor. In addition to her current role, Tania has taught law at Georgetown University, the University of Western Ontario, the Australian National University, Monash University, and Bond University. Tania undertook her Master of Laws at Harvard Law School and her Ph.D in law at the University of Cambridge. She has published widely in the areas of public international law and international economic law. She is the author of *Cultural Products and the World Trade Organization* (2007) and a member of the Indicative List of Governmental and Non-Governmental Panelists for resolving WTO disputes and the Roster of Panelists to assist in the resolution of trade disputes between parties to the Energy Charter Treaty. Tania has provided expert advice and training to entities such as the Australian Department of Foreign Affairs and Trade, the WTO, the World Health Organization, Telstra and the McCabe Centre for Law and Cancer.

LAUREN WIGHT is a policy officer in the Office of Best Practice Regulation within the Australian Department of Finance and Deregulation. Lauren is part of a team responsible for assisting departments and agencies to meet the Australian Government's and Council of Australian Governments' best practice regulation requirements. She has worked on a wide range of regulatory proposals in areas including the labour market, tertiary education and health. She has a degree in finance from the Australian National University.

THAM SIEW YEAN, Ph.D (Rochester), is Professor in international trade and a principal research fellow at the Institute of Malaysian and International Studies (IKMAS), Universiti Kebangsaan Malaysia. She has research interests and publications in foreign direct investment, economic integration and trade in services (including education services). She has served as a consultant in national and international agencies such as the Malaysian Productivity Corporation, MITI, the Ministry of Human Resources, and the Ministry of Higher Education, as well as the United Nations Economic and Social Commission for Asia and the Pacific (UNESCAP), Asian Development Bank, Asian Development Bank Institute, World Bank Institute, and the World Bank. Her recent publications include 'Evolution of Trade Policy Formulation in Malaysia' in *Complexity of FTAs: A Key Issue in Malaysian Trade Policy* (2010); and 'Trade in Higher Education Services in Malaysia: Key Policy Challenges', *Higher Education Policy* 23 (2010).

RUOSI ZHANG is Counsellor in the Trade in Services Division of the WTO Secretariat. She has been working with the WTO Secretariat since 2003 and is responsible for logistics and express delivery services. Before that, she was researcher in international law at the Institute of Law, Chinese Academy of Social Sciences. She received BA and LLM Degrees from Peking University of China and an LLD degree from University of Paris V in France.

FOREWORD

Roberto Azevêdo,
WTO Director-General

Domestic regulation of services has a significant impact on the liberalization of trade in services. WTO members have agreed to negotiate a set of disciplines to ensure that such regulations are not unduly burdensome on trade. This book contains analyses and case studies from academics, regulators and trade experts.

Some of the contributions explore the scope or limitations of WTO legal principles to promote domestic regulatory reform. Others provide case studies on how domestic regulation is implemented in practice and the potential trade consequences. The case studies include a discussion of country-specific challenges and experiences in regulating important service sectors, such as finance, telecommunications, distribution, legal services, education, health, postal and logistics services, as well as the role of regulatory impact analysis. The book concludes with some reflections on what needs to be done to address the interface between domestic regulation and trade in services.

The new generation of services trade agreements is increasingly concerned with addressing regulatory issues. By examining the scope and potential of WTO legal principles against the backdrop of actual regulatory experiences, this book ventures onto new ground. Anyone familiar with WTO negotiations on domestic regulation will certainly appreciate the demand from both trade and regulatory communities for this type of information.

The book will help trade negotiators learn more about regulatory objectives and challenges and, in turn, how best to shape trade disciplines that would take these into account. Equally, those concerned with the regulation of services sectors will gain a greater understanding of how WTO legal principles can help promote and consolidate rather than impede domestic regulatory reform.

This book is a timely and valuable contribution to a better understanding – both in Geneva and across the globe – of the sensitive and sometimes complex interplay between the push for liberalization and the demands for domestic regulation.

DISCLAIMER

The opinions and conclusions contained in this publication are the sole responsibility of the individual authors. This includes contributions prepared by staff of the World Trade Organization (WTO) Secretariat. None of the chapters purports to reflect the opinions or views of WTO members or the Secretariat. Any citation of the chapters should ascribe authorship to the individuals who have written the contributions. This book should not be viewed as advancing any form of legal interpretation or any policy position, and no views or analysis in this publication should be attributed to the WTO, its Secretariat or its members.

ACKNOWLEDGEMENTS

As editors, we would like to express our sincere thanks to the authors whose contributions appear here. We are grateful for their interest in this book project. It is their combined expertise and insights into the trade consequences of regulation, WTO legal principles, services trade and regulatory practices in key sectors, which makes this volume unique. We are also grateful to Anthony Martin and Ross McRae from the WTO Information and External Relations Division for guiding the publication through the production process and for their assistance in preparing the manuscript. We would also like to thank Finola O'Sullivan for her encouragement and support since the beginning of the project. We are also grateful to Hamid Mamdouh, the director of the WTO Trade in Services Division, for his encouragement. Last but not least, we would like to thank Jean-Marie McAdams, Hattie de Varreux and Clemence Moreau for their combined assistance with earlier drafts of this book.

ABBREVIATIONS

3PL	third party logistics
AANZFTA	ASEAN–Australia–New Zealand Free Trade Agreement
ABA	American Bar Association
ACCA	Australian Competition and Consumer Act 2010 (Cth)
ACCC	Australian Competition and Consumer Commission
ACTIS	ASEAN–China Agreement on Trade in Services
ADR	alternative dispute resolution
AFAS	ASEAN Framework Agreement on Services
AJCEP	ASEAN–Japan Comprehensive Economic Partnership
AKFTA	ASEAN–Korea Free Trade Agreement
APEC	Asia-Pacific Economic Cooperation
ASEAN	Association of Southeast Asian Nations
AtB	at the border
ATM	automatic teller machine
BPO	business process outsourcing
BPR	basic postage rate
BtB	behind the border
BWA	Broadband Wireless Access
CA	Certification Authority
CAGR	compound annual growth rate
CCM	Competition Commission of Mauritius
CDO	collateralized debt obligation
CGE	computable general equilibrium
CPI	consumer price index
CT	China Telecom
DSU	WTO Understanding on Rules and Procedures Governing the Settlement of Disputes
EAC	East African Community
ECHR	European Convention on Human Rights
ECJ	European Court of Justice
ECON	Committee on Economic and Monetary Affairs
ECtHR	European Court of Human Rights

EGSM	Extended Global System for Mobile Communications
ETF	exchange trade fund
ETP	Economic Transformation Plan
FDI	foreign direct investment
FIC	Foreign Investment Committee
FIEA	Financial Instruments and Exchange Act (Japan)
FIPB	Foreign Investment Promotion Board (India)
FSA	Financial Services Agency (Japan)
G20	Group of 20
GATS	General Agreement on Trade in Services
GATT	General Agreement on Tariffs and Trade
GDP	gross domestic product
GSM	Global System for Mobile Communications
IBA	International Bar Association
ICJ	International Court of Justice
ICT	information and communications technology
ICTA	Information and Communication Technologies Authority (Mauritius)
IIA	international investment agreement
ILD	international long distance
IMF	International Monetary Fund
ISRO	Indian Space Research Organisation
IT	information technology
ITES	IT-enabled services
ITR	international telecommunications regulation
ITU	International Telecommunication Union
J-REIT	Japanese real estate investment trust
LAN	National Accreditation Board (Lembaga Akreditasi Negara)
LDC	least developed country
LPI	Logistics Performance Index (World Bank)
MAFTA	Malaysia–Australia Free Trade Agreement
MCI	Medical Council of India
MFN	most favoured nation
MII	Ministry of Information Industry (China)
MIIT	Ministry of Industry and Information Technology (China)
MJEPA	Malaysia–Japan Economic Partnership Agreement
MNZFTA	Malaysia–New Zealand Free Trade Agreement
MOHE	Ministry of Higher Education (Malaysia)
MOU	Memorandum of Understanding
MPFTA	Malaysia–Pakistan Free Trade Agreement
MPT	Ministry of Post and Telecommunication (China)
MQA	Malaysian Qualifications Agency

MQF	Malaysian Qualifications Framework
MRA	Mutual Recognition Agreement
MSP	mobile service provider
NAFTA	North American Free Trade Agreement
NCBE	National Conference of Bar Examiners
Netcom	China Net Communications
NGN	next generation network
NIE	New Institutional Economics
NOBC	National Organization of Bar Counsel
OBPR	Office of Best Practice Regulation (Australia)
OECD	Organisation for Economic Co-operation and Development
PHEI	private higher education institution
PIN	personal identification number
PKI	public key infrastructure
PMR	OECD Product Market Regulation
PT	Permit to Teach
PTA	preferential trade agreement
REIMS Agreement	Remuneration for Exchange of International Mail Service
RG	Registrar General
RIA	regulatory impact analysis
RIS	regulation impact statement
RTA	regional trade agreement
SIDS	small island development state
SIM card	subscriber identity module card
SME	small and medium-sized enterprise
SMS	Short Message Service
SOE	state-owned enterprise
SPS	sanitary and phytosanitary
SPS Agreement	WTO Agreement on the Application of Sanitary and Phytosanitary Measures
TBT	technical barriers to trade
TBT Agreement	WTO Agreement on Technical Barriers to Trade
TEU	Treaty on European Union
TRI	Trade Restrictiveness Index
TRIPS Agreement	WTO Agreement on Trade-Related Aspects of Intellectual Property Rights
UBE	Uniform Bar Examination (United States)
UCC	Uganda Communications Commission
UNCTAD	United Nations Conference on Trade and Development
UPC	Universal Postal Convention

UPU	Universal Postal Union
USF	universal service fund
USO	universal service obligation
USPS	United States Postal Service
USSD	Unstructured Supplementary Service Data
VoIP	Voice over Internet Protocol
VSAT	very small aperture terminal
WHO	World Health Organization
WPDR	Working Party on Domestic Regulation
WPPS	Working Party on Professional Services
WTO	World Trade Organization
WTO Agreement	Agreement Establishing the World Trade Organization

1

An introduction to domestic regulation and GATS

AIK HOE LIM AND BART DE MEESTER

1 Introduction

International trade in services is governed principally by regulatory measures. Unlike trade in goods, border measures in the form of tariffs and quotas are not the main barriers to trade. This peculiarity of services trade is due to the manner by which services are produced and consumed. Due to the intangible and non-storable nature of services, suppliers and consumers often have to be in physical proximity to each other for the transaction to be completed. For this reason, economists have traditionally considered services to be non-tradable across borders and have paid little attention to it in trade theory.

Yet, in today's global economy, trade in services is very much a tangible phenomenon – representing over one-fifth of international trade. With technological improvements, there are now greater possibilities for services to be supplied over a distance. Moreover, services trade as defined by the first multilateral agreement on this subject, the General Agreement on Trade in Services (GATS), encompasses not only cross-border trade (Mode 1), but also the consumption of services abroad (Mode 2), commercial establishment of service suppliers in another territory (Mode 3) and the presence of foreign natural persons for the supply of services (Mode 4). Given that the GATS modal coverage goes beyond traditional product-based trade flows, a far wider range of measures fall under the scope of the agreement.

While disciplines under the General Agreement on Tariffs and Trade (GATT) are confined to the cross-border flow of goods, GATS marked an important extension to measures affecting both the service (i.e. the product) and the service supplier (i.e. the producer). The expanded coverage of GATS reflected the nature of services sectors where regulations are more often than not directed at the service supplier rather than at the service itself. For instance, unlike the situation with goods, quality standards are often not based on the characteristics of the service, but on the competence and performance of the service supplier. What this meant is that with GATS, trade negotiations would venture into areas of internal regulation never before recognized as trade policy. This raised one of the most difficult issues in international trade, namely, the relationship between trade liberalization and domestic regulatory autonomy. The pragmatic solution utilized by the drafters of the GATS was to distinguish between three types of services measures:

- quantitative restrictions on entry/establishment (including legal form requirements), whether discriminatory or not;
- discriminatory measures modifying the conditions of competition in favour of national services and service suppliers;
- domestic regulations that are neither discriminatory nor quantitative in nature.

The GATS framework by design defined measures falling under the first two categories as market access and national treatment limitations. These are subject to the disciplines of GATS Articles XVI and XVII, and negotiations to progressively eliminate them.

The third category of measures would not be considered as necessarily imposing trade restrictions. For want of a better term, they constitute 'domestic regulations' from the perspective of GATS and are therefore not subject to progressive liberalization. It is no accident that the GATS Preamble explicitly recognizes the right of members to regulate and introduce new regulations on the supply of services in order to meet national policy objectives. Nevertheless, the agreement also foresaw that domestic regulations may have trade-restrictive effects and mandated the establishment of relevant disciplines under GATS Article VI:4. Given the pervasiveness of domestic regulation in services sectors, a clear identification of trade-restrictive effects, intended or unintended, as well as the criteria to be used in evaluating the unnecessary burdensomeness of regulation has been fraught with difficulty. At the same time, there is increasing evidence that regulatory constraints have an important and significant effect on services trade, and may even negate the gains from external trade liberalization.

By way of an introduction, the following sections provide some background on the GATS negotiations on domestic regulation disciplines for readers who may not be familiar with this body of work. They also serve to outline the issues which are addressed in this book and to introduce the chapters.

2 The services regulatory challenge of open markets

Services sectors in many countries have undergone a major transformation over the last three decades, moving away from a model where services were provided often as a function of government to one where services are provided on a competitive and commercial basis. The degree of change, however, varies across regions and sectors. Historically, several infrastructural and social services, such as telecommunications, transport and public utilities, as well as essential consumer services, such as education and health, have been directly provided by government entities, usually in monopoly situations.

In many of these sectors, governments have progressively transformed their role from that of a primary supplier to being a supervisor or regulator of competitive markets. In other sectors, where there has always been strong private sector involvement, technology and market globalization has made the task of regulation ever more complex with the emergence of either new services or the involvement of an expanded range of private actors. The shift towards private or joint public–private provision of services has often resulted in more and not less regulation and has been described as the rise of the so-called 'regulatory state' (Majone 1997; Glaeser and Shleifer 2003). Indeed, the experience of Organisation for Economic Co-operation and Development (OECD) countries has been that the regulation of services markets has increased just as sectors were privatized and opened up to competition (Blundell and Robinson 2000). In developing countries, the establishment of new regulations, laws, contracts, institutions, regimes and processes have also been an important feature of infrastructure reforms associated with telecommunications, transport and public utilities (Eberhard 2007).

Through the regulatory framework, governments may wish to increase welfare by correcting market distortions, minimizing the impact of externalities and preventing anti-competitive practices. Specific characteristics of services markets make the use of regulation particularly important. Services are generally considered to be intangible and non-storable, and their supply often requires an interaction between the supplier and consumer. This implies that users frequently cannot easily assess the quality of the service until they have consumed it. Through regulation, governments seek to avoid that service suppliers exploit such information asymmetries. For instance, regulation may impose information requirements to inform consumers in advance, or impose qualification requirements for professionals, or licensing requirements that seek to ensure the competence of the service supplier and, thus, the quality of the services provided. Unlike goods, it is difficult if not impossible to subject services to any form of *ex ante* physical testing. Thus, regulations will often be attached to the competence and conduct of the service supplier.[1] This explains why in services there is often greater emphasis on the qualification requirements of the service supplier as a way to indirectly control the quality of the services provided.

In the context of developing countries, a frequently cited concern is the need for some form of government intervention to ensure that markets contribute to poverty reduction and to help bring about inclusive and sustainable development.[2] This policy objective may sometimes be pursued through regulation which aims to ensure that services are available to all citizens at equitable conditions, no matter their location or income. In the case of infrastructure services, for instance, universal service obligations may sometimes require expansion of the network to remote areas or affordable pricing for poorer segments of the population. Furthermore, the provision of certain services may create negative externalities – the costs of which are insufficiently borne by the parties themselves. For instance, heavy road transport or intensive tourism could strongly affect the environment. Excessive risk-taking by financial institutions can undermine the financial stability of all countries and create macroeconomic tensions around the world. Box 1.1 provides a list of regulations typically used to achieve certain policy objectives.

Liberalization of services markets has thus required not just the removal of market access constraints but also the implementation of new regulation or re-regulation to ensure regulatory quality and efficiency, transparent processes, as well as appropriately mandated regulatory bodies. At the same time, it has been well noted in economic literature that regulation may be captured by special interest groups, and thus flourish for reasons totally unrelated to addressing market failure or development needs (see e.g. Stigler 1971; Peltzman 1976). Governments are thus subject to lobbying by those groups seeking to ensure that privileges and rents stemming from regulation are maintained. In such cases, even when regulatory intervention is warranted on public policy

[1] See *Technical Standards in Services: Note by the Secretariat*, WTO doc. S/WPDR/W/49, 3 September 2012.

[2] See Cook *et al.* 2004: 11; *Services, Development and Trade: The Regulatory and Institutional Dimension, Note by the Secretariat*, UN doc. TD/B/C.I/MEM.3/11, 15 December 2011, p. 7.

BOX 1.1 EXAMPLES OF SERVICES-SPECIFIC REGULATION TO PURSUE PUBLIC POLICY OBJECTIVES

Equitable access

Sectors: In the transport or telecommunications sectors, governments often want remote regions to be served, regardless of profitability. Basic equity objectives may prompt governments to ensure that all citizens have access to education and essential health care at low or zero costs.

Measures: Cross-subsidization schemes to ensure that revenues in profitable areas are reinvested in favour of underdeveloped regions or persons in financial need; licensing conditions which include 'universal service obligations' (e.g. commercial hospitals are required to treat a certain percentage of patients free of charge, or postal and telecommunications services must be provided at equal conditions across the country, regardless of profitability considerations).

Consumer protection

Sectors: With regard to professional, financial or health services, the complexity of the service that is provided makes it very difficult for consumers to appreciate quality or safety prior to consumption. Service suppliers may exploit such information asymmetries.

Measures: Prudential and other technical standards to be complied with by service suppliers; transparency-related publication requirements on costs, risks, side-effects, among others, to enable the consumer to make informed decisions; education and training requirements to ensure competence; mandatory professional liability insurance.

Reduction of environmental impacts and other negative externalities

Sectors: Road and air transport cause pollution and noise; tourism could put the environment under stress and disturb natural habitats.

Measures: Traffic restrictions over weekends, during night hours or in sensitive areas; zoning laws and building codes; tax/subsidy-schemes to mobilize funds for preservation of cultural heritage.

Macroeconomic stability

Sectors: Financial institutions may engage in imprudent lending or design complex financial instruments that are insufficiently understood. As a consequence, depositors may lose confidence and withdraw their money, inter-bank lending may suffer, credit supply to the real economy be hampered, and so forth.

BOX 1.1 (*cont.*)

Measures: To ensure stability, financial institutions must comply with measures such as minimum capital requirements; higher capital reserves when new financial instruments are provided; diversify assets to limit exposure to individual clients; and regularly reporting on their activities.

Avoidance of market dominance and anti-competitive conduct

Sectors: Concerns about anti-competitive conduct arise in sectors prone to market concentration, including services with network effects and interconnection needs (e.g. transport and telecommunications) and liberalized former monopolies (e.g. postal and courier, education and energy).

Measures: Limitations on market shares; introduction of price surveillance or mandatory price caps; interconnection guarantees; government-mandated technical standards to replace company-specific requirements.

grounds, governments may be 'bought' into relying on those measures that benefit the interests of a few at the expense of the general good.

The complexity and diversity of services regulation also implies that regulators who are less experienced or have fewer resources might be more easily 'captured' by special interest groups even if they intend to act in pursuit of the 'public interest'.[3] Regulations may in such situations seek to reduce market contestability and thereby protect incumbent suppliers from competition. To what extent such regulatory actions can be disciplined under a trade agreement, how to distinguish protectionism from the pursuit of legitimate domestic objectives, and what should the due balance be between the goal of trade liberalization and domestic regulatory autonomy, have all been major sources of tension.

3 GATS context

GATT addresses this tension by focusing on non-discrimination which is its primary discipline. From this perspective, it follows that measures applied at the border, such as a quota or tariff, would be subject to trade disciplines. Since these measures can only be applied to foreign goods, they are the natural and legitimate concern of trade negotiations.

3 See the discussion of political economy considerations underlying regulatory intervention in WTO 2012: 75–6.

Once the goods have entered the territory they might be subject to so-called 'behind the border' or 'non-tariff' measures in the form of internal regulations. Although such measures may have trade effects, GATT has traditionally been careful not to venture too far into subjecting internal regulations to trade disciplines and has mainly focused on ensuring non-discrimination through the observance of national treatment. That being said, due to the prominence of non-tariff measures, successive GATT rounds have expanded or strengthened disciplines on regulatory measures, including through improvements to the WTO Agreement on Technical Barriers to Trade (TBT Agreement) and the negotiation of a new Agreement on the Application of Sanitary and Phytosanitary Measures (SPS Agreement).

In the case of services trade, the starting point has always been the 'behind the border' measures. Most services restrictions are not applied at the border and are found in a country's internal regulation. Thus, unlike the case for goods trade, there was no convenient shortcut of focusing on border measures as explicit trade barriers. Rather, the challenge for services was to identify from the wide range of internal regulations those which can be considered to be trade restrictions and subject to liberalization commitments. Ultimately, GATS undertook an implicit ranking of measures as instruments of protection. First, quantitative restrictions affecting entry and establishment, whether discriminatory or not, may serve to protect the incumbent service supplier from protection. Such limitations have a general effect on market contestability and would thus be a form of trade restriction. Second, discriminatory measures on foreign services and service suppliers serve to modify conditions of competition in favour of domestic services and service suppliers. The trade-restrictive impact of such measures is evident.

The GATS confines liberalization to the absence of six types of market access measures (Article XVI) and national treatment discrimination (Article XVII). Market access restrictions are defined as six listed types of measures, mainly of a quantitative, quota-type nature (GATS Article XVI:2). National treatment violations are measures that, either *de jure* or *de facto*, modify the conditions of competition in favour of national services or service suppliers. Such market access or national treatment measures can be maintained only in those service sectors for which no specific commitments have been inscribed. In sectors where bindings have been undertaken, such measures violating the market access or national treatment obligation can only be used if they have been specifically listed as limitations to the commitment. Traditionally, trade negotiations focus on the removal of these limitations. Outside of these provisions, governments have by and large unfettered autonomy to decide the shape and content of the remaining regulatory framework.

4 Negotiating disciplines on domestic regulation

Yet, services trade may be affected by non-discriminatory economy-wide or sector-specific regulations relating to the environment, public safety, zoning, consumer protection and competition policy. While such regulations are necessary, they can determine the conditions for the entry and operation of service suppliers in several ways. First, the choice of the regulatory instrument is important in achieving the required policy objective, as some may be more trade-friendly than others. Admittedly, distinguishing between a legitimate policy objective and disguised protectionism in the instrument of choice is far from obvious. Second, even if the instrument is optimal, there is the question of whether more could be done to administer the regulation in a transparent and less trade-burdensome manner. Third, regulatory frameworks for services tend to involve many agencies with different objectives, authority and requirements. Such fragmentation may occur at both the national and international level, and regulatory cooperation between agencies and the recognition of experience, qualifications and standards can do much to help lessen the cost of compliance for the service supplier and enhance international trade.

Thus, while GATS has been careful not to suggest that domestic regulations are trade barriers, it acknowledges that they could potentially be trade restrictive. Two major concerns are involved: how to ensure that regulations serve legitimate policy objectives and are not used as an alternate form of protectionism; and how to mitigate the unintended trade-restrictive consequences of national differences in regulatory requirements, as well as the manner in which they are administered. GATS Article VI:4 contains a negotiating mandate to develop any necessary disciplines that seek to ensure that regulatory requirements and procedures (i.e. licensing, qualifications and technical standards) do not constitute unnecessary barriers to trade in services. Article VI:4 indicates that the disciplines are intended to ensure that domestic regulations are, among others:

(a) based on objective and transparent criteria, such as competence and the ability to supply the service;
(b) not more burdensome than necessary to ensure the quality of the service;
(c) in the case of licensing procedures, not in themselves a restriction on the supply of the service.

Pending the entry of new disciplines, GATS Article VI:5 imposes a standstill obligation. Members are to refrain from applying measures that would nullify or impair a specific commitment, which are incompatible with the criteria set out in Article VI:4, and could not have reasonably been expected at the time when the commitments were made. This discipline thus applies to new measures of domestic regulation. Apart from Article VI:5, GATS also contains a number of general obligations that promote good governance. These include obligations on transparency, as well as on the availability of judicial, arbitral or administrative tribunals or procedures for review of decisions at the request of an affected service supplier, and appropriate remedies where justified (GATS Articles III and VI:2). Where the procedures are not independent of the agency entrusted with the administrative decision concerned, members have to ensure that procedures in fact provide for an objective and impartial review (*ibid.*). For sectors where specific commitments are taken, there are additional obligations to ensure that all measures of general application are administered in a reasonable, objective and impartial manner; that the competent authority informs applicants of the decision concerning the application or its status; and that there are adequate procedures to verify the competence of professionals of any other member (GATS Article VI:1, 3 and 6).

GATS disciplines on domestic regulation could be said to share similar objectives to those espoused by good regulatory practices.[4] The latter typically recommend the design of objective, criteria-based and transparent rules to promote efficiency and to lessen the scope for discretionary decision-making (Mamdouh 2010). The discourse on regulation has also sought to promote regulatory reform and audits, and the establishment of institutions empowered that are legally and functionally independent of any market actor. Key questions have been: the economic impact of regulation, including on trade and investment; the potential economic

[4] For instance, see Lafont 2005; Eberhard 2007; 'APEC-OECD Integrated Checklist on Regulatory Reform', available at www.oecd.org/regreform/34989455.pdf.

and trade costs of regulatory measures; and how such impacts might be alleviated through better design and administration of regulations (UNCTAD 2010). Although trade disciplines and good regulatory practices appear to share common principles of transparency, non-discrimination, impartiality and objectivity, and necessity, how to transform such principles into disciplines on domestic regulation has been far from obvious.

5 Principles and issues in the negotiations

Domestic regulation under GATS Article VI was one of those areas which members decided to set aside for finalization at a later stage. At the end of the Uruguay Round, members could not reach consensus on how to treat non-discriminatory non-quantitative measures, which would be outside the scope of Article XVI (market access) and Article XVII (national treatment), but could still have an important effect on trade in services. Failure to reach agreement on domestic regulation was not too surprising as, more than any other area in GATS, it would have to address the thorny issue of the acceptable balance between trade liberalization and regulatory flexibility.

Thus, the negotiating mandate under GATS Article VI.4 and the subsequent Decision on Domestic Regulation set forth a three-fold work programme. Members were tasked with developing generally applicable disciplines (i.e. horizontal disciplines); disciplines as appropriate for individual sectors of groups thereof; and the development of general disciplines for professional services. In 1995, a Working Party on Professional Services (WPPS) was created and it produced two results in the accountancy sector: the elaboration of voluntary Guidelines for Mutual Recognition Agreements or Arrangements in the Accountancy Sector; and the WTO 1998 Disciplines on Domestic Regulation in the Accountancy Sector (Accountancy Disciplines). These disciplines apply only to that sector and only where specific commitments have been made for accountancy. Although the Accountancy Disciplines were completed in 1998, they are not yet in force. At that time, members decided to integrate them into GATS at the end of the current round of negotiations, along with any other disciplines that may be developed. Those negotiations eventually became part of the Doha Development Agenda, which have not yet been concluded.

Despite having no legal effect as yet, the Accountancy Disciplines have been influential in shaping the further negotiations which were undertaken by the Working Party on Domestic Regulation (WPDR), the body which succeeded the WPPS. The Accountancy Disciplines contained detailed provisions on licensing requirements and procedures, qualification requirements and procedures, and technical standards. They focused mainly on procedural matters, such as transparency and other good governance requirements with respect to the administration of domestic regulation. Some of these provisions elaborate on provisions which already exist in GATS.

The main achievement of the Accountancy Disciplines was to create a so-called 'necessity test', which required WTO members to ensure that measures relating to licensing requirements and procedures, technical standards, and qualification requirements and procedures are:

> not prepared, adopted or applied with a view to or with the effect of creating unnecessary barriers to trade in accountancy services. For this purpose, Members shall ensure that such measures are not more trade restrictive than necessary to fulfil a legitimate objective.

This potentially powerful test would allow WTO members to challenge other members on the necessity of a measure to achieve a particular 'legitimate objective'. The provision provides an open-ended definition of such objectives, among other things, the protection of consumers, quality of the service, professional competence, and the integrity of the profession. Although not yet tested, this provision suggests that while members would not be constrained in what they consider to be legitimate objectives, they might have to consider the trade implications of the regulatory instrument of choice and whether a less trade-restrictive option could be used.

Since the conclusion of the Accountancy Disciplines, WTO members have been approaching the domestic regulation disciplines from a horizontal perspective, the rationale behind such an approach being that it would be more efficient to formulate one set of general disciplines that would be applicable to all services sectors rather than to negotiate separate disciplines for each sector. There was also a concern that if negotiators were instead to follow a sectoral approach, this might result in an interminable 'pre-negotiation' as to the choice and order by which sectors might be taken up. Inevitably, for some sectors it might be difficult to obtain necessary political support to launch negotiations. Moreover, there was a prevailing view at that time that although services sectors might differ greatly in their specific characteristics, there was considerable similarity in the underlying economic and social reasons for regulatory intervention. Based on this logic, it seemed to follow that it would be feasible to develop general disciplines which would be applicable across a range of sectors, as they would address basic transparency and good governance requirements.

However, as the negotiating experience of the last fifteen years has shown, horizontal disciplines have by no means been easy to negotiate. While at a theoretical level there might be common economic and social reasons for regulation, there are also considerable differences between sectors in terms of their regulatory intensity, practices and specific policy objectives. For instance, in network-based services such as telecommunications, transportation and energy services, the key regulatory problems often relate to the prevention of anti-competitive behaviour through the control of essential infrastructure or facilities. On the other hand, the emphasis in regulations in professional services is on ensuring that suppliers are competent and that services meet a particular standard. Such concerns reflect the difficulties which consumers may have in assessing quality and the need to prevent suppliers from exploiting information asymmetries. Thus, disciplines on domestic regulation in professional services may naturally gravitate towards issues concerned with competence and the ability to supply a service, while those on network services will seek to curb collusion, ensure access to essential infrastructure, independence of the regulator, and so on. Finding the right balance in one instrument to satisfy such different objectives has been a considerable challenge.

It is thus perhaps not surprising that the work on horizontal disciplines has focused mainly on trade impediments which may arise from procedural and administrative requirements, such as cumbersome or opaque licensing and qualification procedures, and less on the necessity of the substantive requirements that may be involved in obtaining authorization to supply a service. The disciplines have also sought to carefully define their scope as comprising five types of measures: licensing requirements; licensing procedures; qualification requirements; qualification procedures; and technical standards.

It is difficult to summarize the elements contained in the text and the respective proposals, as at the time of writing the negotiations are still ongoing and consensus has not yet been reached on all the elements that should be included in the disciplines. Nevertheless, it can be said that in the negotiations, consideration has been given to creating disciplines based on the following regulatory principles.

5.1 Legal certainty and transparency

Often, a major obstacle faced by service suppliers when seeking to provide services in another WTO member is the opaqueness and uncertainty of the rules and procedures that they have to comply with. A key objective in the disciplines has been to bring about greater transparency and certainty to the regulatory environment in which service suppliers have to operate. A number of efforts can contribute to reducing information asymmetries, such as:

- publication and availability of information on regulations and procedures;
- specification of reasonable time periods for responding to applications for licences;
- information as to the reasons why an application was rejected;
- notification on what information is missing in an application;
- specification of reasonable time periods for responding to applications;
- information on procedures for the review of administrative decisions.

The problems of a lack of transparency can be compounded by long and complex procedures for authorization to supply a service. Such complexity may serve to hide protectionist intentions. Simplification of procedures will facilitate service suppliers and reduce the opportunities for hidden protectionism. Nonetheless, in many services sectors, the characteristics of the service supplied may not always allow for very simple procedures to be adopted. For instance, several authorities may need to be involved to ensure the quality of the service, to avoid any negative impact on the environment or to enable public consultations. The challenge for the disciplines has been to define principles that allow for transparent and simplified procedures but do not curtail necessary substantive requirements.

In addition to transparency on the regulatory framework, service suppliers may legitimately expect that rules (e.g. assessment criteria for an application) and procedures (e.g. deadlines) will not be modified with a view to treating applicants unfairly. In the event that regulations need to be modified, due process would generally require that applicants should have a reasonable time period to adjust to amended criteria or procedures. Such principles, which are by no means unusual, are often embedded in regulations and procedures. What is the appropriate balance between legal certainty and regulatory flexibility, and what are the procedural instruments to achieve that balance, are questions that have not been resolved.

5.2 *Impartiality and objectivity*

It is well recognized that efficient outcomes are best achieved when decisions are independent from any commercial interests or political influence. Service suppliers typically want to be assured that assessments by regulatory and supervisory authorities for authorization to supply a service, should any be required, will be conducted in a reasonable, impartial and objective manner. A key objective of the negotiations has thus been to formulate disciplines which would ensure that decisions by competent authorities avoid exercising excessive discretion in the administration of regulations. While there is common agreement that the formulation of criteria can be vitally important to ensure objectivity, there are important differences between regulatory cultures. Some jurisdictions provide their regulators with wide-ranging discretionary powers, including the possibility to consider factors other than those contained in the criteria. Others see the actions of their regulators to be fully circumscribed by predetermined criteria. In such a case, discretion is exercised in the choice of criteria rather than in the evaluation of the case. Ultimately, whatever the regulatory culture, the challenge of disciplines is to establish a set of disciplines that would help ensure that the regulator acts fairly, without bias or external influence.

5.3 *Recognition*

Trade in services would be greatly facilitated if there were common standards for service suppliers. However, achieving such wide-scale international harmonization is unlikely. This is why in trade agreements WTO members have been encouraged to create arrangements to recognize the relevant educational qualifications and professional experience that a service supplier may have obtained abroad. For this reason, GATS Article VII allows for recognition measures as long as there are adequate provisions for other members to negotiate accession or achieve recognition of their requirements and certificates. However, there is a certain tension between Article VII and the most favoured nation (MFN) obligation of GATS to 'accord immediately and unconditionally to services and service suppliers of any other Member treatment no less favourable than that it accords to like services and service suppliers of any other country'.

Thus, GATS Article VII.3 instructs members not to accord recognition in a manner which would constitute a means of discrimination between countries in the application of its standards or criteria for the authorization, licensing or certification of service suppliers, or a disguised restriction on trade in services. Members are also encouraged to base recognition on multilaterally agreed criteria, wherever appropriate, and are urged to work in cooperation with relevant intergovernmental and non-governmental organizations toward the establishment of common international standards in the area of services. The objective behind the domestic regulation disciplines would be to further elaborate on the principles which WTO members should abide by when according recognition, including the manner by which international standards are developed.

5.4 Necessity

A recurring principle in trade agreements is the requirement that the measure used to achieve a certain legitimate objective is the 'least trade-restrictive reasonably available'. Necessity tests establish the WTO consistency of a measure based on whether the measure is 'necessary' to achieve certain policy objectives. These tests reflect the balance in WTO agreements between two important goals: preserving the freedom of WTO members to set and achieve regulatory objectives through measures of their own choosing, and discouraging members from adopting or maintaining measures that unduly restrict trade. Necessity tests typically achieve this balance by requiring that measures which restrict trade in some way (including by violating obligations of an agreement) are permissible only if they are 'necessary' to achieve the member's policy objective. In so doing, the necessity tests confirm the right of members to regulate and to pursue their policy objectives.

GATS Article VI:4 indicates that the disciplines shall aim to ensure that measures of domestic regulation do not constitute unnecessary barriers to trade in services. Similar language can be found in TBT Agreement Article 2.2 and SPS Agreement Article 5.6. The 'necessity tests' under these agreements focus on whether a legitimate objective chosen by a WTO member could equally be achieved by means of a reasonably available alternative that is less trade-restrictive. Governments should thus assess, when adopting regulations, whether they could use an alternative measure that would be equally able to achieve the policy objective chosen, but which would be less trade restrictive. Using 'necessity' tests similar to those found in the TBT or SPS Agreements in disciplines on domestic regulation has been a highly contentious issue in the negotiations. For some members, such requirements are viewed with concern as they fear that their autonomy to choose certain policy objectives might be excessively restricted. On the other hand, proponents of the principle of such a test argue that the disciplines would be significantly devalued if they did not contain a means to address unnecessarily burdensome requirements or disguised trade restrictions. Moreover, WTO dispute panel and Appellate Body decisions have consistently focused on the necessity of the *measure* used to achieve the specified objective and not the necessity of the objective itself.[5]

6 Objectives and structure of the book

It is against the difficult context of crafting trade disciplines on domestic regulation that this book explores regulatory principles and practices, and their implications for international trade in services. With some notable exceptions,[6] much of the writing on services trade has focused on the challenges of eliminating traditional barriers, namely, the six types of market access limitations as defined by GATS Article XVI, and Article XVII limitations on national treatment. Existing literature on domestic regulation has tended to focus on the application of general economic and legal principles. Less has been written on how regulatory principles and practices might actually relate to trade principles and disciplines. The 'regulatory world' and the 'trade policy world' seem to exist in separate but parallel universes. Yet, as economies continue to integrate and barriers to foreign market entry reduce, many of the challenges and problems in international trade in services are surfacing in the realm of regulation. It thus seemed opportune to put a collection of economic and legal essays together with sector-specific cases reflecting on services trade, regulatory challenges and experiences.

Indeed, sector regulators are often unaware of how trade disciplines might be relevant for their regulatory interventions. At the sector level, there have been many studies on the economic impact of different regulatory approaches and measures, their relative efficiency in attaining specific public policy goals and the problems encountered. Despite their potential relevance to trade policy, such regulatory studies rarely take trade concerns explicitly into account. Trade negotiators, on the other hand, are often not familiar with evolving regulatory practices nor do they necessarily have knowledge of the regulatory challenges faced in specific sectors. A basic purpose of this book, through a

[5] See *'Necessity Tests' in the WTO: Note by the Secretariat*, WTO doc. S/WPDR/W/27/Add.1, 18 January 2011.

[6] For instance, see Krajewski 2003; Findlay and Sidorenko 2003; Mattoo and Sauvé 2003; Wouters and Coppens 2007; Vranes 2009 on domestic regulation.

collection of essays and case studies, is to help bridge some of this gap by contributing to the relatively small body of work on regulatory issues affecting services trade.

Parts I and II recall the theoretical underpinnings of the purpose of regulation, the problems that they are typically intended to resolve and their potential consequences for services trade. Tinne Heremans provides a concise but comprehensive overview of the rationale and purpose behind regulation, the expected outcomes from regulation in a given sector and the different approaches taken. This is followed by Hildegunn Kyvik Nordås, who reviews the empirical literature on the costs and benefits of domestic regulation for services trade, and its related welfare effects. The two chapters are interrelated, as they look at the economic rationale and consequences of regulation. However, while she similarly concludes that regulation can lower entry barriers and improve welfare, she points to research which shows that it may not always do so. Not all regulation successfully corrects market failures, and complying with regulation is not costless.

The economic perspective on regulation and trade is followed by legal essays which delve deeper into each of the main domestic regulation principles which trade negotiators have been seeking to craft to reduce the impact of regulatory diversity, to simplify and to make procedures more transparent and to avoid unnecessary complexity or disguised restrictions. Andrew Mitchell and Tania Voon reflect upon the meaning and potential scope of reasonableness, impartiality and objectivity in GATS Article VI:1, taking account of relevant case law and the underlying purpose of the provision. In doing so, they consider the breadth and strength of Article VI:1 as a discipline on domestic regulatory conduct and its possible boundaries. Markus Krajewski focuses on the balance between legal certainty and regulatory flexibility and discusses this balance in the context of international trade law, in particular the framework for the liberalization of trade in services. He highlights that embedded in the concept of legal certainty is the general principle of transparency as stipulated in GATS and the need for open and predictable regulatory processes. Panagiotis Delimatsis offers an overview of the issues relating to whether a necessity test should be adopted in the draft disciplines. By analysing the types of measures covered and the meaning of necessity in WTO case law, he demonstrates why the issue matters from a policy perspective and why it has had such a divisive impact to date. Joel Trachtman explores both the usefulness of mutual recognition as a tool for the international liberalization of services and the risks which it poses. He then considers how these risks could be addressed, particularly for capacity-constrained developing countries.

Part III seeks to illustrate some of the problems and regulatory issues affecting services trade through country and sector-specific case studies. Some of the studies in this section focus on a particular regulatory experience or challenge; others discuss general approaches, mechanisms or solutions that have been applied across a range of sectors. There is no 'one-size-fits-all' package of regulatory issues affecting trade in services, nor is there commonality in regulatory responses to liberalization. Nevertheless, the case studies help shed light on how some of the issues which have been discussed in the domestic regulation disciplines have surfaced or been addressed at the sector level. The case studies cover: professional services; infrastructure-related services such as telecommunications and postal; financial services; education and health services; logistics and distribution services. Each of these sectors are characterized by somewhat different regulatory governance structures and challenges. They raise some common problems of the type discussed in the negotiations of horizontal domestic regulation disciplines but also some very specific regulatory issues for international trade in services.

Erica Moeser and Laurel Terry examine how globalization of the practice of law is affecting the regulatory structure governing access to it in the United States. They document the currents that are running strongly in the direction of creating greater opportunities for lawyers to practise their profession across both state and national borders. Henry Gao reviews the reforms that China has had to take in the telecommunications sector as a result of WTO accession. In particular, he discusses how the regulatory framework has balanced the goals of fostering competition, providing universal service and protecting public morals. He also examines how these goals are pursued through various regulatory practices. Krishna Oolun continues the theme of telecommunications by discussing the Mauritian experience of creating an information and communications technology regulator with defined statutory powers. He describes in greater detail how regulatory practices (in terms of licensing, scarce resources management, access and interconnection to network resources, and technical standards and harmonization) were used in the regulatory framework to achieve the policy objectives set for the sector.

The case study on postal services by Siva Somasundram and Iain Sandford examines regulatory issues of competition and universal service obligations, which are somewhat similar to those faced in the telecommunications sector. They draw from the experience in Australia and elsewhere, and address the broad concern of how to regulate liberalized postal markets, as well as the nexus between trade rules and postal regulations, both domestic and international. The case study focuses on the policy and regulatory tensions in ensuring universal service obligations, competition issues and the appropriate role and form of regulation in such markets.

Moving to a qualitatively different set of regulatory issues, there are two case studies on financial services. The first of these by Joan Apecu, Irene Kaggwa Sewankambo and Yusuf Atiku Abdalla describes the trade and regulatory challenges of mobile banking. The case study describes the operation of mobile money services in Uganda and highlights the regulatory challenges confronting two separate authorities, the Uganda Communications Commission and the Bank of Uganda. With the rapid development and evolution of mobile money services, both authorities found existing frameworks ineffective and convergence was required between telecommunications and financial regulation regimes. In contrast, the second financial services case study focuses on the domestic regulation experiences of the mature and highly developed financial services sector of Japan. In this case study, Masamichi Kono, Koichi Iwai and Yoshitaka Sakai discuss how objective and transparent domestic regulations which protect consumers and ensure predictability and stability can support and promote financial services liberalization.

Education and health services are two sectors which share many common regulatory features. Many governments are required to provide education and health as public services. Universal access to such services may also be a public policy objective and government-owned facilities are typically heavily subsidized. At the same time, privately provided education and health is growing strongly, especially in developing countries. Supply of services in both sectors is also increasingly international, raising significant trade and regulatory challenges. The case study by Tham Siew Yean and Nik Kamal Nik Mahmod examines how a new regulatory framework on private higher education in Malaysia had to be developed in order to promote education exports whilst also ensuring quality and access. Rupa Chanda and Pralok Gupta, on the other hand, examine the challenges faced by the prevailing regulatory environment for hospital and telemedicine services, and discuss how India's trade in health services could be improved through reforms in domestic regulations.

The last two sector case studies are on logistics and distribution services. The logistics services sector brings together a range of transportation, warehousing and freight handling services dealing with the flow of inputs from initial suppliers to final customers of products. Distribution services are also concerned with managing the flow of economic activity, connecting producers, wholesale traders and importers of goods, on the one hand, with end-consumers, on the other. Suppliers of logistics services and distribution services thus share a fairly similar set of regulatory issues. Ruosi Zhang in her case study on logistics services in China examines the fragmented nature of domestic regulation affecting them, the implementation of which falls across multiple governmental departments and agencies. She evaluates the repercussions that current domestic regulation has on the performance of the service and the gap between the regulatory framework and the international business reality of the sector. Tomer Broude and Lior Herman, on the other hand, focus their case study on the impact of domestic regulation on the market structure in the retail distribution services sector and its ultimate effects on consumer food prices. Taking Israel, a small and relatively liberalized developed economy, they analyse some forms of domestic regulation which may constitute impediments to entry of foreign enterprises to the Israeli market. They then consider the trade impact of such regulations on retail food distribution services, as well as on food prices.

The final case study is not on a specific sector but on the role of regulatory impact analysis (RIA) and its potential contribution to easing trade and regulatory issues. Such assessments, which began in OECD countries in the 1980s, have become more widespread and evolved into an instrument of regulatory reform, encompassing a mixture of deregulation, re-regulation and initiatives to improve the effectiveness of regulatory instruments. Regulatory governance embraces the wider issues of transparency (through the openness of consultation and the decision-making process); accountability (of regulators and appeal mechanisms); efficiency (maximizing the benefits to the whole community, taking into account the costs); adaptability (flexibility over time); and coherence (across government and between governments). Many of these issues have been highlighted in the preceding sector studies. Thus, whilst Darrell Porter and Lauren Wight describe the Australian model for RIA, which is in turn based on other principles, the lessons from their specific experience could have wider applicability in terms of how to address tension between domestic regulation and international trade.

Based on the discussion of regulatory principles and the case studies, the concluding chapters of the book in Part IV seek to draw some insights for the unfinished business of negotiating GATS disciplines on domestic regulation. Hamid Mamdouh in his chapter reflects on the GATS experience of services liberalization and negotiations, and underscores that regulatory issues need to be addressed as a supplement to market access and national treatment commitments. He also provides some ideas on how regulatory principles could be used to address two key aspects of the services liberalization challenge: the design of rules and the establishment of institutional frameworks which facilitate rather than hinder trade. By way of a conclusion, our final chapter identifies the generic regulatory themes that emerge from the issues discussed in the preceding studies and essays. Several purposes are served by this identification. First, this better informs the ongoing challenge of ensuring that services trade liberalization and regulation are complementary in creating competitive services markets. Second, it acts as a form of reality check on the range of issues for which regulators and trade negotiators need to find common solutions. Third, it provides an opportunity to reflect on the approach taken in the negotiations on domestic regulation disciplines and to consider whether there might be other ways and means that should be explored.

In many ways, this volume represents work in progress, and much more is certainly needed to better understand the relationship between services trade and domestic regulation. What the case studies show is that regulators and trade negotiators often share common challenges, such as ensuring that objectives are pursued through transparent, objective, relevant and impartial regulations and procedures. There is certainly a need for greater dialogue and interaction between the two communities. On that basis, we hope that this book will help promote this interaction and in turn shed light on why the development of trade disciplines in this area has been so complex, as well as how that task could be supported by regulatory cooperation and capacity building.

References

Blundell, J. and Robinson, C. (2000), *Regulation Without the State: The Debate Continues*, Readings 52, London: Institute of Economic Affairs

Cook, P., Kirkpatrick, C., Minogue, M. and Parker, D. (2004) (eds.), *Leading Issues in Competition, Regulation and Development*, Cheltenham: Edward Elgar

Eberhard, A. (2007), *Infrastructure Regulation in Developing Countries: An Exploration of Hybrid and Transitional Models*, Working Paper No. 4, Washington, DC: Public–Private Infrastructure Advisory Facility

Findlay, C. and Sidorenko, A. (eds.) (2003), *Regulation and Market Access*, Canberra: Asia Pacific Press

Glaeser, E. and Shleifer, A. (2003), 'Rise of the Regulatory State', *Journal of Economic Literature* 41(2): 401–25

Krajewski, M. (2003), *National Regulation and Trade Liberalization in Services: The Legal Impact of the General Agreement on Trade in Services (GATS) on National Regulatory Autonomy*, The Hague: Kluwer

Lafont, J.-J. (2005), *Regulation and Development*, Cambridge: Cambridge University Press

Majone, G. (1997), 'From the Positive to the Regulatory State: Causes and Consequences of Change in the Mode of Governance', *Journal of Public Policy* 17(2): 136–67

Mamdouh, H. (2010), 'Services Liberalization, Negotiations and Regulations', paper presented at the Liberalisation of Trade in Services Conference convened by the Cordell-Hull Institute and hosted by the Australian Department of Foreign Affairs and Trade, in Sydney, Australia, 10–12 December

Mattoo, A. and Sauvé, P. (eds.) (2003), *Domestic Regulation and Service Trade Liberalization*, Washington, DC: World Bank

Peltzman, S. (1976), 'Toward a More General Theory of Regulation', *Journal of Law and Economics* 19(2): 211–40

Stigler, G. (1971), 'The Theory of Economic Regulation', *Bell Journal of Economics and Management* 2(1): 3–21

UNCTAD (2010), *Implication of International Trade and Trade Agreements for Primary Health Care: The Case of Services*, Geneva: United Nations Conference on Trade and Development

Vranes, E. (2009), 'The WTO and Regulatory Freedom: WTO Disciplines on Market Access, Non-Discrimination and Domestic Regulation Relating to Trade in Goods and Services', *Journal of International Economic Law* 12(4): 953–87

Wouters, J. and Coppens, D. (2007), 'Domestic Regulation Within the Framework of GATS' in K. Byttebier and K. Van der Borght (eds.), *WTO Obligations and Opportunities: Challenges of Implementation*, London: Cameron May Publishers

WTO (2012), *World Trade Report 2012: Trade and Public Policies – A Closer Look at Non-Tariff Measures in the 21st Century*, Geneva: World Trade Organization

PART I

Impediments to services trade, regulatory theory and principles

2

Why regulate? An overview of the rationale and purpose behind regulation

TINNE HEREMANS

1 Introduction

The starting point for any economist is the superiority of the market mechanism of free exchange in efficiently allocating resources and thereby maximizing social welfare. However, in order for that 'invisible hand' to perform its winning act, the market needs to display certain characteristics:

- there must be a large number of producers of homogeneous products who are sufficiently small and identical so as not to be capable of exercising a great deal of influence on the price level (price-takers) of those products;
- all market participants must have full information about the prices and quality of all products available in the market;
- there should be neither 'externalities' nor 'public goods'.

If these conditions are not met, society's scarce resources will not be put to their highest valued use and the market is deemed to suffer from so-called market failures, which could possibly justify regulatory intervention. As we will see, the characteristics of many services sectors make them particularly susceptible to market failures.

2 Economic theories of regulation

It is common in economic literature reviews[1] to sketch a picture of two opposing schools of thought on regulation: the public interest and the private interest theory of regulation.[2] Yet, it seems more accurate as well

[1] See, among others, Philipsen 2003 and den Hertog 2012.

[2] See Hägg (1997: 337, 356–7), who rejects the strict public/private interest theories divide and believes that both 'mirror' two distinct historical phases in economic research,

as useful to interpret the various economic theories of regulation as valuable pieces of the same regulation puzzle.[3] Therefore, in this chapter the different theories will be grouped under the more encompassing categories of the 'corrective' and 'redistributive' functions of regulation (see e.g. Musgrave 1959). The corrective function of regulation should be understood as aiming at market as well as contract failures. The redistributive function of regulation points to the capture of regulatory processes by private interest groups to extract benefits at the expense of other societal actors (hence 'redistribution').

2.1 *Corrective function of regulation*

As mentioned above, real markets tend to diverge from the ideal of a perfectly competitive market. Welfare economists identified these market failures as harmful to social welfare and investigated the available corrective government instruments (i.e. regulation, taxes and subsidies). Even though a real theory on regulation was never their objective, welfare economists' insights into market failures form an essential part of any discussion of the corrective function of regulation. It should be stressed, however, that early welfare economics simply presumed a benevolent government. In other words, they assumed that government intervention would be a possible low-cost response to market failures without actually examining the interaction between the political process and market failures.[4] Hence, their contribution should be seen as lying in the identification of different instances of market failure where corrective government intervention might be desirable.

emphasizing the corrective and the redistributive impact of public regulation, respectively, and interprets the recent economic theories (new economics of organizations, new institutional economics and agency theory) as providing for a reconciliation of the corrective and redistributive view.

3 Hägg (1997: 337).

4 In his seminal article 'The Problem of Social Cost', Ronald Coase developed the idea that when transaction and information costs are absent (or very low), bargaining between parties will lead to an efficient outcome regardless of the initial assignment of property rights. Hence, he suggested that an *alternative solution for the 'externality' problem* could be the *mutually beneficial bargaining* between the affected parties (the disadvantaged party would 'buy out' the benefit obtained from the 'externality' by the other party) (Coase 1960). However, as will be considered below, such an ideal world with very low transaction costs will rarely exist and externalities will therefore often be too 'complex', for example, involving too many parties, to be remedied through contracting (so-called 'missing markets').

These rudimentary insights were supplemented and refined by new economic theories, among others, transaction cost economics, information economics and agency theory, that can be grouped under New Institutional Economics (NIE). After Coase drew the attention of economists to the engine of the market mechanism – that is, bargaining-contracting – and its potential for solving apparent market failures (self-correcting mechanisms of the market) (Hägg 1997: 337, 356–7), the ensuing research also developed thorough insights into the failings of contracting itself. Consequently, this analysis of contract failure has become an integral part of any present-day discussion on market failures. NIE examines the alternative institutional arrangements, such as public governance through regulation, from the perspective of their contribution to transaction costs savings or the overall promotion of contracting. Through its study of regulations as possible institutional solutions to contracting problems, NIE thus gradually refines the analysis of the corrective function of regulation.[5]

2.2 *Types of market and contract failures*

2.2.1 Market power

Several factors may cause producers to become more powerful than their competitors and evolve from price-takers into price-setters.[6] Since such market power generally leads to inefficient market outcomes from society's point of view,[7] governments attempt to restore the competitive process by means of competition law and other more indirect forms of regulation.

One of the services sectors where the high level of concentration has met with great suspicion from regulators is the audit services market. The consecutive failures and scandals in the audit market sparked a variety of

5 Such as natural circumstances (e.g. scale economies in infrastructure), cartel-agreements, barriers to entry, among others.

6 Market power can lead to allocative inefficiency, productive inefficiency and X-inefficiency, which is the gap between ideal and actual allocative efficiency.

7 Article 33 of the *Proposal for a regulation of the European Parliament and of the Council on specific requirements regarding statutory audit of public-interest entities*, COM(2011) 779, 30 November 2011. Contrast with the rejection of this mandatory rotation in the Committee on Economic and Monetary Affairs (ECON) *Opinion report on the proposal for a regulation of the European Parliament and of the Council on specific requirements regarding statutory auditing of public-interest entities (COM(2011)0779 – C7–0470/2011 – 2011/0359(COD)).*

regulatory initiatives. One policy proposal, which forms the object of heated debate within the EU legislator, is the imposition of a mandatory rotation of audit firms.[8] Aside from guaranteeing greater independence from their clients, the European Union believes that such mandatory rotation could break the dominance of the so-called Big Four(Deloitte, Ernst and Young, KPMG and PricewaterhouseCoopers) and enhance competition.

In some circumstances, however, market power will be the result of a natural monopoly. A natural monopoly is present if average production costs are lowest when concentrated in one sole firm. This typically occurs if the activity requires very large fixed-cost investments relative to the demand, and there are thus significant economies of scale and scope involved. A classic example is infrastructure services like telecommunications, transportation or energy, which require great network-related investments. With regard to these infrastructure investments, additional players in the market might then only amount to an unnecessary duplication of these fixed costs. Given the danger that such monopolists would abuse their market power, in the past these services were often entrusted to companies in public ownership. Today, however, many of those former monopolistic sectors have been liberalized, and the predominant approach towards such markets with natural monopoly characteristics has shifted towards regulation. It was realized that, even if certain essential facilities, such as an electricity grid or a railway network, display these natural monopoly characteristics, this does not prevent other parts of the service provision process being opened up to more competition. Yet, to allow for such competition, some degree of regulation is necessary, especially with regard to the incumbent or essential facility owner's conduct. Examples of such regulation are obligations to give reasonable and non-discriminatory access to infrastructure to third parties, and transparency requirements regarding important data on, for example, transmission costs.

2.2.2 Information asymmetry and bounded rationality

Probably one of the most problematic assumptions in the perfectly competitive market model is that of perfect information. Consumers are presumed to possess perfect information on the price and quality of the products in the market, so they are able to choose the product

[8] Nelson (1970) was the first to distinguish between 'search goods' and 'experience goods'. Darby and Karni (1973) added the category of 'credence goods'.

corresponding most closely to their preferences. Often, however, acquiring this information will prove too 'costly', and there will be a situation of asymmetric information where one party possesses more, or better, information regarding the (potential) transaction. Due to their inherent characteristics, services markets are particularly susceptible to such information asymmetries. Indeed, given that services are often intangible and non-storable or involve the delivery of highly customized products, it will be difficult for consumers to gather the necessary quality information.

Goods and services can be divided into three categories based on the availability and cost in the market of information about their characteristics. With 'search goods' (e.g. clothes), their properties can be determined in advance by means of inspection at a reasonable cost. 'Experience goods', however, can only be assessed after they have been consumed and thus rely on repeat purchasing. Given their inherently intangible and non-storable nature, as well as their often customized character, most 'non-complex' services will be difficult to inspect *ex ante* and will thus fall into this category. One example of such a service is a haircut provided by a hairdresser. Lastly, 'credence goods' are deemed to be of such a complex or technical nature that it would require prohibitively large investments (information costs) on the customer's side to obtain the expertise and technical knowledge needed to evaluate the quality of the good or service. Hence, even after consuming the service or good, the customer will be unable to assess its quality (Kay and Vickers 1990: 223, 229). Typical examples of credence goods are professional services, for example, medical and legal services. Indeed, the demand for many professional services stems precisely from this information asymmetry: consumers want to buy advice from the better informed professional.[9] Yet, even the most optimal treatment by a doctor does not necessarily lead to the healing of a complicated disease (Akerlof 1970). Similarly, the loss of a trial by a lawyer can be the consequence of a weak case on the facts rather than professional underperformance. Hence, clients will have difficulty evaluating the quality of the professional service even after it has been provided. This information

[9] See also Weingast (1980: 81, 85), who notes that even assuming that the consumer can obtain quality information through repeated purchase of care for 'minor problems', there is no 'necessary connection between the quality at this level and quality under the more serious category of treatment in life-threatening situations'.

gap will often be exacerbated by the lack of repeat purchasing taking place in these markets. Most people are unlikely to recurrently require the services of a lawyer, architect or medical specialist. Hence, for transactions involving credence goods to occur, there will have to be a large amount of trust by clients that the producer or service provider will perform optimally in their interest.

The information asymmetry in these markets for 'experience goods' and 'credence goods' make them susceptible to a severe demand-side problem. To be precise, if high-quality producers and service providers cannot credibly communicate their entitlement to such trust, the risk of an adverse selection dynamic arises. Consumers who cannot judge the quality of each product or service and separate the bad (lemons) from the good will only be willing to pay the price at which average quality services and goods are valued. Consequently, high-quality service providers/producers will not be sufficiently rewarded for their services and will leave the market. Their exit will further lower the average quality provided in the market and create a downward spiral up to the point where only the 'lemons' are left (the 'market for lemons' problem).[10]

In addition, information asymmetry can also produce a typical hidden action or moral hazard problem once a contractual relationship is entered into. Indeed, in conventional principal–agent situations,[11] where the 'principal' (client) needs to induce the 'agent' (service provider) to act in the client's interest instead of behaving opportunistically (Shapiro 1986: 845), the principal cannot observe the actions of the agent, there is a realistic danger of opportunistic 'hidden action'. In an ideal world, parties construct the right incentives for cooperation by drawing up a complete and enforceable contract laying down all mutual rights and obligations. Yet, in reality, enforcement will be difficult as parties will often be unable *ex post* to observe or assess the actions of the other party. In addition, for complex 'credence' services, it will often be

[10] In an 'agency game', the principal decides whether or not to put a valuable asset under the control of the agent. If the principal puts the asset under the agent's control, the agent decides to cooperate or appropriate. Cooperation is productive, creating, for example, a surplus from trade or a profit from investment. The parties then divide the product of cooperation between them, so both of them benefit. Appropriation is redistributive, meaning that no cooperative surplus is created but rather the agent benefits at the expense of the principal (Cooter and Ulen 2000: 185).

[11] In an agency game, once the principal has decided to invest, the agent gains more from appropriating (opportunistic behaviour) than from cooperating (Cooter and Ulen 2000: 186).

impossible for the client *ex ante* to lay down the exact attributes of 'a reasonable service' and make his payment contingent upon this (Arruñada 2006: 51, 53). Moreover, several complex services involve a degree of professional judgement for which the service provider should be allowed a measure of individual discretion (see e.g. Jolls *et al.* 1998). Hence, both the lack of information as well as the necessary degree of discretion will make any contract drawn up inevitably 'incomplete' and leave the door open for opportunistic behaviour by the professional-agent: the so-called moral hazard.

Whereas traditional economic theory assumes people behave rationally, over the last two decades economists, assisted by psychologists, have started to nuance this supposition (Hanson and Kysar 1999a; 1999b; Bar-Gill 2008, in debate with Epstein 2008). They found that people are limited in their potential to process information and for instance resort to 'rules of thumb' or heuristics that will not always lead to the decision expected from a rational person in that particular situation. Overall, the use of such 'rules of thumb' can nonetheless be seen as a rational manner to save on information costs. Traditional economists attempt to downplay the implications of such 'irrational behaviour'. For instance, the 'law of large numbers' will be relied upon in basic model to wash out these individual errors and ensure that group behaviour as a whole will be rational. Nevertheless, it seems that the arguments for considering 'bounded rationality' as a genuine market failure are becoming more and more powerful. Indeed, recent scholars have convincingly argued that the impact of these decision-making failures on the consumers' side will often be reinforced by rational producer actions attempting to manipulate the market based on these failures (Klein and Leffler 1981). Hence, this combination of bounded rationality on the side of consumers with market manipulating behaviour on the side of producers could add strength to the demand for regulatory intervention.

Another market where these asymmetric information and bounded rationality problems are pervasive is that of financial services. The complexity of many financial products and activities is of such magnitude that without the necessary trust these markets simply broke down, as was witnessed during the 2007 to 2008 financial crisis. At the 'micro-level', the complexity of the financial products and services not only makes it hard for consumers to assess their quality, but also risks inducing financial agents to undertake 'hidden action' and, for example, use their clients' assets for risky investments to which the clients would not agree if they knew (and could understand) the actual level of risk involved.

These information problems have led regulators to impose tough mandatory disclosure requirements upon financial agents regarding the nature and risk of the product or service. More far-reaching, and related to the finding that consumers are poor risk-estimators and statisticians, some regulators have even imposed an obligation on financial intermediaries to assess the risk profile of particular clients and only provide them with investments of a risk level below or corresponding to that profile.

However, failure of the contract mechanism does not necessarily rule out a market-friendly solution, since the market often appears quite capable of correcting itself. Hence, repeat-purchasing allows consumers to counter the information problems related to experience goods. In markets where there is little repeat purchasing by individual consumers, such information can nonetheless surface in the long term via reputations of service providers on the basis of past performances. In addition, investments in specific assets[12] (such as brand names (advertising), luxurious offices and specialized education, among others) which cannot be recuperated if the firm or service provider is driven out of business or prevented from further exercising that particular profession will ensure that producers have no incentive to cheat on quality and thus signal to consumers that they can expect qualitative services.[13] Furthermore, advertising allows producers to voluntarily disclose information regarding their products and thereby reduce search costs for consumers. In addition, producers can signal their commitment to quality by providing product guarantees or warranties.

2.2.3 Externalities

An externality arises when a transaction creates unintended costs or benefits for a third party. Such costs or benefits are external to the specific bargain and will not automatically be taken into account in the purchase or sales decision of the parties. For instance, when a client chooses a less-qualified, low-cost architect, he or she does not calculate the social cost imposed upon third parties by a low-quality service. The collapse of a badly designed building could then impose a negative effect on third

[12] For a more elaborate treatment of the asset specificity theory, see Heremans 2012: 33–7.

[13] The Coase theorem holds that, in the absence of transaction costs, the outcome of such negotiations will be economically efficient regardless of how the law allocates property rights, since the parties involved will choose transactions that maximize their joint utility and thus social welfare (Coase 1960: 1).

parties. On the other hand, high-quality work of a litigation lawyer not only furthers the client's case but also has the positive effect of creating 'good case law' and thus furthering 'the rule of law' to the benefit of society as a whole. However, the social gain from this positive external effect is not part of the main transaction, and the market is thus likely to under-supply legal services of this quality. In summary, the lack of internalization of social costs or benefits might lead to services of a suboptimal quality level, as well as to the over- or under-provision of certain services.

The financial crisis of 2007 to 2008 painfully highlighted the pervasiveness of externalities in financial services markets. Indeed, by pursuing risky profit-maximizing strategies, such as providing sub-prime mortgages and collateralized debt obligations (CDOs), the actions of some financial institutions almost led to a complete breakdown of financial markets, with the inevitable severe knock-on effects on the economy as a whole. The interconnectedness of the financial system, as well as its dependence on trust, has led regulators to impose stricter capital and liquidity requirements, diversification obligations, and transparency and structural reforms, among other measures.

Since Coase, the externalities problem is often described as one of missing or incomplete markets. If the affected third party were able to negotiate with the consumer or service provider, this would lead to a socially optimal outcome (den Hertog 2012: 25, 44–5). By bargaining on the basis of what his safety from construction accidents is worth to him ('reservation price'), the third party could induce the others to internalize the costs their actions would impose upon him. However, in the event of a 'true or complex externality', there tend to be so many third parties (multilateral relationship) that the occurrence of negotiation becomes illusionary (prohibitive transaction costs). Hence, a private law failure is added to the market failure. All in all, it is possible that the transaction costs of public intervention will be lower than the transaction costs of bargaining. A typical example of such public intervention would be safety and environmental regulation. Hence, the provision of tourism services could be restricted by environmental laws forbidding mass tours to be organized in fragile ecosystems such as the Galapagos Islands.

2.2.4 Public goods

Public goods constitute a special type of positive externality. Typically, the consumption of these goods cannot be restricted to those who have paid for them (non-excludability), causing free-rider behaviour and thus an under-supply of such goods in the market. Moreover, one person's use of the good will have no consequences for its consumption by others (non-rivalry). Classical examples of public goods include national defence, the production of information, and street lights. The provision of public goods thus requires government intervention in some way or another.

2.2.5 Non-economic objectives

Although the dividing line between economic and non-economic objectives is far from clear-cut, certain regulatory objectives indeed seem to go beyond a 'mere' correction of the failing market mechanism and, rather, aim to alter the undesirable outcome of this market process.[14] Such pure, non-economic objectives could include redistribution, fairness, individual freedom and ethics, among others. Goals such as environmental and consumer protection could also legitimately be pursued beyond their economically efficient level based on other non-economic considerations.

Service suppliers in postal, telecommunications, health and educational markets, for example, typically face universal service obligations, which seek to ensure that these services are universally accessible, regardless of the remoteness of a region or of the financial means of a consumer, and thus irrespective of the profitability for the supplier. In the past, these services were often provided by state monopolies precisely for this reason. Now that these markets have been opened up for competition, governments seek to impose such universal service obligations via, for example, licensing requirements and subsidies.

2.3 Redistributive function of regulation

The assumption of a benevolent government attributed to the Public Interest Theory did not persuade all economists and was, moreover, contradicted by a growing empirical literature on the inefficient functioning of various regulated economic sectors.[15] As a result, several new theories of regulation set out to provide a more realistic analysis of the phenomenon of regulation. These theories share the view that regulation is largely the result of lobbying and rent-seeking by interest groups. Accordingly, rather than as a response to market failure, regulatory

[14] For references to such empirical studies, see Hägg 1997: 337, 340.
[15] For a critical discussion, see Posner 1974: 335, 341–3.

measures are perceived as instances of government failure where private interests succeeded in capturing the relevant political actors to pursue their own agenda. Even though a strict antagonism between 'public interest' and 'private interest' theories of regulation amounts to a misleading simplification, it does clarify that the theories grouped here treat regulation mainly as a 'redistributive means' – redistributing wealth to private interest groups at the expense of other societal actors.

Regulatory capture theory has its roots in political science.[16] Despite its lack of theoretical foundations (Stigler 1971: 1, 3) preventing it from growing into a full-blown explanatory theory, it deserves credit for raising awareness of private interest groups' intervention in the regulatory process through its research on the capture of agencies by the regulated branches of industry.

Chicago economists subsequently developed what is often referred to as the Economic Theory of Regulation, where regulation is understood as a process by which interest groups seek to promote their private interests. Stigler, who is seen as the founder of this Chicago School of thought, saw government as the supply-side and industry as the demand-side of protective regulation (Posner 1974: 344–50). Hence, regulation was largely the result of business demand for protection against competition. When looking deeper into industry demand for regulation, Posner suggested that industries, especially those where cartelization was infeasible or costly, would be inclined to push for protective regulation. In heterogeneous and non-concentrated industries, regulation is thus likely to replace cartel agreements (Peltzman 1976). However, this single (industry) interest view was nuanced by Peltzman who described politicians as arbitrating between the dispersed 'uninformed' voters (power of votes) and focused industry interest groups (power of pressure groups).[17]

Becker (1983: 395–6) later reintroduced some element of public interest into the perception of the regulatory process by arguing that competition between different interest groups ('pressure groups') will lead to a socially optimal outcome if these groups enjoy equal political power (1983: 383–5). Thus, competition between equally influential groups is expected to lead to a socially desirable outcome with gains for society

[16] Posner 1974: 341–3.

[17] Becker (1983: 371, 384) states that his 'analysis of non-cooperative competition among pressure groups can unify the view that governments correct market failures and what has seemed to be a contrary view that governments favour the politically powerful'. See also Hägg 1997: 337, 345–6.

rather than dead-weight losses. Becker (1985: 344) deduced this from his finding that pressure groups have an incentive to demand the most efficient regulation, since regulations generating dead-weight costs discourage the political power of the benefited group, whereas they encourage the power of those groups whose welfare has been harmed:

> No policy that lowered social output would survive if all groups were equally large and skilful at producing political influence, for the opposition would always exert more influence than proponents.
>
> (Olson 1965)

In 1965, Olson had already developed his Collective Action Theory, looking into the parameters for the successfulness of interest groups.[18] The main problem confronting such interest groups is the potential for members to free-ride on the lobbying efforts. Hence, to facilitate monitoring of members and lower the organizational transaction costs, pressure groups should ideally be small, well-organized and single-issue oriented (e.g. professional associations). The consumer group that bears the cost of the regulation should, on the contrary, be large and dispersed. Given the relatively small costs imposed on each separate individual and the high costs of bargaining among such isolated actors, their incentives to prevent the regulation from being adopted will be small.

One of the criticisms of the Chicago Theory of Regulation was its lack of interest in the 'supply side of regulation', that is, the actual dynamics of the political and administrative process responsible for this regulation. These dynamics form precisely the research object of the Public Choice Theory.[19] Public Choice Theory compares the political scene to a market in which individuals try to maximize their utility. Politicians support particular legislative measures in exchange for votes, budgetary contributions or prestige. Citizens and interest groups pursue their preferences using their voting power as well as financial influence. Hence, legislation is seen as a product provided by politicians in response to the demand of voters and private interest groups.

A branch of the Public Choice Theory focused on the damaging consequences of the phenomenon of rent-seeking (Cooter and Ulen 2000: 290). Through the adoption of protective regulation, interest groups attempt to reduce competition in order to acquire artificial rents

[18] This theory was mainly developed by the Virginia School, with representatives such as Tullock and Buchanan. For an overview, see Buchanan *et al.* 1980.

[19] See in particular Buchanan and Tullock 1962 and Buchanan *et al.* 1980.

(the rent-seeking hypothesis). A rent is the difference between the revenue from producing a good and the cost of its production. In a competitive market, such rents are dissipated and product prices are driven down to the optimal level. By artificially limiting competition, however, a wealth transfer (the rent) from consumers to producers will occur. Apart from distributive concerns, such rent-seeking behaviour also raises objections from an efficiency point of view, that is, the resources employed by producers to capture this wealth transfer create a pure dead-weight loss (waste) to society.

It is clear that part of the explanation for the highly regulated nature of the services sector in the European Union is to be found in such rent-seeking activity. Within the European Union, it is estimated that there are about 800 regulated professions to which access is restricted on the basis of professional qualifications. While for many professions, this may be perfectly logical, sometimes there is a strong suspicion that this primarily reflects a profession's desire to restrict competition.

2.4 *Why* ex ante *regulation above* ex post *liability?*

Tort law generally steps in where costs are imposed (damage) outside a market transaction setting and where Coase-style voluntary bargaining offers no solution due to prohibitively high transaction costs (Shavell 1984). The classical setting for tort liability is the occurrence of complex negative externalities involving a large number of potential victims or tortfeasors (one who is guilty of tort).

Tort law and regulation attempt to create the right incentives for mutually beneficial bargaining between the two parties to take place. However, they do so in a fundamentally different manner. Most prominently, tort liability is only imposed *ex post* and has an indirect *ex ante* deterrent effect. Regulation, on the other hand, compels certain conduct *ex ante* and thus directly interferes with the private transaction. In his seminal article, Shavell (1984: 360–1) set out four factors that determine the optimal choice between the application of regulation and liability law.

Generally the private parties involved will be best informed about the pertinent risks and will therefore be in the best position to decide on the optimal amount of precaution to be taken. However, the correct estimation of certain risks may require complex analyses that are beyond the budget or intellectual capacity of the individual parties. In that case, government regulation has the advantage of spreading the costs of information gathering and processing over several potentially harmful situations.

If the damage is of such magnitude that the potential wrong-doer will be unable to compensate it when found liable (insolvency risk or incapacity to pay), his incentive to take care will be suboptimal. In determining his level of precaution, he will only take into account the accident costs up to the amount of his own total assets.[20] Damages exceeding his 'wealth' will thus fail to induce the potential injurer to internalize all the social costs of his activity (Shavell 1984: 363). At that point, *ex ante* regulation will be more efficient in provoking the desired behaviour. For example, excessive speculation by hedge funds causing financial markets to become unwarrantedly volatile will not be sufficiently deterred by possible tort liability, since such hedge funds will be unable to refund the damage done to financial stability of the system as a whole.

If the damage is spread out over many victims or if a considerable time period elapses before it surfaces, victims might have suffered only minor harm individually or might fail to identify the cause. Therefore, they may lack sufficient incentives to sue. Such a significant reduction in the probability or threat of liability suits would lead to a suboptimal amount of care-taking on the side of potential injurers.[21] In that case regulation is likely to be the more efficient deterrent.

A final factor in the balance between liability and regulation is the costs involved in administrating the respective systems. The tort liability system entails public costs linked to the functioning of the legal system (including conducting trials, employing judges and empanelling juries) and private expenses borne by the parties in the pursuit of their claim or defence (time, effort and legal expenses) (Shavell 1984: 365). The adoption as well as the enforcement of regulation involves its own public costs. Private regulatory costs are generated in the process of complying with the prescriptions of the regulation. All in all, the tort process involves the clear advantage of only producing costs when an accident actually happens.

In conclusion, the optimal quality incentives will probably be provided through a combination of liability law and regulation.[22]

[20] See Cooter and Ulen 2000: 335–6 on the way expected damages influence the incentives to take precaution on the side of the injurer.

[21] However, often settlements will be able to avoid expensive trials.

[22] When discussing the regulation of professional services, Ogus *et al.* 2003 distinguish between entry and conduct regulation. However, when traditional economic regulation

3 Types of regulation

Even if failure of the market mechanism combined with private law failure calls for government intervention, economic theory will still call for the *least market interfering instrument* to be used. For example, to address information asymmetry, information regulation will merely 'inject' missing information into the market to facilitate the functioning of the market mechanism, whereas regulatory standards interfere directly with the quality or safety of the products being provided in the market.

Regulation can be divided into, on the one hand, structural and entry regulation and, on the other hand, conduct regulation.[23] Structural and entry regulation affects the market structure itself by, for example, only allowing a service provider to enter the market when it fulfils certain preconditions. Examples include licensing and qualification requirements, planning restrictions, among others. Conduct regulation attempts to influence the behaviour once in the market and includes price regulation, advertising restrictions and quality standards, among others.

A selection of regulatory instruments will be briefly discussed in function of their *degree of interference with the market mechanism* as well as *their point of intervention*, that is, before entering the market or while 'behaving' in the market.

3.1 Entry and structural regulation

3.1.1 Licensing

If an occupation or activity is subject to licensing, only those individuals or firms who are granted a licence or permit will be allowed to perform it. The granting of such a licence will generally depend on the applicant meeting certain requirements (education, training, minimum quality standards and 'fitness', among others). Licensing thus attempts to influence the quality of the service before its provision (*ex ante*) and controls the input (i.e. education, and training and experience) rather than

(e.g. regulation of natural monopolies) is included in the categorization, it makes sense to speak of structural regulation which then includes entry regulation. See Kay and Vickers 1990: 223.

[23] For an overview of the empirical research on the effects of professional licensing, see Svorny 2000: 296, 309–14. Licensing can also be motivated by other motives, such as the desire to restrict the quantity of that activity, for example, to prevent over-fishing, limit the amount of fire-arms being sold or protect natural monopolies.

the output.[24] The underlying assumption is that there is a strong complementary relationship between the licensing requirements, for example, investments in human capital (input), and the quality of the service provided (Ogus 2004: 215). Hence, the provision of professional services will typically be conditional on the service supplier having obtained a licence based on certain educational requirements. Similarly, to provide educational services, a school will need to obtain a licence attesting to its fulfilment of certain criteria (e.g. training of its teachers and adequacy of infrastructure) deemed necessary for qualitative education.

Clearly, licensing is a very intrusive instrument with considerable administrative costs (checking all individual applications) as well as potential welfare losses caused by the limiting of competition. By excluding lower quality, and thus cheaper, services from the market, consumer choice is reduced. Such paternalistic restraint of consumer choice would only seem appropriate if low quality provision entails disastrous consequences or great societal repugnance (*ibid.*). Yet, the difficulty in formulating clear and enforceable standards defining 'proper performance' for certain complex services often also motivates the choice for a case-by-case, *ex ante* screening process (Leland 1979: 1335, 1337).

With regard to the licensing of professional occupations, excluding the lowest quality providers from the market should increase the average quality level, thus alleviating the information problems that risk resulting in adverse selection (the lemons problem)[25] as well as the moral hazard agency failure (Stigler 1971). In principle, certification would address these information problems in a less market interfering manner. However, if the bounded rationality of individuals, for example poor risk assessments, is taken into account, there could be a paternalistic justification for preventing individuals from choosing low quality services. More importantly, licensing may also be justified as preventing the serious externalities from malperformance by *ex ante* excluding 'incompetent' service providers.

However, it is clear that licensing practices are at risk of being abused by private interest groups to restrict competition and acquire monopoly gains (Ogus 2004: 215).

[24] Shapiro 1986: 843–4. For a critical perspective, see Svorny 2000: 303–4.
[25] Shapiro 1986: 843. For a critical appraisal of these arguments, see Svorny 2000: 305–6.

3.1.2 Restrictions on organization

Related to licensing are the entry restrictions flowing from certain market organizational measures aiming to control, in terms of location or quantity, the establishment of service providers. A typical example is pharmacies and other health services, where governments sometimes limit freedom of establishment in order to ensure a universal service provision.

3.2 Conduct regulation

3.2.1 Information regulation

Information regulation attempts to 'inject' missing information into the market. Hence, information remedies 'merely' control the degree and content of information that is or should be disclosed, so as to facilitate the functioning of the market mechanism without directly interfering in it. The administrative costs of formulating and enforcing such information requirements are relatively low.

Mandatory disclosure duties (for example via labelling, on product characteristics such as price, composition or risks) seek to provide consumers with the optimal amount of information while still leaving consumer choice intact. However, excessive mandatory disclosure duties run the risk of information overload. A typical example mentioned above are the extensive information duties imposed on financial agents regarding the nature and riskiness of the financial products on offer. Also in other services markets, such as energy services, operators will be obliged to fully disclose the components of their price calculations to facilitate the comparison between different providers.

Whereas advertising is generally an efficient instrument of voluntary information disclosure which increases transparency in the market, some regulation on false or misleading information will usually be indispensable.

A certification system can inform consumers on the investments made in training and education by professionals by allowing them to use a specific title or certificate which sets them apart from other professionals in the same field. Ideally, certification has the advantage of signalling quality without creating entry barriers for lower quality providers. In reality, however, certification may become the standard in the market, to the extent that only the supply of certified services remains. New entrants will then have no option but to conform.[26]

[26] For an in-depth discussion, see Netz 2012: 99.

3.2.2 Regulatory standards

Regulatory standards (safety, quality and technical) directly impose a certain quality or safety level in the market, thereby reducing consumer choice.

Although standards considerably interfere with the market mechanism, information regulation will not suffice if services are of too complex a nature for consumers to obtain or process all the relevant information needed to determine their preference. In addition, the bounded rationality of consumers, for example failure to make adequate risk estimates, can justify imposing standards. Furthermore, mandatory disclosure duties will not protect third parties against possible externalities. Hence, construction services need to comply with many standards, for example, energy efficiency standards. Not only do such standards contribute to reducing the negative external effect of energy consumption on the environment, but they also remove the need for clients to conduct complex technical assessments on the beneficial level of insulation, among others.

The administrative costs involved with standards will be relatively high. These include the cost of formulating standards, monitoring compliance and enforcement. Standards will also entail compliance costs for the regulated sector, as well as other indirect costs. Such indirect costs include productive inefficiencies as well as the stifling effect on innovation. In addition, the difficulty in setting the optimum standard could lead to considerable allocative inefficiency. For example, prudential regulation imposing capital requirements on banks will have to find a balance between providing a sufficient buffer against financial downturn and misfortunes, and allowing banks to fulfil their important function of financing the economy.

Furthermore, standard-setting processes are vulnerable to rent-seeking activity by pressure groups and risk resulting in inefficient standards that allow those private interest groups to exploit competitive advantages and limit the entry of new players.

3.2.3 Price controls and fee restrictions

Economists generally do not favour the use of price regulation because this could distort price signals and undermine a well-functioning competitive market. In the past, such price controls were often adopted with distributional objectives in mind. They have mostly been replaced by other economic instruments such as subsidies and taxes.

Nevertheless, in the case of a natural monopoly, price controls are deemed unavoidable, even if the precise modalities remain highly problematic.[27] As discussed above, a monopolist lacks the incentives to charge prices at an allocatively and productively efficient level. In certain liberalized services markets, such as energy and telecommunications, where competition is still too weak to lead to efficient pricing, regulators often impose price caps. Similarly, the universal service obligation in health and energy services is often pursued via price controls.

4 Conclusion

This chapter has provided an overview of the economic rationale for regulation and the instruments utilized. In doing so, it has reflected on a more refined understanding of the market mechanism (and thus of market failures) as pioneered during the 1960s, under the impulse of Robert Coase (1960). Attention was turned to the core function of the market, that is, the dynamic process of bargaining among self-interested private actors which leads to the efficient allocation of resources.[28] Or, in other words, voluntary bargaining among private parties producing 'cooperative surpluses'[29] that benefit society as a whole. Hence, as long as individuals can freely bargain, an efficient allocation of resources should occur.

Yet in reality, as explained in this chapter, there will often be obstacles to such efficient exchange and cooperation, the so-called transaction costs.[30] Still, such a potential breakdown in the bargaining process does not inevitably call for regulatory or corrective intervention. Indeed, a first, less interfering, answer to transaction costs are facilitative law rules. Facilitative law, encompassing contract and property law, seeks to create the environment for welfare-enhancing bargaining.[31] Hence, such rules aim to protect property rights and to streamline the exercise of the

[27] *Ibid.*

[28] This dynamic bargaining perspective replaced the earlier more static image of a centralized auctioneer allocating resources according to individuals' preferences.

[29] The term 'cooperative surplus' denotes the value created by moving resources to more valued uses.

[30] These include search costs, negotiating costs and enforcement costs (Cooter and Ulen 2000: 87–91).

[31] Even though these rules also control the conduct of private parties, they can always be overruled by private agreements between the affected parties, depend upon private

freedom of contract, thereby reducing the costs of defending one's property and of concluding transactions, and thus facilitating cooperation and exchange between individuals more generally (Cooter and Ulen 2000: 288–9; Kerber 2008: 66). For instance, since many market transactions do not amount to a direct exchange but involve some degree of postponed performance, parties might shy away from bargaining due to the perceived risk of non- or inadequate future performance. Indeed, it will often be profitable for a party to defect after the other party has performed, thereby preventing the socially optimal outcome of cooperation. For those instances, contract law amounts to a transaction-costs saving instrument which ensures the enforceability of the mutually agreed upon commitments and thus induces the parties to conclude the mutually beneficial bargain. In other words, contract law facilitates the efficient functioning of the market mechanism. Evidently, economists favour laws that facilitate rather than 'correct' or replace the market mechanism.[32]

By refining our understanding of the market mechanism as a dynamic bargaining–contracting process, Coase also deepened the concept of market failure. A market will only truly fail if transaction costs are prohibitively high, and even facilitative law cannot 'reconstruct' the bargaining process. In other words, only if there is a market failure combined with a private law failure, is there potentially a case for regulatory intervention.

Regulation or market correcting law can then be understood as the instrument whereby the state implements its collectivist system. In other words, the state attempts to induce or force individuals to behave in a manner that they are unlikely to do voluntarily, in order to reach certain collective or public interest goals that cannot be achieved by the market due either to market failure (and private law failure) or to their non-economic character (e.g. redistribution and individual freedom). Non-compliance is (generally) sanctioned by the state itself and backed by criminal or administrative sanctions. Hence, in contrast to facilitative law, regulation limits the freedom of action of individuals in the interest of what the state perceives to be the common good.

enforcement and are backed by private sanctions. In essence, the freedom of choice so fundamental to the market mechanism is safeguarded to the greatest extent.

[32] Cooter and Ulen (2000: 93) explain this normative Coase theorem as stating that the law should be structured so as to remove the impediments to private agreements.

References

Akerlof, G.A. (1970), 'The Market for 'Lemons': Quality Uncertainty and the Market Mechanism', *Quarterly Journal of Economics* 84(3): 488–500

Arruñada, B. (2006), 'Managing Competition in Professional Services and the Burden of Inertia' in C.D. Ehlermann and I. Atanasiu (eds.), *European Competition Law Annual 2004: The Relationship Between Competition Law and the (Liberal) Professions*, Oxford: Hart Publishing

Bar-Gill, O. (2008), 'Behavioral Economics of Consumer Contracts, the Exchange', *Minnesota Law Review* 92(749): 749–802

Becker, G.S. (1983), 'A Theory of Competition Among Pressure Groups for Political Influence', *Quarterly Journal of Economics* 98(3): 371–400

Becker, G.S. (1985), 'Public Policies, Pressure Groups, and Dead Weight Costs', *Journal of Public Economics* 28(3): 329–47

Buchanan, J.M., Tollison, R.D. and Tullock, G. (1980), 'Towards a Theory of the Rent-Seeking Society', College Station: Texas A&M University Press

Buchanan, J.M. and Tullock, G. (1962), *The Calculus of Consent*, Ann Arbor: University of Michigan Press

Coase, R.H. (1960), 'The Problem of Social Cost', *Journal of Law and Economics* 3: 1–44

Cooter, R.B. and Ulen, T. (2000), *Law and Economics*, Boston: Addison-Wesley

Darby, M.R. and Karni, E. (1973), 'Free Competition and the Optimal Amount of Fraud', *Journal of Law and Economics* 16(1): 67–88

Epstein, R.A. (2008), 'The Neoclassical Economics of Consumer Contracts', *Minnesota Law Review* 92(803): 810–16

Hägg, P.G. (1997), 'Theories on the Economics of Regulation: A Survey of the Literature from a European Perspective', *European Journal of Law and Economics* 4(4): 337–70

Hanson, J.D. and Kysar, D.A. (1999a), 'Taking Behavioralism Seriously: The Problem of Market Manipulation' *NYU Law Review* 74(3): 630–749

Hanson, J.D. and Kysar, D.A. (1999b), 'Taking Behavioralism Seriously: Some Evidence of Market Manipulation', *Harvard Law Review* 112(7): 1420–572

Heremans, T. (2012), *Professional Services in the EU Internal Market*, Oxford: Hart Publishing

den Hertog, J., (2012), 'Economic Theories of Regulation' in R. Van den Bergh and A. Pacces (eds.), *Regulation and Economics*, Encyclopedia of Law and Economics IX, Cheltenham: Edward Elgar

Jolls, C., Sunstein, C.R. and Thaler, R. (1998), 'A Behavioral Approach to Law and Economics', *Stanford Law Review* 50: 1471–550

Kay, J. and Vickers, J. (1990), 'Regulatory Reform: An Appraisal' in G. Majone (ed.), *Deregulation and Re-regulation*, London/New York: Pinter

Kerber, W. (2008), 'European System of Private Laws: An Economic Perspective' in F. Cafaggi and H.M. Watt (eds.), *Making European Private Law*, Cheltenham: Edward Elgar

Klein, B. and Leffler, K.B. (1981), 'The Role of Market Forces in Assuring Contractual Performance', *Journal of Political Economy* 89(4): 615–41

Leland, H.E. (1979), 'Quacks, Lemons, and Licensing: A Theory of Minimum Quality Standards', *Journal of Political Economy*, 87(6): 1328–46

Musgrave, R.M. (1959), *The Theory of Public Finance*, New York: McGraw-Hill

Nelson, P. (1970), 'Information and Consumer Behavior', *Journal of Political Economy* 78(2): 311–29

Netz, J. (2012), 'Price Regulation: Theory and Performance' in R. Van den Bergh and A. Pacces (eds.), *Regulation and Economics*, Encyclopedia of Law and Economics IX, Cheltenham: Edward Elgar

Ogus, A. (2004), *Regulation*, Oxford: Hart Publishing

Ogus, A., Paterson, I. and Fink, M. (2003), *The Economic Impact of Regulation in the Field of Liberal Professions in Different Member States, Research Report for the European Commission*, Vienna: Institute for Advanced Studies

Olson, M. (1965), *The Logic of Collective Action*, Cambridge: Harvard University Press

Peltzman, S. (1976), 'Towards a More General Theory of Regulation', *Journal of Law and Economics* 19(2): 211–40

Philipsen, N.J. (2003), *Regulation of and by Pharmacists in the Netherlands and Belgium: An Economic Approach*, Maastricht: Intersentia

Posner, R.A. (1974), 'Theories of Economic Regulation', *Bell Journal of Economics and Management Sciences* 5(2): 335–58

Shapiro, C. (1986), 'Investment, Moral Hazard, and Occupational Licensing', *Review of Economic Studies* 53(5): 843–62

Shavell, S. (1984), 'Liability for Harm Versus Regulation of Safety', *Journal of Legal Studies* 13(2): 357–74

Stigler, G.J. (1971), 'The Theory of Economic Regulation', *Bell Journal of Economics and Management Sciences* 2(1): 3–21

Svorny, S. (2000), 'Licensing, Market Entry Regulation' in B. Bouckaert and G. De Geest (eds.), *The Regulation of Contracts*, Encyclopedia of Law and Economics III, Cheltenham: Edward Elgar

Weingast, B.R. (1980), 'Physicians, DNA Research Scientists and the Market for Lemons' in R.D. Blair and S. Rubin (eds.), *Regulating the Professions*, Lexington: Lexington Books

3

Domestic regulation: what are the costs and benefits for international trade in services?

HILDEGUNN KYVIK NORDÅS

1 Introduction

Services have been considered non-tradable and therefore outside the scope of trade policy-making until quite recently. A logical consequence is that explicit policy barriers to cross-border trade in services are rare. What segments markets for tradable services is therefore largely in the realm of domestic regulation.[1] Both the General Agreement on Trade in Services (GATS) and a number of regional trade agreements (RTAs) aim at developing disciplines on domestic regulation. GATS Article VI states that disciplines on qualification requirements and procedures, technical standards and licensing requirements shall be established to ensure that regulation is not more burdensome than necessary to ensure the quality of the service. Such disciplines are, however, yet to be established, but a reference paper on pro-competitive domestic regulation in telecommunications has been included in a number of World Trade Organization (WTO) members' GATS schedules of commitments, and some RTAs have quite detailed disciplines on domestic regulation in this sector.[2]

The region where services market integration runs the deepest is the European Union. The Treaty of Rome of 1957 had already granted full market access for the signatories through cross-border trade as well as the movement of capital and labour, while the Internal Market Act aimed at removing barriers to the implementation of the letter as well as the intention of the Treaty of Rome. Nevertheless, domestic regulation turned out to be a formidable obstacle to the integration of services markets. In the words of the European Commission, 'a decade after the envisaged completion of the internal market, there is still a huge gap between the vision of an integrated European Union economy and the

[1] See Jensen 2011 for a discussion on which services are tradable.
[2] See for instance the United States–Australia Free Trade Agreement.

reality as experienced by European citizens and providers'.[3] Hence, a Services Directive aiming at lowering regulatory barriers to trade was introduced in 2006. Against this backdrop, this chapter will focus on empirical work on the European Union and the telecommunications sector.[4]

2 Which sectors are regulated and why?

Regulation can be divided into two broad categories: regulation that aims at protecting consumers; and regulation that aims at restraining dominant firms from exploiting their market power.[5] Licensing and related quality and qualification requirements in professional and financial services are examples of regulation in the first category. The market failure that such regulation aims at correcting is asymmetric information, where service providers possess information that is superior to that available to the consumer. For instance, a badly designed bridge may collapse after many years or medical treatment may have harmful, long-term side-effects. In either case, the consumer may not be able to spot and avoid negligent service providers. When the consequences of negligence are grave and the cost of regulation moderate, regulation may enhance welfare.

Industries that are subject to network effects, economies of scale or two-sided markets are examples of the second category. *Ex ante* regulation may be necessary to prevent incumbents in telecommunications and other network industries from exploiting their market power. In this case, a lack of regulation constitutes an entry barrier to foreign as well as local potential entrants. The WTO Reference Paper on telecommunications addresses this problem and encourages countries to introduce pro-competitive regulation so that foreign suppliers have access to infrastructure and ultimately the consumer. Pro-competitive regulations and prudential regulations in the telecommunications and financial sector,

[3] Directive 2006/123/EC of the European Parliament and of the Council of 12 December 2006 on services in the internal market [2006] OJ L376/36, 27 December 2006 ('Services Directive').

[4] Interested readers are referred to Francois and Hoekman 2010 for a comprehensive literature survey on services trade and policy, whose brief discussion of domestic regulation is not repeated here.

[5] Of course, pro-competitive regulation also ultimately benefits the consumer, but the distinction is still useful, since the regulatory measures are typically quite different in the two categories.

respectively, are found to be positively related to trade and investment (Kox and Nordås 2007).

Telecommunications, finance and professions in the health sector are regulated in almost every country. Beyond these, it is surprising how countries differ regarding how many and which services sectors are regulated. The EU database on regulated professions, for instance, reveals that the number of regulated professions ranges from 47 in Estonia to 404 in the Czech Republic; and the unweighted average is 157.[6]

A possible reason for such diversity in the approach to regulation may be differences in the legal framework (e.g. civil versus common law) and differences in the division of labour between the public and the private sector. As noted by La Porta *et al.* (2008), rules and regulations are deeply rooted in legal origins. The burden of entry regulation, for instance, varies systematically among legal traditions, countries with common law having lighter entry regulation but stronger protection of investors. In countries where government plays a major role through government ownership and publicly provided services, an absence of regulation need not imply that entry barriers are low.

3 Indicators of domestic regulation

Empirical research on the relationship between domestic regulation and trade in services requires measures of both domestic regulation and trade in services. Services trade data are available at a relatively aggregate level from balance of payment statistics from the International Monetary Fund and the Organisation for Economic Co-operation and Development (OECD). One of the few sources of information on domestic regulation that are comparable across countries and over time is the OECD Product Market Regulation (PMR) indices in non-manufacturing sectors. It contains information on regulation in three broad areas: state control; barriers to entrepreneurship; and barriers to trade and investment. There is specific information on licensing and permit systems, the extent to which international standards are adopted or encouraged,

[6] Author's calculation based on information at the European Commission website, available at http://ec.europa.eu/internal_market/qualifications/regprof/index.cfm?action=homepage. The database contains information on regulated professions in the European Economic Area and Switzerland. It constitutes a transparency measure in relation to Directive 2005/36/EC of the European Parliament and of the Council of 7 September 2005 on the recognition of professional qualifications [2005] OJ L255/22, 30 September 2005.

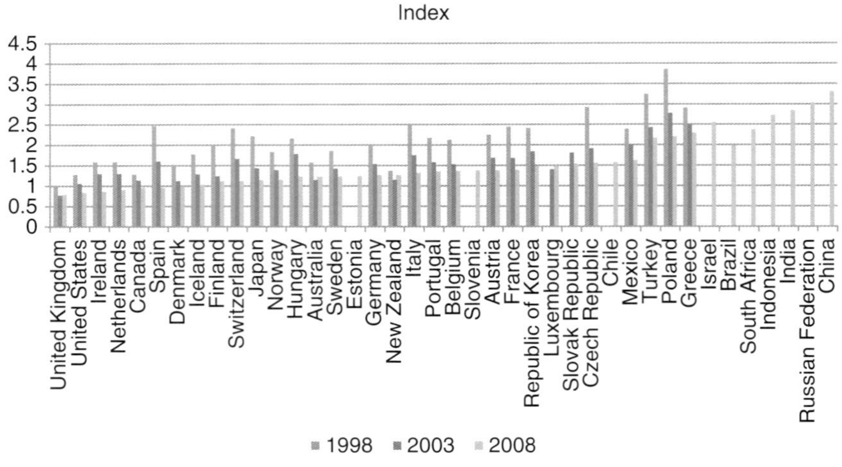

Figure 3.1 OECD product market regulation indices
Source: OECD.

mutual recognition agreements and, in the case of professional services, more detailed information on qualification requirements and procedures for recognition is provided. Thus, information on domestic regulation that comes close to the GATS Article VI definition can be extracted from the PMR, but to my knowledge there are no studies that single out this specific information for empirical analysis. The PMR is presented in Figure 3.1, where the most recent year (2008) includes all OECD countries and six large non-members.[7] The values range from 0 (least burdensome) to 6. OECD countries are ranked according to the PMR index value in 2008, while the non-OECD countries are ranked separately.

The regulatory burden has declined over time in most countries. Non-OECD countries by and large have more burdensome regulation than OECD countries, although Brazil scores better than four other OECD countries. It should be noted that the PMR indices mainly capture regulation 'on the books', and do not fully capture to what extent and how regulation is implemented. The PMR has been used in a number of empirical studies that relate regulation to economic performance, including trade performance.

[7] The next issue of the PMR will be published in 2013/14.

Regulation may impose cost-raising restrictions on services providers or it may erect entry barriers.[8] Cost-raising regulations not only deter foreign suppliers, but also inhibit the competitiveness of local firms. Thus, several studies have found that the level of cost-raising domestic regulation is negatively associated with both imports and exports as well as inward and outward foreign direct investment (FDI) in services.[9] Indeed, empirical studies analysing trade and investment flows in OECD countries conclude that domestic regulation has a stronger marginal effect on trade and investment flows than explicit barriers to trade and investment (Kox and Nordås 2007; Nordås and Kox 2009).

Non-discriminatory regulation may *de facto* impose higher costs on foreign than local service suppliers. Foreign suppliers must learn how to deal with an unfamiliar regulatory environment and compliance costs are often at least partly duplicated in each market a firm enters. A lack of recognition of qualifications obtained abroad implies that service providers must retrain in the host country or engage local staff with the required qualifications. Different standards could imply that foreign service suppliers must redesign their product or restructure their business model to meet the host country requirements, depending on whether regulation relates to processes or products. Differences in regulation may, in other words, be a considerable barrier to international trade in its own right.

The OECD PMR indicators have been used for empirical analyses of the trade and FDI effects of both the level and differences in regulation. These studies construct indicators of bilateral differences in regulation and introduce them in gravity regressions that explain bilateral services trade flows, FDI flows or the relative importance of trade versus FDI.[10] Pica and Mora (2005) introduced the absolute value of the difference in PMR index values between country pairs as a measure of regulatory heterogeneity in a gravity equation that explains bilateral FDI in services. They found that FDI flows are negatively associated with this measure. Interestingly, it appears that FDI does not necessarily flow from heavily

[8] As noted above, regulation may also lower entry barriers, but such pro-competitive regulation is not captured in the PMR.

[9] An early study is Golub *et al.* 2003, who found that domestic regulation is negatively associated with inward FDI as well as exports of services.

[10] The gravity equation relates bilateral trade or FDI to relative market size and relative trade costs. The methodology has been subject to refinements in recent literature, demonstrating a number of weaknesses in the standard approach. Nevertheless, the qualitative findings in the studies reported here appear to be robust to such refinements.

regulated to lightly regulated countries, but rather among countries with the same level of regulation. A possible explanation is that firms that are used to dealing with heavy-handed regulation at home find it easier to deal with regulation abroad as well, and vice versa.

Kox and Lejour (2006) and Kox and Nordås(2007; 2009) took a similar approach. However, they argued that countries with the same score on the PMR index may well have different regulatory structures and designs. They therefore constructed a more fine-grained indicator of regulatory heterogeneity based on whether or not country pairs gave the same answers to individual questions in the PMR questionnaire. Regulatory heterogeneity was found to have a relatively large impact on FDI. Financial services and computer services appeared to be most sensitive to differences in regulation.

Nordås and Kox (2009) also analysed how the level and heterogeneity of domestic regulation affect the choice of mode of servicing foreign markets. It is first noticed that the relative importance of commercial presence has increased over time, albeit trade and FDI are complements rather than substitutes in most services sectors. The exceptions to this finding are financial services where modes of supply appear to be independent, and transport services where cross-border trade and investment appear to be substitutes.

When modes of supply are complementary, regulation that raises the cost of establishing a firm also impedes cross-border trade. However, the relative importance of commercial presence in services trade among country pairs tend to be higher the more similar the regulatory regime. A possible explanation is that commercial presence requires more commitment of resources and compliance with regulation than cross-border trade. Finally, it appears that inward FDI in services falls off more sharply with distance the more restrictive is domestic regulation. The disadvantage of remoteness is, in other words, amplified by regulation.

Simple regressions correlating the PMRs to FDI stocks and services trade, controlling for gross domestic product (GDP), shows the correlations reported in Table 3.1.[11] It is noticeable that regulation not only hampers inward investment and imports of services, but also inhibits the outward orientation of local service suppliers. In fact,

[11] The regression relates the log of FDI stocks and the log of trade flows, respectively, to the PMR index value, controlling for the log of GDP. All coefficients are significant at a 1 per cent level.

Table 3.1 *Correlations PMR, services FDI stocks and services trade*

	Inward FDI	Outward FDI	Imports	Exports
PMR	−0.83	−1.60	−0.50	−0.43

Note: Estimated by author using OECD data on services trade and investment stocks.

outward FDI appears to be more affected by home country regulation than inward FDI.

4 Trade liberalization under different market structures

The empirical literature on domestic regulation and services trade is relatively sparse for good reason. Comparable information on regulation across countries outside the OECD area is not readily available, and services trade data are patchy. One way of getting around this problem is to analyse trade liberalization under different market conditions, assuming implicitly or explicitly that the market structure is a result of domestic regulation.

Several theory papers have taken this approach. A general finding is that cross-border trade is more likely to raise welfare than the establishment of commercial presence in the event of a cartel or oligopoly in the liberalizing country. The reason for this is that, in the absence of pro-competitive regulation, the foreign firm would join the cartel, earn a profit beyond the normal return to capital and expatriate some or all of the profits. A welfare loss occurs when expatriated profits exceed the welfare gains from additional imported services varieties and increased competition from foreign providers (Francois and Wooton 2001; Wong *et al.* 2006).

Konan and Van Assche (2007) incorporated an imperfectly competitive telecommunications sector in a computable general equilibrium (CGE) model for Tunisia and simulated the welfare effect of trade liberalization in this sector under a cartel and duopoly scenario, respectively.[12] They assumed that if the sector were liberalized without imposing regulation on the incumbent supplier, one foreign firm would enter and

[12] They first estimated the demand elasticity and the Lerner mark-up conditions for a monopoly, a cartel, oligopoly and monopolistic competition in the telecommunications sector.

form a cartel with the incumbent. This is contrasted with a scenario where one foreign firm enters and a Cournot duopoly would ensue. In the first case, trade liberalization would result in a welfare loss, mainly due to repatriation of profits by the foreign company, while in the latter case there would be a welfare gain.

A promising empirical approach is to use firm-level data to conjecture the competitiveness and openness of markets. Kox and van Leeuwen (2013) estimated the optimal scale of business services firms in thirteen EU Member States and argued that, in a fully competitive market with no entry or exit barriers, all firms would converge towards the optimal scale and achieve the same level of productivity. They found that rigid labour markets and restrictions on closing a business could explain that firms operated on an inefficient scale. They also tested whether import penetration improves productivity and found that firms tend to narrow the productivity gap towards the best firms in their size class, but competition from imports did nothing to change the distribution of firms on size classes. The paper stopped short of exploring to what extent import penetration is a function of domestic regulation. An interesting extension and promising subject of future research would be to explore direct effects on productivity and indirect effects through imports.

An important insight from this research is that the welfare gains from trade liberalization depend on the market structure. In network industries, pro-competitive domestic regulation may be a precondition for welfare-enhancing trade liberalization. In inherently competitive industries in contrast, deregulation could strengthen the welfare gains from trade liberalization.

5 EU internal services market

The EU treaties have removed barriers to trade and movement of capital and labour, and domestic regulation accounts for remaining policy barriers to services trade. EU legislation in a number of services areas aims at creating integrated services markets through regulatory reforms. The most important is the Services Directive of 2006.[13] A number of impact analyses preceded the entry into force of the Services Directive.

[13] The Services Directive covers commercial services accounting for about 40 per cent of EU GDP. It does not cover financial services, transport, postal services, audiovisual services and telecommunications. These are covered by other EU Directives, while social services are mainly outside the scope of the common market.

The most common methodology was to construct a quantitative measure of regulatory burden in each EU Member State and use the gravity model, a general equilibrium model, or both, to simulate the trade and welfare effects of reducing or eliminating the regulatory barriers.[14]

These studies predicted that the implementation of the Services Directive would increase intra-EU services trade by 5 per cent to 60 per cent, boost services FDI by 20 per cent to 40 per cent and raise GDP by between 0.3 per cent and 1.5 per cent. Different results can partly be explained by the coverage of the analyses in terms of countries, sectors, time-frame and whether or not both trade and FDI are considered. In addition, early studies assumed that the Services Directive would entail the country of origin principle. A service supplier that complies with the home country regulation should, in that case, be able to provide services in all EU Member States without being subject to licensing or other forms of permits or authorization in the host country. The country of origin principle was, however, met with fierce opposition and was dropped from the final version of the Services Directive.

The European Commission has recently published a study which makes a preliminary assessment of the impact of the Services Directive (Monteagudo *et al.* 2012). The study used information on the presence or absence of twenty authorization requirements in fifteen services sectors covering about 20 per cent of EU GDP.[15] Before the Directive was implemented, legal services were the most regulated sector followed by retail trade and architecture. However, the sectors where the regulatory indices went down the most were travel agencies, tourist guides, construction and real estate agents. The estimated impact of the reduction in regulatory burden that actually took place was a 4 per cent increase in services FDI and about 7 per cent additional services trade. This is substantially below the *ex ante* estimates. The authors explain the difference mainly by the fact that their study looked at actual deregulation rather than assuming that regulatory barriers would be eliminated.

The EU study finally estimated the impact of the Services Directive on labour productivity and welfare. The most important source of labour productivity gains was less onerous domestic regulation facing service suppliers in their home market, while increased competitive pressure

[14] See Copenhagen Economics 2005; Breuss and Badinger 2006; Kox and Lejour 2006; and De Bruijn *et al.* 2008.

[15] These were scored and aggregated into an index of barriers to intra-EU trade and investment before and after the implementation of the Services Directive.

from foreign suppliers was not important. The estimated labour productivity gains in the sectors included were entered as exogenous shocks to a CGE model, and an increase in GDP of about 0.8 per cent for the European Union as a whole, varying across countries from 0.3 per cent to 1.5 per cent, was estimated.[16] The impact on GDP is, in other words, similar to that obtained from the pre-Services Directive studies, even if the estimated trade effect is much smaller. In the EU study, the productivity gains mainly stem from a less burdensome regulatory environment at home, which was not considered in most of the pre-Services Directive studies.

An important policy lesson from the EU internal market experience is that the levels, as well as differences in regulation, constitute a formidable barrier to trade in services. Reducing regulatory barriers results in more trade, but first and foremost it improves the productivity and thus the competitiveness of local firms.

6 Telecommunications

At the time the WTO telecommunications Reference Paper was introduced in the mid-1990s, there was consensus that incumbent dominant providers should be subject to *ex ante* regulation that forced them to give entrants access to their network on reasonable terms. Since then, the telecommunications sector has developed almost beyond recognition. The Internet has largely substituted for fixed line traffic in OECD as well as in a number of developing countries, while the proliferation of 3G and 4G mobile networks to some extent blurs the distinction between wired and wireless access to the Internet. Moreover, from the consumers' point of view, telecommunications, broadcasting and content constitute a bundle of services purchased from a single provider often at a flat subscription fee.

Convergence between broadcasting, broadband and wireless Internet platforms calls into question whether traditional access regulation serves its purpose. Moreover, the deployment of next generation networks (NGNs) is so expensive that often only one network provider can be sustained, with the possible exception of large metropolitan areas. There appears to be a growing consensus that one needs to strike a balance between incentives to invest in new technology, on the one hand,

[16] The CGE model used was the EU Directorate General for Economic and Financial Affairs QUEST.

and competitive markets at the current point in time, on the other. What is the right balance depends on the market structure, level of income, geography and population density in each case.[17] Recent research has argued that, under uncertainty, more investment in NGN occurs if the entrants are forced to share the incumbent's investment costs. Risk sharing where operators jointly deploy and share the cost of NGN would also yield higher investment rates than traditional access regulation (Nietzsche and Withies 2011). The Australian government is of the view that the markets under-invest in NGN, and has opted to build a national broadband network as a government-funded infrastructure project.[18]

The convergence of communications services platforms, and the bundling of communications services and content raise new regulatory issues with international dimensions. The telecommunications provider is typically a regulated domestic firm, while the content providers are unregulated, but typically large multinational companies. Little empirical work has been done on the relation between trade and regulation in this setting. The welfare effect of domestic regulation on a local telecommunications firm which sells access to unregulated foreign content providers has, however, been analysed by Faros *et al.* (2009) from a theoretical standpoint. They make a case for traditional *ex ante* access regulation provided that the regulated access price allows the telecommunications operator to recover its long-run marginal cost. *Ex post* regulation, in contrast, could allow the (unregulated) foreign content provider to exploit its market power and shift excessive profits to its home country. Traditional access regulation may, in other words, raise the telecommunications profits which, in turn, could generate more investment in NGN when content and communications services are complementary.

The relations between telecommunications firms and content providers have become a contentious issue for regulators. It was hotly debated at the recent International Telecommunication Union (ITU) treaty meeting, as will be further discussed in section 7. For now it is noted that very little empirical research is available on the relationship

[17] See e.g. OECD 2011; ITU Regulation Toolkit, available at www.ictregulationtoolkit.org/en/index.html; and the EU regulatory framework for electronic communications, available at http://europa.eu/legislation_summaries/information_society/legislative_framework/index_en.htm.

[18] See www.nbn.gov.au/about-the-nbn/.

between electronic communications, electronic content regulation and international trade – a gap that urgently needs to be filled to inform policy-making.

7 Harmonization or mutual recognition?

Regulatory convergence stimulates services trade and investment. There are several ways that governments can reduce regulatory heterogeneity. International standards are probably most practical in cases where regulation is of the prudential or pro-competitive sort, and there is consensus on what constitutes best practice. Examples are the Basel agreements on regulation of financial services and the international telecommunications regulations (ITRs) under the auspices of the ITU.

But even in these cases best practice regulation changes with technology and market structure. Thus, amendments of regulations in the financial services sector became imperative following the financial crisis that started in 2007. By the same token, with the emergence of high-speed Internet and related services, the current ITRs, last amended in 1988, are ripe for an overhaul. Nevertheless, in both cases new regulation has been met with controversy and only eighty-nine countries signed the new ITR that was debated during the ITU treaty meeting in Dubai in December 2012. Among the countries that felt that the treaty did not adequately ensure a free market in Internet services were EU Member States, India, Japan and the United States.

Regulatory harmonization is even more difficult to achieve in areas where regulatory principles are less well established and where there are different views on whether or not regulation is necessary. As we saw in section 2, which services are subject to regulation varies substantially across countries even within the European Union. Furthermore, whether or not a sector is regulated does not necessarily reflect how open the sector is to foreign trade. In the building industry, for instance, some countries regulate the architect and engineering inputs, while others rely on building codes and their enforcement, leaving engineering and architecture unregulated. Which of these approaches is more conducive to trade is an open question.

The experience of the European Union illustrates the difficulties of regulatory harmonization. Pelkmans (2012) notes that early attempts at regulatory harmonization came about by using the least common denominator. The end result was a detailed, complex and costly uniform set of regulations. The Services Directive takes a somewhat different perspective. It seeks to simplify administrative procedures in all EU Member States and indicates that harmonized forms could be introduced by the European Commission. The Services Directive calls for authorization schemes to be used sparingly and for mutual recognition of authorizations. Mutual recognition of professional qualifications has been introduced in Directive 2005/36/EC.[19]

Mutual recognition reduces regulatory barriers to trade and investment, while allowing for regulatory discretion and diversity. Mutual recognition is not without problems, however. It was, for instance, not politically possible to introduce the origin principle in the Services Directive, which would have implied that licences, qualifications and authorizations awarded in one Member State would be valid in all Member States. What is not politically possible within the European Union is probably not possible in regional trade agreements, GATS or a possible new international services agreement either. Therefore, some progress towards harmonization on best practice regulation where such consensus exists, mutual recognition among like-minded countries, and intentional agreements to simplify regulation are probably the most realistic prospects.

8 Conclusion

The empirical literature on the relationship between domestic regulation and services trade is relatively sparse, for good reason. Comparable information on domestic regulation that can be used in empirical analysis is not readily available and services trade data is patchy. Furthermore, conceptual problems related to measuring services trade flows persist. In telecommunications, for instance, trade involves a flow of services in one direction and payments for the services in the opposite direction. The latter part is often missing because telecommunications operators do not always charge for terminating each other's traffic. If traffic is asymmetric, operators typically agree on net payments, in which case information on gross flows may not be available. If traffic is more symmetrical, so-called bill and keep agreements are common. This means that telecommunications operators bill their customers for traffic, including traffic that originated on a foreign operator's network, but keep the proceeds. In this

19 Directive 2005/36/EC of the European Parliament and of the Council of 7 September 2005 on the recognition of professional qualifications [2005] OJ L255/22, 30 September 2005.

case, no payments are involved and no transactions are recorded on the countries' balance of payments.

Two-sided markets are also common in services (e.g. information communications technology services and content, distribution and advertising, and many more). In such markets, prices may not reflect costs if one side pays in order to attract customers. Moreover, in some cases, one side of the market is regulated, while the other is not. The most tradable services are typically characterized by such market structures. A growing literature exists on the economics of regulation, but the trade aspect is rarely dealt with. Adding the trade dimension to models of regulation and bringing them to microdata would be a useful and promising area for future research. A problem is that firm-level data are typically confidential and only national research teams have access to them. As long as this remains the case, empirical research is limited to impact analysis of reforms in single countries or common markets such as the European Union.

The Services Directive, as well as other sector-specific Directives and Regulations, constitute natural experiments and a rich source of future empirical research on the relationship between domestic regulation and services trade. It also provides a reality check since what cannot be achieved within the European Union is unlikely to succeed in less comprehensive trade agreements, for instance GATS.

Caution is needed when analysing the relationship between domestic regulation and services trade. First, domestic regulation often imposes entry barriers rather than tariff-equivalent trade costs. Standard gravity estimates of the impact of regulatory reforms may therefore not be suitable. Second, differences in regulation impose trade costs that may be at least as trade restricting as the level of regulation. What matters is not only how much regulation there is but also how similar it is to, or how well it is recognized by, major trading partners. Finally, regulatory barriers to trade in services will always exist. Simulating the trade effect of eliminating regulatory barriers may therefore not be very helpful. Going forward, the impact of future regulatory reforms on competitiveness and productivity would be augmented if harmonized with major trading partners.

References

Breuss, F. and Badinger, H. (2006), 'The European Single Market for Services in the Context of the Lisbon Agenda: Macroeconomic Effects of the Services Directive' in *Deepening the Lisbon Agenda, Studies on Productivity, Services and Technologies*, Vienna: Austrian Federal Ministry of Economics and Labour

Copenhagen Economics (2005), *Economic Assessment of the Barriers to the Internal Market for Services: Final Report*, Copenhagen: Copenhagen Economics

De Bruijn, R., Kox, H. and Lejour, A. (2008), 'Economic Benefits of an Integrated European Market for Services', *Journal of Policy Modeling* 30(2): 301–19

Faros, Ø., Kind, H.-J. and Sørgard, L. (2009), 'Domestic Regulation and International Trade', *Journal of Industry, Competition and Trade* 9(1): 1–16

Francois, J. and Hoekman, B. (2010), 'Services Trade and Policy', *Journal of Economic Literature* 48(3): 642–92

Francois, J. and Wooton, I. (2001), 'Market Structure, Trade Liberalization and the GATS', *European Journal of Political Economy* 17(2): 389–402

Golub, S., Nicoletti, G., Hajkova, D., Mirza, D. and Yoo, K.-W. (2003), *Policies and International Integration: Influences on Trade and Foreign Direct Investment*, OECD Economics Department Working Papers 359, Paris: Organisation for Economic Co-operation and Development

Jensen, B.J. (2011), *Global Trade in Services: Fear, Facts, and Offshoring*, Washington, DC: Peterson Institute for International Economics

Konan, D.E. and Van Assche, A. (2007), 'Regulation, Market Structure and Service Trade Liberalization', *Economic Modelling* 24(6): 895–923

Kox, H. and Lejour, A. (2006), 'The Effects of the Services Directive on Intra-EU Trade and FDI', *Revue économique* 57(4): 747–69

Kox, H. and Nordås, H.K. (2007), *Services Trade and Domestic Regulation*, OECD Trade Policy Working Paper 49, Paris: Organisation for Economic Co-operation and Development

Kox, H. and van Leeuwen, G. (2013), 'Market Selection and Scale Inefficiency: A New Methodology Applied to EU Business Services', *Structural Change and Economic Dynamics* 25: 77–94

La Porta, R., Lopez-de-Silanes, F. and Shleifer, A. (2008), 'The Economic Consequences of Legal Origins', *Journal of Economic Literature* 46(2): 285–332

Monteagudo, J., Rutkowski, A. and Lorenzani, D. (2012), *The Economic Impact of the Services Directive: A First Assessment Following Implementation*, European Economy Economic Papers No. 456, Brussels: European Commission

Nietzsche, R. and Withies, L. (2011), 'Access Regulation and Investment in the Next Generation Networks: A Ranking of Regulatory Regimes', *International Journal of Industrial Organization* 29(2): 263–72

Nordås, H.K. and Kox, H. (2009), *Quantifying Regulatory Barriers to Services Trade*, OECD Trade Policy Working Paper 85, Paris: Organisation for Economic Co-operation and Development

OECD (2011), *Next Generation Access Networks and Market Structure*, OECD Digital Economy Papers 183, Paris: Organisation for Economic Co-operation and Development

Pelkmans, J. (2012), *Mutual Recognition: Economic and Regulatory Logic in Goods and Services*, Bruges European Economic Research Papers 24/2012, Bruges: Department of European Economic Studies

Pica, G. and Mora, J.V.R. (2005), *FDI, Allocation of Talents and Differences in Regulation*, CEPR Discussion Paper 5318, London: Centre for Economic Policy Research

Wong, C.Y.P., Wu, J. and Zhang, A. (2006), 'A Model of Trade Liberalization in Services', *Review of International Economics* 14(1): 148–68

PART II

Legal perspectives on WTO principles and domestic regulations

4

Reasonableness, impartiality and objectivity

ANDREW MITCHELL AND TANIA VOON

1 Introduction

Similar to the General Agreement on Tariffs and Trade (GATT), the General Agreement on Trade in Services (GATS) imposes requirements of reasonableness and impartiality on World Trade Organization (WTO) members with respect to their administration of certain measures. This general obligation of procedural fairness offers a potentially powerful mechanism for ensuring equitable treatment for traded services and service suppliers beyond the substantive disciplines of WTO law, such as those related to discrimination. Yet, the provision has been subject to relatively little extended commentary or jurisprudence, perhaps because of an underlying concern about the sovereignty implications of WTO dispute settlement organs assessing the reasonableness of WTO members' administration.

Further exploration of the requirements of GATS Article VI:1 is warranted, not only due to the potentially wide-reaching nature of the provision itself (particularly in view of the importance of licensing, access and similar decisions in the context of trade in services), but also due to the existence of corresponding concepts of reasonableness in other GATS provisions. For example, references to objectivity, impartiality and reasonableness appear elsewhere in the GATS domestic regulation provision, Article VI. GATS Article VI:2(a) provides that where judicial, arbitral or administrative review of administrative decisions affecting trade in services is 'not independent' of the agency that made the decision, members must ensure that the review procedures 'in fact provide for an objective and impartial review'. GATS Article VI:3 requires that members' competent authorities advise decisions 'within a reasonable period of time' after the submission of a complete application for authorization to supply a service on which the member has made a specific commitment.

In addition, a number of telecommunications-specific disciplines refer to objectivity, impartiality or reasonableness. For example, the GATS

Annex on Telecommunications (which applies to all WTO members) requires members to 'ensure that any service supplier of any other Member is accorded access to and use of public telecommunications transport networks and services on *reasonable* and non-discriminatory terms and conditions, for the supply of a service included in its Schedule' (section 5(a), emphasis added). Developing country members may, consistent with their level of development, place certain 'reasonable conditions on access to and use of telecommunications transport networks and services' (section 5(g)). Other relevant provisions appear in the telecommunications Reference Paper,[1] which more than eighty-two WTO members have adopted as an additional commitment in their GATS schedules.[2] For example, section 5 of the Reference Paper requires regulators' decisions and procedures to be 'impartial with respect to all market participants'. Procedures for the allocation and use of scarce resources such as frequencies must be 'carried out in an objective' manner (section 6), and interconnection with major suppliers must be provided on 'cost-oriented rates that are . . . reasonable' (section 2.2(b)).

This chapter contains a legal analysis of the meaning and potential scope of GATS Article VI:1, taking account of relevant case law and the underlying purpose of the provision. We begin by providing an overview of Article VI:1 and explaining its general relationship to GATT Article X:3(a) and to the pronouncements of panels and the Appellate Body on the latter provision. We then identify the boundaries of GATS Article VI:1 by considering its textual limitations to particular service sectors (those in which specific commitments are undertaken), particular measures (those of general application affecting trade in services), and particular conduct in relation to those measures (their administration). Finally, we consider the core concepts of reasonableness and impartiality at the heart of both GATS Article VI:1 and GATT Article X:3(a), in view of the limited case law to date, characterizing them as due process provisions that potentially incorporate both procedural and substantive protections. We conclude that the breadth and strength of GATS Article VI:1 as a discipline on domestic regulatory conduct is yet to be fully realized.

1 WTO Negotiating Group on Basic Telecommunications, Reference Paper, 24 April 1996. The Reference Paper is reproduced in WTO 1997.

2 *Regulatory Issues in Sectors and Modes of Supply*, WTO doc. S/WPDR/W/48, 13 June 2012, para. 89 (counting EU Member States individually).

2 Overview of GATS Article VI:1 and relationship to GATT Article X

The words 'reasonable', 'objective' and 'impartial' appear together in GATS Article VI:1, which specifies:

> In sectors where specific commitments are undertaken, each Member shall ensure that all measures of general application affecting trade in services are administered in a reasonable, objective and impartial manner.

This provision corresponds with GATT Article X:3(a), which states:

> Each Member shall administer in a uniform, impartial and reasonable manner all its laws, regulations, decisions and rulings of the kind described in paragraph 1 of this Article.

Paragraph 1 of GATT Article X refers to '[l]aws, regulations, judicial decisions and administrative rulings of general application, made effective by any [Member], pertaining to the classification or the valuation of products for customs purposes, or to rates of duty, taxes or other charges, or to requirements, restrictions or prohibitions on imports or exports . . ., or affecting their sale, distribution, transportation', among others.

The reasoning of the Appellate Body and WTO panels in adopted reports concerning the meaning of concepts such as measures 'of general application' and the 'administ[ration]' of measures in GATT Article X may provide relevant guidance to WTO tribunals interpreting the same concepts in GATS Article VI:1 because the two provisions form part of the same treaty. Thus, GATT Article X provides relevant 'context' for the interpretation of GATS Article VI:1 within the meaning of Article 31(1) of the Vienna Convention on the Law of Treaties,[3] and the WTO jurisprudence on GATT Article X sheds light on the meaning of that provision. Similarly, the Appellate Body has previously referred to WTO case law on the general exceptions in GATT Article XX in interpreting the general exceptions in GATS Article XIV,[4] and vice versa.[5] The Appellate Body also recently, for example, described the national treatment provision of GATT Article III:4 as relevant 'context' in interpreting the non-discrimination obligations in Article 2.1 of the WTO Agreement on Technical Barriers to Trade (TBT Agreement) and thus

[3] Opened for signature on 23 May 1969 and entered into force on 27 January 1980.
[4] For example, see Appellate Body Report on *United States – Gambling*, para. 305.
[5] For example, see Appellate Body Report on *Brazil – Retreaded Tyres*, para. 143.

considered its previous findings on GATT Article III:4 'instructive' in interpreting TBT Agreement Article 2.1.[6]

Before turning to the interpretation of the different components of GATS Article VI:1, it is worth noting the apparent hesitation of some WTO panels, and perhaps the Appellate Body, in finding a violation of the corresponding GATT provision. The panel in *United States – Stainless Steel (Korea)* cautioned in 2000 that GATT Article X:3(a) was 'not . . . intended to function as a mechanism to test the consistency of a Member's particular decisions or rulings with the Member's own domestic law and practice; that is a function reserved for each Member's domestic judicial system, and a function WTO panels would be particularly ill-suited to perform'.[7] In a similar vein, the Appellate Body stated, with respect to GATT Article X:3(a), in 2004 that 'allegations that the conduct of a WTO Member is biased or unreasonable are serious' and therefore 'should not be brought lightly' and 'must be supported by solid evidence . . . reflect[ing] the gravity of the accusations inherent in claims' under that provision.[8]

These statements depict a view of claims under GATT Article X:3(a) (and, by extension, GATS Article VI:1) as substantively different to claims under most other WTO provisions, and in some way more sensitive. Perhaps a claim of violation of the reasonableness requirements of these provisions could even be seen as questioning a WTO member's good faith.[9] However, as one panel has noted in the context of GATT Article X:3(a):

> a WTO Member is free to challenge another Member's compliance with its WTO obligations without being taken to call into question another Member's good faith. This is reflected in Article 3.10 of the DSU which states that 'the use of the dispute settlement procedures should not be intended or considered as contentious acts'.[10]

Accordingly, like GATT Article X:3(a), GATS Article VI:1 is properly regarded as imposing an obligation on WTO members akin to other WTO obligations. A claim of violation of this provision does not

[6] Appellate Body Report on *United States – Clove Cigarettes*, paras. 100, 176 and 180.

[7] Panel Report on *United States – Stainless Steel (Korea)*, para. 6.50. See also Panel Report on *United States – Hot-Rolled Steel*, para. 7.267.

[8] Appellate Body Report on *United States – Oil Country Tubular Goods Sunset Reviews*, para. 217.

[9] Cf. Appellate Body Report on *EC – Sardines*, para. 278 (indicating that WTO tribunals should presume that members act in good faith); Appellate Body Report on *United States – Offset Act (Byrd Amendment)*, para. 298 (emphasizing that a failure to act in good faith would require more than simply establishing a WTO violation).

[10] Panel Report on *China – Raw Materials*, para. 7.739.

necessarily encompass an allegation of bad faith; nor need a panel ruling on such a claim make a determination on the member's compliance with its domestic laws and regulations (Mitchell 2008: 173).

3 Scope of GATS Article VI:1

As Delimatsis (2006: 13, 19–28; 2007: 96–103) explained, the scope of GATS Article VI:1 is limited in several respects. In particular, the provision on its terms applies only:

- in sectors where specific commitments are undertaken;
- to measures of general application affecting trade in services;
- to the way in which measures are administered.

We consider each of these conditions in turn below.

3.1 Sectors where specific commitments are undertaken

Regarding the first condition on the application of GATS Article VI:1 ('sectors where specific commitments are undertaken'), GATS Article XXVIII(e)(i) defines a sector of a service, with respect to a specific commitment, as 'one or more, or all, subsectors of that service, as specified in a Member's Schedule'. Thus, in order for the obligation in Article VI:1 to apply to a given member in a particular service sector, that member must have made commitments in that sector pursuant to Part III of GATS (headed 'Specific Commitments') in relation to market access (GATS Article XVI), national treatment (GATS Article XVII) or additional commitments (GATS Article XVIII). Whether this condition is satisfied will depend on the correct interpretation of the member's Schedule of Specific Commitments, which may itself be a complicated task.[11]

3.2 Measures of general application affecting trade in services

The reference in GATS Article VI:1 to 'measures of general application affecting trade in services' contains several different elements that need to be defined: the relevant measure must be 'of general application' and 'affecting' 'trade in services'. A measure that may be challenged in the WTO is broadly defined as 'any act or omission attributable to a WTO

[11] See e.g. Appellate Body Report on *United States – Gambling*, paras. 158–213; Appellate Body Report on *China – Publications and Audiovisual Products*, paras. 228–412.

Member'[12] and may include, for example, legislation, regulations, and administrative or judicial decisions (see generally Yanovich and Voon 2005: 115–63). As for whether a measure affects trade in services, the Appellate Body has stated in the context of GATS Article I (which defines the scope of the Agreement) that this depends on whether 'trade in services' is taking place and whether the measure 'affects' such services.[13] GATS Article I:2 defines 'trade in services' as the supply of a service by one of four modes of supply, and the notion of affecting services will be broadly construed.[14]

More complicated is the reference to measures 'of general application'. Neither panels nor the Appellate Body have opined on the meaning of this phrase in the context of GATS Article VI:1, but some clarification exists in the context of GATT Article X. In particular, the Appellate Body has stated that GATT 'Article X does not deal with specific transactions, but rather with rules "of general application"'.[15] A WTO panel has also explained, with respect to GATT Article X:2, that a measure of general application includes a measure that 'affects an unidentified number of economic operators, including domestic and foreign producers' and may be a 'country-specific measure' (but not a measure specific to a particular company or shipment).[16] Other WTO panels have gone further, suggesting that even a ruling in an individual case (such as concerning a specific importer) could be a measure of general application within the scope of GATT Article X:1 if it 'establish[es] or revise[s] principles or criteria applicable in future cases'.[17] Put differently, 'a Member's actions in a single instance might be evidence of a lack of uniform, impartial and

[12] Appellate Body Report on *United States – Corrosion-Resistant Steel Sunset Review*, para. 81.

[13] Appellate Body Report on *Canada – Autos*, para. 155.

[14] For example, see in the context of GATS Art. I:1, Appellate Body Report on *EC – Bananas III*, para. 220, as cited in Appellate Body Report on *Canada – Autos*, para. 158.

[15] Appellate Body Report on *EC – Poultry*, para. 111.

[16] Panel Report on *United States – Underwear*, para. 7.65 (followed in Panel Report on *Thailand – Cigarettes (Philippines)*, para. 7.773). The Appellate Body upheld the panel's finding that the measure at issue was a measure of general application: Appellate Body Report on *United States – Underwear*, p. 21.

[17] Panel Report on *Thailand – Cigarettes (Philippines)*, para. 7.773, quoting Panel Report on *Japan – Film*, para. 10.388. See also Panel Report on *United States – Corrosion-Resistant Steel Sunset Review*, para. 7.310 (the panel's findings on GATT Art. X:3(a) were not appealed: Appellate Body Report on *United States – Corrosion-Resistant Steel Sunset Review*, para. 6); Panel Report on *Thailand – Cigarettes (Philippines)*, para. 7.128, which relates to a claim under the Agreement on Implementation of Article VII of the General Agreement on Tariffs and Trade 1994 ('Agreement on Customs Valuation'). The panel's

reasonable administration of its laws' only if they 'have a significant impact on the overall administration of the law, and not simply on the outcome in the single case in question'.[18] Following similar reasoning, a measure affecting trade in services may be regarded as a measure of general application falling within the scope of GATS Article VI:1 if it applies to a range of instances or establishes principles for the future.

3.3 *Administration of measures*

Regarding the limitation in GATS Article VI:1 to measures being 'administered', the panel in *United States – Gambling* stated:

> The Panel is of the view that Article VI:1 does not apply to measures of general application themselves but, rather, to the *administration* of these measures. Article VI:3 imposes transparency and due process obligations with respect to the processing of applications for authorization to supply in a sector where specific commitments have been undertaken. Therefore, Articles VI:1 and VI:3 contain disciplines of a procedural nature.[19]

Similarly, the Appellate Body made clear in *European Communities – Bananas III* and *European Communities – Poultry* that relevant provisions of GATT Article X apply not to members' measures in themselves but rather to the publication and administration of members' measures. Claims relating to the 'substantive content' of particular measures rather than their publication or administration 'must be determined by reference to provisions of the covered agreements other than Article X of the GATT'.[20]

The Appellate Body subsequently clarified in *European Communities – Selected Customs Matters* that these statements 'do not exclude . . . the possibility of challenging under Article X:3(a) the substantive content of a legal instrument that regulates the administration of a legal instrument of the kind described in Article X:1',[21] where administration refers to

findings on GATT Art. X:1 and the Agreement on Customs Valuation were not appealed: Appellate Body Report on *Thailand – Cigarettes (Philippines)*, paras. 4, 6 and n. 11.

[18] Panel Report on *United States – Hot-Rolled Steel*, para. 7.268; the panel's findings on GATT Art. X:3(a) were not appealed. See also Panel Report on *United States – Offset Act (Byrd Amendment)*, para. 7.145.

[19] Panel Report on *United States – Gambling*, para. 6.432 (original emphasis).

[20] Appellate Body Report on *EC – Poultry*, para. 115, citing Appellate Body Report on *EC – Bananas III*, para. 200. See also Panel Report on *United States – Corrosion-Resistant Steel Sunset Review*, para. 7.293; Panel Report on *Argentina – Hides and Leather*, para. 11.76.

[21] Appellate Body Report on *EC – Selected Customs Matters*, para. 200.

'putting into practical effect, or applying, a legal instrument'.[22] The same broad reading of administration (Mitchell and Sheargold 2009: 1, 11) might apply to the interpretation of GATS Article VI:1, allowing a challenge to the substance of a measure that is 'administrative in nature'[23] in the sense that it governs the administration of another measure or 'provid[es] guidance on the meaning of specific requirements of a measure'.[24]

4 Substance of GATS Article VI:1: reasonable, objective, impartial

4.1 GATS Article VI:1 as a requirement of due process

The requirement to accord reasonable, objective and impartial administration of services measures under GATS Article VI:1, like the corresponding provision in GATT Article X:3(a), provides an example of the incorporation into the WTO agreements of administrative law principles such as due process.[25] Also known as 'procedural fairness' or 'natural justice', due process may be regarded as both a general principle of law and a principle of customary international law (Franck 1995: 7–8; Mitchell 2008: 146–53) within the meaning of Article 38(1)(c) and (b), respectively, of the Statute of the International Court of Justice (widely viewed as an informal listing of the sources of public international law) (see e.g. Koskenniemi 2000: xi). Due process may encompass both procedural and substantive elements (della Cananea 2009: 295–6), including the bias rule (decision-makers not to have an interest in the outcome of their decision); the hearing rule (persons who may be adversely affected by the decision to have an opportunity to present their case); and the 'no evidence' rule (decision-makers to base their decision on evidence and reasons) (Mitchell 2008: 147–9). The notion of impartiality in GATS Article VI:1 relates most clearly to the bias rule, while the notion of reasonableness relates most clearly to the no evidence rule. The requirement of objectivity (which appears in GATS Article VI:1 but

[22] Appellate Body Report on *EC – Selected Customs Matters*, para. 224 (emphasis omitted) (quoted in Panel Report on *United States – COOL*, para. 7.821).

[23] Panel Report on *Argentina – Hides and Leather*, para. 11.70; the Panel Report was not appealed.

[24] Panel Report on *United States – COOL*, para. 7.833; the panel's findings on GATT Art. X:3(a) were not appealed.

[25] See Appellate Body Report on *United States – Shrimp*, para. 183 (regarding GATT Art. X:3(a)).

not in GATT Article X:3(a), which refers instead to uniformity) may incorporate aspects of all three rules.

Due process requirements are also clearly reflected in various provisions of the WTO Understanding on Rules and Procedures Governing the Settlement of Disputes (DSU) (Mitchell 2008: 153–7; Mitchell and Sheargold 2009: 6–8). For example, DSU Article 11 requires WTO panels to 'make an objective assessment of the matter before it, including an objective assessment of the facts of the case and the applicability of and conformity with the relevant covered agreements'. Panels cannot include citizens of WTO members whose governments are parties or third parties to the dispute (Article 8.3); disputing parties must have sufficient time to prepare their submissions (Article 12.4); and the Appellate Body must address each issue properly raised in the appeal (Article 17.12). The Appellate Body has elaborated on the significance of due process within the WTO dispute settlement mechanism as follows:

> Due process is a fundamental principle of WTO dispute settlement ... Due process is intrinsically connected to notions of fairness, impartiality, and the rights of parties to be heard and to be afforded an adequate opportunity to pursue their claims, make out their defences, and establish the facts in the context of proceedings conducted in a balanced and orderly manner, according to established rules. The protection of due process is thus a crucial means of guaranteeing the legitimacy and efficacy of a rules-based system of adjudication.[26]

Cases on the due process requirements of the DSU could be informative in relation to the due process requirements of GATS Article VI:1. Of course, GATS Article VI:1 (and GATT Article X:3(a)) is concerned not with the due process to be accorded by WTO panels in resolving WTO disputes, but with the due process to be accorded by administrative decision-makers and other actors involved in the administration of laws and regulations within WTO members. In that sense, GATS Article VI:1 is perhaps more analogous to provisions in the various trade remedies agreements regarding the way in which members' domestic authorities make decisions concerning the imposition of anti-dumping, countervailing or safeguard measures. The Agreement on Subsidies and Countervailing Measures, for example, requires members (through their relevant authorities) to:

- give interested parties ample opportunity to present evidence (Article 12.1);

[26] Appellate Body Report on *Thailand – Cigarettes (Philippines)*, para. 147.

- provide reasons for the imposition of countervailing duties (Article 22.5);
- maintain procedures for prompt independent review of administrative actions (Article 23).

Similar provisions apply in the context of other WTO agreements, such as the Agreement on Trade-Related Aspects of Intellectual Property Rights (TRIPS Agreement) with respect to decision-making on the enforcement of intellectual property rights and review of such decisions (Mitchell 2008: 158–9). The content and case law on the application of all these provisions could provide relevant guidance in understanding the content of GATS Article VI:1.

4.2 Guidance from GATT Article X:3(a) on reasonableness and objectivity

Given the dearth of substantive case law on GATS Article VI:1, the case law on GATT Article X:3(a) may be informative in understanding the threshold requirements of GATS Article VI:1. As foreshadowed above, the terms 'reasonable' and 'impartial' appear in both GATS Article VI:1 and GATT Article X:3(a), while the term 'uniform' in GATT Article X:3(a) is substituted by 'objective' in GATS Article VI:1. While each of these requirements is separate and independent,[27] the different terms encompass some common concepts and considerations.[28] Similarly, the Appellate Body has stated that the phrases 'neutral in application and administered in a fair and equitable manner' in Article 1.3 of the Agreement on Import Licensing Procedures and 'administer in a uniform, impartial and reasonable manner' in GATT Article X:3(a) are, 'for all practical purposes, interchangeable'.[29] Nevertheless, below, we focus on the interpretation by panels and the Appellate Body of reasonableness and impartiality under GATT Article X:3(a), since these terms are also explicit in GATS Article VI:1.[30]

[27] See Panel Report on *China – Raw Materials*, para. 7.740; Panel Report on *Dominican Republic – Import and Sale of Cigarettes*, para. 7.383 (the panel's findings on GATT Art. X:3(a) were not appealed).

[28] See e.g. Panel Report on *China – Raw Materials*, para. 7.707; Panel Report on *Argentina – Hides and Leather*, para. 11.86.

[29] Appellate Body Report on *EC – Bananas III*, para. 203.

[30] On the notion of objectivity within the law, see Kramer 2007.

The notion of reasonableness is common to numerous jurisdictions (see e.g. Bobek 2009: 311, 314–23) and many aspects of private, public, domestic and international law (see MacCormick 1999: 1578–9). Panels have defined 'reasonable' within the meaning of GATT Article X:3(a) as 'in accordance with reason', 'not irrational or absurd', 'proportionate', 'sensible', and 'within the limits of reason, not greatly less or more than might be thought likely or appropriate'.[31] Impartial has been said to mean 'not partial; not favouring one party or side more than another; unprejudiced, unbiased, fair', such that impartial administration refers to 'the application or implementation of the relevant laws and regulations in a fair, unbiased and unprejudiced manner'.[32] Accordingly, the panel in *China – Raw Materials* stated that 'the aim of Article X:3(a) is to ensure that traders are treated fairly and consistently when seeking to import from or export to a particular WTO Member'.[33] Accordingly, application of the provision may 'requir[e] an examination of the real effect that a measure might have on traders operating in the commercial world', including 'whether there is a possible impact on the competitive situation due to alleged partiality, unreasonableness or lack of uniformity in the application of customs rules, regulations, decisions, etc.'.[34] This focus on the effects of administration on commercial operations is reflected in the cases on GATT Article X:3(a) discussed below.

From a procedural perspective, panels have found violations of GATT Article X:3(a) due to unreasonableness and/or impartiality on the basis of extensive delays in decision-making,[35] the use of a methodology not supported by any domestic law in force at the relevant time,[36] and a procedure by which private persons may assist customs officials that contains the inherent 'possibility of revealing confidential business

[31] Panel Report on *Dominican Republic – Import and Sale of Cigarettes*, para. 7.385 (referring to *The New Shorter Oxford English Dictionary* (5th edn, Oxford University Press, 2002) vol. II, p. 2482) (quoted in Panel Report on *United States – COOL*, para. 7.850); the panel's findings on GATT Art. X:3(a) were not appealed. See also Panel Report on *China – Raw Materials*, para. 7.696.

[32] Panel Report on *China – Raw Materials*, para. 7.694.

[33] Panel Report on *China – Raw Materials*, para. 7.708 (citing Panel Report on *EC – Selected Customs Matters*, para. 7.108).

[34] Panel Report on *Argentina – Hides and Leather*, para. 11.77.

[35] Panel Report on *Thailand – Cigarettes (Philippines)*, para. 7.969; the panel's findings on GATT Art. X:3(a) were not appealed. Cf. Panel Report on *United States – Hot-Rolled Steel*, para. 7.277 (conduct including delays found not to violate GATT Art. XX:3(a)).

[36] Panel Report on *Dominican Republic – Import and Sale of Cigarettes*, paras. 7.386–7.388 and 7.394.

information'.[37] However, in view of the substantive aspects of due process mentioned above, GATT Article X:3(a) and GATS Article VI:1 could also potentially be used to address substantive matters: that is, not merely the way in which decisions are taken in administering particular measures but also the substance of those decisions. This possibility seems to be emerging in some of the more recent cases.

The panel in *China – Raw Materials* raised concerns not only about uncertainty in terms of procedure but also arbitrariness,[38] in the context of GATT Article X:3(a). In that case, the panel stated that, in challenging an 'administrative process' under Article X:3(a), the complainant 'must show that the identified features of the challenged administration necessary lead to an inconsistency with Article X:3(a)', which may be achieved by demonstrating that those features 'pose a very real risk of non-uniform, partial [or] unreasonable administration' or 'a very real risk to the interests of the relevant parties'.[39] The panel found that China's system for the allocation of export quotas necessarily involved unreasonable (and non-uniform)[40] administration contrary to GATT Article X:3(a) due to 'the lack of any definition, guidelines or standards in how the 32 Local Departments in charge of Foreign Trade' should apply the potentially determinative criterion of 'operation capacity'.[41] For procedural reasons, the Appellate Body declared moot and of no legal affect the panel's findings regarding the operation capacity criterion.[42] Nevertheless, the panel's approach suggests a limit to the amount of unbridled, unguided discretion that may be granted to a decision-maker (say, authorizing the supply of a service).

Moving further from the realm of the procedural towards the substantive, the panel in *United States – COOL* indicated that an assessment of whether administration is reasonable must be undertaken on a case-specific basis and taking account of 'its objective, cause or the rationale behind it'.[43] In that case, the panel found a violation of GATT

37 Panel Report on *Argentina – Hides and Leather*, paras. 11.94 and 11.101.
38 Cf. Panel Report on *United States – COOL*, n. 1080 (referring to the analysis regarding the chapeau to GATT Art. XX in Appellate Body Report on *Brazil – Retreaded Tyres*, para. 226).
39 Panel Report on *China – Raw Materials*, para. 7.708 (emphasis omitted). Cf. Appellate Body Report on *EC – Selected Customs Matters*, para. 201.
40 Panel Report on *China – Raw Materials*, para. 7.752.
41 Panel Report on *China – Raw Materials*, paras. 7.738, 7.743, 7.745 and 7.746.
42 Appellate Body Report on *China – Raw Materials*, para. 235.
43 Panel Report on *United States – COOL*, para. 7.851. See also Panel Report on *Thailand – Cigarettes (Philippines)*, para. 7.951.

Article X:3(a) on the basis of unreasonable administration through a letter from the US Secretary of Agriculture. The letter by its terms pertained to the implementation of a certain labelling rule, yet it recommended that industry voluntarily adopt certain practices in labelling meat that were stricter than the practices required under the rule. According to the panel, no 'justifiable rationale' for this discrepancy existed, and 'the language of the letter may . . . have caused uncertainty and confusion'.[44] These reasons suggest a willingness by the panel in the course of assessing the Article X:3(a) claim to engage with the substance of the decision-maker's role and reasons in administering a measure in a particular way. Going further, a violation might be regarded as arising from a particular decision (provided that its impact is sufficiently widespread, as discussed above), 'if the decision is one that no reasonable person could have reached upon any reasonable evaluation of the relevant factors' (MacCormick 1999: 1586). This raises the important question whether an assessment of reasonableness is a question of fact as it is usually regarded in other branches of law (MacCormick 1999: 1595); whether that is the case in the context of proceedings before a WTO panel, of course, has implications for the scope of any appeal.

5 Conclusion

The existing interpretation and application of GATT Article X:3(a) in WTO disputes offers an important basis for understanding the nuances and complexities of GATS Article VI:1, in the absence of significant case law on the provision itself. Against the background of existing decisions, a WTO tribunal in a future dispute squarely raising GATS Article VI:1 will be well placed to avoid the intuitive reluctance to find a violation of, or even rule on this provision, knowing that Article VI:1 need not be linked to the good faith of WTO members or impinge on their sovereignty. In this way, the potentially powerful due process discipline of Article VI:1 can be brought to bear in appropriate circumstances. These circumstances are relatively limited, being dependent on the commitments to particular service sectors made in the relevant member's GATS schedule, and on the identification of the challenged measure as a measure of general application. The conduct challenged must also be administrative, but the Appellate Body's more flexible approach to

[44] Panel Report on *United States – COOL*, para. 7.859.

defining 'administration' in GATT Article X:3(a) increases the likely scope of applicability of GATS Article VI:1. As for the notions of reasonableness, impartiality and objectivity that are central to Article VI:1, while their application to particular instances must be determined on a case-by-case basis, the possibility exists that they could extend to sanction not merely procedural but also substantive unfairness. GATS Article VI:1 could therefore provide a significant form of protection to WTO members' service suppliers, who face a range of administrative decisions and procedures regarding their supply of services in the jurisdictions of other members.

References

Bobek, M. (2009), 'Reasonableness in Administrative Law: A Comparative Reflection on Functional Equivalence' in G. Bongiovanni, G. Sartor and C. Valentini (eds.), *Reasonableness and Law*, Heidelberg: Springer

Delimatsis, P. (2006), 'Due Process and "Good" Regulation Embedded in the GATS: Disciplining Regulatory Behaviour in Services Through Article VI of the GATS', *Journal of International Economic Law* 10(1): 13–50

(2007), *International Trade in Services and Domestic Regulations: Necessity, Transparency, and Regulatory Diversity*, Oxford: Oxford University Press

della Cananea, G. (2009), 'Reasonableness in Administrative Law' in G. Bongiovanni, G. Sartor and C. Valentini (eds.), *Reasonableness and Law*, Heidelberg: Springer

Franck, T. (1995), *Fairness in International Law and Institutions*, Oxford: Clarendon Press

Koskenniemi, M. (2000), 'Introduction' in M. Koskenniemi (ed.), *Sources of International Law*, Aldershot: Ashgate

Kramer, M. (2007), *Objectivity and the Rule of Law*, Cambridge: Cambridge University Press

MacCormick, N. (1999), 'Reasonableness and Objectivity', *Notre Dame Law Review* 74(5): 1575–603

Mitchell, A.D. (2008), *Legal Principles in WTO Disputes*, Cambridge: Cambridge University Press

Mitchell, A.D. and Sheargold, E. (2009), 'Global Governance: The World Trade Organization's Contribution', *Alberta Law Review* 46(4): 1061–80

WTO (1997), *World Trade Organization: Agreement on Telecommunications Services (Fourth Protocol to General Agreement on Trade in Services)*, 36 ILM 354, 367

Yanovich, A. and Voon, T. (2005), 'What is the Measure at Issue?' in A. Mitchell (ed.), *Challenges and Prospects for the WTO*, London: Cameron May

5

Balancing legal certainty with regulatory flexibility

MARKUS KRAJEWSKI

1 Introduction

The concept of legal certainty is a central element of most legal systems in the world (Maxeiner 2008: 28). It can be associated with the rule of law, but variations exist concerning its exact contours and its relative importance vis-à-vis other fundamental legal principles. In particular, legal certainty is often contrasted with principles of justice or rightfulness (von Arnauld 2006: 638). Indeed, a formal understanding of legal certainty which focuses on issues of stability and consistency does not guarantee a fair and just outcome. More fundamentally, even though legal certainty is one of the most effective safeguards against governmental and administrative arbitrariness, it offers no protection against unjust or unfair laws. How can the potential for conflict between legal certainty and justice be solved?

Writing shortly after the breakdown of the Nazi dictatorship, the German legal philosopher Gustav Radbruch (1946: 107) gave this answer: 'The conflict between justice and legal certainty should be solved in such a manner that positive law should be considered supreme even if it is unjust or unreasonable unless the conflict between positive laws and justice reaches such an intolerable level that the statute – as 'incorrect law' – has to yield to justice' (author's translation from German). Even though this famous quote aimed predominantly at reconciling extreme forms of injustice with legal positivism, it highlights the fundamental importance of legal certainty in modern constitutionalism and legal philosophy and the difficulty of balancing legal certainty with justice.

More often than not, the conflict between legal certainty and justice will not involve extreme forms of injustice, but laws, legal practices or administrative decisions which are no longer considered to be an adequate articulation of justice or other values of a society. In such a situation, the conflict will not be solved by setting aside the positive law or practice, but by adapting it to new situations and new consideration.

At this point, legal certainty may become an obstacle to regulatory flexibility because of the static notion of legal certainty which aims at preserving the status quo. Arguably, the balance between legal certainty and regulatory flexibility requires procedures and mechanisms which strike a balance between legitimate expectations and the need for a stable and secure legal environment, on the one hand, and the necessity to react to new developments and challenges which may not have been known previously or which have been subject to different value judgements previously, on the other.

This chapter focuses on the balance between legal certainty and regulatory flexibility and discusses this balance in the context of international trade law, in particular the framework of the liberalization of trade in services. The central argument of the present contribution is that legal certainty as developed in national and international legal regimes contains sufficient elements to strike the necessary balance. It may even be argued that a comprehensive understanding of legal certainty already contains such a balance. The conflict is hence a conflict between regulatory flexibility and a narrow concept of legal certainty which is reduced to stability in favour of those who benefit from the status quo.

2 Notion and contents of legal certainty in constitutional and administrative law

Considering the presence of the principle of legal certainty throughout a variety of legal systems in the world, it would be futile to try to develop a uniform understanding of the concept and its contents. Nevertheless, certain elements are generally associated with the principle of legal certainty in national legal orders. Legal certainty is usually an element of constitutional or administrative law, which suggests that the dominant function of this principle concerns the protection of individual rights vis-à-vis governmental activities.

Before considering some elements of legal certainty, it should be noted that a significant part of contemporary US legal scholarship seems to deny the relevance, even the possibility or desirability, of legal certainty (Maxeiner 2008: 33–5). Yet, the difference between US and 'European' legal thinking seems to be more of a methodological or even philosophical nature concerning the question whether the application of the law through courts can ever be certain or whether striving for legal certainty remains an unattainable goal. In addition, US scepticism of the notion of legal certainty seems to focus on the judiciary and does not necessarily address issues of legislation or administration. In any event, it is doubtful whether many legal scholars in the United States would deny any relevance in the US legal system for the elements considered as aspects of legal certainty mentioned below.

A first, and central, aspect of legal certainty concerns ideas of legal clarity. Law must be known to those who should adhere to it. Usually this requires publication of the relevant provisions or the announcement of administrative decisions to the addressee (von Arnauld 2006: 167–97; Maxeiner 2007: 549). Another aspect of legal clarity concerns the language used in provisions and decisions: it must be clear and non-contradictory (von Arnauld 2006: 226–35, 252–69; Maxeiner 2007: 549). These requirements show the close relation between the idea of legal certainty and that of transparency. Furthermore, legal clarity requires precision regarding the contents (von Arnauld 2006: 240–52). The latter may be more relevant for specific rules than for general principles (Braithwaite 2002: 50), but it is generally accepted that a vague rule does not provide for legal certainty.

In addition to clarity, legal certainty requires the binding nature of the law and of court or administrative decisions (Maxeiner 2007: 549). A particular problematic issue of this aspect concerns the adoption and implementation of retroactive laws or the retroactive application of a law. The general principle of *nullum crimen sine lege* prohibits the retroactive application of criminal law to actions committed before the adoption of the law which criminalized the respective action. It is often thought that this principle is part of a general principle of law which restricts the retroactive application or implementation of a statute to the detriment of an individual. Non-retroactivity is a key element of legal certainty (Raitio 1993: 187 ff). The notion that rules and regulations are predetermined is closely connected with non-retroactivity and is therefore also a central aspect of legal certainty (Paunio 2009: 1469).

Another, perhaps the oldest, element of legal certainty is stability (Paunio 2009). Stability of the legal environment is closely connected with protection of legitimate expectations (Bradley and Ewing 2010: 697). Individuals need to rely on actions and decisions of government agencies and officials which have been taken in their favour or which confer a benefit to them. The central question in this context is, however, if and how those agencies and officials are allowed to change their policies and withdraw certain benefits or decisions. Legitimate expectations and the right to adopt necessary changes need to be balanced. A similar issue arises in the case of consistent practice of an authority (Bradley and

Ewing 2010: 699). In some legal systems, this notion of legal certainty may even amount to a binding nature of such practices vis-à-vis the authority itself (von Arnauld 2006: 423–42).

This brief and necessarily non-comprehensive explanation of some central elements of the idea of legal certainty highlights two important aspects which are relevant for the subject of this chapter: first, the notion of legal certainty is not an absolute concept, but a matter of degree. As law is expressed through language and applied by human beings, it cannot provide for absolute certainty. Apart from this fundamental characteristic of law as a social institution, legal certainty is also a matter of degree because it needs to be balanced with other requirements of a modern legal system. Second, the notion of legal certainty is of particular relevance in the relationship between the individual subject of the law and the state or the government in its legislative, administrative and judicial functions. Legal certainty is therefore closely connected with the protection of individual rights.

3 Legal certainty in European and international law

3.1 European law

Legal certainty is one of the fundamental principles of the law of the European Union (Raitio 1993: 125 ff; Hartley 2010: 160). It can be based on the principle of the rule of law considered to be one of the core values of the European Union in Article 2 of the Treaty on European Union (TEU) and on the general principles of the law referred to in TEU Article 6. The principle comprises similar elements to the ones mentioned in the previous section, including publication of legal acts, precision and clarity, restriction of retroactivity, the protection of vested rights and legitimate expectations (von Arnauld, 2006: 489–99, with references to the case law; Hartley 2010: 161–2).

As a general rule, the principle of legal certainty requires that an individual is able to predict the legal consequences of her or his actions (von Bogdandy 2001: 359). The case law of the European Court of Justice (ECJ) which consistently applied and specified the principle of legal certainty indicates that the individual perspective is the *raison d'être* of legal certainty (von Arnauld 2006: 499). According to the ECJ, the principle of legal certainty 'requires that rules of law be clear and precise and predictable in their effect, so that interested parties can ascertain their position in situations and legal relationships governed by European

Union law'.[1] The core element of legal certainty under EU law is therefore the notion of predictability for the individual (Hartley 2010: 161).

Closely related to EU law is the European Convention on Human Rights (ECHR), which is also incorporated into EU law on the basis of TEU Article 6(3). The European Court of Human Rights (ECtHR) in Strasbourg developed legal certainty as an element of human rights law based on the requirement that limitations of human rights are 'prescribed by law' as stated in ECHR Articles 8 to 11 (von Arnauld 2006: 536). According to the ECtHR, clarity, precision and accessibility of the law are central elements of that requirement.

In the *Sunday Times* case, the ECtHR held:

> the law must be adequately accessible: the citizen must be able to have an indication that is adequate in the circumstances of the legal rules applicable to a given case. Secondly, a norm cannot be regarded as a 'law' unless it is formulated with sufficient precision to enable the citizen to regulate his conduct: he must be able – if need be with appropriate advice – to foresee, to a degree that is reasonable in the circumstances, the consequences which a given action may entail. Those consequences need not be foreseeable with absolute certainty: experience shows this to be unattainable. Again, whilst certainty is highly desirable, it may bring in its train excessive rigidity and the law must be able to keep pace with changing circumstances.[2]

This quote indicates that the ECtHR, like the ECJ, considers individual predictability to be one of the key elements of legal certainty. However, it is also clear that the ECtHR not only takes the predictability and expectations of the individual into account, but also the necessity to balance legal certainty with a potential for adaptability of the law.

3.2 General public international law

Legal certainty does not feature prominently in general public international law, which may be largely due to the relative absence of individual rights in international law. However, there are also certain elements in that body of law which can be associated with legal certainty. The principle of *pacta sunt servanda* (Article 27 of the Vienna Convention on the Law of Treaties) is evidence of the binding nature of the law.

[1] *LVK – 56 EOOD* (C-643/11) (2013, nyr), para. 51; Raitio 1993: 14.

[2] *Sunday Times v. United Kingdom*, Case No. 6538/74, ECtHR, 26 April 1979, para. 49.

Furthermore, Article 62 of the Vienna Convention contains an extraordinary right to terminate an agreement if there is a fundamental change of circumstances 'which was not foreseen by the parties'. This seems to indicate that international law recognizes certain aspects of predictability as a general value of the law. In its judgment concerning the *Gabcikovo-Nagymaros Project*, the International Court of Justice (ICJ) pointed out that Article 62 can only be invoked if the unforeseen circumstances serve the 'stability of treaty relations' in international law.[3] Predictability and stability, as well as the binding nature of the law, are therefore elements which exist as principles of public international law, but they are not as clearly linked to individual expectations and the need to be able to assess the legal consequences of one's actions as in domestic or European law. It is therefore safe to conclude that legal certainty has only a weak basis in general public international law.

3.3 *International investment law*

Predictability, stability and the protection of legitimate expectations are of predominant relevance in the law protecting foreign investments based on international investment agreements (IIAs). Typically, these agreements contain the requirement to afford the investor 'fair and equitable treatment', a clause which has frequently been applied in investor–state dispute settlement proceedings in recent years.[4]

First and foremost, fair and equitable treatment relates to the protection of legitimate expectations of the investor.[5] Such expectations can be based on the domestic legal framework in general[6] or on the behaviour of officials and agencies, such as specific promises or presentations about a particular legal or factual situation.[7] Investment tribunals ruled that an investor does not have to expect sudden or fundamental changes

[3] *Gabcikovo-Nagymaros Project (Hungary/Slovakia)*, ICJ, Judgment of 25 September 1997, p. 7 (65), para. 104.

[4] For a recent overview and attempt to classify the caselaw, see Potesta 2012.

[5] The investor's legitimate expectations are the 'dominant element' of the fair and equitable treatment standard according to the tribunal in *Saluka Investments B.V. v. Czech Republic*, UNCITRAL Arbitration, Partial Award of 17 March 2006, para. 304. See also Fietta 2006: 385.

[6] Dolzer and Schreuer 2008: 134; *CMS Gas Transmission Co. v. Argentine Republic*, ICSID Case No. ARB/01/8, Award of 12 May 2005, para. 277.

[7] *Metalclad Corp. v. United Mexican States*, ICSID Case No. ARB(AF)/97/1, Award of 30 August 2000, para. 85 ff.

of the law relevant to the respective investment. Yet, the fair and equitable treatment principle does not include a guarantee that the circumstances of the investment remain unchanged.[8] It should also be noted that legitimate expectations must be based on information available to the investor at the time the investment was made.[9] In other words, an investor can base his or her expectations on the law as it stands at that time, but future developments are not relevant in this context.

A second fundamental element of the fair and equitable standard relates to the stability, predictability and consistency of the legal and business environment (Dolzer 2005b: 105). The tribunal in *CMS – Argentina* stated that a 'stable legal and business environment is an essential element of FET [fair and equitable treatment]'.[10] In this context, reference is often made to the objective and purpose of investment treaties. Based on the Preambles to these agreements, which frequently refer to the intention to create favourable conditions for investments, tribunals have concluded that guaranteeing a stable and predictable investment climate is one of the central purposes of these agreements. The protection of a stable and predictable legal and business environment is closely linked to the investment framework which the investor can legitimately expect.[11]

Many cases which involved claims under the fair and equitable treatment standard concerned changes in the legal and regulatory framework relating to the investment, such as the revocation of environmental permits or measures imposed to stabilize the currency. While tribunals have often declared that states have the sovereign right to regulate, including changes in the legislation, they have nevertheless granted the investor compensation if the investor secured specific contractual promises with the government or received reassurances from government officials that the investment framework would remain stable (Potesta 2012: 19 ff). In addition, tribunals have assessed whether the exercise of legislative power was arbitrary or unreasonable in cases of changes in the legal system.

[8] *Saluka Investments B.V. v. Czech Republic*, UNCITRAL Arbitration, Partial Award of 17 March 2006, para. 305.

[9] *AES Summit Generation Ltd and AES-Tisza Erömü Kft v. Republic of Hungary*, ICSID Case No. ARB/07/22, Award of 23 September 2010, para. 9.3.8.; Dolzer 2005a: 968.

[10] *CMS Gas Transmission Co. v. Argentine Republic*, ICSID Case No. ARB/01/8, Award of 12 May 2005, para. 274.

[11] See also Dolzer and Schreuer 2008: 133, who treat transparency, stability and legitimate expectations as elements of one category.

The treatment of legal certainty in international investment law shows once more that the principle is of particular relevance for the protection of individual rights. In this context, it is important to note that IIAs traditionally do not aim at a balance between investor rights and the state's right and obligation to regulate economic activities. Instead, investment agreements predominantly seek to protect the investor. Furthermore, it is worth noting that many investment tribunals have interpreted the term 'legitimate expectations' without considering the legitimacy of the expectations of the investor, but assessed whether the investor could have reasonably expected the respective changes in law or policy.

3.4 WTO law

Contrary to international investment law, legal certainty does not seem to be a central element of World Trade Organization (WTO) law. While the principle has been evoked from time to time in dispute settlement proceedings as an element of the multilateral trading system,[12] a cursory search of the case law suggests that legal certainty has not played a significant role in the decisions of the panels and the Appellate Body. This relative low profile of the principle of legal certainty seems to coincide with its weak status in general public international law. Legal certainty does not exercise significant authority in relations between states which face each other on the basis of sovereign equality. There are, however, a few instances in WTO law in which the notion of legitimate expectations is of relevance.

The first concerns non-violation complaints in accordance with General Agreement on Tariffs and Trade (GATT) Article XXIII:1(b), General Agreement on Trade in Services (GATS) Article XXIII:3 and WTO Understanding on Rules and Procedures Governing the Settlement of Disputes (DSU) Article 26. According to settled case law, a non-violation complaint requires that the measure which is challenged could not reasonably have been expected by the complaining member.[13] In applying this notion, panels have considered whether the

[12] For example, see the submissions of Guatemala (Third Party) in Panel Report on *Mexico – Tax Measures on Soft Drinks*, para. 5.75: 'Firstly, Guatemala considers the WTO dispute settlement mechanism to be a system that brings legal certainty to trade relations between Members'.

[13] See Panel Report on *Japan –Film*, paras. 10.76–10.77, based on earlier practice.

measure was introduced or anticipated at the time a tariff concession was made, and whether the measure coincided with general policy goals pursued by the responding state.[14] Given the special nature and the reduced relevance of the non-violation complaints in the WTO legal system, it would be difficult to argue that the relevance of legitimate expectations for these complaints suggests that the protection of legitimate expectations is a general principle of WTO law, in particular since non-violation complaints are not based on the violation of WTO law.

Similar to non-violation complaints, GATS Article VI:5 also contains a reference to legitimate expectations. According to this provision, a member shall not apply licensing and qualification requirements and technical standards that nullify or impair such specific commitments in a manner 'which could not reasonably have been expected of that Member at the time the specific commitments in those sectors were made'. The provision resembles the requirements of a non-violation complaint and can in fact be understood in a similar manner.

Unlike the other multilateral trade agreements, the Agreement on Trade-Related Aspects of Intellectual Property Rights (TRIPS Agreement) contains some provisions which directly refer to legitimate interests of the right holder. For example, TRIPS Agreement Article 13 restricts limitations or exceptions of exclusive rights to 'certain special cases which ... do not unreasonably prejudice the legitimate interests of the right holder'.[15] Based on this, the panel in *United States – Section 110(5) Copyright Act* linked this provision to the principle of legal certainty, stating that the notion of 'certain special cases' required that 'an exception or limitation in national legislation must be clearly defined'. The panel continued: 'However, there is no need to identify explicitly each and every possible situation to which the exception could apply, provided that the scope of the exception is known and particularised. This guarantees a sufficient degree of legal certainty'.[16] It is not surprising that the TRIPS Agreement seems more receptive to the notion of legal certainty than other areas of WTO law, as it aims at the protection of individual legal rights, whereas the interstate relationship is more prevalent in the agreements on trade in goods and services.

[14] *Ibid.* para. 10.79; Panel Report on *EC –Asbestos*, para. 8.291 ff.

[15] Similar provisions can be found in TRIPS Agreement Arts. 17, 26(2) and 30.

[16] Panel Report on *United States – Section 110(5) Copyright Act*, para. 6.108.

4 Legal certainty and domestic regulation in the GATS context

The previous two sections showed that the principle of legal certainty contains a number of different elements. Some of them can also be found in GATS, even though they have not (yet) been specifically linked to that principle due to reasons explained above.

4.1 Transparency and clarity of commitments

Transparency is a general principle of GATS as stipulated in the Preamble to the agreement. It contributes to an open and predictable regulatory framework (Krajewski 2003: 126). GATS Article III requires that members publish, or otherwise make publicly available, measures of general application which affect trade in services. The obligation to make relevant rules and provisions known to those affected by them or required to adhere to them is a central element of legal clarity which contributes to legal certainty (Delimatsis 2008a: 93).

Issues of legal clarity also arise concerning the contents of the GATS Schedules of Specific Commitments of WTO Members. In *United States – Gambling*, the panel (as confirmed by the Appellate Body) pointed to the importance of clarity and precision of the commitments.[17] According to the panel, this requirement, which can be found in the Scheduling Guidelines, can also be based on the principle of transparency as enshrined in the GATS Preamble. The panel also referred to the Appellate Body ruling in *EC – Computer Equipment*, which found that 'the security and predictability of "the reciprocal and mutually advantageous arrangements directed to the substantial reduction of tariffs and other barriers to trade" is an object and purpose of the WTO Agreement, generally'[18] and applied this principle to the GATS commitments as well.[19]

It should be noted that the principle of security and predictability of the multilateral trading system is not associated with legitimate expectations of the WTO members or even individual service suppliers. In *EC – Computer Equipment*, the Appellate Body clearly stated that security and predictability of concessions does not allow an 'interpretation of a concession in the light of the "legitimate expectations" of exporting

[17] Panel Report on *United States – Gambling*, para. 6.106; Appellate Body Report on *United States – Gambling*, paras. 188–9.

[18] Appellate Body Report on *EC – Computer Equipment*, para. 82.

[19] Panel Report on *United States – Gambling*, para. 6.108; Appellate Body Report on *United States – Gambling*, paras. 188–9.

Members, i.e., their *subjective* views as to what the agreement reached during tariff negotiations was'.[20]

4.2 Domestic regulation

In addition to GATS Article III and the requirement of clear and precise scheduling, GATS Article VI, which addresses domestic regulation, is of central relevance for the balance between legal certainty and regulatory flexibility. Paragraph 1 of the Article requires members to ensure that all measures of general application affecting trade in services are administered in a reasonable, objective and impartial manner. Relying on case law concerning the respective provision in GATT (GATT Article X:3(a)), Delimatsis (2007: 28) argued that GATS Article VI:1 requires members to 'abide by the sound regulatory principles of consistency and predictability when administering their domestic regulations'. GATS Article VI:1 therefore also contains an aspect of legal certainty at least concerning the application of measures. However, the provision does not apply to the measures themselves and is therefore not applicable if the relevant measures are changed.

GATS Article VI:2 contains the obligation to establish independent review mechanisms for administrative decisions affecting trade in services. Such reviews may serve the principle of legal certainty if they ensure compliance of those decisions with the law (binding nature of the law). They may also facilitate the consistent application of the law by various administrative institutions and bodies, which also supports the principle of legal certainty.

The most important (potential) set of rules addressing domestic regulations are the disciplines negotiated under the mandate of GATS Article VI:4. WTO members have been engaged in negotiations under this mandate since 1995. The first concrete result of the negotiations under this mandate was the adoption of the Accountancy Disciplines by the Council for Trade in Services, in 1999.[21] The Accountancy Disciplines contain further specifications regarding the transparency requirement. Furthermore, they require that the conditions for licensing requirements and procedures shall be pre-established, publicly available and objective.

20 Appellate Body Report on *EC – Computer Equipment*, para. 82 (original emphasis).

21 *Disciplines on Domestic Regulation in the Accountancy Sector*, WTO doc. S/L/64, 17 December 1998. For a critical review of these disciplines, see Trolliet and Hegarty 2003: 150–3.

Requiring that the relevant regulations and procedures exist prior to a decision about a licence can also be considered an element of legal clarity.

After the adoption of the Accountancy Disciplines, WTO members began to negotiate on disciplines applying to all sectors. These negotiations have not yet been finalized.[22] The most controversial aspect of the negotiations concerns the necessity test. GATS Article VI:4(b) provides that future disciplines shall aim to ensure that such domestic regulations are, among other things, 'not more burdensome than necessary to ensure the quality of the service'. WTO members have debated the desirability, contours and elements of a necessity test at great length.[23]

While a necessity test would not directly be considered an element of legal certainty, elements of legal clarity emerged in the context of the debates on the necessity test in the negotiation process in the follow-up to the Chair's Draft in 2009. In his progress report of 2011, the Chair reported proposals for disciplines on licensing qualifications and requirements which included the notion of clarity. The relevant proposal requires members to ensure 'that licensing and qualification procedures for the purpose of obtaining authorization to supply a service are [simple,] reasonable, clear and relevant'.[24] The idea that rules are 'simple' or as 'simple as possible' is also taken up in other proposals.

Another aspect of legal certainty can be found in paragraph 11 of the Chair's Draft of 2009 which requires the pre-establishment of licensing requirements and procedures, qualification requirements and procedures, and technical standards.[25] Such a requirement would not be aimed at regulatory inflexibility and should not be construed to refer to regulatory stability in the same way as in the context of the fair and equitable treatment clause in investment law (see section 3.3). Instead, the notion of pre-establishment in the context of paragraph 11 of the Chair's Draft requires that a decision to award or withhold a licence or to accept or reject an application should be based on criteria which were in force at the date of application. In other words, laws should not be applied retroactively (see section 2 on non-retroactivity). However, laws can be changed during the application process and a balance needs to be struck

[22] See Krajewski 2008a: 178–92 for an analysis of the negotiations until 2007.

[23] For an overview, see Delimatsis 2008b: 385 ff.

[24] *Disciplines on Domestic Regulation Pursuant to GATS Article VI:4: Chairman's Progress Report*, WTO doc. S/WPDR/W/45, 14 April 2011, paras. 17 and 31, p. 25 (brackets in the original).

[25] *Ibid*. para. 11, p. 17.

between the regulatory flexibility and the applicant's expectation of legal certainty. Such a balance can be achieved through transparency about changes in the law and communication of changes to the applicant as suggested in an alternative proposal for paragraph 11 which states: 'Where pending applications are to be examined under amended or replaced measures, the Member shall promptly inform all applicants and provide reasonable time to such applicants to adapt their applications to such amended/new measures'.[26] Indeed, providing reasonable time for the applicant to react to any changes in the law takes the position of the applicant into account without unduly restricting regulatory flexibility.

Even though it is difficult to predict whether and which of these elements will be taken up in the final draft of the disciplines, it is significant to note that at least some members seem to move away from adopting a strong necessity test and seem to focus more on elements of legal certainty. A requirement for rules to be clear and simple lies at the heart of legal clarity. Two points are worth mentioning. First, while some aspects of legal certainty have been part of the negotiations on domestic regulation, other elements, in particular the protection of legitimate expectations or stability of the legal environment, have not played an important role in this context. It can therefore be assumed that those elements of legal certainty which have the greatest potential to conflict with regulatory flexibility will not be part of the disciplines on domestic regulation. Second, regardless of the scope of the disciplines it should be kept in mind that panels and the Appellate Body may be called upon to interpret and apply these disciplines should they become binding. As a consequence, these institutions will determine whether a rule was clear or simple at the end of the day. This raises fundamental questions about the capacity and legitimacy of these institutions to adjudicate on matters of domestic regulatory concern.[27]

5 Conclusion: regulatory flexibility and legal certainty – what role for disciplines on domestic regulation in the WTO?

According to the GATS Preamble, WTO members recognize the right of members to regulate and to introduce new regulations on services. This suggests that WTO members were mindful of the impact trade liberalization might have on domestic regulatory autonomy (Krajewski

[26] *Ibid.*
[27] On the same problem concerning necessity, see Krajewski 2008b: 397–404.

2003: 57). The right to introduce new regulations is a prominent recognition of the need for regulatory flexibility and policy space of WTO members. Legal certainty must therefore not impede on the right to regulatory flexibility. This raises the question how GATS law and future disciplines on domestic regulation can achieve a balance between the two concepts.

The analysis of the concept of legal certainty in different national and international legal systems showed that a number of elements of the principle generally do not conflict with regulatory flexibility. They concern the notions of legal clarity, in particular the requirements of transparency and the use of an understandable, that is, 'simple' language. In addition, elements of good administrative practice, such as the objective, impartial and consistent application of the law, do not seem to conflict with legal certainty. Lastly, the general binding nature of the law is not an impediment to regulatory flexibility.

As shown by the case law on the fair and equitable treatment principle in IIAs, the protection of legitimate expectations is particularly problematic vis-à-vis regulatory flexibility. It should be noted that the current draft of the disciplines on domestic regulation does not refer to legitimate expectations or the stability of the legal and regulatory environment. This recognizes the fact that the disciplines on domestic regulation do not confer individual rights even though their adoption may benefit investors and service providers. Legal certainty and regulatory flexibility are therefore best served if neither the disciplines nor any future jurisprudence on GATS provisions incorporate legitimate expectations or elements of stability which have a tendency to impede changes in the legal and regulatory system.

In conclusion, it should be recalled that legal certainty requires transparent, objective and impartial regulations. At the same time, these regulations must be sufficiently flexible to react to new challenges and changes of societal values or policy choices. GATS disciplines should require that any such changes are implemented in open and predictable processes, but should not place an unnecessary burden on regulatory flexibility.

References

von Arnauld, A. (2006), *Rechtssicherheit*, Tübingen: Mohr Siebeck

von Bogdandy, A. (2001), 'Rechtsgleichheit, Rechtssicherheit und Subsidiarität im transnationalen Wirtschaftsrecht: Zur unmittelbaren Anwendbarkeit des

Art. 81 Abs. 3 EG-Vertrag und des WTO-Rechts', *Europäische Zeitschrift für Wirtschaftsrecht* 12: 357–65

Bradley, A.W. and Ewing, K.W. (2010), *Constitutional and Administrative Law*, 15th edn, Harlow: Pearson

Braithwaite, J. (2002), 'Rules and Principles: A Theory of Legal Certainty', *Australian Journal of Legal Philosophy* 27: 47–82

Delimatsis, P. (2007), 'Due Process and "Good" Regulation Embedded in the GATS', *Journal of International Economic Law* 10(1): 13–50

(2008a), 'Article III GATS' in R. Wolfrum, P.-T. Stoll and C. Feinäugle (eds.), *WTO: Trade in Services*, Leiden: Martinus Nijhoff

(2008b), 'Determining the Necessity of Domestic Regulations in Services: The Best is Yet to Come', *European Journal of International Law* 19(2): 365–408

Dolzer, R. (2005a), 'The Impact of International Investment Treaties on Domestic Administrative Law', *NYU Journal on International Law and Politics* 37(4): 953–72

(2005b), 'Fair and Equitable Treatment: A Key Standard in Investment Treaties', *International Lawyer* 39(1): 87–106

Dolzer, R. and Schreuer, C. (2008), *Principles of International Investment Law*, Oxford: Oxford University Press

Fietta, S. (2006), 'Expropriation and the "Fair and Equitable" Standard: The Developing Role of the Investors' "Expectations" in International Investment Arbitration', *Journal of International Arbitration* 23: 375–99

Hartley, T.C. (2010), *The Foundations of European Union Law*, 7th edn, Oxford: Oxford University Press

Krajewski, M. (2003), *National Regulation and Trade Liberalization in Services*, The Hague: Kluwer Law International

(2008a), 'Article VI GATS' in R. Wolfrum, P.-T. Stoll and C. Feinäugle (eds.), *WTO: Trade in Services*, Leiden: Martinus Nijhoff

(2008b), 'Comment: Quis Custodiet Necessitatem? Adjudicating Necessity in Multilevel Systems and the Importance of Judicial Dialogue' in M. Panizzon, N. Pohl and P. Sauvé (eds.), *GATS and the Regulation of International Trade in Services*, Cambridge: Cambridge University Press

Maxeiner, J. (2007), 'Legal Certainty: A European Alternative to American Legal Indeterminacy', *Tulane Journal of International and Comparative Law* 15(2): 541–608

(2008), 'Some Realism about Legal Certainty in the Globalization of the Rule of Law', *Houston Journal of International Law* 31(1): 27–46

Paunio, E. (2009), 'Beyond Predictability: Reflections on Legal Certainty and the Discourse Theory of Law in the EU Legal Order', *German Law Journal* 10(11), 1469–93

Potesta, M. (2012), 'The Doctrine of Legitimate Expectations in Investment Treaty Law', Society of International Economic Law (SIEL), Third Biennial Global Conference, 9 July 2012

Radbruch, G. (1946), 'Gesetzliches Unrecht und übergesetzliches Recht', *Süddeutsche Juristenzeitung* 1: 105–8

Raitio, J. (1993), *The Principle of Legal Certainty in EC Law*, Dordrecht: Kluwer

Trolliet, C. and Hegarty, J. (2003), 'Regulatory Reform and Trade Liberalization in Accountancy Services' in A. Mattoo and P. Sauvé (eds.), *Domestic Regulation and Service Trade Liberalization*, Washington, DC: Oxford University Press/World Bank

6

Who's afraid of necessity? And why it matters?

PANAGIOTIS DELIMATSIS

1 Introduction

One of the most contentious issues of the Working Party on Domestic Regulation (WPDR) mandate has been the requirement that the new disciplines ensure that the covered measures do not constitute *unnecessary* barriers to services trade nor are more burdensome than *necessary* to ensure the quality of the service. This has been considered to encompass a so-called 'necessity test', similar to those included in other WTO agreements such as General Agreement on Tariffs and Trade (GATT) Article XX, Agreement on Technical Barriers to Trade (TBT Agreement) Article 2.2 or Agreement on the Application of Sanitary and Phytosanitary Measures (SPS Agreement) Article 5.6. World Trade Organization (WTO) members appear to be divided on this particular issue; and this is regardless of their level of development. This chapter intends to offer a succinct overview of the issues relating to the adoption of a necessity test. It will do so by first analysing the meaning of necessity as crystallized through WTO case law. Then, it demonstrates why the issue of necessity matters from a policy perspective and why it has had such a divisive impact.

2 Interpretation of the notion of necessity in other WTO agreements

Since the inception of GATT, necessity tests have formed part of the contract, providing flexibility and 'breathing space' to regulators. Necessity has been traditionally considered as the prevailing proxy for the identification and the discipline of protectionist or unduly burdensome regulatory behaviour. It is through the application of a necessity test that the GATT/WTO adjudicating bodies have attempted to draw the dividing line among competing values – those of promoting trade and the pursuit of legitimate policy objectives. Necessity typically forms part of a WTO provision that encompasses a positive obligation or an exception which can be raised as an affirmative defence to justify derogation from the WTO obligations. In the first case, necessity is typically accompanied by an open-ended list of public policy objectives. Examples include TBT Agreement Article 2.2 or SPS Agreement Article 5.6. In the second case, the provision entailing an exception includes a closed list of objectives to narrow down the possibility of deviating from a given WTO obligation. This, however, does not mean that such exceptions will be construed narrowly.[1] Probably the opposite is true, if one considers cases such as the *United States – Shrimp*[2] or *United States – Gambling*.[3]

Again, an otherwise WTO-inconsistent measure can only be maintained if it comes within one of the objectives set out in the closed list. Such provisions can provide for an exception to a particular provision, such as GATT Article XI:2(b) or paragraph 5(e) of the General Agreement on Trade in Services (GATS) Annex on Telecommunications, or can entail a general exception, that is, they can apply to all measures coming within the purview of a particular agreement. The most extensively discussed provision of this type is GATT Article XX. For necessity tests that are part of an affirmative defence, the WTO adjudicating bodies clarified that it is for the respondent to bear the burden of proof.[4] On the other hand, in the case of positive obligations, the complaining party is required to adduce evidence to prove that a certain measure is unnecessary.[5]

Over the years, the GATT/WTO interpretation of the concept of necessity has converged across the WTO agreements. First, this has happened in the interpretation of the various subparagraphs of GATT[6] Article XX and then expanded to other WTO agreements. Quite unsurprisingly, the WTO adjudicating bodies gained inspiration from the dispute settlement reports during the GATT years (i.e. findings related

[1] See Appellate Body Report on *EC – Hormones*, para. 104. Contrast with the case law within the European Union: among various cases, see *Van Duyn* (41/74) [1974] ECR 1337, para. 18.

[2] In this case, the Appellate Body accepted that the protection of living natural resources could fall within the scope of GATT Art. XX(g), neglecting the GATT negotiating history pointing to the contrary.

[3] In this case, both the panel and the Appellate Body endorsed a broad definition of public morals and public order.

[4] Appellate Body Report on *United States – Wool Shirts and Blouses*, pp. 15–16.

[5] Appellate Body Report on *EC – Sardines*, para. 323.

[6] Cf. GATT Panel Report on *Thailand – Cigarettes*, para. 74.

to the meaning of GATT Article XX) to interpret not only similar provisions entailing an affirmative defence (e.g. GATS Article XIV), but also provisions encompassing the concept of necessity within a *positive* obligation (i.e. TBT Agreement Article 2.2).[7]

Thus, necessity in WTO agreements has been interpreted in a manner that surpasses the narrow confines of a particular WTO agreement. It has become a universal concept, the very core of which remains essentially the same regardless of the agreement where it is to be found. This includes:

- less trade restrictiveness;
- justiciability of means (measures) and not ends (policy objectives);
- balancing of certain factors;
- comparison between alternatives.

As the analysis below will show, the principle of necessity has nowadays virtually acquired constitutional value (cf. Trachtman 2008: 208). Its main trait, that is, the comparison of alternatives, which implies balancing and a cost-benefit or proportionality analysis, resembles the types of inquiry that constitutional courts typically conduct at the domestic level. Necessity has acquired a WTO meaning. This is corroborated by *United States – Gambling*, where the Appellate Body found that the standard of necessity is an objective standard whose independent and objective assessment lies with the WTO adjudicating bodies. The principle of necessity already constitutes the WTO heuristic device *par excellence* for limiting to very specific cases deviations from WTO law. This is particularly done through the identification and comparison of alternatives, which has become the conceptual tool for ascertaining the 'necessity' of a given measure.

2.1 Necessity in a provision entailing an exception to WTO obligations

In *United States – Spring Assemblies*,[8] the concept of necessity under Article XX was already tied to an examination of whether a satisfactory and effective alternative existed. Less ambiguously, the *United*

[7] In *Australia – Apples*, the Appellate Body underscored that, by virtue of Agreement Establishing the World Trade Organization (WTO Agreement) Art. II:2, all WTO provisions, regardless of the WTO agreement in which they are to be found, constitute context relevant to the interpretation of each other when the wording so allows: Appellate Body Report on *Australia – Apples*, para. 173, n. 285.

[8] GATT Panel Report on *United States – Spring Assemblies*, para. 58.

States – Section 337 GATT panel stated that a measure cannot be regarded as necessary under GATT Article XX(d) when an alternative measure which the regulating state could reasonably be expected to employ, and which is not inconsistent with other GATT provisions, is available to it.[9] Thus, already in this early judgment, emphasis is put on the important role that alternative measures can play in assessing the necessity of the impugned measure. In *Korea – Beef*, a hallmark case regarding the interpretation of the concept of necessity, the Appellate Body found that the term 'necessary' can refer to a range of degrees of necessity; an indispensable measure can be just as 'necessary' for the WTO purposes as a measure which can make a significant contribution to the pursuit of a given objective.[10] In the latter case, however, alternative measures exist which could also be adopted by the respondent to a WTO dispute. In that case, the Appellate Body suggested that the examination of necessity would involve a sequential process of 'weighing and balancing',[11] in which the impugned measure and the various alternatives will be compared against a series of factors.

While this appears to be an open-ended list, the WTO adjudicating bodies focused on three factors in particular:

- the relative importance of the interests or values at stake;
- the extent of the contribution made by the measure to the achievement of the relevant objective;
- the trade restrictiveness of the measure.

The Appellate Body noted in *Brazil – Tyres* that the weighing and balancing process is 'a holistic operation that involves putting all the variables of the equation together and evaluating them in relation to each other after having examined them individually, in order to reach an overall judgment'.[12] However, the three factors do not seem to carry the same weight. In early cases, it became clear that the most vital is the relative importance of the objective pursued, as the comparison of possible alternatives must be carried out 'in the light' of the importance of the interests or values at stake.[13] This, however, could have the adverse

[9] GATT Panel Report on *United States – Section 337*, para. 5.26.
[10] Appellate Body Report on *Korea – Beef*, para. 161.
[11] See also Appellate Body Report on *China – Publications and Audiovisual Products*, para. 242.
[12] Appellate Body Report on *Brazil – Tyres*, para. 182.
[13] Appellate Body Report on *United States – Gambling*, para. 307.

consequence of inducing WTO members to take the most restrictive measures when they seek a high level of protection without worrying about the impact on trade.[14] To avoid this, the Appellate Body underscored that the more restrictive a given measure is, the greater its contribution to the pursuit of the objective must be. In turn, the greater the contribution of a measure to the objective pursued, the more likely is it to be found 'necessary'. In particular, with respect to the actual contribution of the measure to the pursuit of the objective, the Appellate Body clarified that a measure can be deemed necessary if it is apt, or designed, to produce a material contribution to the attainment of the objective pursued. This can be demonstrated through quantitative projections in the future, or qualitative reasoning based on hypotheses that can be tested.[15] More crucially, the Appellate Body noted that the relevant measure should be designed in a manner that the trade restrictiveness of the measure can be outweighed by the other two factors.

The WTO adjudicating bodies will not consider as possible alternative whatever measure the complainant proposes. Instead, for a measure to qualify as a genuine alternative and thus be subject to comparison with the impugned measure, the proposed alternative measure has to achieve the level of protection sought by the regulating state equally effectively,[16] while generating a lower level of trade restrictiveness when compared to the impugned measure. If the complainant succeeds in bringing forward such an alternative measure and establishing a presumption regarding the effectiveness of the measure, the respondent's last resort is to show that the measure is not, in fact, reasonably available. For instance, the respondent may seek to show that the alternative measure is theoretical in nature, or that it would not be capable of adopting it due to prohibitive costs or substantial technical difficulties.[17]

More recently, the Appellate Body confirmed in *United States – Gambling* that the findings on the concept of necessity under GATT are also relevant for Article XIV, the general exception provision under

[14] Cf. the admonition of SPS Agreement Art. 5.4 suggesting that members, when setting their level of protection, have to take into account the objective of minimizing negative trade effects.

[15] Cf. Appellate Body Reports on *China – Publications and Audiovisual Products*, para. 253, and *Mexico – Soft Drinks*, para. 74 (stating that a measure can still be 'necessary' even if it cannot be guaranteed to achieve the objective pursued with absolute certainty).

[16] The Appellate Body clarified that it is members' prerogative to set the level of protection they deem appropriate: Appellate Body Report on *Australia – Apples*, para. 342.

[17] *Ibid.* paras. 309–11.

GATS.[18] However, it also bears noting that the *Mexico – Telecoms* panel, when interpreting paragraph 5(e) of the GATS Annex on Telecommunications and the necessity standard enshrined therein, found that a measure making merely a contribution to the achievement of the objective would satisfy the necessity requirement.[19]

2.2 *Necessity in a WTO positive obligation*

In this subsection, we will examine two WTO provisions which may be particularly relevant for the interpretation of a possible necessity test under the mandate of GATS Article VI:4. These provisions are TBT Agreement Articles 2.2 and 5.6. Similar to GATS Article VI:4, these two provisions also entail positive obligations. One trait of the type of necessity test examined here is that the relevant provisions include an *illustrative* list of objectives, thereby creating a broad leeway for the exercise of regulatory autonomy by the responding WTO member. The objectives mentioned in this illustrative list, as well as those mentioned in other WTO agreements, can be regarded as reference points for the identification of other objectives of equal importance.[20] Another difference with the general exception provisions examined in the previous subsection relates to the allocation of the burden of proof. When a positive obligation is at stake, it is for the complainant to make a *prima facie* case, that is, adduce evidence and arguments sufficient to establish that the impugned measure creates an unnecessary barrier to trade. For this, the complainant will have to prove that the measure chosen is more trade restrictive than necessary to achieve the attainment of a legitimate objective. In this exercise, however, a common characteristic with the necessity test under the previous subsection is that it is, again, for the *complainant* to identify alternative measures.

2.2.1 TBT Agreement Article 2.2

This provision requires that WTO members' technical regulations do not create unnecessary trade obstacles. More specifically, technical regulations should not be more trade restrictive than necessary to fulfil a legitimate objective, taking into account the risks that the non-fulfilment of this objective would create. In *United States – COOL*, the Appellate

[18] Appellate Body Report on *United States – Gambling*, para. 291.
[19] Panel Report on *Mexico – Telecoms*, paras. 7.337–7.343.
[20] Appellate Body Report on *United States – Tuna II (Mexico)*, para. 313.

Body confirmed that the initial burden of proof under this provision lies with the complainant. It noted that, in most cases, the complainant would seek to identify a less restrictive alternative which would be equally effective to pursue the relevant objective and reasonably available to the respondent.[21] Earlier, in *United States – Tuna II (Mexico)*, the Appellate Body clarified the meaning of the standard of necessity under TBT Agreement Article 2.2. It suggested at the outset that, similarly to GATT Article XX and GATS Article XIV, this provision involves a relational analysis of factors such as the trade restrictiveness of the technical regulation at issue; the degree of contribution that it makes to the pursuit of the objective; and the risks that the non-fulfilment of the relevant objective would create. Interestingly, the Appellate Body stated that TBT Agreement Article 2.2 allows for some trade restrictiveness; rather, what it attempts to discipline is those technical regulations that exceed 'what is necessary to achieve the degree of contribution that a technical regulation makes to the pursuit of a legitimate objective'.[22]

As in the case of general exceptions provisions, the Appellate Body emphasized that a sequential process takes place also in the case of TBT Agreement Article 2.2. Panels should begin with the identification and evaluation of the factors mentioned above or any additional factors in specific cases and then, in a second step, proceed to confirm the result of this analysis by comparing the measure with possible alternatives, which may be less restrictive, while being reasonably available and making an equivalent contribution to the relevant legitimate objective, taking account of the risks non-fulfilment would create. Panels could stop at the very first step of this inquiry if they found that one of the factors were not met, for instance, that the impugned technical regulation were not trade restrictive or that it were not suitable to make a contribution to the pursuit of the relevant objective.

A careful examination of the test applied under this provision and the one under the general exception provisions reveals that the three factors are virtually identical. For the first two, that is, the trade restrictiveness and the actual contribution to the realization of the objective, the similarity cannot be doubted. As to the third component of the test, that is, the risks of non-fulfilment, the Appellate Body suggested that the comparison among the impugned measure and the various alternatives should be conducted *in the light* of the nature of the risks at issue and

21 Appellate Body Report on *United States – COOL*, para. 379.
22 Appellate Body Report on *United States – Tuna II (Mexico)*, para. 319.

the gravity of the consequences that the non-fulfilment of the legitimate objective would bring about. Arguably, an examination of the relative importance of the legitimate objective is implied in this endeavour. This is also implicit in the Appellate Body's statement in *United States – COOL* that 'the relevant objective is the benchmark against which a panel must assess the degree of contribution made by a challenged technical regulation, as well as by proposed alternative measures'.[23] Contrary to the necessity test under the general exceptions provisions, the Appellate Body has not clarified whether there is a hierarchy among the factors to be assessed. It is safe to say that, at least, the factors to be assessed should outweigh the trade restrictiveness of the technical regulation.

2.2.2 SPS Agreement Article 5.6

SPS Agreement Article 5.6 establishes a requirement for WTO members not to adopt or maintain sanitary and phytosanitary (SPS) measures[24] that are 'more trade-restrictive than required' to achieve members' level of protection, taking into account technical and economic feasibility. Although the term 'necessary' is not mentioned, contextual elements such as SPS Agreement Article 2.2 lead to the plausible conclusion that a necessity test is part of Article 5.6. The Appellate Body found as much in *Australia – Apples*.[25] Footnote 3 to this provision provides that, for a measure to be regarded as violating this obligation, another measure should be reasonably available to the regulating WTO member, taking into account technical and economic feasibility, which is equally effective, but *significantly* less trade restrictive. In *Australia – Salmon*, the Appellate Body clarified that a three-prong test is included in this provision and thus the complainant needs to demonstrate that another, alternative measure cumulatively meets three conditions:

- is reasonably available taking account of economic and technical feasibility (reasonable availability);
- achieves the member's chosen level of protection (effectiveness);
- is significantly less trade restrictive than the SPS measure contested (trade restrictiveness).[26]

[23] Appellate Body Report on *United States – COOL*, para. 387.
[24] Cf. Appellate Body Report on *Australia – Apples*, para. 171 ff.
[25] *Ibid.* paras. 339 and 363.
[26] Appellate Body Report on *Australia – Salmon*, para. 194.

It is only under the third condition that a comparison (or balancing) will take place between the chosen measure and the proposed alternative.[27]

Footnote 3 is important for two reasons: first, because it links the concept of necessity with a long-standing jurisprudence established in the GATT *acquis* and the interpretation of GATT Article XX; and second, because it emphasizes the importance of the comparison of alternatives when assessing necessity.[28] At the same time, the SPS Agreement drafters did not want any alternative measure to prevail over the chosen measure and thus they required the beneficial effects on trade to be 'significant' if the alternative measure is to be chosen. The footnote does not give an indication as to the scope of the term 'significant'. However, the provision seems to imply a *de minimis* threshold, below which an alternative measure, even if it still is less trade restrictive, cannot cancel out the initial choice of the regulating WTO member. This means that, like TBT Agreement Article 2.2, SPS Agreement Article 5.6 implies that some trade restrictiveness is allowed. Nevertheless, contrary to TBT Agreement Article 2.2, the SPS Agreement provision raises the bar for the complaining party, as it would need to prove that the alternative measure that it suggests entails a significantly lower degree of trade restrictiveness. Panels have interpreted this third condition as implying an assessment of whether choosing the alternative measure would lead to a significantly increased market access.[29] At the same time, the poor analysis in those panel reports demonstrates the difficulty for both the judiciary and the parties to the dispute to assess and to measure this threshold in a straightforward way. In various cases, the panels were in fact content with stating that the respondent did not refute the complainant's argument that the proposed alternative met the third requirement of the SPS Agreement Article 5.6 test.[30] Indeed, for the most part, the complainants in those SPS cases rather focused on challenging the respondents' contention that the proposed alternative met their appropriate level of protection.

[27] Appellate Body Report on *Australia – Apples*, para. 337. [28] *Ibid.* para. 363.

[29] For instance, see Panel Report on *Australia – Salmon*, para. 7.151.

[30] Cf. Panel Report on *Australia – Apples*, paras. 7.1264–7.1265. Even more striking is the panel's legal analysis in Panel Report on *Japan – Agricultural Products II*, para. 8.95 and n. 332 (reversed subsequently by the Appellate Body for disregarding the rules relating to the allocation of the burden of proof).

3 Assessing the necessity of domestic regulations in services: why so much fuss?

Through the adoption of regulatory disciplines pursuant to GATS Article VI:4, GATS essentially aims to facilitate drawing the line of equilibrium between the multilateral interest in progressive liberalization of trade in services and each WTO member's interest in preserving its regulatory autonomy. Such a fine line has traditionally been drawn in the WTO through the use of proxies that allow for balancing on a case-by-case basis to ensure equality of competitive opportunities among the service suppliers active in a given market, without unnecessarily hampering members' regulatory freedom. Necessity does nothing else than express members' shared understanding that substantive WTO obligations should not be deviated from lightly.[31] Constructive ambiguity, which has been a common drafting method in WTO history, leaves the WTO judiciary without any guidance on the collective preferences of the WTO membership. In the absence of any such guidance, the identification of the common intention of members regarding a given issue can only be based on judicial constructions, which inevitably cause controversy.[32]

3.1 A generally applicable necessity test

One of the most contentious aspects of the WPDR mandate has proved to be the requirement addressed to the Council for Trade in Services, enshrined in GATS Article VI:4(b), to ensure, through the developed disciplines, that the covered measures are 'not more burdensome than necessary to ensure the quality of the service'. This requirement has become known as the 'necessity test'. The objective of such a provision would be to prohibit measures that exceed what is necessary to ensure the quality of the service provided or, arguably, the achievement of any other legitimate, public policy objective. While the inclusion of a broad necessity test in the Draft Accountancy Disciplines was unproblematic, the possibility of including a necessity test applicable across all services sectors (i.e. horizontally) has created controversies and animated discussions within the WPDR. The main argument against a necessity test appears to relate to its adverse impact on WTO members' sovereign right

[31] Cf. Appellate Body Report on *United States – Gambling*, para. 308.

[32] See, among many examples, the interpretation of the Schedules of Commitments in the *United States – Gambling* case.

to regulate, and the fact that negative trade effects are not required for a measure to be found 'unnecessary'.[33] The right to regulate permeates the WTO agreements.[34] In the case of services, it is explicitly referred to in the GATS Preamble. Recently, the Appellate Body regarded this right as an '*inherent* power enjoyed by a Member's government', which nevertheless is to be exercised in harmony with the WTO obligations assumed by a member.[35]

Developing countries are mainly concerned about their regulatory *flexibility*, whereas developed ones seem to care mostly about their regulatory *sovereignty*. On the other hand, it seems that there are two main arguments for the inclusion of a necessity test.

The first relates to the text of GATS Article VI:4 and the mandate itself. Indeed, the notion of necessity is reflected in the introductory text of Article VI:4, with the reference in the first sentence to '*unnecessary* barriers to trade in services', and in subparagraph (b) of Article VI:4 to 'not more burdensome than *necessary*' (author's emphasis). Crucially, and contrary to similar provisions such as TBT Agreement Article 2.2 or SPS Agreement Article 5.6, GATS Article VI:4(b) does not use the term 'not more trade restrictive than necessary'. As a given measure can be burdensome without necessarily restricting trade at the same time, this discrepancy begs the question as to whether the GATS drafters intended to give a broad scope to this provision when compared to the corresponding SPS Agreement and TBT Agreement provisions. This can reasonably be argued, notably when one takes into account that the negotiating history of GATS Article VI:4 reveals that, at one point, the European Union brought forward a proposed text using the term 'trade restrictive' which, however, did not find its way into the final text of Article VI:4 as adopted in the Uruguay Round. At the same time,

33 See *Views on the Issue of the Necessity Test in the Disciplines on Domestic Regulation: Communication from Brazil, Canada and the United States*, WTO doc. S/WMDR/W/44, 22 March 2011, paras. 2–3.

34 See e.g. Panel Report on *United States – Tuna II (Mexico)*, para. 7.436 (where the panel stated that the elaboration of legitimate objectives is the prerogative of the member adopting a measure). Again, in certain cases and depending on the WTO provision at stake, the WTO adjudicating bodies will be required to make an objective assessment of the objective that a member pursues, and this may include a determination of legitimacy. See Appellate Body Reports on *United States – COOL*, paras. 371–2 (when interpreting TBT Agreement Art. 2.2) and *United States – Tuna II (Mexico)*, paras. 313–14 (when interpreting TBT Agreement Art. 2.4).

35 Appellate Body Report on *China – Publications and Audiovisual Services*, para. 222 (author's emphasis).

it bears mention that the negotiating history within the WPDR reveals a shared understanding that the necessity test of Article VI:4 refers to the trade restrictiveness of the covered measures.

The second argument relates to the need to include a certain test which will allow a distinction between trade distortive measures and genuine regulatory interventions. It is no coincidence that the mandate includes a necessity test or that the concept is to be found in the TBT and SPS Agreements. The GATS drafters had realized that a yardstick was needed to assess the covered measures. In the European Union, most of the cases relating to this type of measures are assessed based on the proportionality test, which includes necessity as one of its elements. Necessity tests form part of WTO members' 'comfort zone'. Over four decades of GATT/WTO case law on necessity ensure security and predictability of judicial interpretations. In addition, necessity tests in various forms (reasonableness, proportionality, necessity and means-ends tests) have existed and have been systemically interpreted in most domestic jurisdictions, as well as included in various regional trade agreements or common market arrangements. The most prominent in the latter category are the European Union, MERCOSUR and the Trans-Pacific Strategic Economic Partnership. Thus, regulators, judicatures and economic actors alike are familiar with the type of balancing of competing interests that a necessity test requires. This is an obvious advantage of a necessity test when compared to a series of alternative tests that have been proposed during WPDR negotiations.

3.2 Alternatives to necessity

3.2.1 A 'disguised restriction' test

Due to objections expressed by several WTO members against the application of a necessity test across services sectors, the proposed test was replaced by a requirement that the covered measures should not be 'disguised restrictions on trade in services'.[36] Such a test is not ambiguity-free. It mirrors the language of the chapeau of GATT Article XX and GATS Article XIV.[37] The concept of 'disguised restriction' under WTO law has been associated with discrimination and the manner a certain

[36] Working Party on Domestic Regulation, *Disciplines on Domestic Regulation Pursuant to GATS Article VI:4: Informal Note by the Chairman*, Second Revision, 20 March 2009, para. 2.

[37] Also in SPS Agreement Arts. 2.3 and 5.5 or GATS Art. VII:3.

measure is applied or administered.[38] In *United States – Gasoline*, the Appellate Body opted for a broad reading of 'disguised restriction' suggesting that concealed or unannounced restriction does not exhaust the term.[39] For instance, disguised discrimination and restrictions resulting in arbitrary or unjustifiable discrimination appear to be equally included in this term. However, WTO case law suggests that a disguised trade restriction does not necessarily entail discrimination. In this category, one could classify measures that have a limiting trade effect that is not merely inadvertent or unavoidable, but rather a foreseeable violation of WTO obligations.[40] It is submitted that this alternative test will inevitably be interpreted according to previous WTO case law which classified disguised trade restrictions as several acts or omissions, such as the treatment of similarly situated trading partners in a different manner; the lack of serious, good faith consultations with other trading partners to find a multilateral solution; or the fact that significant costs that are only incumbent on the exporters are not taken into account when regulating. Hence, just as with the application of a necessity test, under the new 'disguised trade restriction' test, the existence of less trade restrictive alternatives and the comparison of regulatory conduct in similar situations will be important evidence for the WTO judiciary. In fact, in a worst-case scenario, this test allows for judicial activism, as it does not require any balancing, contrary to the necessity test.

3.2.2 'Relevance' test

An alternative wording to necessity would require that the covered measures be 'relevant to the supply of the services to which they apply'.[41] A 'relevance' test would be construed as a 'soft' necessity test. As clarified in *United States – Shrimp*, the adopted measures should then not be necessary, but at least directly connected with, or primarily aimed at, the objective pursued, revealing a close and genuine relationship between means and ends. This test would again operate similarly to a necessity test, notably if we consider the judicial restraint in cases involving

[38] Cf. the chapeau of GATS Art. XIV or para. 5(d) of the GATS Annex on Telecommunications.

[39] Appellate Body Report on *United States – Gasoline*, p. 25.

[40] *Ibid.* p. 28.

[41] Working Party on Domestic Regulation, *Disciplines on Domestic Regulation Pursuant to GATS Article VI:4: Informal Note by the Chairman*, Second Revision, 20 March 2009, para. 11.

objectives of great importance (e.g. protection of public health) and the description of necessity as a continuum in *Korea – Beef*.[42]

3.2.3 'Restriction on the service supply' test

This test is focused on licensing and qualification procedures and is based on the wording of GATS Article VI:4(c). This test should be read as requiring the abolition of those procedures that have restrictive effects on trade in services. However, restrictive effect cannot be assessed as such; rather, it should be evaluated against an objective. More specifically, in order to be meaningful, this test would entail an assessment of the restrictive effect of a given measure against the objective pursued and the contribution to this objective, and thus require showing that the contribution of the measure is so significant in a given context that it outweighs the restrictive effect of the measure. Thus, once again, the importance of the objective, the contribution of the measure to the attainment of the objective and its trade restrictiveness are all elements that will be part of a holistic analysis. Contrary to a necessity test, however, such a test – just like the other alternative tests proposed – may not call for a comparison of alternatives.

3.2.4 Necessity test and its alternatives: a tentative comparison

Legally speaking, the non-incorporation of a necessity test in the future GATS Article VI:4 disciplines would go against the letter and spirit of WTO members' legal mandate.[43] Crucially, it would also prevent the effective enforcement of the prospective disciplines because, in the end, the WTO judiciary would need to do some balancing either based on existing legal benchmarks or judicially created ones. Elements of a necessity test would be applied in every type of balancing that the WTO judiciary would conduct even under the alternative tests discussed above. In that case, members would have missed the unique opportunity to design themselves a test that would encompass concepts and elements that would allow for more flexibility when regulating, while protecting other members' right to trade based on WTO law.[44]

42 Appellate Body Report on *Korea – Beef*, para. 161.

43 In this direction, see Australia's intervention in *Report of the Meeting held on 19 and 20 June 2006*, WTO doc. S/WPDR/M/35, 14 August 2006, paras. 7–8.

44 For a proposal, see Delimatsis 2010.

4 Conclusion

This chapter was aimed at deciphering the concept of necessity in a succinct manner and identifying the possibility of its inclusion in the future GATS Article VI:4 disciplines. It has argued that necessity has been a conceptual tool and an indispensable proxy commonly used by the WTO judiciary in the quest for striking a balance between the competing rights of expanding trade and regulatory autonomy. Just as in various jurisdictions, it appears that the concept is also gradually becoming a principle of constitutional value within the WTO. The composite test that necessity implies, including the concepts of (less) trade restrictiveness, the justiciability of means (measures) and not ends (policy objectives), the balancing of certain factors, and the comparison between alternatives, is worth reconsidering within the WPDR. The results of these negotiations will not only affect GATS, but also many preferential trade agreements that pledged to incorporate the results of these negotiations in their respective legal frameworks.

References

Delimatsis, P. (2010), 'Concluding the WTO Services Negotiations on Domestic Regulation: Hopes and Fears', *World Trade Review* 9(4): 643–73

Trachtman, J. (2008), 'Regulatory Jurisdiction in the WTO' in W. Davey and J. Jackson (eds.), *The Future of International Economic Law*, Oxford: Oxford University Press

7

Mutual recognition of services regulation at the WTO

JOEL P. TRACHTMAN

1 Introduction

Mutual recognition is a useful tool for international liberalization in particular contexts. However, it has two types of limit, and to the extent that it may exceed these limits, it poses two important types of risk.

The first limit of mutual recognition is set by the degree and importance of achievement of the relevant regulatory goal: the degree to which the foreign regulation achieves the goals of the domestic regulatory scheme, and the importance of meeting these goals. Thus, the first risk is that mutual recognition is implemented in a way that sacrifices important regulatory goals without adequate justification – without 'sufficient' achievement of the regulatory goal. States may, at times, accept compromises of their regulatory goals, but they should not do so unless they are compensated with enhanced welfare from free trade or from other sources. The second limit of mutual recognition relates to the material capacities of developing countries. The risk is that mutual recognition is established by developed countries in a way that disadvantages services exports of developing countries.

Mutual recognition as developed in the European Union has managed the first risk through a nuanced deliberative process that includes both legislative and adjudicative capacity, and has experienced only an attenuated form of the second risk, due in large part to the relative economic homogeneity of EU Member States.

This chapter argues that mutual recognition of services regulation at the WTO (World Trade Organization), as a type of liberalism, must be embedded in a process of governance that has two components. First, mutual recognition can only take place to the extent of satisfactory essential harmonization: to the extent that states can legitimately agree on an appropriate level of regulatory protection. This political process is necessary in order to establish an agreed minimum level of regulation.

Second, mutual recognition cannot be permitted to leave poor countries at a disadvantage in international trade. Therefore, essential harmonization must be established in a way that protects poor countries. This will require technical assistance, transfer of resources and accommodation of difference.

After defining critical terms below and providing a jurisdiction-based understanding of recognition, this chapter examines the current WTO legal doctrine. This doctrine generally declines to adopt the broad judicially enforced doctrine of equivalence that has emerged in the European Union, but the WTO does have limited capacity for case-by-case judicial evaluations of equivalence: judicial findings that the home or exporting country regulation satisfies the regulatory concerns of the host or importing country. Nor does the WTO include the internal legislative will or capacity to legislate rules of essential harmonization, as has been common within the European Union. While essential harmonization is indeed a necessary predicate for mutual recognition, the WTO does not have the internal capacity for significant essential harmonization. On the other hand, the WTO has the capacity to refer to other organizations' normative efforts as sources of essential harmonization.

Looking beyond the WTO itself to plurilateral or regional arrangements for mutual recognition, this chapter evaluates the risk that these arrangements may violate the most favoured nation (MFN) principle of WTO law. This is more than a technical issue, as plurilateral or regional arrangements for mutual recognition may adversely affect the competitive position of excluded states. This substantive issue raises special concerns to the extent that the excluded states are poor countries. Even if poor countries are not arbitrarily excluded, it is difficult and costly for them to participate meaningfully in efforts toward essential harmonization and mutual recognition. Thus, the MFN obligation may be understood as a potential source of protection for poor countries against being disadvantaged by mutual recognition initiatives.

In order to develop a coherent analysis of mutual recognition at the WTO, it is useful to begin with careful delineation of the meaning of relevant terms. Once we define terms carefully, we see that mutual recognition itself is not a form of governance.

1.1 Recognition

Recognition, in simple legal terms, is a choice of law rule. It is a selection by importing (or host) countries of the rule of the home or exporting country, to the exclusion of the rule of the importing country. Pure recognition regimes diminish barriers to trade by dismantling importing country regulatory barriers: because the importing country law is inapplicable, it cannot serve as a barrier. In this sense, recognition is, by its nature, purely deregulatory (presuming that the exporting country rules are less onerous than the importing country rules). Thus, recognition is not so much a rule of governance in the normal sense, but a rule of choice of governance. In light of this deregulatory bias of pure recognition, it is a choice of reduced governance. Recognition, at its core, entails an agreement to compromise local regulatory autonomy, by accepting that the exporting country regulation is 'good enough'. So, we cannot lightly accept the compromise implicit in recognition arrangements.

This chapter argues that the context of recognition arrangements, in terms of the possibility for externalization, the possibility for detrimental regulatory competition, and the possibility for discrimination against outsiders, is critical to an understanding of the utility of recognition arrangements. States may regard these concerns as they determine whether to engage in recognition arrangements. In addition, institutional mechanisms may be established to reduce the harmful effects of externalization, regulatory competition and discrimination. Essential harmonization is a critical component of these mechanisms. It should be clear that the value of engaging in mutual recognition will depend entirely on the context, both factual and institutional.

In the field of services, recognition may address either foreign regulatory standards, or foreign licensing and other qualification decisions. In this chapter, I focus on regulatory standards as a first general approximation because licensing or other qualification *decisions* will necessarily be dependent on, or will incorporate, regulatory standards.

1.2 Mutual

When added to 'recognition', the word 'mutual' denotes narrow reciprocity. You recognize my regulation, and I will recognize yours. In this sense, it is a trade concept – a concept of reciprocal liberalization – much more than it is a governance or regulatory concept. The question answered by mutuality is how does one state compensate the other for its recognition. This question is not relevant from the standpoint of an examination of the legal and public policy aspects of recognition itself. Therefore, for the purposes of this chapter, I focus simply on recognition.

1.3 *Essential harmonization*

Essential harmonization is not necessary to recognition but, to the extent that the regulation at stake is meaningful, host or importing countries would be expected, before agreeing to recognition, to check the partner's regulation to ensure that it satisfies the host or importing country's regulatory goals, and, to the extent that it does not, to require modifications to the partner's regulation to ensure that it does. To the extent that a general minimum standard of harmonization can be agreed in a legislative context, this is understood as 'essential harmonization'.

Essential harmonization plays two roles. First, it is a product of multilateral legislation. Exporting countries, or at least their exporting firms, are required to comply with harmonized standards, or to forego the benefits of exporting the relevant services. Second, by serving as a predicate for recognition, it serves as an agreement on the scope or depth of regulatory competition. States are permitted to apply higher standards to their own suppliers, but regulatory competition might be expected to suppress the application of standards above the level of the essential harmonization. The political process of essential harmonization provides an opportunity to decide collectively how far states will accept pressure on their standards from regulatory competition. By accepting recognition on the basis of essential harmonization, states accept competitive incentives to reduce the cost of the regulation that they apply to their own suppliers to the level required by the essentially harmonized rule.

1.4 *Equivalence*

Although there is some ambiguity in the literature, 'equivalence' is not the same thing as 'recognition'. I follow Joseph Weiler's suggestion that the relevant judicial doctrine, announced by the European Court of Justice (ECJ) in *Cassis de Dijon*, is best termed 'functional equivalence' or, in this chapter, simply 'equivalence' (Weiler 2005: 45). Equivalence, as compared to mutual recognition, is a more particular, case-based finding that the home or exporting country regulation is equivalent (in the sense of satisfying the regulatory goal) to the host or importing country regulation. Mutual recognition, on the other hand, involves broad and automatic recognition of foreign regulation, without case-based evaluation.

Thus, under a doctrine of equivalence, an administrative agency or a court might find that the home state regulation is functionally equivalent to (that it satisfies the regulatory concerns of) the host state regulation.

One way of understanding the relationship between equivalence and recognition is in terms of the institution that makes the decision. Thus, equivalence is a case-by-case determination, based on a standard, and usually administered by a court. Recognition is a legislatively (or treaty) determined rule, usually established by a legislature or an administrative agency.

2 Jurisdictional analysis of recognition

A rule of recognition is best understood as a rule of allocation of regulatory authority: of jurisdiction. That is, recognition simply means that the recognizing (host) state defers to the recognized (home) state in connection with the specified regulatory authority. So, for example, if the subject of the recognition is the prudential regulation of banking institutions, as in the EU Second Banking Directive (1989/646/EC), then perhaps Germany, as host state, defers to the United Kingdom, as home state, in connection with the prudential regulation of UK banks doing business in Germany.

Recognition is the opposite of a jurisdictional rule of territoriality, assuming that the foreign supplier is either engaging in conduct (territorial conduct) or is producing effects (territorial effects) in the recognizing state. Recognition involves deference by territoriality to nationality: that is, the recognizing state transfers regulatory authority to the recognized state, despite the fact that whatever negative outcomes may occur will be experienced in the recognizing state.

The expected benefit of recognition includes not just reduced costs of compliance for international companies, but also enhanced regulatory competition. On the other hand, if we assume the beneficial character of regulation, competition diminishes the authority of regulators, jeopardizing their ability to maximize the public interest. The scope for regulatory innovation is equally great under recognition and territoriality-based national treatment. However, proponents of regulatory competition would argue that the incentives for innovation are stronger under recognition.

The greatest problem with recognition is the risk of externalization: these risks must be compared with the benefits that are expected from greater competition. Moreover, it is worth asking whether there is a structure that would provide the benefits of competition with reduced risks of externalization. Of course, externalization reduces the benefits of competition, and what we are really seeking is a structure that has aggregate benefits greater than the other available structures. Thus, again, territoriality-based national treatment, or managed recognition (as described below), would allow host states to forestall externalization by imposing their own regulation. More interestingly, managed recognition would provide an opportunity for states to reveal their anti-externalization preferences in negotiation over essential harmonization. This process requires states to revisit – and perhaps to modify – their preferences for regulation. As states use these processes to modify their regulation, democratic accountability for harmonization agreements becomes important.

In the EU context, a process that Nicolaïdis and Shaffer (2005: 290) have termed 'managed mutual recognition' has been the rule in a number of areas. The more refined approach of 'managed recognition' would utilize one or more of the following instruments, all derived from EU practice, to reduce the risk of externalization:

- *Judicial examination of equivalence.* 'Equivalence' could be mandated by a court under a general constitutional or treaty-based free trade provision, based on an examination of the home state regulation to determine that they achieve the host state's regulatory goals. Such requirements may be applied pursuant to proportionality or 'least trade restrictive alternative' requirements. It is feasible that these disciplines could be extended to other fields. The result would be that recognition would only be required where the host state's regulatory goals are met by the home state regulation, ensuring against externalization. In the field of services, there is only a limited possibility, discussed below, that WTO panels would apply equivalence. This is because the scope of application of General Agreement on Trade in Services (GATS) Article VI:5, as discussed below, is limited to cases that, in addition to being disproportionate, constitute nullification or impairment of commitments. However, secondary legislation, such as the WTO 1998 Disciplines on Domestic Regulation in the Accountancy Sector (Accountancy Disciplines), may impose equivalence. Indeed, the Accountancy Disciplines provide that: 'A Member shall ensure that its competent authorities take account of qualifications acquired in the territory of another Member, on the basis of equivalency of education, experience and/or examination requirements'.
- *Legislative establishment of essential harmonization.* International integration organizations such as the European Union or the WTO, or international functional organizations, such as the Basel Committee or the International Accounting Standards Board, may engage in

efforts that amount to 'legislative' establishment of essential harmonization. Unlike in the European Union (since the 1987 Single European Act), the international system does not generally provide for majority voting. The European Union often engages in essential harmonization, as a predicate to mutual recognition, to forge the single market. In negotiating harmonization Directives, states understand that the increased regulatory competition that will result from the proposed mutual recognition will place pressure on their ability to maintain regulation that, by definition, is otherwise desirable from a purely local standpoint, having been legislated through presumptively legitimate processes. Before agreeing to mutual recognition, they agree on a minimum level of regulation that will insulate their home regulation from being reduced in unacceptable ways. Furthermore, they exact a *quid pro quo*, both in terms of essential harmonization and in terms of other market liberalization in other areas. It would be difficult for the WTO to take action to harmonize regulation in the services area because such legislative action would generally require consensus. Indeed, the only action taken in connection with domestic regulation so far has been to establish the Accountancy Disciplines.

- *Maintenance of 'safeguards' that would allow states to address threats to their public policy.* EU harmonization and mutual recognition initiatives, such as the Second Banking Directive, contain provisions that allow host states to act in derogation from their ordinary recognition obligations in order to protect the 'general good'. These provisions provide a safeguard against externalization, at least in more egregious cases.

These devices could be used to determine, in specific cases relating to particular regulatory systems, and particular regulatory rules, whether competition or coordination is the superior alternative.

3 Equivalence in GATS

In this section, I review current WTO legal doctrine to achieve an understanding of the extent to which equivalence is part of the WTO legal system relating to services.

GATS Article VI deals with domestic regulation. Much of Article VI only covers sectors in which specific commitments have been undertaken. Article VI:4, which appears to be applicable regardless of the WTO member's commitments, is forward-looking, calling on the WTO Council for Trade in Services to develop any necessary disciplines 'with a view to ensuring that measures relating to qualification requirements and procedures, technical standards and licensing requirements do not constitute unnecessary barriers to trade in services'. Such disciplines would ensure, among other things, that such requirements are 'not more burdensome than necessary to ensure the quality of the service'. This, of course, is not a proportionality requirement per se, but an agreement to develop disciplines based on a proportionality standard.

The Uruguay Round Decision on Professional Services called for the work programme under Article VI:4 to be put into effect immediately as to professional services, and called for the establishment of a Working Party on Professional Services to develop 'the disciplines necessary to ensure that measures relating to qualification requirements and procedures, technical standards and licensing requirements in the field of professional services do not constitute unnecessary barriers to trade'. The decision also established work in the accountancy sector of professional services as a priority, calling for, among other things, the establishment of disciplines referenced in Article VI:4 and the use of international standards. Indeed, accountancy is the only area in which these efforts have borne fruit. It further calls on the Working Party on Professional Services to 'encourage the cooperation with the relevant international organizations as defined under paragraph 5(b) of Article VI, so as to give full effect to paragraph 5 of Article VII'.[1]

The provision of GATS Article VI that imposes present disciplines of interest here is Article VI:5, which is limited to sectors in which the WTO member has undertaken specific commitments, and is further limited to the period prior to the entry into force of disciplines developed under Article VI:4: it is an interim device. During this period, 'the Member shall not apply licensing and qualification requirements and technical standards that nullify or impair such specific commitments in a manner which' does not comply with the following criteria:

(a) are based on objective and transparent criteria, such as competence and the ability to supply the service;
(b) are not more burdensome than necessary to ensure the quality of the service;

[1] GATS Art. VII:5, as discussed below, calls for recognition based on multilaterally agreed criteria, requiring that WTO members 'work in cooperation with relevant intergovernmental and non-governmental organizations towards the establishment and adoption of common international standards and criteria for recognition'.

(c) in the case of licensing procedures, are not in themselves a restriction on the supply of the service.[2]

Focusing on (b), the elements of this test thus require that national measures not nullify or impair a specific commitment in a way that is more burdensome than necessary. In determining whether a member is conforming to these obligations, account is required to be taken 'of international standards of relevant international organizations applied by that Member'.[3] The reference to international standards presumably amplifies the necessity test.[4]

These provisions represented a limited set of disciplines, a compromise and an agreement to engage in further work in the future regarding the application of standards to services. This treatment reflects concerns that the services sector is heterogeneous enough to confound attempts to apply generic disciplines on standards.

In addition, it is possible that necessity requirements under the exceptions provided in GATS Article XIV could require recognition. These provisions, which provide a defence after a finding of violation, have been found to require that the national measure be the least trade restrictive alternative. Sometimes, the least trade restrictive alternative will be simple recognition of the effectiveness of home state regulation.

In addition, the Appellate Body in *United States – Shrimp* seems to have identified an embryonic equivalence requirement in the chapeau of General Agreement on Tariffs and Trade (GATT) Article XX (exceptions). Recall that GATS Article XIV parallels GATT Article XX. The Appellate Body held as follows:

> As we see it, the Panel correctly reasoned and concluded that conditioning market access on the adoption of a programme *comparable in effectiveness*, allows for sufficient flexibility in the application of the measure so as to avoid 'arbitrary or unjustifiable discrimination'.[5]

[2] GATS Art. VI:4.

[3] GATS Art. VI:5 (citation omitted). The omitted footnote defines the term 'relevant international organizations' as 'international bodies whose membership is open to the relevant bodies of at least all Members of the WTO'.

[4] That is, a measure may be viewed as disproportionate in relation to the fact that international measures exist, whereas if the international measures did not exist, the measure might be proportionate. This concept is clearly expressed in the jurisprudence of the ECJ. It is also specifically included in the WTO Agreement on Technical Barriers to Trade.

[5] Appellate Body Report on *United States – Shrimp*, para. 144 (emphasis in original).

A measure requiring foreign regulatory programmes to be 'comparable in effectiveness', as opposed to being 'essentially the same', would comply with the prohibition against arbitrary or unjustifiable restrictions on trade. This appears to function as a 'soft' equivalence discipline, which only arises after a violation of another provision of GATT or, in our context, GATS.

4 WTO legality of mutual recognition in services

Sub-multilateral mutual recognition is a challenge to the MFN non-discriminatory structure of the multilateral trading system. Mutual recognition may be discriminatory in the MFN sense. Mutual recognition under GATS requires that equivalent opportunities are offered to other states. It seems clear that mere mutuality is not a permissible basis for discrimination. There is even a question under WTO law regarding the degree to which regional trade agreements (RTAs) may limit mutual recognition arrangements to their members, as opposed to making recognition available to other WTO members.

Does mutual recognition violate the MFN obligation under GATS Article II? The analysis would be similar to that under GATT Article I:1 (MFN) (see Bartels 2005). This analysis requires review of the scope of MFN obligations (see generally Davey and Pauwelyn 2000). There are two issues. First, does the MFN obligation apply on a service-by-service basis, or does it allow distinctions based on the jurisdiction of origin of the service provider? Second, does it apply to provide WTO members that are not party to a mutual recognition agreement an opportunity to qualify for recognition? There would seem to be a conflict between mutual recognition and a strict understanding of the MFN obligation, to the effect that imported 'like' products from one member cannot be treated differently from 'like' products from other members. Mutual recognition focuses on the regulatory context in which products or services are produced, rather than the actual characteristics of the products or services.

The legal question is whether, and under what circumstances, a state may recognize foreign regulation without recognizing the similar regulation of all WTO members. Recall that in *Canada – Autos*, the Appellate Body confirmed that GATT Article I:1 addresses *de facto*, as well as *de jure*, discrimination. The Appellate Body emphasized the unconditional and broad scope of Article I:1 in finding that mere differential treatment of products originating in different members, regardless of the producer-based rationale, violates Article I:1. Although the Appellate Body did not emphasize this, its interpretation is based on the 'like products' reference of Article I: automobiles are like products regardless of whether their manufacturers have or have not invested in Canada.[6] Given the focus on the Article I:1 reference to the matters referenced in Article III:4 (national treatment), and to 'any advantage', it appears possible that 'like products' treated differently due to different recognition arrangements might result in a violation of MFN.

Thus, while it appears that there is a possible argument that recognition arrangements may be legal under GATS Article II, there seems to be little support for 'closed' recognition as it might appear within a RTA, such as the EU common market. By 'closed' recognition, I mean arrangements that limit the group of states eligible to participate in the recognition arrangements in ways that are not based on regulatory standards.

Even if a recognition arrangement were otherwise illegal under the MFN requirements of Article II, GATS Article VII specifically authorizes recognition of 'standards or criteria for the authorization, licensing or certification of services suppliers', either by agreement or autonomously. Coming immediately after Article VI, which specifically includes 'technical standards', Article VII may be viewed as intended to exclude recognition of technical standards from its terms, but it is not clear why this would be so, and a contrary interpretive argument could be constructed. Of course, some of the same ground may be viewed as already covered by Article VI:5, to the extent that WTO members are prohibited from imposing requirements that are more burdensome than necessary to ensure the quality of the service. Such a proportionality discipline may be viewed as including, to some extent, a requirement of recognition. After all, if the home state regulation is sufficient to achieve the regulatory goal, application of the host state regulation may well be more burdensome than necessary. In addition, paragraph 3 of the Annex on Financial Services permits recognition of 'prudential measures' of another country, either by agreement or autonomously, 'in determining how the Member's measures relating to financial services shall be applied'.

GATS Article VII:1 permits recognition of 'education or experience obtained, requirements met, or licenses or certifications granted in a particular country'. Recognition arrangements have been made in

[6] Appellate Body Report on *Canada – Autos*, para. 85.

connection with a number of free trade areas and customs unions, including most notably the European Union. However, most RTAs do not contain specific recognition commitments.

Recognition arrangements are required to be notified to the WTO. Most recognition arrangements notified to the WTO address recognition of professional qualifications; however, some relate to the recognition of academic qualifications. Recognition arrangements have often been made within RTAs, and also are often made between geographically proximate countries.

In some regional contexts, notably the European Union and the Australia–New Zealand Tasman Mutual Recognition Arrangement, there are arrangements for persons licensed to practise a certain profession in their home country to practise that profession in the territories of other parties to the agreement. However, in most regional and geographic arrangements, the recognition provided is more modest. The negotiation of the specifics of recognition arrangements is often delegated to the relevant private professional bodies. Recognition negotiations are hampered by significant diversity across countries in their licensing requirements, by concerns about the loss of regulatory sovereignty, and by motivations of professionals already licensed to protect their market from competition.

Note that GATS Article VII and paragraph 3 of the Annex on Financial Services do not require recognition but merely authorize it. Although a strong GATS standard of necessity might eventually lead to judicially required equivalence, this is unlikely to be the case under current treaty language. But the necessity test might nevertheless mandate equivalence of some regulations and not others, whereby partial equivalence becomes the operational consequence of the principle of proportionality.

As to mutuality, under GATS Article VII, members that develop mutual recognition arrangements are required to 'afford adequate opportunity for other interested Members to negotiate their accession to such an agreement or arrangement or to negotiate comparable ones with it'.

GATS Article V permits economic integration arrangements. It provides that GATS 'shall not prevent' sub-multilateral agreements for liberalization of trade in services, conditioned on the elimination of discrimination in the national treatment sense. Because it does not require equivalence or harmonization, following GATT jurisprudence in the *Turkey – Textiles* case, it would not provide an exception for equivalence or harmonization from other GATS requirements.

In the *Turkey – Textiles* decision,[7] the Appellate Body examined the relationship between Article XXIV and other provisions of GATT. Under the Appellate Body's decision, it is at least arguable that the exception of GATT Article XXIV is only available with respect to measures that are *necessary* in order to form a free trade area or customs union as defined in Article XXIV. Therefore, it appears that to the extent that WTO members engage in mutual recognition, their mutual recognition arrangements must conform to all the requirements of WTO law, including the MFN requirements of GATS Article II, and/or Article VII.

5 Embedded liberalism I: mutual recognition and essential harmonization at the WTO

The WTO should not be seen as calling for mutual recognition *without* a process of essential harmonization: mutual recognition, as a fundamentally liberalizing rule, should be embedded in appropriate prudential regulation. This prudential regulation will prevent externalization and inappropriate regulatory competition. Essential harmonization is the occasion for a political process that sets the limits for externalization and regulatory competition.

In light of this need for essential harmonization, the WTO is not today institutionally capable of delivering significant mutual recognition arrangements on its own. Nor will it emerge soon as a locus for essential harmonization. Rather, mutual recognition arrangements will develop based on functionally specialized efforts toward essential harmonization, such as the development of international standards for services. These efforts will generally take place in functionally specialized agencies, such as the Basel Committee or the International Organization of Securities Commissions. In limited areas, these essential harmonization arrangements will be incorporated within the WTO system as the basis for recognition arrangements: that is, compliance with these international standards will serve as essential harmonization for the purposes of mutual recognition.

Compliance with these international standards will thus serve as a basis for acceptance of foreign services without cumulative application of host state law: for recognition of the home state regulation or simply of the international regulation. It is in this sense that international

[7] Appellate Body Report on *Turkey – Textiles*.

standardization and mutual recognition are complementary in the multilateral system.

Even if the essential harmonization occurs outside the WTO, GATS Article VII may validate open recognition arrangements, but may call for disapproval of closed recognition arrangements.

6 Embedded liberalism II: mutual recognition and developing countries

For developing countries, plurilateral or multilateral mutual recognition represents a danger of market foreclosure. Developing countries may lack the material capacity to participate, the power to control the agenda, and the resources to comply with harmonized standards established through multilateral processes. They are therefore in danger of failing to benefit even from open mutual recognition, and of finding that harmonized standards and mutual recognition put their non-participating services at a disadvantage compared to services of states that are able to participate in mutual recognition processes. In the 1980s, Japan and the United States feared a 'Fortress Europe'. Today, it is not out of the question for poor countries to fear that mutual recognition will help build the walls of a 'Fortress North'. A nuanced, inclusive and redistributive political process is needed: embedded mutual recognition.

Within the trade and regulation context, poor countries will achieve the greatest possible benefit from MFN-based liberalization in connection with services that are of export interest to them. Mutual recognition arrangements among developed countries, failing to include poor countries, are highly likely to place the services of poor countries at a disadvantage relative to those of countries participating in these arrangements. So, mutual recognition arrangements within north–north preferential trade agreements pose the risk of trade diversion to the disfavour of developing countries. As noted above, this type of closed recognition may violate WTO MFN obligations.

It may well be that a regime of 'open recognition' – allowing all states to submit their regulatory regimes for review and possible acceptance for recognition – would satisfy the requirements of MFN. However, this approach may not provide sufficient market access for developing countries if individual developed countries, or groups of developed countries, establish high standards that are excessively difficult or costly for developing countries to meet. In fact, just as domestic standards may be set to provide protection against imports, it may be that the standards applied in recognition regimes are set by the parties to provide *de facto* protection. To the extent that recognition regimes are established without transparency and input from developing countries to influence their development, this is a risk.

Moreover, it may be excessively costly for developing countries to qualify for recognition, either in connection with their regulatory standards or with their certification arrangements. In connection with the Doha Round, there have been discussions of technical assistance to enable developing countries to participate in, and qualify for, harmonization and recognition processes. Arrangements should be made to ensure that even open recognition arrangements do not place developing countries at a competitive disadvantage, or require developing countries to expend excessive amounts of their own resources in order to comply.

7 Conclusion: mutual recognition and governance

As noted at the beginning of this chapter, mutual recognition is a technique of trade facilitation that involves regulatory deference by importing or host countries. It is perfectly rational for states to decide to compromise some of their regulatory goals as they engage in international commerce. They may do so through recognition without predicate where the value of their regulation is small relative to the value of expanded commerce. Alternatively, they may engage in managed recognition to maximize the combined value of regulation and expanded commerce. Managed recognition would include either harmonization or equivalence regimes.

The WTO has little capacity to produce harmonized rules, but may increasingly select harmonized rules from other regimes as predicates for recognition. Indeed, as discussed above, GATS Article VI may serve as a basis for adjudicated equivalence, but would only serve as a discipline to the extent that the national measure also results in nullification or impairment.

Mutual recognition may also pose dangers to developing country market access. Mutual recognition regimes should be structured so as not to reduce such, and so as not to require excessive amounts of resources. Arrangements for technical assistance may be made to address the latter concern.

Thus, mutual recognition, like any form of liberalism, must be embedded in two ways. First, it should not jeopardize a satisfactory level of prudential regulation. Thus, capacity for harmonization and/or equivalence evaluation will set the limit on the scope of mutual recognition. Second, it should not disadvantage poor countries, either *de jure* through closed recognition among developed countries or *de facto* through harmonization or equivalence conditions that are excessive, or excessively costly, for poor countries.

References

Bartels, L. (2005), 'The Legality of the EC Mutual Recognition Clause under WTO Law', *Journal of International Economic Law* 8(3): 691–720

Davey, W. and Pauwelyn, J. (2000), 'MFN Unconditionality: A Legal Analysis of the Concept in View of its Evolution in the GATT/WTO Jurisprudence with Particular Reference to the Issue of "Like Product"' in T. Cottier, P.C. Mavroidis and P. Blatter (eds.), *Regulatory Barriers and the Principle of Non-Discrimination in World Trade Law*, Ann Arbor: Michigan University Press

Nicolaïdis, K. and Shaffer, G. (2005), 'Transnational Mutual Recognition Regimes: Governance without Global Government', *Law and Contemporary Problems* 68(3–4): 263–318

Weiler, J. (2005), 'Mutual Recognition, Functional Equivalence and Harmonization in the Evolution of the European Common Market and the WTO' in F. Kostoris Padoa Schioppa (ed.), *The Principle of Mutual Recognition in the European Integration Process*, New York: Palgrave Macmillan

PART III

Case studies

Introduction to Part III

In Part III of this book, a number of case studies on domestic regulation in services sectors are presented. These case studies concern the following sectors: legal services, telecommunications, information and communications technology, mobile banking, financial services, higher education, logistical services, postal services and retail food distribution.

These case studies show WTO members' practical experiences in regulating specific services markets, including the challenges they encountered and the results achieved. The studies do not solely include services sectors in well-developed markets in WTO members. They also include experiences of developing countries, which may have limited regulatory experience and capacity when dealing with fast-developing services sectors.

Confronting WTO members' practical experiences with the basic principles discussed in more detail in Part III of this book enables us to test the approach taken in the current negotiations, and the theoretical principles (subject to the negotiations in the Working Party on Domestic Regulation) against practical reality. This confrontation may show how the principles may function in practice, and how the current approaches in the negotiations may need to be adjusted, by taking into account practical difficulties of implementing these principles, for example, 'single window' applications for licences, disciplines on a horizontal rather than a sector-specific basis, the introduction of a necessity test, or the use of international standards. On the basis of this analysis, we provide a number of conclusions and suggestions for 'ways forward' in the final part of this book.

8

Legal services in the United States

ERICA MOESER AND LAUREL S. TERRY

1 Introduction: an evolving regulatory environment

Globalization of the legal profession is understandably affecting the regulatory structure governing access to the practice of law in the United States. The currents are running strongly in the direction of creating greater opportunities for lawyers to engage in trade in legal services and to practise their profession across both state and national borders.

To understand the currents and cross-currents affecting legal practice in the United States, however, one must recognize certain factors. First, the practice of law is regulated by each of the fifty US states, the District of Columbia (Washington, DC) and US territories. Second, access to practise normally requires formal permission to practise on a jurisdiction-by-jurisdiction basis. Third, there are formal structures regulating lawyers once they are admitted. The latter include registration requirements, continuing education requirements and disciplinary structures, to name a few. Some or all of these regulatory structures do not exist in the design of the legal profession in other nations. And, of course, institutions are slow to change as a general matter.

Against this backdrop, there is also considerable clamour for change. Major US law firms seeking access to practise on a global scale are encouraging the removal of barriers to practise in the United States, understanding that the regulators in other nations will be more kindly disposed to permit the entry of US lawyers into overseas markets if there is a recognition that US markets must be open as well.

Interestingly, the push to open access to lawyers from overseas has called attention to the barriers to practise that exist from one US jurisdiction to another for US-licensed lawyers. A by-product of globalization is a new focus on the mobility of US lawyers across state and territorial lines.

2 An overview of the basic US regulatory structure

As noted above, the legal profession in the United States is regulated by each of the fifty states, the District of Columbia (Washington, DC) and US territories – collectively, the jurisdictions. In each US jurisdiction, the regulation of lawyers is typically allocated to the judicial branch of government, whereas the regulation of other professions is an executive or legislative branch function. Typically, the authority for this judicial regulation derives from each jurisdiction's constitution. The *Comprehensive Guide to Bar Admission Requirements* identifies for each US jurisdiction the authority that promulgates its rules for lawyer admission (Moeser and Huismann 2013: Chart 1).

Although there are some federal laws that apply to lawyer regulation, such as the US antitrust laws, the US federal government is not responsible for regulating lawyers, and there is no over-arching federal regulatory body for the legal profession. Moreover, there are debates in the United States about the scope of the US Constitution's enumerated powers, the meaning of the Tenth Amendment, and how much regulatory power over the legal profession the federal government could exercise, even if it wanted to do so.

Regulation in a given US jurisdiction addresses three different time spans in a lawyer's regulatory life: admission to practice, regulation of practice and lawyer discipline.[1] While the highest judicial body in each state typically has the ultimate regulatory authority for all three of these regulatory stages, it is common for the day-to-day regulatory functions to be delegated and to be handled by a different entity than the jurisdiction's highest court. In some states, the same regulatory entity may handle all three stages of lawyer regulation, whereas in other states, there may be separate entities for the three different stages of regulation. For example, the Pennsylvania Board of Law Examiners is empowered by the Supreme Court of Pennsylvania to 'recommend for admission only those individuals who have demonstrated the minimum competency and requisite character necessary to become a member of the bar'.[2] The Disciplinary Board of the Supreme Court of Pennsylvania is an independent agency

[1] Although GATS Art. VI refers to 'qualification' and 'licensing' requirements and procedures, for the US legal profession, these are not 'terms of art' that have precise meanings. Instead of these terms, US lawyers and their regulators often distinguish among 'bar admission rules', ethics or conduct rules, and discipline rules, without noting whether the particular rule would be viewed as a qualification or licensing requirement or procedure under GATS.

[2] See www.pabarexam.org/board_information/mission.htm.

under the Supreme Court's jurisdiction, with exclusive jurisdiction for attorney discipline: 'the purpose of this disciplinary system is to assist the Supreme Court of Pennsylvania in performing its constitutional duty to regulate attorney conduct'.[3]

With respect to admissions, the actual regulatory bodies that exist under the judicial branch bear titles such as the Board of Bar Examiners or the Board of Law Examiners. While most such agencies are entities of the jurisdictions' highest courts, some (particularly in the western part of the United States) are supervised by the particular jurisdiction's state bar. Information about these regulatory bodies is readily accessible on their websites. The National Conference of Bar Examiners (NCBE), the National Organization of Bar Counsel (NOBC), and the American Bar Association (ABA) Section of Legal Education and Admissions to the Bar all provide links to bar admissions authorities. In addition to these online sources, the *Comprehensive Guide to Bar Admission Requirements* (Moeser and Huismann 2013) is published annually in hard copy and online, and it includes detailed information about the relevant regulator in each jurisdiction and the substance of its regulatory requirements.

The licence to practise law is a general one: that is, the licensee is authorized to practise in any field of law in the jurisdiction in which the lawyer is licensed. There is no distinction between barristers and solicitors, to use the terminology from the United Kingdom. In addition to this full admission licence, most US jurisdictions have adopted rules that allow temporary practice by a lawyer licensed in another US jurisdiction. Jurisdictions typically have different rules that apply to temporary *transactional* work by lawyers licensed outside of the jurisdiction, on the one hand, and temporary *litigation* work by lawyers licensed outside of the jurisdiction, on the other hand. The latter type of practice is often called *pro hac vice*. Some US jurisdictions have adopted rules that allow temporary transactional and litigation practice by lawyers licensed outside the United States. Individuals who are practising law in a jurisdiction in which they are not licensed or otherwise permitted to do so are said to be engaged in the unauthorized practice of law. The scope of these reserved activities is broader in the United States than in some other countries, such as the United Kingdom, and includes both litigation and transactional work.

Once the law licence is conferred, it is renewable with no additional testing in the jurisdiction in which it is conferred. Lawyers typically pay

[3] See www.padisciplinaryboard.org/about/history.php.

annual regulatory fees and are required to satisfy continuing legal education requirements; however, they are not subject to retesting. Lawyers are subject to a code of conduct that is typically adopted by the highest court in each jurisdiction. Although virtually all jurisdictions have used the ABA Model Rules of Professional Conduct as a starting template, it is the state professional conduct rules, rather than the ABA Model Rules of Professional Conduct, that provide the binding source of lawyer regulation. Some jurisdictions have adopted the ABA Model Rules verbatim. Some jurisdictions have enacted rules that include only minor variations from the ABA Model Rules. Other jurisdictions, however, have enacted rules that differ in significant respects from the ABA Model Rules. These 'ethics codes', as they are often referred to, include mandatory provisions, the violation of which can subject a lawyer to a range of disciplinary measures, including possible permanent revocation of the lawyer's licence to practise law. These state ethics codes typically include requirements regarding lawyer independence, confidentiality obligations, avoiding conflicts of interest, and rules regarding fee agreements, advertising and partnership with non-lawyers. While there are virtually identical rules in many jurisdictions with respect to certain issues, such as Rule 1.3: Diligence, there are significant variations in other rules, such as those dealing with confidentiality. Each jurisdiction's ethics code is readily accessible. For example, in addition to being available on the jurisdiction's website, links to these ethics codes are available on the website of the ABA Center for Professional Responsibility and the NOBC.[4] The ABA Center for Professional Responsibility website provides additional detail, including charts that provide state-by-state comparisons for particular ethics rules and for other lawyer regulatory issues.

Similar to the admissions and conduct stages of lawyer regulation, the discipline stage of lawyer regulation is handled on a subfederal jurisdictional basis and has been heavily influenced by model policies developed by the ABA. Each jurisdiction has a website with information about its lawyer discipline system. In addition, the websites of the ABA Center for Professional Responsibility and the NOBC include links to each jurisdiction's lawyer discipline system and additional information. The National Lawyer Regulatory Data Bank is a national repository of information concerning public regulatory actions relating to lawyers throughout the United States. The Data Bank provides disciplinary

[4] See www.nobc.org/State_Ethics_Opinions.aspx; www.americanbar.org/groups/professional_responsibility/policy.html.

authorities and bar admissions agencies 'a central repository of information to facilitate reciprocal discipline and to help prevent the admission of lawyers who have been disbarred or suspended elsewhere'.[5] Participation is voluntary, but all states and the District of Columbia, as well as many federal courts and some agencies, provide regulatory information to the Data Bank. In 2009, the US Conference of Chief Justices reached agreements with regulatory representatives from Australia and the European Union to encourage the exchange of information among the relevant regulatory authorities.[6] In August 2013, the ABA House of Delegates voted upon a resolution that urges the highest courts and lawyer regulatory authorities in US jurisdictions to coordinate with their foreign regulatory counterparts and to enter into voluntary arrangements to facilitate the exchange of relevant information, consistent with the jurisdictions' rules regarding the admission, licensure and disciplinary status of lawyers licensed in their respective jurisdictions. It also urges them to adopt the Guidelines for an International Regulatory Information Exchange.[7]

3 Pathways to licensure

The customary route for a lawyer to become licensed begins when the individual graduates from an accredited law school with the juris doctor (JD) degree. Law school typically requires three years of post-baccalaureate study for a total of seven post-secondary years. Most law graduates receive their degrees at the conclusion of the academic year (ordinarily in May) and sit for the bar examination in the state in which they intend to practise during late July.

The bar examination is offered twice each year, in late July and late February. Those who are unsuccessful on an administration may retake the test in the original state or another. A majority of states allow the would-be lawyer to take the bar examination an unlimited number of times. There is strong statistical evidence that most candidates pass the bar examination in the first attempt, and that almost all candidates who repeat the bar examination pass it by the third attempt (Case 2012).

[5] See www.americanbar.org/groups/professional_responsibility/services/databank.html.

[6] These resolutions are available at http://ccj.ncsc.org/Policy-Resolutions.aspx; www.americanbar.org/groups/professional_responsibility/policy/gats_international_agreements/misc.html.

[7] *Report to the House of Delegates*, ABA Resolution 104, August 2013.

While each jurisdiction constructs its own bar examination, the tests are far more similar than different. Typically, one day is devoted to the Multistate Bar Examination, a 200-question multiple-choice test developed by the NCBE.[8] A second day of testing is typically comprised of written examinations with essay questions and performance tests that are crafted nationally or locally. Two jurisdictions use locally crafted multiple-choice examinations, and a few jurisdictions extend testing to three days. The *Comprehensive Guide to Bar Admissions Requirements* (see Moeser and Huismann 2013: Charts 2, 11 and 12) includes information on:

- bar examination fees;
- length, scoring and test components;
- each jurisdiction's character and fitness requirements;
- admission on motion rules;
- other procedural requirements.

Each jurisdiction sets its own passing score on the bar examination, just as each sets its own rules for eligibility. For 2011, an average of 79 per cent of candidates who were graduates of nationally accredited law schools and who took a bar examination in the fifty-six jurisdictions for the first time passed it. For those repeating the bar examination in the same jurisdiction in 2011, 37 per cent passed. Pass rates vary by jurisdiction because of many variables, including the difference in jurisdictions' cut scores (the term for the score required to pass) and the overall ability of the recent law graduates who typically comprise the bulk of the first-time takers in different jurisdictions.[9]

As noted above, all US jurisdictions recognize graduation from an accredited law school as qualifying an applicant to sit for their bar examinations. The US Department of Education recognizes the ABA Council of its Section of Legal Education as the sole accrediting authority for law schools. In ABA terminology, these law schools are 'approved'. Approval (i.e. accreditation) is granted when a law school satisfies the Standards for Approval of Law Schools.[10]

8 A description of this and other nationally developed tests used by jurisdictions to test candidates for licensure can be found at www.ncbex.org.

9 Statistical information compiled by calendar year is available at www.ncbex.org. In particular, see '2012 Statistics', *The Bar Examiner* 82(1): 16–19.

10 The text of the Standards and information about the 202 currently approved law schools are available at www.americanbar.org/legaled.

Another factor affecting eligibility is the character and fitness of the applicant to practise law. The granting of a law licence in every jurisdiction involves some degree of evaluation of the applicant's history and capacity to practise law. The NCBE conducts for a number of jurisdictions character and fitness investigations on applicants seeking either admission to the bar or a limited licence to practise law. The NCBE Character and Fitness Application can be completed online and is not limited to US residents.[11]

The most common alternative to gaining admission to the bar by passing a bar examination is becoming admitted by presenting proof of admission and a record of practice in another US jurisdiction. This type of admission, often referred to as 'admission on motion' or 'admission on foreign licence' – where 'foreign' denotes another US jurisdiction – is permitted in over half of US jurisdictions. Some jurisdictions have additional methods, which are described below.

The trend line has moved toward permitting more mobility of lawyers in recent years and is likely to continue to move in that direction.

4 Trends toward modification of eligibility requirements

There is significant activity in the area of broadening access to practise by lawyers seeking to move across state lines permanently or temporarily. One of the challenges of the first quarter of the twenty-first century is modifying existing regulatory structures to accommodate greater lawyer mobility without breaking faith with the consumers of legal services who depend on regulation to ensure a competent and ethical bar. There are inevitable and unavoidable tensions when these competing interests occasionally collide.

Over the years the principal modifications to the mainstream eligibility requirement of an accredited law degree and passage of the bar examination have been associated with permitting the following categories of applicant to take the bar examination:

- graduates of unaccredited law schools;
- holders of master of laws (LLM) degrees from accredited US law schools;
- lawyers educated outside the United States.

[11] See www.ncbex.org/character-and-fitness.

The degree of permissiveness and variety of approaches is reflected in the *Comprehensive Guide to Bar Admission Requirements* (Moeser and Huismann 2013: Charts 4 and 11–13).

Full admission appears to be the preferred avenue for foreign-educated lawyers. In each year since 2000, there have been more than 1,000 foreign-educated applicants who have successfully passed US state bar examinations (and presumably have continued the process to become fully admitted lawyers).[12] Thirty-two US jurisdictions permit lawyers educated outside the United States to practise the law of their home country (and sometimes third country and international law).[13] Someone holding this type of limited licence is termed a foreign legal consultant. This limited licence is a little-used mechanism. In 2011, only ninety-one individuals were licensed as foreign legal consultants. Of these, forty-seven were authorized in Florida and twenty-three in New York. The remaining twenty-one applied in eight other states.[14] There is little growth in this area as foreign-educated lawyers make strides in obtaining unrestricted licences via the bar examination, motion admission and rules permitting temporary practice.

5 Uniform Bar Examination

Ultimately, the testing of lawyers for licensure may evolve to the point of the adoption of a single common test. Law is the only profession in the United States that has not moved to an examination structure of this type. The Uniform Bar Examination (UBE) is a new development that represents an important advance in this area. Now adopted by thirteen states, it represents a major step forward. Applicants who take the UBE are eligible to seek admission in all of the states that have adopted the UBE without further testing, greatly increasing their mobility through the score portability that this examination offers. States that have adopted the UBE so far include: Alabama, Arizona, Colorado, Idaho, Minnesota, Missouri, Montana, Nebraska, New Hampshire, North Dakota, Utah, Washington and Wyoming.[15]

12 See: www.ncbex.org/publications/statistics; Terry 2013a.

13 See www.americanbar.org/groups/professional_responsibility/committees_commissions/commission_on_multijurisdictional_practice.html.

14 Statistical information compiled by calendar year available at www.ncbex.org. In particular, see '2012 Statistics', *The Bar Examiner* 82(1): 28.

15 Information about the UBE is available at www.ncbex.org.

The UBE offers significant potential to lawyers at the entry level of practice in that it eliminates the need for redundant testing as lawyers move from state to state during their early years of practice.

6 Looking toward the future

With respect to admissions issues, it is unlikely that jurisdictions will abandon the bar examination as a primary mechanism for authorizing the practice of law in the United States. It is more likely that eligibility to take the bar examination will continue to expand to permit lawyers lacking a JD degree from an accredited US law school to attempt it. Underlying all considerations as to the eligibility of an applicant is the legal consumer's interest in being protected by regulators from the incompetent, dishonest or otherwise incapable lawyer, whose limitations may not be easily recognized by a client and whose potential to damage individual lives is significant. The importance of lawyer regulation is recognized throughout the world. For example, when responding to the World Trade Organization (WTO) request for input on the issue of domestic regulation disciplines, the International Bar Association (IBA) observed that lawyers play an essential role in protecting individual political, civil and economic rights; that the rule of law and integrity of the legal system, promoted by lawyers, is vital and important to the highest degree; and that legitimate regulatory objectives include protection of clients and the public generally.[16]

Although it is unlikely that jurisdictions will abandon the bar examination, it is likely that under the auspices of the ABA, there will be initiatives to expand access to the profession to US lawyers wishing to practise across US jurisdictions and to foreign-educated lawyers, particularly those who wish to practise the law of their home country. These initiatives are occurring in the context of encouraging jurisdictions to implement the ABA's model policies. In addition, the UBE offers tremendous potential for permitting newly licensed lawyers to move across state boundaries as they seek employment or the expansion of their ability to serve existing clients. It is reasonable to predict that additional jurisdictions will adopt this approach over the next decade.

[16] See *Communication to the World Trade Organization on the Suitability of Applying to the Legal Profession the WTO Disciplines for the Accountancy Sector*, IBA resolution ATL01/11496697v2, September 2003.

With respect to conduct regulation, the practice of law has changed in dramatic ways in the United States, as it has elsewhere. Lawyer regulation must consider these new developments, which are driven by technology, globalization and market forces. A number of these developments and issues have been set forth in the extensive reports prepared by the ABA Commission on Ethics 20/20, which concluded its work in 2013.[17] Global developments are now regularly discussed at meetings of the Conference of Chief Justices, the NCBE, the NOBC and the ABA. Forums such as these provide an opportunity to discuss regulatory trends, including issues related to 'who' regulates lawyers, 'what' is regulated, 'why' lawyers are regulated, and 'when', 'where' and 'how' such regulation occurs (see e.g. Terry *et al.* 2012). The International Conference of Legal Regulators has now met twice and reflects increased interest in regulatory cooperation and communication. More than 100 professionals from Africa, Asia, Australia, Europe and North America attended the September 2012 inaugural conference in London, including US representatives from the NCBE, the Conference of Chief Justices, the NOBC and the ABA (Terry 2013b).

7 Trade-related implications

Legal services are covered by a number of trade agreements which the United States has signed, including the General Agreement on Trade in Services (GATS), the North American Free Trade Agreement (NAFTA) and more than a dozen bilateral trade agreements (Terry 2010). The United States included legal services in its original GATS Schedule of Specific Commitments.[18] The 2005 US Doha Round GATS 'offer' proposed expanding the US legal services commitments by removing the limitation that US citizenship is required to practise before the US Patent and Trademark Office and by expanding to twenty-four from sixteen the number of state foreign legal consultants listed.[19]

The ABA maintains a website devoted to GATS and legal services. The legal services portions of the US GATS Schedule and the 2005 US

[17] Some of these papers are available at www.americanbar.org/groups/professional_responsibility/aba_commission_on_ethics_20_20/work_product.html.

[18] See *The United States of America: Schedule of Specific Commitments*, WTO doc. GATS/SC/90, 15 April 1994.

[19] See *United States: Revised Services Offer*, WTO doc. TN/S/O/USA/Rev.1, 28 June 2005.

GATS offer, along with a number of other documents relevant to GATS and legal services, are posted on this website.[20] The ABA has taken a leading role in trying to educate US lawyers and regulators about GATS and its potential impact on legal services, including on domestic regulation. The ABA Task Force on International Trade in Legal Services is the successor to the ABA Task Force on GATS Legal Services Negotiations. One of the goals of the ABA Task Force is to educate and provide outreach related to the status of GATS and to provide individuals and entities with a mechanism to provide their input. It includes as regular or liaison members representatives from organizations whose members regulate US lawyer admissions, conduct and discipline.

The ABA has adopted several policies relevant to GATS and legal services, including the 2002 resolution that urged the US trade representative to seek in the Doha Round negotiations practise rights for outbound US lawyers equivalent to the practice rights set forth for inbound foreign lawyers in the ABA Model Rule for the Licensing and Practice of Foreign Legal Consultants and the 2006 ABA resolution that addressed the issue of WTO domestic regulation disciplines.[21] In 2013, upon the recommendation of the ABA Commission on Ethics 20/20, the ABA House of Delegates adopted three resolutions that encourage US states to offer certain admission and practice rights to foreign-licensed lawyers.[22]

Undoubtedly, trade negotiations have had, and will have, influence on the type and rate of change in the area of delivery of legal services. While some commentators have suggested that the federal government of the United States may ultimately pre-empt the constitutionally derived prerogatives of each state to regulate its legal profession, it is more likely that market influences, both at home and abroad, will result in the elimination of barriers. Federal pre-emption is revolutionary, and it is more likely that an evolutionary model will prevail.

At any given moment there are various players on the stage where trade-related issues are concerned. Certainly, the Office of

[20] See www.americanbar.org/groups/professional_responsibility/policy/gats_international_agreements.html.

[21] These relevant policies adopted by the ABA House of Delegates are available at www.americanbar.org/groups/professional_responsibility/policy/gats_international_agreements/relevant.html.

[22] Resolutions Revised 107A, Revised 107B and 107C as Amended are available at www.americanbar.org/groups/professional_responsibility/aba_commission_on_ethics_20_20/house_of_delegates_filings.html.

the US Trade Representative has been central in trade treaty aspects of modifying the regulation of the legal profession at home and abroad. The Conference of Chief Justices, the NCBE and the NOBC are national network organizations that facilitate discussions among state regulators of the legal profession. The ABA, particularly the ABA Task Force, has played a central role in facilitating discussions about GATS and legal services, including issues of domestic regulation. The IBA continues to serve as an important source of information and outreach.[23]

8 Conclusion

The regulatory structure of licensing lawyers in the United States is complicated to describe or understand because each jurisdiction determines its own rules, policies and procedures. An excellent source of information on each jurisdiction's admission requirements appears in the *Comprehensive Guide to Bar Admission Requirements* (Moeser and Huismann 2013), which is available online. The website of the ABA Center for Professional Responsibility provides a further source of information on each jurisdiction's regulation of lawyer conduct and disciplinary systems, including charts that show state-by-state implementation of various policies.[24] The website of the NOBC is also a useful resource.

While many of the separate licensing and regulatory structures are similar or parallel, there are many permutations. Regulation is justified as serving the public interest, and particularly the interest of the consumer. As is true in many countries, US lawyers are not regulated based on the type of client they represent. Accordingly, there can be conflicts and tensions between the needs and interests of sophisticated repeat-player clients engaged in global trade and the lawyers who represent them, and the needs and interests of other types of clients, including those who are more vulnerable. Legal profession regulators face the very difficult task of trying to balance all of these needs and interests, while also keeping in mind the need to protect the public and the vitality of the jurisdiction's legal system and rule of law.

In sum, the meaning and purpose of state and national barriers are shifting along with the nature of law practice in a national and global

[23] The IBA recently published its *Revised GATS Handbook*, which is available at http://tinyurl.com/IBA-GATS2013.

[24] See www.americanbar.org/groups/professional_responsibility/policy.html.

economy. Globalization and technology have permanently altered the framework in which law is practised on a local, national and global scale. Structures are changing – too radically and too fast for some and far too slowly for others. Regulators are struggling to keep pace with the mechanics and politics of this inevitable change.

References

Case, S.M. (2012), 'The Testing Column: Persistence on the Bar Exam', *The Bar Examiner* 8(4): 20–3

Moeser, E. and Huismann, C. (2013), *Comprehensive Guide to Bar Admission Requirements 2013*, Chicago/Madison: National Conference of Bar Examiners/American Bar Association

Terry, L.S. (2010), 'From GATS to APEC: The Impact of Trade Agreements on Legal Services', *Akron Law Review* 43: 875–984

(2013a), 'Summary of Statistics of Bar Exam Applicants Educated Outside the US: 1992–2012 (It's not just about New York and California)', Excerpts from National Conference of Bar Examiners, *Bar Admission Statistics 1992–2012*

(2013b), 'Creating an International Network of Lawyer Regulators: The 2012 International Conference of Legal Regulators', *The Bar Examiner* 82(2): 18–27

Terry, L.S., Mark, S. and Gordon, T. (2012), 'Trends and Challenges in Lawyer Regulation: The Impact of Globalization and Technology', *Fordham Law Review* 80(6): 2661–84

9

Telecommunications reform in China: fostering competition through state intervention

HENRY GAO

1 Introduction

As in many developing countries, the telecommunications services sector in China has for a long time been monopolized by the state through the Ministry of Post and Telecommunication (MPT). Established in 1949, the MPT is not only the regulator of telecommunications services, but also the sole owner and operator. Not surprisingly, such monopoly has resulted in the slow growth of the sector. However, such slow growth did not cause major problems in the first thirty years following the founding of the People's Republic of China because there was little mobility among the population, thus little need for long-distance communication. During this period, the telephone was an exclusive luxury available mostly to the government and the military.

As the country started its economic reform in 1979, however, the telecommunications sector started to drag economic growth down. To solve the problem, the Central Committee of the Communist Party of China and State Council issued two directives in 1984 to encourage the development of the telecommunications sector.[1] Recognizing the special importance of telecommunications in the economy, these two directives made the development of the sector a priority, and launched the first of the many waves of reforms to come.[2] Together, these reforms have

[1] For the text of the two directives, see 'Dangdai Zhongguo Youdian Shiye' ['Telecom Industry in Contemporary China'], available at www.1921.org.cn/book.php?ac=view&bvid=89290&bid=1143. As each directive includes six points, they are referred to as the 'Two Six-points'. For the background on the introduction of the two directives, see 'Jiefang Sixiang Dakuayue' ['Liberalizing the Thoughts and Making Big Leaps'], available at www.cnii.com.cn/index/zt/jd90zn/content/2011-06/17/content_886493.htm.

[2] For a detailed history of China's telecommunications reform, see 'Tongxinye Guanghui Licheng he Weida Chengjiu Daxing Wangzhan' ['Grand Internet Exhibition of the Glorious History and Great Achievements of the Telecom Industry'], available at www.cnii.com.cn/index/zt/jd90zn/node_32463.htm.

transformed China, in a mere two decades, from a country with one-tenth of the world's average telephone density (teledensity) level into a country with the highest number of telecommunications networks and subscribers in the world.

In this chapter, we will discuss the objectives and purposes behind China's telecommunications regulation, regulatory practices adopted to achieve these objectives, as well as their implications for international trade.

2 Regulatory goals and practices

In the view of the author, there are three main goals in China's telecommunications regulatory framework: fostering competition, providing universal service and protecting public morals. This section discusses the rationales for these regulatory goals and how China tries to achieve them through various regulatory practices.

2.1 Fostering competition

Because the establishment of telecommunications networks used to require considerable initial investment, telecommunications services were traditionally considered natural monopolies. As technological advances since the 1970s greatly reduced the establishment cost, however, the regulatory philosophy changed and the inefficiencies caused by state-owned monopolies became a bigger problem. This led to the liberalization of the sector across the world in the 1980s and 1990s, which was usually achieved by either privatizing existing monopolies or allowing the entry of newly established private operators.

While recognizing the need to foster a more competitive market, the Chinese government is more concerned with the strategic importance of the telecommunications sector. As noted by the Ministry of Information Industry (MII)[3] in the Tenth Five-year Plan Programme for the Information Industry,[4] the sector is not only a pillar industry that is of infrastructural importance to the national economy, but also a

[3] In 2008, the MII was restructured as the Ministry of Industry and Information Technology (MIIT) after the Commission of Science, Technology and Industry for National Defense, the State Council Informatization Office, and the State Tobacco Monopoly Bureau were merged into the MII. See www.danwei.org/media_guide/regulatory_agencies/miit.php. In this chapter, the ministry is referred to as MII before 2008, and MIIT after 2008.

[4] MII, 'Outline of the Tenth Five-year Plan Programme for the Information Industry', 17 September 2004, available at http://news.xinhuanet.com/st/2004-09/17/content_1992523.htm.

fundamental safeguard to national defence and security. Thus, the Chinese government is wary of allowing the entry into the sector of private firms, either domestic or foreign. Instead, it takes a different approach by boosting competition through administrative intervention. This reform includes four stages:

- 1994: from monopoly to duopoly;
- 1999: vertical division;
- 2002: horizontal division;
- 2008: overall restructuring.

2.1.1 1994: from monopoly to duopoly

After a decade of rapid economic growth, the demand for telecommunications services skyrocketed in the early 1990s. However, as a monopoly, the MPT lacked incentive to improve the quantity and quality of its services. At the same time, the Ministry of Railroads and the Ministry of Electricity each had their own telecommunications network with excess capacities, but they could not provide telecommunications services to the general public, as it was regarded as the exclusive turf of the MPT. To solve the problem, they teamed up with the Ministry of Electronics Industry and lobbied the State Council to establish a new telecommunications company in 1992 (see Harwit 2008: 47–8). In late 1993, the State Council formally approved the establishment of a new operator, China United Communication. Also known as Unicom, the new company was established the following year with ¥ 1.3 billion in registered capital drawing from a consortium of fifteen investors led by the three ministries.

Although it is one of the largest telecommunications carriers in the world today, Unicom was initially blessed with a rather limited business scope, which only allowed the company to fill the gaps left by the MPT by utilizing the surplus capacity of the private networks of the Ministry of Railroads and the Ministry of Electricity and providing local telephone services in areas where the existing network of the MPT had no coverage or insufficient capacity.[5]

In the same year, the operating arm of the MPT was also divested from the ministry to form China Telecom (CT) (see Harwit 2008: 50–3).

[5] State Council, *Guanyu Tongyi Zujian Zhongguo Lianhe Tongxin Youxian Gongsi de Pifu* [*Reply on the Approval of the Establishment of China United Communication Limited Company*], Guohan (1993) No. 178, 14 December 1993, available at www.gov.cn/xxgk/pub/govpublic/mrlm/201012/t20101217_63189.html.

While it was supposed to be an independent company, it was still regarded by the MPT as its preferred choice. To help CT in its competition against Unicom, the MPT resorted to various tactics such as refusing to connect Unicom's network to its own network and charging Unicom prohibitive rates to use the existing network of the MPT. Furthermore, while allowing Unicom to provide domestic local and long-distance services, the State Council decided to keep the most lucrative market segment – international services – exclusively for CT (Harwit 2008: 52–3).

All of these obstacles made it difficult for Unicom to survive, let alone grow. However, with the support of the three ministries, it managed to survive by exploiting the loopholes in the existing framework and engaging in various grey-area activities, such as an aggressive campaign to attract foreign investment (Harwit 2008: 52–9). Nonetheless, by the end of 1997, and with a meagre 3 per cent market share, the prospects for Unicom were rather bleak.

However, its luck finally turned in 1998, when the MPT and the Ministry of Electronics Industry were merged to create the new Ministry of Information Industry (MII). Now safe under the protective wings of the new telecommunications regulator, Unicom embarked on the path of rapid growth.

2.1.2 1999: vertical division

From 1999 to 2000, CT was broken down into three different companies according to the lines of business: the land-line business became the new CT, the mobile business was incorporated as China Mobile, and the satellite communication business was incorporated as China Satellite Communications (Satcom). In addition, the paging business was transferred from CT to Unicom.

Lest anyone mistake the vertical division of CT as an open call for cut-throat competition in the telecommunications market, then MII Minister Wu Jichuan explicitly stated at the founding of China Mobile that the Chinese government wanted 'orderly and cooperative competition' (Harwit 2008: 68). In confirmation, the official Xinhua news agency reported that 'all operators have expressed their willingness to avoid duplicated construction and vicious competition'.

By dividing the old CT according to lines of business, the original intention might well have been to avoid competition and instead encourage companies to focus on their own lines of business without worrying about vicious competition. However, as the example of Unicom has shown, things do not always turn out as intended. Soon after, the companies started to cross over into each other's lines of business. To further complicate the picture, three other companies also joined them in the new telecommunications gold-rush: Jitong Communications (Jitong), which was first established in 1994 to provide Internet services; China Net Communications (Netcom), which was founded in 2000 by the China Academy of Sciences along with three other partners to provide broadband Internet services; and China Railway Communications (Railcom), which was incorporated by the Ministry of Railroads in 2000, after it failed to persuade Unicom to take over its private telecommunications networks. In 2000, they were all granted licences to provide basic telecommunications services.

2.1.3 2002: horizontal division

Even though CT was broken up, it was still the dominant player in the land-line telephone services market. To introduce more competition, the State Council introduced a new plan to restructure the telecommunications sector in late 2001.[6] Under the plan, CT was divided into two companies: the new CT took over the assets and operations of the old CT in the twenty-one provinces in southern China; while the new China Netcom was established by merging the assets of the old Netcom, Jitong and those of the old CT in the ten provinces in northern China.

While the new CT took over the wealthy provinces in the south, it was also responsible for the poorer provinces in western China. Moreover, China Netcom was also allocated Netcom and Jitong, apparently to compensate it for the smaller one-third share of assets it inherited from the old CT. By trying to create two companies of comparable size out of the former monopoly carrier, the Chinese government made it possible for them to compete against each other on an equal footing. Moreover, even though the division was made along geographical boundaries, both companies were allowed to compete in each other's home regions and they took advantage of such opportunities (see Harwit 2008: 72–3). This provided both companies the incentive to improve their services, and it increased competition.

2.1.4 2008: overall restructuring

As the competition in telecommunications services intensified, the Chinese leadership started to realize that excessive competition might

[6] State Council, *Guangyu Yinfa Dianxin Tizhi Gaige Fangan de Tongzhi* [*Notice on the Reform Plan for the Telecom System*], Guofa (2001) No. 36, 17 November 2001.

weaken the overall capacity of the Chinese telecommunications carriers to compete against foreign operators, which were finally officially allowed to enter the Chinese telecommunications market after many years, as the result of China's accession to the World Trade Organization (WTO) in 2001 (Harwit 2008: 73). To foster national champions that could compete against foreign companies, the Chinese government announced a large restructuring project in 2008, which created three giant players: the new CT, which was created from the merger of the old CT, the CDMA mobile business of Unicom and the basic telecommunications services of Satcom; the new China Mobile, which combined the old China Mobile and Railcom; and the new Unicom, which took over the Global System for Mobile Communications (GSM) mobile business of the old Unicom and China Netcom.

After the restructuring, China Mobile emerged as the biggest player in the mobile business with some 400 million subscribers, while CT took top positions in both the fixed-line (220 million subscribers) and broadband (38 million subscribers) businesses.[7] While Unicom did not have dominant positions in any of the three businesses, it was the second largest operator in all three. In summary, the restructuring achieved its purpose, 'creating three highly-competitive players with national network coverage, similar resources and scale, and capacities to compete in all lines of businesses'.[8]

As the above shows, competition was introduced into the sector through administrative intervention, which resulted in the creation of new telecommunications companies sponsored by different ministries, as well as the restructuring of the sector through the division and merger of different companies.

2.2 *Universal service*

Recognizing the key role of telecommunications service as an infrastructure service in economic development, many countries around the

[7] Sina, 'Yunyingshang Gaoguan Tiaozheng Fangan Luoding, Dianxin Chongzu Lakai Xumu' ['Plan on the Reshuffling of Senior Executives of Operators Finalized, Restructuring of the Telecom Industry Unveiled'], available at http://tech.sina.com.cn/focus/telecom_cz2008/.

[8] Ministry of Industry and Information Technology, National Development and Reform Commission, Ministry of Finance, 'Guanyu Shenhua Dianxin Tizhi Gaige de Tonggao' ['Announcement on Deepening Reform of the Telecom System'], 24 May 2008, available at http://tech.sina.com.cn/t/2008-05-24/14022215251.shtml.

world have imposed universal service obligations on telecommunications operators. Generally, universal service can be defined as providing access to a defined minimum telecommunications service of specified quality to all users everywhere and at an affordable price.[9] The need for universal service obligations arises from the fact that there are users, especially those in distant areas, to whom an operator would not provide the services or, in cases where services were provided, would charge a very high price for them, due to the high cost involved in providing such services (see Bobjoseph 2003: 176).

Even though many countries subscribe to the concept of universal service, the content of such a concept can be vastly different. In developed countries, universal service is understood as a telephone in every home (*ibid.*). The focus of the regulation is typically on the provision of services to socially disadvantaged groups such as the unemployed, the disabled, the elderly or the infirm. It would be unrealistic, however, to hold developing countries to the same standard, as they typically lack comprehensive infrastructure and have low teledensities. Instead, the main goal is to make the telephone accessible to people through village payphones, public call offices or telecentres.[10]

For China, universal service is a major problem due to its huge population, vast land area with varied geography, and historically low teledensity rate. The universal service obligation is prescribed in Article 44 of the Telecommunications Regulations, which states that:

> telecommunications service providers shall fulfil their statutory obligation in regard to universal telecommunications service. The MII may, through appointment or tender, determine the substantive obligations of telecommunications services providers in regard to universal telecommunications service. The subsidy policies for universal telecommunications service shall be formulated by the MII together with the Ministry of Finance and the State Planning Commission and subsequently approved by the State Council.
>
> (author's translation)[11]

[9] Communication from the European Commission, *Services of General Interest in Europe*, COM(2000)580, 26 September 1996 [1996] OJ C281/3, para. 14.

[10] Communication from the ITU (International Telecommunication Union), *General Trends in Telecommunication Reform*, 17 June 1999, S/C/W/110/Add. 4, para. 1.6.2.

[11] 'Telecommunications Regulation', promulgated by the State Council on 25 September 2000, available at www.miit.gov.cn/n11293472/n11294912/n11296257/11937080.html.

If a provider fails to fulfil the obligation, it will be subject to the penalties prescribed by Article 70, which include fines and suspension of business operations.

To implement the universal service obligation, the MII established the following goals in the Tenth Five-year Plan Program for the Information Industry: by 2005, the teledensity for the country should exceed 40 per cent, and more than 95 per cent of the administrative villages should have access to the telephone.

As mentioned earlier, CT was the monopoly telecommunications services provider before 1994. As the only operator in the market, it also took sole responsibility for providing universal services. This was mainly achieved through internal cross-subsidization, that is, subsidizing rural operations using revenues generated from urban subscribers. In addition, to help finance the initiative, the government also provides various favourable policies, such as allowing CT to charge initial installation fees for land-line services and to accelerate the amortization of fixed assets.

However, the landscape of the telecommunications services market has changed dramatically since the mid-1990s. On the one hand, there are many new players in the market following the establishment of Unicom in 1994. On the other, CT no longer enjoys monopoly status and the new entrants also compete in the more lucrative market segments such as international direct dialling services. Moreover, with the imminent accession to the WTO, the threat of foreign competition loomed large. As such, it was unfair to impose the universal service obligation solely on CT, as its profit margins had been quickly eroded by competition from new entrants. Instead, the need to protect the domestic operators against competition from foreign providers became more acute, and imposing the universal service obligation might well make the former less competitive against the latter.

As the experiences of many countries have shown, a good way to ensure universal service is through the establishment of a universal service fund (USF). Indeed, the MII has been making plans for the fund since 1998.[12] In 2002, the MII submitted the report *Feasibility Study on the Establishment of the USF* to the Ministry of Finance. Based on the experiences of other countries, the report suggested a USF

[12] 'Xinchanbu Caizhengbu Yijian Xiangzu: Dianxin Pubian Fuwu Jijin Nanchan' ['Telecom Universal Service Fund Stalled due to Disagreement between MII and MOF'], *21st Century Business Herald*, 17 March 2004, available at http://users.nber.org/~wei/data/21%20century%207-14-08.pdf.

drawing from contributions of all operators. However, neither the Ministry of Finance nor the operators found it attractive. The concern of the Ministry of Finance was that such a fund could become the hidden coffer of the MII, and be misused or misappropriated.[13] The operators, on the other hand, worried that compulsory contribution could affect their balance sheet and, therefore, the performance of their shares. Another difficult issue is how to allocate the shares different operators should contribute to the fund. Should it be based on total revenue, or total profits, or profit margins? As a result, the USF plan still remains stalled ten years on.

Instead of the USF, the Chinese government decided to impose universal service obligations on operators through administrative order. In January 2004, the MII launched the Village Connection Project on a trial basis.[14] The project divides the tasks of connecting villages without telephone access among the six operators. As the largest operators, China Mobile and CT were responsible for more than 70 per cent of the villages, with the remaining 30 per cent allocated to the other four operators. The initial trial stage of the project was for two years, and it was further expanded after the initial success. As of 2010, all of the administrative villages have been connected to the telecommunications network.[15]

2.3 Protection of public morals

China regards the regulation of information dissemination as one of the top priorities in its telecommunications regulation. This used to be an

[13] Xi Zhigang, 'Dianxin Pubian Fuwu Jijin Shangwei Jianli de Zhengjie Suozai' ['Main Obstacles to the Establishment of the Telecom Universal Service Fund'], 6 January 2012, available at www.catr.cn/zcfg/zcyj/201106/t20110607_223070.htm.

[14] See MII, 'Nongcun Tongxin Pubian Fuwu – Cuntong Gongcheng Shishi Fangan (Shixing)' ['Rural Telecom Universal Service – Village Connection Project Implementation Plan (Trial)'], 16 January 2004, available at www.cnii.com.cn/20070108/ca395867.htm. See also MII, 'Guangyu zai Bufen Shengqu Kaizhan Cuntong Gongcheng Shidian Gongzuo de Tongzhi' ['Notice on the Trial Run of the Village Connection Project in Some Provinces'], 4 January 2004.

[15] MIIT, 'Quanguo Cuntong Gongcheng 'Shiyiwu' Zongjie ji 'Shierwu' Qidong Dahui Zhaokai' ['Meeting Held to Summarize the Implementation of the National Village Connection Project during the Eleventh Five-year Plan Phase and Launch the Twelfth Five-year Plan Phase'], 26 April 2011, available at www.miit.gov.cn/n11293472/n11293832/n13918169/14098451.html.

easy task prior to the 1990s, when the MPT monopolized the telecommunications sector. With the entry of more carriers and intensified competition among them, however, monitoring the dissemination of information became more and more difficult. While these companies are all state-owned enterprises, they are reluctant to waste resources on such activities, as they do not generate profits. Therefore, the Chinese government opts to use administrative regulations.

According to Article 57 of the Telecommunications Regulations:

> any organisation or individual shall not use telecommunications networks to produce, copy, publish and transmit information having the following contents:
>
> (1) against the Cardinal Principles set forth in the Constitution;
> (2) detrimental to state security, state secrecy, state power and national unification;
> (3) detrimental to state honour and interests;
> (4) instigating ethnic hatred or discrimination and detrimental to national unity;
> (5) detrimental to state religious policy, propagating heretical or superstitious ideas;
> (6) disseminating rumours, disrupting social order and stability;
> (7) disseminating obscenity, pornography, force, brutality and terror or crime-abetting;
> (8) humiliating, slandering others, trespassing the lawful rights and interests of others;
> (9) other contents forbidden by laws and regulations. (author's translation)

As telecommunications is defined widely under Article 2 of the Telecommunications Regulations to include 'the use of wired or wireless electromagnetic systems, or photoelectric systems, to transmit, emit or receive speech, text, data, graphics or any other form of information' (author's translation), the prohibitions in Article 57 cover both telephone (including both fixed-line and mobile) and Internet networks. This is confirmed by the Regulation on the Administration of Internet Information Services, which includes in Article 15 the same list of prohibited information.[16]

Chinese regulation of the dissemination of information is not unique to the telecommunications sector. Both lists mentioned above mirror the

[16] 'Regulation on the Management of Internet Information Services', promulgated by the State Council on 20 September 2000, available at www.net.cn/static/hosting/fa_xinxi.htm.

one under Article 25 of the Regulation on the Administration of Publication.[17] Therefore, the main power does not rest with the MII, but with the other ministries, especially the Ministry of Public Security and Department of Propaganda, which is not part of the central government but a functional division of the Central Committee of the Communist Party of China.

3 Implications for trade

As part of its WTO accession package, China made the following commitments on telecommunications services:

- For basic telecommunications, China has made extensive commitments on both domestic and international fixed-line services, as well as mobile and paging services. On market access, the main limitations are in Mode 3, where foreign carriers can only operate as joint ventures with a 49 per cent (fixed-line and mobile) to 50 per cent (paging) cap on foreign equity. There were some geographical restrictions upon accession, but they were gradually phased out two to six years after accession. For national treatment, there are no restrictions for Modes 1 to 3, while Mode 4 remains unbound except for the horizontal commitments.
- For value-added telecommunications, again the main restrictions on market access are in commercial presence, where foreign equity is limited to 50 per cent, with geographical restrictions removed two years after accession. The commitments on national treatment are the same as those for basic telecommunications.
- On top of its market access and national treatment commitments, China has also agreed to subscribe to the telecommunications Reference Paper. This applies to both basic telecommunications and value-added subsectors, even though the Reference Paper is usually interpreted to apply to basic telecommunications services only.[18]

Among the three types of regulatory practices mentioned above, the first two do not have much impact on trade. This is because these two types of regulations mainly apply to basic telecommunications services,

[17] 'Regulation on the Administration of Publication', promulgated by the State Council on 25 December 2001, amended by State Council on 19 March 2011, available at www.gov.cn/zwgk/2011-03/19/content_1827821.htm.

[18] See the first paragraph of the Reference Paper. See also Gao 2008: 723–4.

which so far have been controlled by state-owned firms, with no foreign investment. By March 2012, China had approved nineteen foreign investment telecommunications companies.[19] They are all in value-added services, such as Internet and information services. Given the highly lucrative nature of the basic telecommunications market in China, it is surprising that foreign carriers have not entered the market. There are several possible explanations.

First, under Chinese regulations, foreign carriers need to have registered capital of ¥ 100 million to provide basic telecommunications services within a province, and ¥ 1 billion to provide the service from one province to another.[20] On top of this, the foreign carrier has to pay a fee of US$ 250 million for each licence for basic telecommunications services.[21]

Second, after many years of discussion, the comprehensive telecommunications law still remains as a draft. Instead, the Telecommunications Regulations have left many important issues undefined and made it difficult for foreign carriers to understand the regulatory practices. As illustrated by the several rounds of reshuffling of telecommunications firms, the basic telecommunications sector is mainly regulated through administrative actions, which may be subject to change. Foreign carriers, on the other hand, prefer to have as much transparency and predictability as possible when making investment decisions.

Third, the choice of partners is limited. Currently, there are only three domestic operators in the basic telecommunications services market. Due to their dominant position in different subsectors, they enjoy high profitability and do not have incentives to collaborate with foreign investors. In addition, due to the limitations on foreign equity, foreign investors may not have full control of the joint venture and this can be a concern for them. For example, some of the biggest carriers in the world,

19 MIIT, 'List of Approved Foreign-invested Telecom Companies', available at http://bzxx.miit.gov.cn:8080/datainfo/miit/miit10063.jsp.

20 'Regulation on the Administration of Foreign Investment in Telecom Companies', promulgated by the State Council on 11 December 2001, amended by the State Council on 10 September 2008.

21 CNII, 'AT&T Toulu zheng Youshui Zhongguo Jiangdi Hezi Dianxin Qiye Paizhaofei' ['AT&T Says It is Lobbying China to Lower License Fee for Telecom Joint Ventures'], 20 March 2006, available at www.cnii.com.cn/20050801/ca341240.htm.

such as AT&T and Cable and Wireless, have reported that they found the joint venture environment difficult.[22]

As to measures taken to protect public morals, some have argued that the blocking and filtering of websites, such as Google, could violate China's WTO commitments.[23] However, as Gao (2011) argued, at least in the case of Google, it is very difficult to establish such violation as a complainant would first need to establish whether or not China had included appropriate commitments in its schedule. Moreover, even if some violation were found, China could still invoke the 'public morals' exception under GATS Article XIV(a).

These regulatory issues illustrate the inadequacy of the existing disciplines in the GATS framework, which mainly focus on market access and national treatment obligations. While, technically, the measures mentioned above do not violate the market access or national treatment commitments, they do have significant effects on the willingness and ability of foreign suppliers to provide the service. Without proper domestic regulation, the process of trade liberalization could well be delayed or even stalled. In particular, liberalization has to be accompanied by rules that can ensure the transparency of the regulations and procedures, the necessity of the regulatory measures chosen and the reasonableness, impartiality and objectivity in administering the regulatory measures.

[22] For the story on AT&T, see 'Shanghai Xintian Zongcai Cizhi, Shoujia Hezi Dianxin Qiye Geqian' ['CEO of UNISITI Quits, First Telecom Joint Venture Facing Trouble'], *Dongfang Daily*, 17 December 2004, available at http://tech.sina.com.cn/t/2004-12-17/1909479006.shtml. For the story on Cable & Wireless, see 'Dadong Dianbao Rushi Jichu Dianxin, Guonei Yunyingshang Jinzhang' ['Cable & Wireless Enters Basic Telecom through Proxy, Domestic Operators Anxious'], *Daily Economic News*, 31 May 2005, available at http://tech.sina.com.cn/t/2005-05-31/0203621951.shtml.

[23] See Computer and Communications Industry Association, *Promoting Cross Border Data Flows: Priorities for the Business Community* (November 2011), available at www.ccianet.org/wp-content/uploads/library/promotingCrossBorderDataFlows.pdf; Google, *Enabling Trade in the Era of Information Technologies: Breaking Down Barriers to the Free Flow of Information* (15 November 2010), available at http://static.googleusercontent.com/media/www.google.com/en//googleblogs/pdfs/trade_free_flow_of_information.pdf. See also Tim Wu, 'The World Trade Law of Censorship and Internet Filtering', (2006) *Chicago Journal of International Law* 7(1): 263, 282; Brian Hindley and Hosuk Lee-Makiyama, *Protectionism Online: Internet Censorship and International Trade Law*, ECIPE Working Paper No. 12/2009, 10–12, available at www.ecipe.org/publications/protectionism-online-internet-censorship-and-international-trade-law; R. McKinnon, Testimony in the Hearing on Google and Internet Control in China.

4 Conclusion: lessons and suggestions

China's experience with telecommunications regulation provides some interesting lessons, especially for developing countries where the state controls the telecommunications sector. Due to space constraints, this chapter will focus on two areas: fostering competition and universal service.

4.1 Fostering competition: alternative approach

For many developing countries, fostering sufficient competition in the telecommunications market is a major challenge. While new competitors can be introduced relatively easily, it is much harder to make them competitive against the former monopoly operator. In this regard, China's experience provides an alternative to the traditional approach. Rather than introducing private operators and then leaving them to market forces, China chose to establish new operators under the patronage of ministries, and guide their development through heavy government intervention. For example, Unicom was sponsored by the Ministry of Electronics Industry, which was eager to break the monopoly of the MPT in the telecommunications market. While both ministries are part of the central government, the power struggle between them made competition not only possible but also intense.

Even after all telecommunications companies were reassigned to the MII, the Chinese government was able to maintain the competitive environment through several measures. First was supervision of personnel. The top executives of these companies are all former government officials and many of them are expected to return to government after serving in the telecommunications companies, typically with a promotion to a higher rank. The promotion decision is based on their performance at the company, such as whether they increased the revenue and profit of the company. This gives them a strong incentive to engage in fierce competition with their peers. Moreover, to prevent them from developing an affinity with any particular firm, the government often reshuffles their positions. This is what happened in the 2008 restructuring. Second was the distribution of key assets. For example, in the 2008 restructuring, the assets and networks of existing companies were reallocated among the three new companies, making them comparable in size and market power, thus making it easier for them to compete against each other.

Of course, such an approach also has its limitations. First, the approach worked well in China, as it has a very large domestic market that is rapidly growing. For countries where the market is small or already saturated, it would be much more difficult for new companies to make inroads into the market and thus it might be wasteful to establish such new companies. Second, there must be substantial control of the telecommunications companies by the government. If the firms are privately-owned, it will be difficult to obtain the necessary approval for the reshuffling from the shareholders. Third, while such an approach can create competitive pressures in the short term, its long-term effects are unclear. For example, even after the 2008 reshuffle, China Mobile still maintains its dominance in the mobile services market. Therefore, to ensure true competition, it might be better to introduce private players and foreign operators rather than relying on state-owned firms.

4.2 Universal service

China's experience with universal service also provides some interesting lessons. First, instead of setting up a universal service fund (USF) like most other countries, China chose to allocate responsibilities for different areas to different operators through administrative intervention. While many commentators argue that the USF is more transparent and fairer, it might not be suitable for developing countries like China for two reasons. First, before the fund can be established, the total cost for providing a universal service must be ascertained through proper cost accounting. Unfortunately, many developing countries do not have the resources to conduct such surveys. Second, the management and operation of the fund also entail significant costs. For example, in many countries, the funds are first collected from the customers by the operators and then sent to the government, which distributes the funds among telecommunications operators. The transaction costs of each step in the process and bureaucratic inefficiency all contribute to USF costs. In contrast, by dividing the responsibilities among operators through administrative intervention, the regulator in China does not need to ascertain the costs of different operators or collect and distribute the funds. This greatly simplifies the process and reduces the regulatory costs.

Second, China takes a practical approach to the means used to achieve the universal service obligation. First, the minimum standard for the obligation is defined in a flexible manner. In rural areas in China, it is not uncommon for villagers to share key resources, such as wells, televisions and telecommunications devices. Thus, instead of targeting one phone for each family, the MII required only two phones for each village, with at least one as a manned public payphone.[24] Such an arrangement serves three purposes: increasing the utility rate of the phone; minimizing the possibility of theft or damage to the equipment; and preventing the termination of the service due to not paying the monthly line rental. Second, in terms of the technological requirements, China allows both traditional land-line and new wireless services, including mobile, radio and satellite telephone services. This helps to reduce the costs for operators, as certain technology, such as land-lines, might be prohibitively expensive for certain regions due to geographical problems.

4.3 *Role of domestic regulations*

At the same time, the Chinese approach is not without shortcomings, many of which also illustrate the need to have proper rules on domestic regulation at the WTO level. First is the need to have sufficient regulation for a given sector. For some countries and sectors, the main problem seems to be too many regulations. But this is not necessarily the case for every country and sector. For China, sectors like telecommunications have been directly controlled by the state and thus there was no need to introduce regulations. However, as the former monopoly has been broken down and more competition is introduced, the regulatory framework needs to be strengthened rather than dismantled, so as to protect new entrants from dominance by large players in the sector.

Second is the transparency issue, which is related to the last point. Without proper regulations in place, the government can simply regulate the sector through administrative discretion. This is not very conducive to building up a competitive market, as the operators will not have the predictable regulatory environment they would need in making business decisions, and thus will be much more hesitant in taking risks against the dominant supplier.

Third is the need to tailor the rules on domestic regulation to specific sectors. As different sectors have different characteristics, a 'one-size-fits-all' approach for rules on domestic regulation might not be the best solution to all the problems facing a diverse range of sectors. On the

[24] See MII, 'Nongcun Tongxin Pubian Fuwu – Cuntong Gongcheng Shishi Fangan (Shixing)' ['Rural Telecom Universal Service – Village Connection Project Implementation Plan (Trial)'], 16 January 2004, available at www.cnii.com.cn/20070108/ca395867.htm.

contrary, they might sometimes backfire. Of course, it might not be realistic to have specific rules for each individual sector, or even sub-sector, as that would simply take too long to draft and even longer to reach agreement among WTO members. Instead, one feasible alternative is to group the sectors according to their shared traits. For example, those sectors which are natural monopolies and directly controlled by the government could fall into one group, while the other sectors which have long been subject to the competitive forces of the market could form another category. With the first group, the primary objective should be fostering competition, while the second group apparently would benefit from government regulations that would remedy the undesirable negative externalities resulting from over-competition. This would ensure that whatever rules on domestic regulations come into place, they could help advance rather than hinder the regulatory objective in the sector.

References

Bobjoseph, M. (2003), *The WTO Agreements on Telecommunications*, Bern: Peter Lang

Gao, H. (2008), 'Telecommunications Services, Reference Paper' in W. Rüdiger and P.-T. Stoll (eds.), *WTO: Trade in Services*, Max Planck Commentaries on World Trade Law VI, Leiden: Brill Publishers, 718–47

(2011), 'Google's China Problem: A Case Study on Trade, Technology and Human Rights under the GATS', *Asian Journal of WTO and International Health Law and Policy (AJWH)* 6: 347–85

Harwit, E. (2008), *China's Telecommunications Revolution*, Oxford: Oxford University Press

10

Information communications technology: the Mauritian experience of regulation and reform

KRISHNA OOLUN

1 Introduction

This chapter presents the evolution of the information and communications technology (ICT) sector in Mauritius and the advances made in defining clear institutional, policy, legal and regulatory frameworks which have positively influenced trade in the ICT services. The case study analyses the pre-existing conditions that facilitated competition in telecommunications thus paving the way to making ICT a key pillar for the development of the Mauritian economy through its Cyber Island Strategy. The study also reviews the prominent role played by the sector ministry and the ICT regulator in fostering widespread application of modern technologies and reporting on the ensuing economic benefits for the country.

The ICT sector definition for Mauritius conforms to the recommendations of the United Nations (ITU 2010) to ascertain a scientific measurement of sector outputs. It thus includes manufacturing and services industries whose products capture, transmit or display data and information electronically. It comprises wholesale and retail trade, communications, business services such as call centres, software development, website development and hosting, multimedia, IT consulting and disaster recovery centres. Since 2008, ICT training has been excluded from the definition.

Section 2 presents the demographic, political and economic context of Mauritius, and describes how policy actions have influenced development of the ICT sector. Section 3 details the key elements of the regulatory reforms, and shows how actions to create clear institutional, policy, legal and regulatory frameworks have contributed to the creation of a vibrant ICT sector. Section 4 examines the outcomes and outputs of the reforms especially as regards impact on the economy and trade. Finally, section 5 provides an assessment of the successful execution of the strategic reform process. It also provides some concluding comments describing lessons learned, and highlights the remaining challenges emerging from the experience of Mauritius.

2 Demographic, political and economic context

Situated off the coast of Africa in the Indian Ocean, Mauritius has few natural resources to support economic development. Since gaining independence in 1968, however, successive governments have, through specific well-targeted strategies, sought to ensure national wealth and development by diversifying the Mauritian economy from its original dependence on the production of sugar-cane to textile production, tourism, financial services and ICT, the latter being the subject of interest in this study.

The government also pursued a strategy of turning Mauritius into a service-oriented regional hub, partly by creating the conditions for a low-tax gateway to investment from other countries, thus spurring the need for reliable ICT networks and services. The service sector for 2011 accounted for 70.5 per cent of Mauritius's gross domestic product (GDP). Foreign investment has been strong, largely due to a positive investment climate led by good governance and a stable political environment, a democratic and open economy, a modern legal framework, regulatory efficiency and a reliable system of state justice. Mauritius is ranked twentieth in the World Bank (2011) report *Doing Business 2011*, which ranks countries according to their ease of doing business.

The government recognized in the late twentieth century that telecommunications and ICT hold great promise for small island economies such as Mauritius. In that regard, Mauritius started its telecommunications sector reform in 1998. This subsequently paved the way to defining ICT as an important pillar of the Mauritian economy and has now set the scene for future avenues of development in terms of business process outsourcing (BPO) and IT-enabled services (ITES), which is one of the net positive externalities of that reform process.

3 Telecommunications reform process

As an initial step, key institutional decisions were taken. The Ministry of Information and Communication Technology was established in 1997 to handle policy formulation. The operation role was left exclusively to Mauritius Telecom Ltd, created as a private company in 1992 with the government as majority shareholder. In line with the World Trade Organization (WTO) General Agreement on Trade in Services (GATS) commitments (GATS 1998), the telecommunications sector was to open up progressively to full competition and to end all state monopolies and exclusivity rights in both domestic and international services by 2004. Accordingly, the earlier Telecommunications Act of 1988, which established a legal framework catering to the needs of telecommunications services of a state-owned monopoly, was replaced by the Telecommunications Act of 1998 to pave the way to the emergence of a free and democratized telecommunications market on the island.

Subsequently, in an effort to reduce the cost of doing business and to promote the application of ICT in Mauritius, the government brought forward the liberalization of the telecommunications sector by one full year to 1 January 2003. Recognizing the need to bring regulation up to date in light of convergence and to promote affordable and adequate access to quality ICT services through functional market-driven competition and regulatory principles in a trouble-free networked information and knowledge society, Parliament passed the Information and Communication Technologies (ICT) Act in late 2001, effectively creating the Information and Communication Technologies Authority (ICTA) and the National Regulatory Authority, which has the status of a body corporate.

Indeed, Mauritius has so far demonstrated full compliance with the six-criteria framework set out in the WTO Reference Paper on telecommunications services:

- competitive safeguards;
- Interconnection;
- universal service;
- public availability of licensing criteria;
- independent regulators;
- allocation and use of scarce resources.

3.1 Policy-making

The key to the ICT sector development has been the constant formulation of national strategic plans since 1998 and the reviewing of legislation thereunder. The latest is the *National ICT Strategic Plan 2011–2014* (NICTSP 2011), which gives significant policy guidance to successfully embracing the knowledge economy and responding to the changes happening in the sector. The *NICTSP 2011–2014* builds on previous plans, makes recommendations to turn the ICT sector into the main pillar of the island's economy and proposes that Mauritius positions itself as a regional ICT hub to consolidate trade in ICT services. The plan contains eight strategic areas of intervention:

- development of a comprehensive broadband strategy for Mauritius;
- reviewing the legal and regulatory ICT environment;
- an institutional revamp;
- a human resource strategy to meet the needs of the industry;
- promotion of Mauritius as a credible ICT destination;
- promotion of the adoption of ICT services;
- reviewing the e-government strategy;
- strengthening the cybersecurity framework.

Not only has the government, through the Ministry and the ICTA, defined a clear framework, but it has also followed up with the necessary policy measures as well as legislative decisions, which have been revised regularly to adapt to the changing ICT landscape and to make the ICT market appealing and attractive to flagship companies and foreign investment. Recently, the Ministry has also defined policies to circumvent challenges facing ICT businesses as a whole, and has elaborated the *National Broadband Policy 2012–2020* (NBP 2012). This is all in line with the government's recognition of the importance of continually monitoring policies linked to sector reform programmes.

3.2 Legal and regulatory framework

The Ministry and the ICTA have pursued measures aimed at bridging the digital divide; lowering the cost of telecommunications; establishing the right eco-system to permeate the use of ICT throughout the country; making access to the Internet a citizen's basic right; and, more importantly, establishing the country as a safe and reliable ICT destination – capitalizing on the existing bilingual workforce, modern ICT infrastructure and good governance within the country to promote trade in ICT services. Policy formulation has been accompanied by the definition and adoption of clear legal and regulatory measures aimed at implementing policy and creating the environment necessary to promote investment and use of ICT. The Regulatory Institutional Framework was defined in 2001, with the creation of the ICTA through the Information and Communication Technologies Act.

A new licensing framework was introduced in July 2003, and the ICTA invited prospective operators to apply for licences. The 2003 ICT Regulations structure the licensing framework into three categories: commercial, private network and engineering. The commercial licence category defines three types of licences: infrastructure provider, networking service provider and network application provider. The infrastructure provider is authorized to set up the physical infrastructure for operators and service providers. The networking service provider, for its part, is allowed to offer networking services, including the provision of network capacity, to service providers. The network application provider offers services to the general public.

Furthermore, the Competition Act of 2007 established the Competition Commission of Mauritius (CCM) to promote competition and to deter anti-competitive practices. There is a statutory Memorandum of Understanding (MOU) which recognizes that, in certain aspects of ICT regulation, the CCM and the ICTA have overlapping powers, and in which the scope of intervention of both institutions is clearly described. There is general agreement that the ICTA acts *ex ante*, while CCM acts *ex post*; they collaborate in market definition and market power regulation.

The government has further enhanced the regulatory framework to comply with international best practices by introducing various other statutes to consolidate the sector and to position Mauritius as a safe and secure destination for ICT and BPO investments. These include:

- Computer Misuse and Cybercrime Act, in 2003;
- Electronic Transactions Act, in 2000 (amended in 2008);
- Independent Broadcasting Act, in 2000 (amended in 2009);
- Copyright Act, in 1997 (amended in 1999 and 2000);
- Postal Services Act, in 2002;
- Data Protection Act, in 2004 (amended in 2009).

3.3 *Information and Communication Technologies Authority*

The ICTA is managed and administered by the ICT Board, consisting of a chairperson and six other members appointed by virtue of their qualifications, expertise and experience in the subject matter. The executive arm of the ICTA is headed by an executive director, who has around eighty employees under administrative control. The executive director oversees the running of five departments: Engineering, Information

Technology, Finance and Administration, Marketing and Communications, and Service Regulation and Legal Affairs.

Since its creation in June 2002, the ICTA took responsibility for liberalizing the Mauritian ICT sector and bringing in new entrants for the benefit of consumers. The regulator had thus been involved primarily with the following main functions:

- tariff rebalancing;
- determination of licensing structures;
- licensing of services;
- interconnection of networks while ensuring fair access to such networks;
- dispute resolution among operators;
- determination of telecommunications numbering;
- spectrum management;
- consumer safeguard and information;
- quality of service standards for a range of services;
- universal service/access management.

After instituting the basic regulatory framework, the ICTA subsequently embarked on the process of consolidating regulation, and has created a forward-looking and flexible regulatory framework to enable it to transform and to remain a resilient organization in response to the constant technological changes and convergence. The framework is built on an adaptive regulatory model called the 'continuum of perspectives on competitive reform in the telecommunications regulatory framework' (Oolun 2007), with very strong change management attributes (see Figure 10.1).

The salient features of this model are:

- A basic continuum, starting with the centrally controlled, government-focus approach to meeting public policy objectives through the welfare state, and moving to the fully liberal, decentralized and market-oriented approach to achieving the objectives by establishing independent institutions to address specific matters such as policy-making, legislation, regulation, operation, competition, consumer issues and dispute resolution.
- Four milestones marked as nodes 1 to 4 are identified as the 'policy processes'. The first one is the WTO commitment to introduce competition in telecommunications. The second milestone is reforming the legislative framework to provide the necessary legislative instruments to legally allow the changes. The third is the onset of liberalization, and the final one is the introduction of full competition.

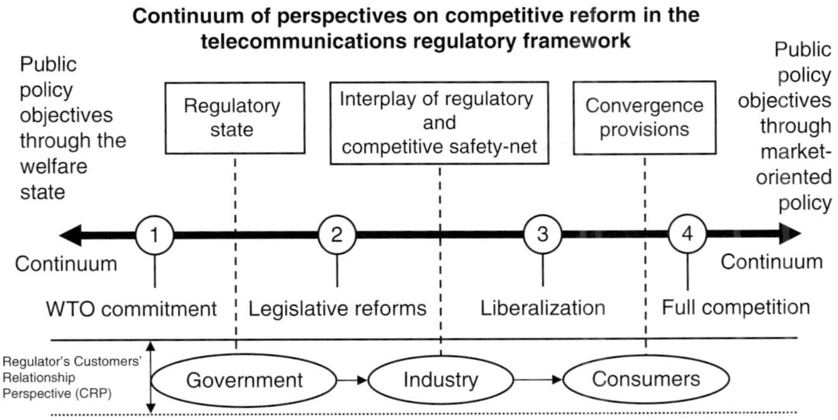

Figure 10.1 Adaptive regulatory model
Source: Oolun 2007.

- Regulatory reform is a process that takes time and is not deemed to be completed in a grand manner by a single person or one particular government in power. Thus, small increments will be brought at different points in time by different persons to add value to the reform process. The Lindblom incremental model is used to move across the continuum of perspectives (Lindblom and Woodhouse 1993).
- There are three 'regulatory measures' blocks recognized to aid the transition between the identified milestones. The 'regulatory state' is the onset of regulatory practices to achieve public policy objectives. The 'interplay of regulatory and competitive safety-net' allows liberalization to happen in practice. 'Convergence provisions' allow full competition to achieve the market-oriented policy that kindles the knowledge society.
- The movement from left to right across the continuum is an adaptive process in a value chain regarding regulatory reform in the country.

As Mauritius moved through the process, a 'change management' strategy, led by a team from the ICTA and hinged on an evolutionary model, was adopted. The combined effect of the application of the framework and the provisions of the ICT Act has allowed the ICTA to establish several milestones in the ICT sector. Some of these, directly linked to making a positive contribution to the Mauritian economy, are described.

3.3.1 Licensing

With the view to opening up the sector, the ICTA had received a profusion of applications. The 'beauty contest' model, which is open and non-discriminatory, was chosen for evaluation. Applicants were required to convince the ICTA, in a public hearing exercise, that their project proposal was viable for them to be considered for the grant of a licence. The ICTA had thus approved applications from fourteen companies to enter the domestic telecommunications market, ten for international long distance (ILD) and one each for fixed-line, payphone, Internet and mobile services. The ICTA was also one of the first National Regional Authorities at that time to licence Voice over Internet Protocol (VoIP) service providers to allow them to offer cheaper international calling rates to users. Annual licence fees ranged between US$170,400 for an ILD licence to US$34,000 for an Internet telephony licence, US$265,000 for fixed-line and mobile licences, and US$1,600 for Internet and payphone licences. The licence issued to each of the companies contains terms and conditions that are indiscriminate and transparent, and which have been finalized through extensive consultation. In fact, copies of the licences and the list of licensees are published on the ICTA website for enhanced transparency. The licensing regime adopted in 2003 has been a major driver for development of the sector and for bringing foreign direct investment from overseas telecommunications and ICT companies into Mauritius.

3.3.2 Interconnection and tariff rebalancing

The ICTA had published a model interconnection agreement in January 2003 to set out the regulatory framework for operators to enter into interconnection agreements. Wholesale prices, such as the Interconnection Usage Charges, are determined by the ICTA. The major decisions thus taken by the ICTA have affected both the wholesale and retail level offers, and have allowed:

- carrier pre-selection for international calls (2004);
- calling party pays regime and cost-based interconnection charges to mobile operators (2004);
- minimum termination charges for international calls terminated in Mauritius (2006);
- cost-based interconnection charges to fixed-line operators with zero access-deficit charges (2006 and revised in 2008).

These decisions have not only assisted interconnected operators in terms of their business case, but have also ensured competitive voice call tariffs to end-users within various markets.

3.3.3 Numbering

The efficient management and administration of this scarce national resource is essential, especially in a multi-operator environment. The ICTA took over the management of the numbering plan from the incumbent state-owned Telco and re-engineered through extensive public consultations and determined that the following actions were important for consolidating competition in the sector:

- migration towards an eight-digit numbering plan by September 2013;
- numbering allocation procedures, which has been in place since December 2004;
- carrier selection strategies introduced in December 2004;
- introduction of number portability three years after the migration to the eight-digit numbering plan.

3.3.4 Radio spectrum management and reform

Radio spectrum management has been one of the important priorities for the regulator. After establishing the Mauritian Spectrum Allocation Chart in 2003, in accordance with the ITU Radio Regulations allocation table, the ICTA deepened the spectrum reform through the following:

- the policy decision taken in February 2003 to allocate spectrum for the Global System for Mobile Communications (GSM) on the 1800MHz band. To date, the three mobile operators are operating on both the 900MHz and 1800MHz bands for the provision of mobile telephony and data services in Mauritius;
- the introduction of spectrum refarming (the reallocation of frequencies) of the 1800MHz band for the purpose of deploying DCS1800 mobile networks, as well as spectrum refarming of the 2.1GHz band and allocation of this band to IMT2000 services;
- the review of the licensing regime to include individual licensing, class licensing and licence exemption for Broadband Wireless Access (BWA) services to enable the deployment of BWA technologies such as WiMAX;
- the introduction of spectrum planning and international coordination for Digital Terrestrial Television Broadcasting, and reorganization of

the 900MHz band and opening of the Extended GSM (EGSM) band to cater for new services;

- the adoption of a decision in June 2012 on 'Additional Spectrum for the Terrestrial Component of the International Mobile Telecommunications (IMT) in the 1800MHz Band' to release additional spectrum for operators to provide high-speed mobile broadband services such as 4G-LTE, in line with the *National Broadband Policy 2012–2020* to gear Mauritius towards greater broadband uptake for innovative services.

3.3.5 Public key infrastructure

The public key infrastructure (PKI) is a cybersecurity infrastructure that verifies the identities of people, websites, computer programs and applications on the Internet, and also secures online transactions through the use of digital certificates. In the PKI, the Certification Authority (CA) issues digital certificates to end-users. A digital certificate on the Internet is similar to an identification card in the real world. The CA verifies the identity of the end-user and publishes certificates in an online repository where people can verify each other's certificate. The ICTA is the controller of the CA, which is the apex trust agency for the Mauritian PKI. It approves the methods used by the CA to verify the identity of a subscriber before granting or renewing a subscription for a certificate. Thus, in May 2012, the technical infrastructure required for the issuance of the digital certificate was installed at the premises of the ICTA and, one CA has also been licensed. Through the Mauritian PKI, the ICTA intends to create the right environment for the take-up of e-commerce and e-business in a secure and trusted environment, which is yet another bold step in promoting trade in ICT services.

3.3.6 Standards and harmonization

The ICTA has as a function under section 18(1)(b) of the ICT Act to 'provide economic and technical monitoring of the information and communication industry in accordance with recognised international standard practices, protocols and having regard to the convergence of technology'. Under section 18(1)(n) of the Act, the ICTA must 'ensure the safety and quality of every information and communication services including telecommunication service and, for that purpose, determine technical standards for telecommunication network, the connection of customer equipment to telecommunication networks'. In addition, the ICTA:

- ensures industry compliance with mandatory standards that, among others, cover electromagnetic interference and health issues;
- performs homologation of telecommunications and radio communications apparatus;
- determines technical standards where necessary to:
  - avoid disruption to telecommunications networks;
  - ensure interoperability of the standard telephone service;
  - minimize radio communications interference;
  - protect public health and safety;
- follows the work of the relevant ITU-T study groups and attends study group meetings;
- represents Mauritius in international conferences on telecommunications to ensure compliance with standards harmonization.

3.3.7 Economic regulation

Effective economic regulation in Mauritius has primarily been the regulatory interventions on the pricing of international bandwidth access. Much has been accomplished in terms of falling prices for international connectivity, especially from 2002 to 2012, when various cost-based determinations were made by the ICTA in accordance with section 31 of the ICT Act on tariffs. One of the price determinations, for example, addressed the issue of the high costs of monopoly international bandwidth on the SAT3/SAFE undersea cable, spurring the incumbent to lower prices. In that period, the price of a full-circuit E1 (2Mbps capacity) from Mauritius to Paris fell by as much as 84 per cent. A similar picture is applicable in terms of bilateral half circuits with an average reduction of up to 77 per cent on the selected routes.

Such measures leading to the effective reduction in international bandwidth prices have spurred economic opportunities, including in the ICT sector, with call centres and BPO gaining significant growth in the years following such price reductions.

3.3.8 Universal service and access

While market-based outcomes are generally left to the workings of competitive forces, the need to ensure universal access and service to telecommunications to all has also been ensured. Following the setting up of the operational framework of the USF in October 2008, the ICTA has been tasked with the management of the said fund, ranging from the collection of monies from licensed operators to the disbursement of funds to selected recipients who have been earmarked for the concretization of universal services, as decided upon by the ICTA Board. By law, disbursement is made to operators who are designated by the ICTA, following a bidding exercise open to all operators and after the designated operators enter into an agreement with the ICTA with a commitment to meeting specified targets. Four USF projects are presently run under this mode:

- provision of free Internet access in post offices;
- provision of free WIFI Internet access in municipalities and district councils;
- provision of entry level Internet access (256 kilobits per second) to households at a subsidized monthly rate of MUR 200 (30 Mauritian rupees to US$1);
- provision of satellite bandwidth to the outer islands of Mauritius to ensure that telecommunications services are offered at a uniform tariff, regardless of the physical location of the users.

4 Outcomes of the sector reform

For the purpose of this chapter, the foundation used to provide a concise outlook of the outcomes of the ICT sector reform in Mauritius from an economic and trade perspective is characterized by a quantitative analysis of key economic indicators underpinning the contribution of the ICT sector to the Mauritian economy. This is done in terms of the contribution to:

- employment;
- value added in the ICT sector and contribution to GDP;
- investment.

4.1 Employment

The number of large establishments (i.e. those employing ten or more people) operating in the ICT sector has been rising, from 88 in 2004 to 137 in 2011 (see Figure 10.2).

The number of employees in those establishments increased constantly as illustrated in Figure 10.3. Interestingly, it went up by 2.3 per cent, from 12,826 in 2010 to 13,116 in 2011, despite the smaller number of establishments in 2011 compared to 2010. This has resulted in a constant increase in the share of employment in the ICT sector over the total employment in Mauritius between 2004 and 2011 (see Figure 10.4).

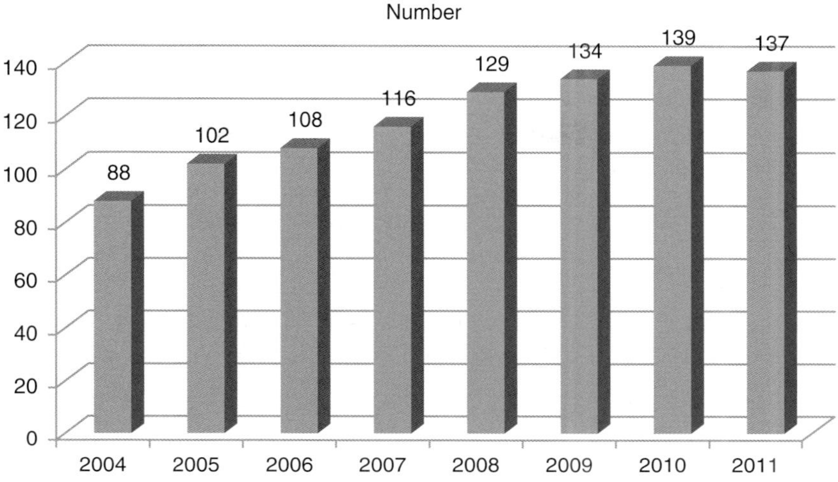

Figure 10.2 Number of large establishments in the ICT sector, 2004–2011
Source: Statistics Mauritius, 2012.

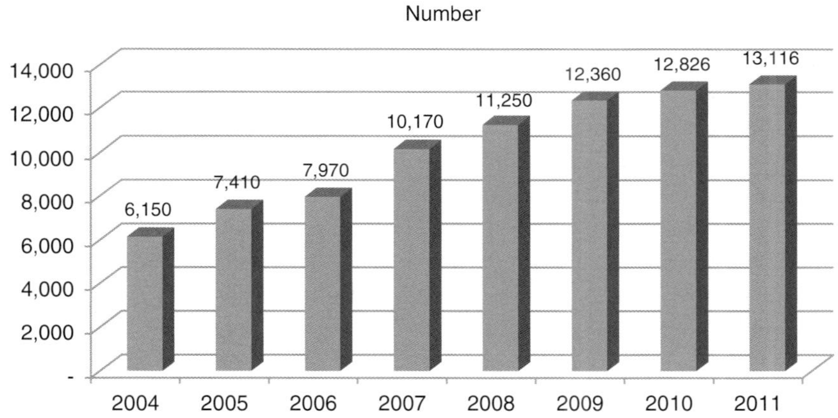

Figure 10.3 Number of employees in large establishments in the ICT sector, 2004–2011
Source: Statistics Mauritius, 2012.

4.2 Value added and contribution to GDP

With the spotlight firmly on the ICT sector as the emerging third pillar of the Mauritian economy, it is important to establish the significance of the ICT sector to GDP and, by extension, to economic growth, over the past few years. Between 2004 and 2011, the performance of the ICT

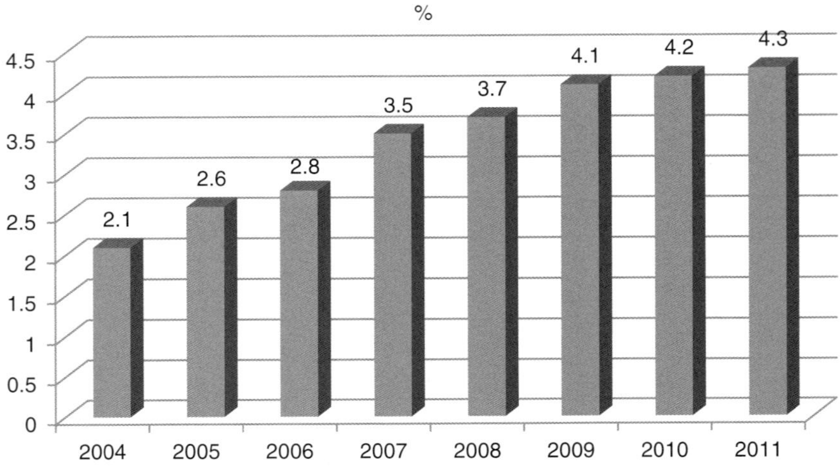

Figure 10.4 Share of employment (in %) in the ICT sector over total employment, 2004–2011
Source: Statistics Mauritius, 2012.

sector in terms of the value added of the sector has been on a constant rise as clearly revealed in Figure 10.5. By the end of 2011, the contribution of the ICT sector towards value added stood at MUR 19,004 million compared to MUR 7,565 million in 2004. In other words, the contribution of the ICT sector has more than doubled over a seven-year period.

In 1997, the contribution of the ICT sector to the total GDP stood at a mere 3.7 per cent, stagnating at around 4.0 per cent from 1999 to 2002. In 2004, this figure was 4.9 per cent, suggesting that the ICT sector was not yet as important compared to the others, and was still in the process of establishing itself as a 'support' pillar of the Mauritian economy. This is in contrast with the agricultural sector, which contributed 6.3 per cent to GDP in 2004. From 2004 onwards, the contribution of the ICT sector has almost constantly risen, reaching 6.7 per cent in 2011 (see Figure 10.6).

In terms of real growth (after removing price effects), the ICT sector fared particularly well over the period 2002 to 2011, averaging an annual growth rate of 14.7 per cent. Figure 10.7 shows that the annual growth in the value added generated by the ICT sector was well beyond Mauritius's overall annual GDP growth for the corresponding years. Moreover, the period from 2002 to 2003 delivered the most substantial growth rate for the sector – an increase by 32.6 per cent, which is directly correlated

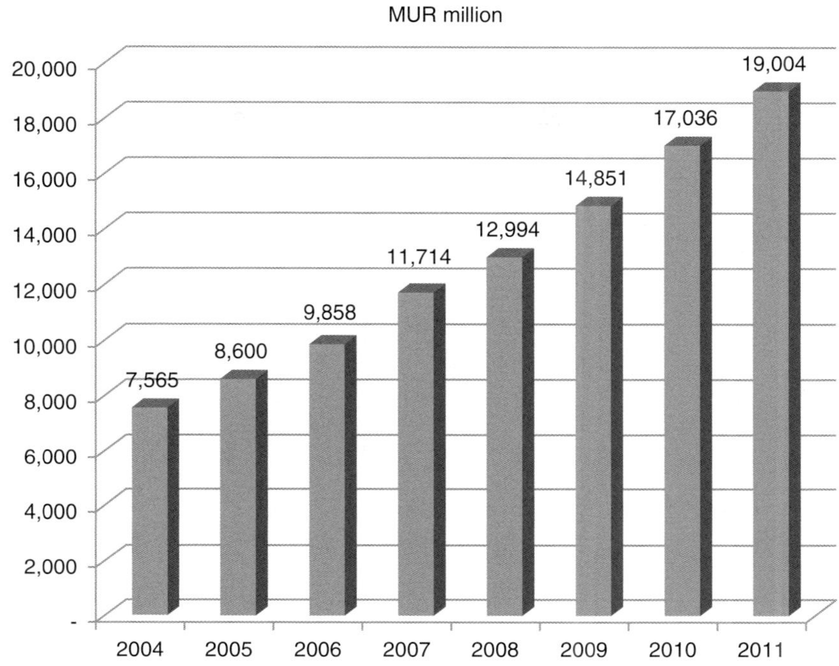

Figure 10.5 Value added for the ICT sector, 2004–2011 (MUR million)
Source: Statistics Mauritius, 2012.

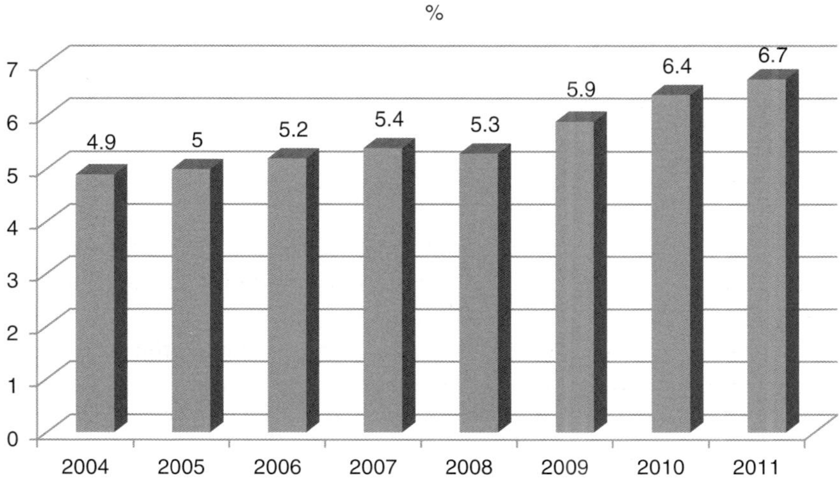

Figure 10.6 Contribution (in %) of the ICT sector to GDP, 2004–2011
Source: Statistics Mauritius, 2012.

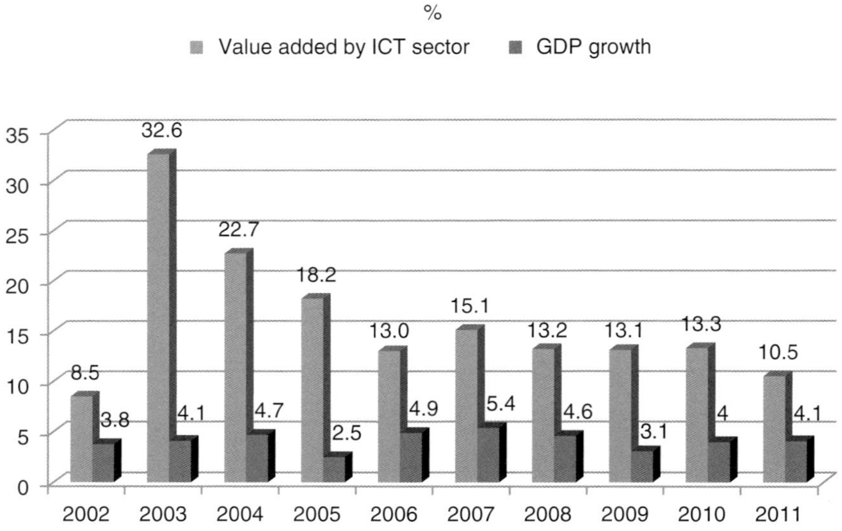

Figure 10.7 Growth of value added (in %) by the ICT sector relative to the overall annual GDP growth, 2002–2011
Source: Statistics Mauritius, 2012.

to the implementation of the policy for the ICT sector liberalization and issue of new licences. By 2005, the growth rate had returned to normal after the positive one-off shock of the liberalization. It stabilized after 2006 with a reduced trend, yet it remained in double digits throughout the period to 2011. Keeping a growth rate of over 10 per cent in the coming years will be a challenge.

4.3 External trade in services

While it is noted in Figure 10.8 that the total imports for ICT goods and services have ranged between MUR 9,005 million in 2007 and MUR 8,899 million in 2011, imports of ICT services have been increasing (see Figure 10.9), which correlates with the objective of essentially making Mauritius an ICT services hub.

Similarly, exports of ICT goods and services between 2007 and 2011 varied between MUR 4,764 million and MUR 4,988 million (see Figure 10.10), while the export of ICT services has constantly risen during the same period (see Figure 10.11).

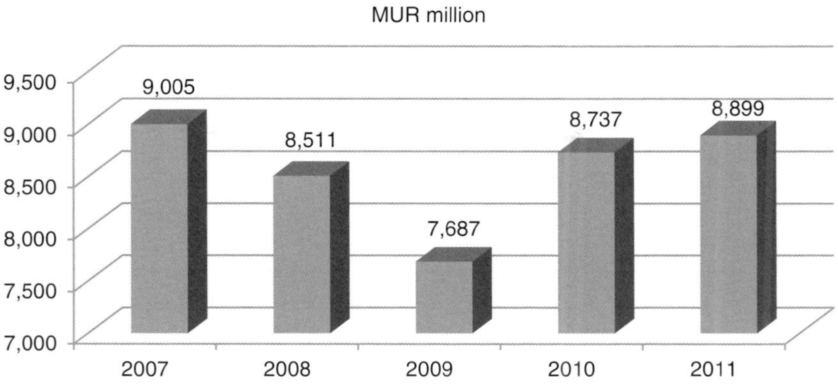

Figure 10.8 Total imports of ICT goods and services, 2007–2011 (MUR million)
Source: Statistics Mauritius, 2012.

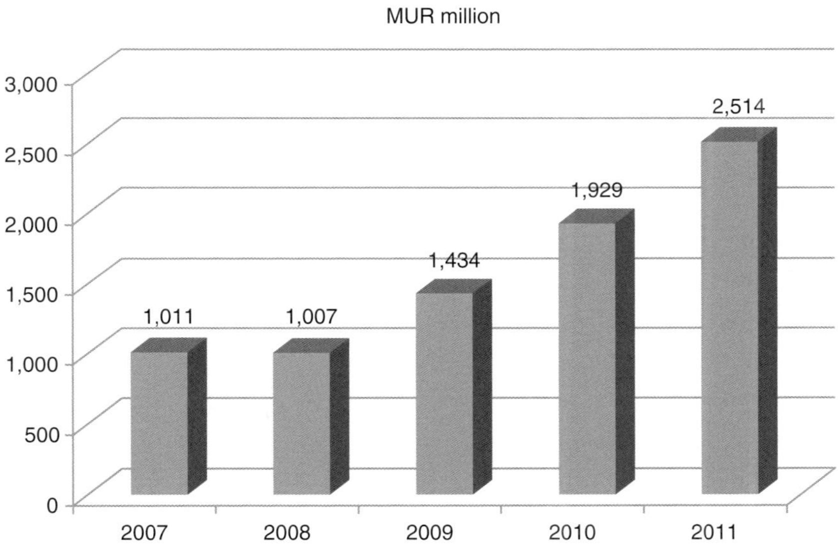

Figure 10.9 Total imports of ICT services, 2007–2011 (MUR million)
Source: Statistics Mauritius, 2012.

4.4 Contribution to investment

According to Statistics Mauritius, it is reported that out of the total amount of public sector investment expenditure in 2002, MUR 1,300 million were directed towards telecommunications-based projects, while MUR 300 million went towards cybercity related projects. It is further

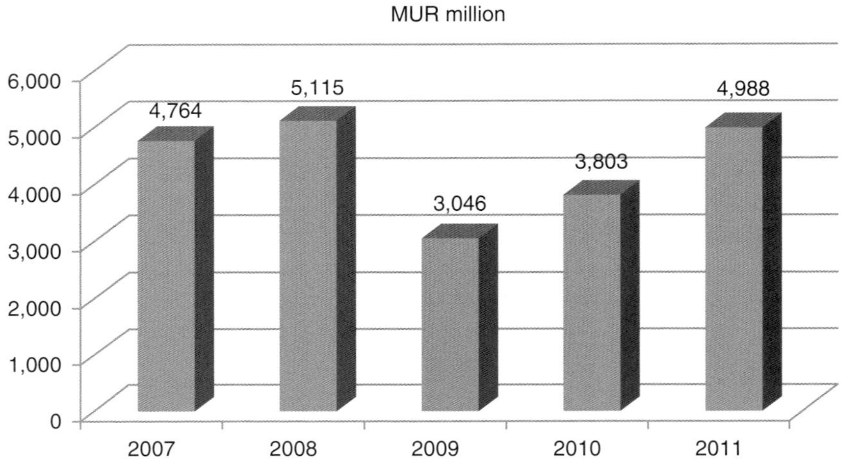

Figure 10.10 Total exports of ICT goods and services, 2007–2011 (MUR million)
Source: Statistics Mauritius, 2012.

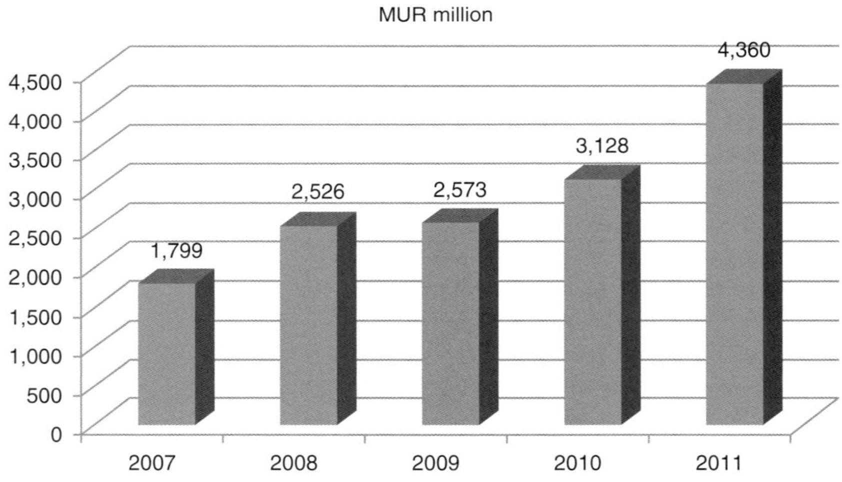

Figure 10.11 Total exports of ICT services, 2007–2011 (MUR million)
Source: Statistics Mauritius, 2012.

reported that MUR 1,665 million had been invested in cybercity projects by 2003. To complement this picture, the overall investment from the private sector pertaining mainly to ITES and BPO suggests that a total of MUR 1.45 billion had been invested up to September 2005. Added to that amount are the investments made by private operators who were granted licences to operate in the sector. A total of some MUR 2 billion was recorded from one mobile operator, Mahanagar Telephone Mauritius Limited (MTML), and the eight international operators between 2003 and 2008. Between 2008 and 2012, the actual amount of realized investment amounted to MUR 726 million for the BPO companies. It has been further established that the distribution of the level of investment by activity was as follows:

- call centres (36 per cent);
- BPO (31 per cent);
- software development (18 per cent);
- disaster recovery (12 per cent);
- online education (2 per cent);
- multimedia (1 per cent).

5 Conclusion: lessons learned and challenges

The policies and regulatory frameworks defined following the WTO commitments provided a strategic vision and had established national goals regarding ICT, while elaborating specific policies to achieve those goals. In the Mauritian case, the WTO commitments had come before the regulatory frameworks were created. This did not pose any particular problem because the regulatory reform was adopted as an ongoing process with constant adaptation as per the model developed in Figure 10.1; on the other hand, it was easier to embark on the reform process. The success of this reform is also built on years of clear and comprehensive policy and regulatory development, as well as on the effective implementation of various initiatives to support the growth of the ICT sector and build an investor-friendly environment.

The liberalization of telecommunications in January 2003, which was the starting point, allowed many operators to start activities in 2004, thus leading to a plethora of competitive services and pricing available for consumers. The reform also created the ICT sector as a new vector for economic growth and trade for Mauritius. The ICT sector has now effectively become the third pillar of the Mauritian economy, with a GDP contribution of 6.7 per cent, a turnover of US$1 billion and directly employing some 15,000 people, with flow-on benefits for many more. ICT services and BPO have become a key factor for the economic growth of Mauritius.

Within this context, a number of good practices can be identified:

- compliance with the six-criteria framework of the WTO Reference Paper on telecommunications services;
- defining an adaptive regulatory reform model and implementing same with the right management structure;
- creating a conducive environment to attract new investments and players;
- consolidating the regulatory and legislative frameworks as an ongoing reform process;
- developing efficient management strategies in the use of scarce resources;
- defining institutional framework and responsibilities to achieve objectives;
- setting transparent and fair licensing processes through stakeholders' involvement.

On the other hand, there are a few challenges that were faced and which had to be confronted in working towards the reform process:

- *Promoting investment in infrastructure*: as a small island development state (SIDS), it is normally difficult for an operator to find the right economies of scale in order to obtain sufficient returns on the infrastructure investment. Being aware of this, the ICTA adopted a technology- and service-neutral approach to allow mobile infrastructures to be used for fixed service as well. This allowed entry of two players who invested in infrastructure development.
- *Costing model*: choosing the right costing model for the incumbent's network cost determination has been very challenging. Whilst many regulatory literatures mention the benefits of the long-run, incremental costs, it was not possible to apply it in the case of Mauritius, given that all simulations gave results which would have increased the costs of the network elements.
- *Benchmarking*: most of the alternative licensed operators in Mauritius come from Europe and, as such, have a European regulatory culture. During consultation exercises on regulatory matters, they tend to force their views on subjects like unbundling, numbering and spectrum administration because they want the framework to be benchmarked against that in Europe, where they already operate. The ICTA has always had to counter those challenges by coming up with solutions and regulatory measures tailored to the local context, with the result that many of its decisions are challenged at the level of the ICT Appeal Tribunal.

Promoting and supporting the ICT sector towards becoming and staying an important pillar of the Mauritian economy in the future entails addressing the following challenges:

- producing and attracting the required number of qualified ICT workers;
- identifying new market opportunities;
- re-engineering the ITES and BPO industry while leveraging on the strengths and mix of capabilities spanning both local and global domain knowledge.

In this regard, policy actions are already under way to address those challenges:

- an ICT Centre of Excellence has been set up to create a talent pool that matches industry needs;
- an annual ICT and BPO international meeting has been held in Mauritius since 2011 to create a platform for buyers, sellers and other stakeholders, which will allow sector consolidation through concerted strategies.

Drawing from its experience, the ICTA confirms that there is no one-size-fits-all solution to successfully regulating an ICT market, especially in a SIDS. But by being aware of the processes to be adopted, such as holding public consultations to identify risks, setting milestones which operators need to achieve, and allowing operators to develop a culture of marketing new services within a predefined level of quality standards as set by the regulator to drive demand, regulators can be more confident of achieving the developmental goals of ICT within their respective countries. Furthermore, regulators should take advantage of the various existing regulatory tools and ensure that they develop an ICT regulatory toolkit, similar to the one established jointly by the ITU and the World Bank, and make sure that they use the right tools available depending on the situation.

More generally, the experience of the ICTA shows that licensing and qualification requirements in ICT, especially with regard to standards and the effective use of scarce resources such as the spectrum, do not really constitute barriers to trade. It should be viewed as an enabler and a means of allowing operators to evolve in a trouble-free environment. In that regard, the layered approach to licensing is favoured, with a clear set of domestic regulations governing the physical up to the network layers, while the application layer, which is of more interest from the trade perspective, should be left completely deregulated to allow for innovations and enhanced trade. This should be the approach to be adopted by WTO members in trying to negotiate a set of horizontal domestic regulation disciplines for telecommunications and ICT.

References

GATS (1998), *General Agreement on Trade and Services at the World Trade Organization: Reference Paper in Telecommunications 1998*, Geneva: World Trade Organization

ITU (2010), *Core ICT Indicators 2010*, Geneva: International Telecommunication Union

Lindblom, C.E. and Woodhouse, E.J. (1993), *The Policy-Making Process*, 3rd edn, Englewood Cliffs: Prentice-Hall

NBP (2012), *The National Broadband Policy 2012–2020*, Government of Mauritius

NICTSP (2011), *The National ICT Strategic Plan 2011–2014*, Government of Mauritius

Oolun, M.K. (2007), *Sustained Regulatory Reforms in Telecommunications: Strategy for Emergence of a Knowledge Economy*, MBA dissertation, Leicester: Leicester University

World Bank (2011), *Doing Business 2011: Making a Difference for Entrepreneurs*, Washington, DC: World Bank

11

Regulation of postal services in a changing market environment: lessons from Australia and elsewhere

SIVA SOMASUNDRAM AND IAIN SANDFORD

1 Introduction

The digital revolution and the exponential growth of the Internet have led to radical changes in the ways in which countries conduct their commerce, communicate and store information. Coupled with the digital revolution, the last several decades have also seen a fundamental rethink of the role of the state in the economy. Broadly, the past reliance in many countries on state control and regulation has given way to a greater emphasis on competition, trade openness and market forces.

This chapter, drawing from the experience in Australia and elsewhere, considers some of the key issues raised by these trends in relation to the regulation of postal services.[1] It seeks to address the broad concern of how best to regulate by focusing on: the policy and regulatory tensions in ensuring universal service obligations (USOs) in postal markets that are, or are being, liberalized; typical competition issues arising in liberalized postal markets; as well as the appropriate role and form of regulation in such markets. In addition, the chapter examines the impact of international trade rules (in particular the WTO General Agreement on Trade in Services, GATS) on the postal sector and some of the problems arising out of the nexus that exists between trade rules and postal regulations (both domestic and international).

The chapter proceeds as follows. In section 2, as background, we provide a short overview of postal services and the contemporary environment in which postal service providers operate. In section 3, we outline the nature of postal USOs and explore, in particular, some of the key policy challenges postal regulators face in designing USOs in liberalized postal markets. In section 4, we explore competition issues that arise in

[1] Postal services are broadly defined as services involving the collection, sorting, transport and delivery of postal items.

relation to postal services where competition is permitted in relation to some services. We then, in section 5, consider the relevance of GATS to defining the reserved services in postal markets and the relationship with certain Universal Postal Union (UPU) rules.[2] Finally, in section 6, we conclude by distilling a series of regulatory lessons that may be extracted from our survey of the pertinent issues.

2 Background: a rapidly evolving environment

The global postal sector has evolved dramatically over the last twenty years. Traditionally, the sector consisted of two significant players: state-owned monopolies providing basic mail services; and privately owned courier companies supplying parcels and expedited mail services. However, since the early 1990s, two forces have radically transformed the sector.

First, the introduction of market-oriented postal reforms in many countries has resulted in public postal monopolies being corporatized (i.e. legally transformed into state-owned enterprises run as independent, commercial enterprises) or privatized (partially or completely).[3] These reforms have also seen the introduction of competition in various segments of the postal supply chain. Emulating the regulatory approach to other network industries such as telecommunications and electricity, the reforms have sought to ensure competitive supply in those segments not characterized by economies of scale and sunk costs (see e.g. Cohen and Chu 1997).

Second, within this new business environment, another coincidental phenomenon, the information technology (IT) revolution and the advent of new electronic communication technologies, has globalized the sector and created new challenges and opportunities. Greater broadband penetration, the rise of the Internet, and the prevalence of social media networks have contributed to a substitution from physical mail to electronic communications (IPC/BCG 2012: 25). That substitution is

[2] The UPU is the specialized agency of the United Nations responsible for the legal and other frameworks governing the international exchange of mail and aims 'to secure the organization and improvement of the postal services' (Constitution of the UPU Art. I.2).

[3] For example, see Crew *et al.* 2009: 2–8. Examples of postal operators that have been corporatized include the Australian Postal Corporation (Australia Post), New Zealand Post Ltd (NZ Post) and Royal Mail Holdings plc. (Royal Mail). Privatized postal operators include Deutsche Post AG (Deutsche Post), Singapore Post Ltd and Pos Malaysia Berhad.

ongoing and is reflected in the consequential decline in physical mail volumes since the late 1990s. It has brought into question the very relevance of physical mail (IPC/BCG 2012: 17). On the flipside, however, postal service providers are well positioned to capitalize on the ongoing e-commerce revolution to tap growing and new market segments, such as parcels and digital mail (IPC/BCG 2012: 39–47).

These developments all make for some very exciting and challenging times for postal regulators in designing the appropriate regulatory frameworks needed to ensure USOs, fair competition and the maximization of public welfare.

3 USOs in liberalized postal markets

The UPU requires its member countries to ensure that all 'users/customers enjoy the right to a universal postal service involving the permanent provision of quality basic postal services at all points in their territory, at affordable prices' and that their designated postal operators deliver on these services (Universal Postal Convention (UPC) Article 3.1). However, member countries are free to define the scope and the level of these services taking into account population needs and national conditions (UPC Article 3.2).

In most countries, USOs have typically involved the imposition of a range of requirements on the designated postal operator relating to:

- type of services covered;
- quality of covered services in terms of accessibility, speed and frequency;
- their pricing, through measures such as uniform postage rates and price caps, aimed at securing affordability.[4]

Such USOs have been justified on various grounds, including their provision of an important public good (in essence a functioning communications network) and their positive redistributive and social impacts.[5]

Traditionally, the *quid pro quo* for undertaking these sometimes onerous USOs has been for governments to grant their designated postal operators exclusive monopoly rights over all or particular segments of domestic postal markets. The reserved services were seen as necessary to enable designated postal operators to fund and meet their USOs.

[4] Ambrosini *et al.* (2006: 23–38).
[5] For a discussion of these justifications, see e.g. Cremer *et al.* 2008.

Without the reserved services, the viability of USOs were considered at risk, as designated postal operators were potentially unable to support the losses made on the high cost services from the reduced profits brought about by competition on the low cost services (see e.g. Crew and Kleindorfer 1998: 104).

The emergence of increasingly dynamic and liberalized postal markets has necessarily brought USOs and reserved services under greater policy scrutiny. The debate has tended to focus on two main issues: the need for USOs to better address market realities and national specificities; and how to reduce the reserved services to promote competition without risking USOs.

On the first issue, the pressing concern for postal regulators is not to abandon USOs altogether but to ensure that they are reflective of market needs and that the social and economic trade-offs surrounding them are optimized. The USOs of many countries, however, appear to mandate unnecessary service levels and artificially low tariffs and are often not flexible enough to adapt to market realities.

For example, in countries where businesses and government typically generate the bulk of the mail, USOs that set tariffs below costs for such mail indirectly subsidize these large mailers (Walsh 2002: 265–76). Whether such tariffs are the outcome of a proper cost-benefit analysis reflective of market developments or that of political imperatives is often not clear. Further, the changing commercial context sometimes requires revision of the balance struck in the relevant policy settings, as has occurred in Australia and the United Kingdom.

Australia's incumbent operator, Australia Post, is legislatively required to provide a bulk mail service that allows private firms to tend pre-sort bulk mail letters at specified facilities for delivery within Australia (as part of the reserved services) at a discount to the basic postage rate (BPR). The discount is meant, in part, to reflect the estimated avoided upstream transport cost prior to lodgement.[6] The applicable tariff was, until recently, scrutinized by the Australian Competition and Consumer Commission (ACCC, Australia's competition authority), and tariff increases had to be 'approved' by it.[7] Recognizing the competitive

[6] Australian Postal Corporation Act 1989 (Cth), s. 32A.

[7] See e.g. *Price Notification Declaration for Australia Post's Reserved Letter Services*, 23 February 2011; and ACCC 2011. The Australian legislative framework provides for an ACCC 'no objection' regime with the Australian government ultimately responsible for approving any tariff increases.

impacts of electronic substitution and the need for Australia Post to meet changing consumer demands without being hampered by lengthy tariff surveillance processes, the Australian government disbanded the regime in October 2011.[8]

The United Kingdom has gone a step further in removing bulk mail altogether from its USOs. Again, that decision was in response to increasing competition in the UK bulk mail market, the fact that users did not appear to require uniform pricing, and the need to give the incumbent operator, Royal Mail, greater commercial freedom.

Another common fixation of the USOs in many countries is with the speed and frequency of mail delivery. In particular, next-day services (or the next two days for some larger countries) and the availability of six-day collection and delivery services are often a focus. Market evidence in many countries, however, suggests that consumers are not too concerned with these parameters as opposed to the affordability and predictability of the USO services.[9] But the political context in many countries requires retention of such service attributes despite the significant operational costs they impose on USO-constrained operators and the clear benefits from achieving a service level mix driven more by market demands.[10]

A matter that is currently under-explored is the scope for USOs to capitalize on the digital revolution and, in particular, the opportunities created by the ability to replace physical delivery by 'e-delivery'.[11] The laws of many countries either do not or are not explicit enough to countenance the USOs being satisfied by e-delivery or other electronic

8 See *Price Notification Declaration (Australia Post Letter Services) (No. 2) 2011*, 18 October 2011 and the accompanying *Explanatory Statement*.

9 See e.g. TNS BMRB 2012: 9–10, reporting that UK consumers may tolerate significant reductions in USO service levels, including the loss of a Saturday service and certain first class mail attributes; BCG 2011, reporting on a survey of the mail usage and value placed on current service parameters by consumers in fourteen countries.

10 The ongoing US debate on eliminating Saturday service is an example. The United States Postal Service (USPS) estimates that it would lose up to US$18 billion a year by 2015 if the US government failed to grant it the freedom, among other things, to eliminate the Saturday service and reduce the service standards for US first class mail. Matters are currently before the US Congress, while the US Postal Regulatory Commission has challenged USPS estimates of the net financial benefit to be gained from eliminating the Saturday service (see e.g. USPRC 2011; USPS 2011).

11 An example of e-delivery would be to have inbound physical mail opened, scanned and electronically transmitted to recipients. This creates the opportunity to have the corresponding physical mail actually delivered at a time and location convenient to both the postal operator and the recipient.

means. This may be a wasted opportunity given the efficiency gains and cost reductions that are potentially to be had. The recent experience of Itella Corporation, Finland's USO-constrained operator, is a case in point.[12]

On the second issue, namely, promoting competition without risking USOs, the challenge for postal regulators is not whether the reserved services can coexist with competition in the postal sector but rather in defining the parameters of that relationship given the overlay of USOs.

In an increasingly competitive environment, postal operators must be able to operate efficiently and in a manner that is commercially flexible. However, commercial logic can often be incongruous with the public policy objectives embodied in USOs, and there is always a risk that a monopolist supplier will rent-seek or leverage its position to act unfairly against competitors. This three-way balancing act between commercial flexibility, USOs and the need for fair competition defines the challenge for postal regulators on this front (see e.g. Crew *et al.* 2009: 3).

Defining the scope of USOs is central to getting this balance right. A clear definition helps determine the true cost of their provision. Whichever methodology is used,[13] the cost of USOs is normally defined as the loss that they generate. A proper understanding of that loss enables governments to assess – as the next steps in developing the appropriate regulatory framework – the financial consequences for any USO-constrained operator, how to fund the loss, as well as its overall welfare consequences. In turn, a fair and correct analysis of USO costs enables governments to continually scrutinize the *quid pro quo* rationale for any reserved services and to delimit their scope.

The regulatory outcomes of this type of analysis have necessarily been country-specific and varied. Indeed, it has, in some countries, resulted in the total abolition of reserved services backed with mechanisms (such as licences or formal agreements with government)

[12] Itella's limited experiment with e-delivery in 2010 was considered inconsistent, among other things, with Finland's USO laws, as these laws did not recognize e-delivery. For relevant commentary, see e.g. Okholm and Winiarczyk 2012: 2.

[13] There is extensive literature on the methods to measure the cost of USOs. Some studies have relied on the Net Avoided Cost method, used first in the telecommunications industry. Under this method, USO costs are measured by the impact of USOs on the financial performance of the USO-constrained operator. Other studies have favoured methods that take into account a broader range of factors (see e.g. Gallet and Tolledano 1997; Crew and Kleindorfer 1998: 103).

guaranteeing the provision of the required USOs.[14] A number of alternative ways to fund USOs have been adopted in these countries including:

- direct public compensation to cover the net costs of the USO-constrained operator;
- cost sharing arrangements such as special universal service funds, to which all operators contribute and from which the net costs are reimbursed;
- zero compensation on the basis that USOs mandate a nation-wide delivery network with consequent efficiencies of scale representing a significant commercial advantage.[15]

In other countries, the analysis has caused the retention of the reserved services but with postal regulators focused on fine-tuning their scope with a view to promoting competition. In Australia, for example, in an effort to introduce greater competition in the letter market, the scope of the reserved services was reduced in 1994 by, among other things, the lowering of the weight and tariff thresholds defining the reserved services.[16]

4 Competition issues

Problems relating to anti-competitive conduct can, in general, be placed into one of two categories: unilateral anti-competitive conduct by a single organization with market power; and concerted anti-competitive conduct by more than one organization.[17] In this section, we consider, in line with this broad framework, competition problems that potentially arise with respect to postal services, together with some brief illustrations of how such issues have arisen in practice. The specific regulatory context of the postal sector presents a regulatory challenge involving

[14] Sixteen EU Member States were required to abolish their reserved services by 2010 and the remaining eleven by 31 December 2012 (EC Directive 2008: L52/20). Other examples include Colombia, Peru, New Zealand, Nicaragua and Singapore. For relevant country experience commentary, see e.g. Zhang 2008: 386.

[15] See e.g. EC Directive 2008: L52/6; Zhang 2008: 385–6.

[16] Under the Australian Postal Corporation Amendment Act 1994 (Cth), the weight threshold defining a reserved mail item was reduced from 500g to 250g. In addition, the tariff threshold for competition was reduced from ten to four times the BPR. Exemptions also apply for document exchanges, carriage of letters within organizations, and carriage of newspapers, magazines, books and catalogues: Australian Postal Corporation Act 1989 (Cth), ss. 29–30.

[17] A third category, control of anti-competitive mergers, is not relevant to this chapter.

balancing the risk of market failure (and hence the need for pro-competitive regulatory action) on the one hand, with the risk of regulatory failure, on the other.

4.1 Unilateral competition issues in the postal sector

The benefits of competitive forces for public welfare do not require actual competition in a market. These forces discipline an incumbent's pricing and quality so long as there is *potential* for a competitor to offer competing goods or services. Thus, even in markets where there are few incumbent suppliers, competitive forces still operate, provided barriers to entry are low.

Frequently, however, barriers to market entry are not low, raising policy issues about how best to pursue public welfare. At least four kinds of barriers to entry exist in markets relevant to the postal sector.

First, it is sometimes the case that government measures create legal barriers to entry on the basis that restricting competition is judged beneficial. For instance, the existence of a legal monopoly for letter mail in many countries, including Australia, creates a legal barrier to entry to this specific market. As described above, this is the result of a policy choice made, given the public benefits associated with USOs and the need to fund them. A key issue is where to delimit the USO-constrained operator's monopoly in order to permit competition in other areas.

Second, even in cases where formal legal or regulatory barriers are not imposed, barriers to market entry may exist in the form of a dominant firm's ability to affect entry conditions to keep out potential competition. Sometimes such 'market power' will simply arise from the firm's control of high levels of goodwill, a unique product or a particularly efficient means of production or distribution. In such cases, there is usually little public benefit to intervention by regulators, since the firm has reached its position of dominance in a market by out-competing its rivals through the value it offers to consumers. Thus, few competition problems are associated with the brand equity that incumbent postal service suppliers have built in these ways. Regulatory interventions that erode the value of the incumbent's position carry a risk of also eroding those consumer benefits that explain its dominance in the first place.

Third, in other cases, a firm's power to affect conditions of entry to one market can arise through its dominance of another market. Thus, a supplier that can command high profits in one market (e.g. the market for delivery of letter mail in which the supplier has a statutory monopoly) could use that position to deter rivals from competing in a different market (e.g. the market for parcels). This could happen, for instance, if the dominant supplier in one market uses high returns from the first market to offer significant discounts in a different market, for example, through reduced prices or bundling of various services. In this way, the firm with market power could effectively cross-subsidize its offering in the different market, reducing the ability of competitors to make profitable sales. This is usually viewed as an abuse of market power and is frequently subject to prohibitive regulation.

There are frequent allegations of this kind of misuse of market power in postal markets.[18] In the European Union, for instance, such questions have been addressed in the context of claims that Deutsche Post used revenues from its profitable letter mail monopoly to finance a strategy involving below-cost sales in the competitive business parcel market (Commission Decision 2001); and that La Poste Belge improperly conditioned the availability of discounts for letter mail (services exclusively reserved to La Poste Belge) to non-use of a different company's service in the market for overnight business to business (B2B) services, a market in which La Poste Belge and the other company competed (Commission Decision 2002).

In Australia, the ACCC has been given regulatory functions in relation to postal services, including in relation to tariff regulation[19] and accounting transparency to assure competitors of Australia Post that it is not unfairly competing by cross-subsidizing its competitive services with revenues from the reserved services.[20]

[18] For example, see *UPS Europe SA v. Commission (Deutsche Post AG intervening)* (T-175/99) [2002] All ER (D) 307 (Mar), in which a European affiliate of United Parcel Service claimed that Deutsche Post was able to acquire a controlling interest in its competitor in the express market, DHL, only as a result of the revenue it obtained on its reserved services.

[19] Price notification provisions appear in Part VIIA of the Australian Competition and Consumer Act 2010 (Cth) (ACCA). They apply to 'notified services' and 'declared persons'. Following a 2011 review, surveillance of Australia Post pricing relates only to certain reserved letter services: see *Price Notification Declaration (Australia Post Letter Services) (No. 2) 2011*. Under this Declaration and the ACCA, Australia Post must notify the ACCC, among other things, if it plans to increase the price of a relevant service.

[20] Part 4A of the Australian Postal Corporation Act 1989 (Cth) permits the ACCC to require Australia Post to keep records about its reserved services to enable the ACCC to scrutinize

A fourth situation can arise where a firm has market power through its control of the infrastructure necessary for the delivery of a service, since the need to access or recreate such infrastructure is itself a barrier to the entry of competitors. Thus, by denying access, or through pricing such access highly, the infrastructure owner can influence the ability of competitors to compete in markets that rely on such infrastructure.

This is an issue for postal markets, since the cost of establishing collection and distribution networks can be high, particularly if the service to be offered contemplates a wide geographical reach. Given this dynamic, the fact that USO-constrained operators, by definition, have universal coverage, can provide a significant advantage when funding is either by a monopoly or public investment. Since the infrastructure necessary for the collection and distribution of reserved mail (e.g. retail shops, collection and delivery boxes, and logistics) can also be used for other services (e.g. pick-up and delivery of parcel mail, express delivery services, and retail services through shops), control of universal postal infrastructure can create an advantageous competitive position in markets beyond the reserved mail market in which the USOs apply.

Examples are common where postal operators have been identified as enjoying an infrastructure advantage that could be misused in order to affect the conditions of entry to markets in which competition is allowed. For this reason, several countries have imposed 'access' obligations on USO-constrained operators.

In the liberalized New Zealand market, for instance, NZ Post is required to grant access to its network (effectively allowing competitors to insert mail into the network at different points) on non-discriminatory terms through a deed of understanding between the corporation and its state shareholder.[21] In October 2009, there were agreements in place to provide access to twenty-seven competitors, including access pricing agreements with six.[22]

In Australia, the ACCC is given power to inquire into disputes about the terms and conditions, including price of access, relating to bulk mail interconnection arrangements.[23] This approach is significant given

whether or not Australia Post is cross-subsidizing from its reserved services to the services it provides in competition with others.

21 The deed (and a 2010 amendment relating to certain service standards) is available at www.nzpost.co.nz/about-us/postal-legislation/deed-of-understanding.

22 See NZ Post, 'Securing a Universal Postal Service', available at www.nzpost.co.nz/about-us/media-centre/media-archive/2009/securing-a-universal-postal-service.

23 Part 3 of the Australian Postal Corporation Regulations 1996.

the increasing importance of bulk mail in the small-letter category of the reserved service. To date, no dispute has been considered under these provisions, but the ACCC has circulated a draft guide for managing such disputes (ACCC 2012).

Imposing access obligations, however, carries risks. By imposing obligations to allow competitors to use a firm's facilities on certain terms, access regulation attenuates property rights and reduces incentives for investment, innovation and potentially the ability of the firm to compete effectively.

The experience of Royal Mail under the UK network access regime is an example. Access to Royal Mail's downstream postal network was, in the past, subject to licensing conditions, including price controls. Access tariffs were set with reference to the head-room margin between the corresponding retail and access services. The regime was considered highly intrusive and required approvals through a slow and detailed regulatory process for many operational and commercial decisions. Royal Mail's ability to adjust its access prices in the face of competition was severely constrained (Eccles 2009: 349–53). The new UK regulatory framework[24] moves from a licence-based system to one involving a light touch of general authorizations with regulatory conditions. Price regulation is limited to the tariffs of the universal services and network access only and, in the case of the latter, a 'margin squeeze' price control has been adopted to ensure Royal Mail does not misuse its position to squeeze the margins of those accessing its network (see e.g. Oates 2012: 2–3).

4.2 Concerted anti-competitive action

Concerted action within the postal market is not typically considered in analyses of the postal sector. Indeed, at a domestic level, the normal approach in countries with competition laws is for those operations of postal operators not enjoying legal exclusivity to be subject to cross-sectoral competition laws proscribing horizontal arrangements among competitors.

A particular issue arises, however, because of the fundamentally national basis of USO-constrained operators. Each operator delivers universal services within a national jurisdiction. In order to offer services that

[24] Postal Services Act 2011 (UK).

allow mail to cross into other jurisdictions for ultimate delivery, different operators convene to determine the terms for such deliveries, particularly the terms of remuneration for international mail. This potentially gives rise to a competition issue where postal operators are actual or potential competitors in postal markets.

This issue has been explored through proceedings to exempt an arrangement between European USO-constrained operators from the EU rules proscribing horizontal price fixing. The European Commission has considered an agreement for the Remuneration for Exchange of International Mail Service (REIMS Agreement) on several occasions. The agreement provides for greater cost-orientation of terminal dues (compared to those negotiated under the UPU framework) and contemplates penalties for failure to meet certain service quality requirements. In its decisions, the European Commission found that the REIMS Agreement provides for price fixing and has an appreciable effect on trade in the European Economic Area (see e.g. Commission Decision 2004: recitals 94–103). However, the European Commission exempted the REIMS Agreement from the applicable competition rules, on grounds including that there were benefits to consumers (in the form of increased quality of service and reduced cross-subsidization) (Commission Decision 2004: recitals 105–58). It nonetheless imposed conditions, including in relation to non-discriminatory access to REIMS terminal dues on the same conditions for non-party postal operators (Commission Decision 2004: recitals 169–72 and Article 3).

Regulatory action in relation to concerted anti-competitive conduct by operators has not been a feature of the Australian postal sector.

5 Trade rules and postal regulation

Trade agreements, be it those of the WTO or preferential trade agreements (PTAs), have reinforced and driven market-oriented postal reform in many countries. This has occurred primarily in two ways. First, trade agreements have provided a means of locking in already enacted (and future) domestic postal reform measures and market access guarantees through international treaty obligations. Second, for many countries, trade agreements have proven to be the necessary stimulus for undertaking domestic postal reform on the back of wider market opening and other regulatory commitments agreed to in trade negotiations (see e.g. Zhang 2008: 394–9).

Given these impacts, and the increasing prevalence of trade agreements, postal regulators must necessarily be better informed of trade rules and mindful of their implications for postal regulations (domestic and international).

The nexus between trade rules and postal regulations is multifaceted, complex and still evolving. To illustrate the complexities, we focus on some of the core rules of GATS[25] and their relevance to and impact on two key issues of the postal sector: defining and securing the reserved services; and the terminal dues system of the UPU.

5.1 Reach of trade rules and the reserved services

GATS, in principle, covers any 'service in any sector except services supplied in the exercise of governmental *authority*' (GATS Article I:3(b), authors' emphasis). This means that no service sector is *a priori* excluded from the application of GATS. The only services excluded are those supplied in the exercise of governmental authority.

GATS defines such excluded services narrowly as 'any service which is supplied neither *on a commercial basis*, nor in *competition with one or more service suppliers*' (GATS Article I:3(c), authors' emphasis). Accordingly, the fact that a service is supplied by a governmental body is irrelevant. Rather, both the stipulated criteria must be satisfied for the exclusion to apply to any service, including a service supplied by a governmental body.

Unfortunately, GATS does not elaborate on these criteria. Each criterion can be the subject of varying interpretations and that indeterminacy is problematic for delimiting the scope of GATS (see e.g. Luff 2002: 76–7; Alverno 2003: 8; Leroux 2006).

It has, for example, been suggested that the supply of a service on a commercial basis presupposes supply aimed at a profit or a financial return (Leroux 2006: 354) or strategic behaviour (see e.g. Adlung 2006: 463). Similarly, there is uncertainty as to what the concept of 'in competition with one or more service suppliers' actually means. It is not clear whether the criterion is limited to actual competition between existing suppliers or includes potential competition from likely entrants or the accessibility of alternative supplies by consumer movements or electronic

25 As many of the core rules of PTAs relating to cross-border trade in services either replicate or build on those of GATS, the issues canvassed in this section are also potentially relevant to the relationship between PTA rules and postal regulations.

means (Adlung 2006: 465). These rules on the scope of GATS have two main implications for postal regulators in defining and securing the reserved services.

First, the governmental status of an operator supplying the reserved services in a WTO member is insufficient on its own to exclude such services from the ambit of the non-discriminatory and market access rules of GATS. These services may be subject to GATS if they can in some way be characterized as being supplied on a commercial basis and in competition with one or more service suppliers. Accordingly, in seeking to ring-fence the reserved services from trade rules, the regulatory focus must be on carefully defining the scope and characteristics of the reserved services in light of these rules rather than on the status of the operator supplying these services.

Second, the definitional uncertainties relating to the exclusion for 'services supplied in the exercise of governmental authority' means that even the best defined reserved services may not be secure from the reach of GATS. One could, for example, argue that the reserved services are typically supplied for a fee in most countries and are, therefore, commercial in nature and subject to GATS.[26] Ironically, the legal form and governing frameworks of the postal operator supplying the reserved services could also have a bearing. If the operator is a private company or a statutory corporation with a mandate to return dividends to its owners and/or operate 'in a manner consistent with sound commercial practice',[27] one could again argue that the operator is in effect supplying the reserved services on a 'commercial basis'. In short, postal regulators should avoid relying on definitional exclusions that are highly qualified and open to conflicting interpretations to carve out their reserved services from the reach of trade disciplines. Explicit carve-outs which specifically reference the concerned reserved services, such as those sought by Australia in some of its PTAs,[28] appear to provide for a more secure legal foothold for ring-fencing the reserved services.

[26] *Communication from New Zealand: Negotiating Proposal for Postal/Courier Services*, WTO doc. S/CSS/W/115, 6 November 2001, para. 17.

[27] Australian Postal Corporation Act 1989 (Cth), s. 26.

[28] See e.g. Cross-Border Trade in Services Chapter, Australia-United States Free Trade Agreement, Art. 10.12 (express delivery services). The notes to the Chapter clarify that, in the case of Australia, Art. 10.12 does not cover the reserved services of Australia Post.

5.2 Trade rules and the terminal dues system

The terminal dues system of UPU provides for the payments that a postal administration makes to another[29] for the costs of handling and delivering cross-border letter post items[30] in the country of destination.

From the perspective of trade rules, the terminal dues system is potentially problematic because of: the differentiated treatment it accords to postal services to, from and as between developing and developed countries, respectively (the terminal dues to be paid by developing countries tend to be lower, on average, than those paid by developed countries);[31] and the right it grants the designated postal operators of UPU member countries to enter into separate bilateral or multilateral agreements applying other payment mechanisms (UPC Article 27.9) or to invoke reservations against the system (UPC Articles 28.11 and 29.8). There is a dearth of comprehensive data on the number and scope of such agreements. However, anecdotal evidence suggests that these agreements are becoming increasingly prevalent and that they cover not only differentiated terminal dues but also matters such as parcels remuneration, service quality, border clearance processes and operational matters.

These facets of the terminal dues system raise the question as to whether it is consistent with the most favoured nation (MFN) principle of GATS which requires each WTO member, in respect of 'any *measure* covered' by GATS, to extend to the 'services *and* service suppliers' of any other WTO member 'treatment *no less favourable* than that it accords to *like services and service suppliers of any other country*' (GATS Article II:1, authors' emphasis).[32]

[29] The applicable rules are set out in the UPC and the Letter Post Regulations of the UPU. The UPC, the Letter Post Regulations and the Parcel Post Regulations provide for the common rules applicable to the services for the international exchange of letter post and parcel post items between UPU member countries.

[30] There is a separate remuneration system for services related to parcel post items: UPC Art. 33 and Parcel Post Regulations, Art. RC 192.

[31] UPC Arts. 28, 29.3, 29.4 and 29.5. Generally, under these rules, the terminal dues payable by developed countries for mail flows between themselves and to developing countries are higher than those payable by developing countries for mail flows between themselves and to developed countries. This is because the terminal dues payable by developed countries are ostensibly based on the actual costs of processing, delivery and transport with a relevant domestic tariff in the destination country used as a proxy for such costs. In contrast, the terminal dues payable by developing countries are based on worldwide average costs.

[32] The GATS MFN obligation is a general obligation in that it applies to all measures and service sectors covered by GATS and not just those in respect of which a WTO member has undertaken specific commitments.

The debate on this issue has tended to focus on two key matters: whether the terminal dues system is a 'measure' covered by GATS; and whether the services and service suppliers involved in delivering letter post items from developing countries are 'like' those from developed countries and whether they are treated less favourably under the terminal dues system.

Although a discussion of MFN is, strictly speaking, beyond the scope of a chapter on domestic regulation, these issues deserve two brief observations. First, in relation to the issue whether terminal dues constitute a measure amenable to analysis under GATS, we note that GATS covers 'any measure' (GATS Article XXVIII(a)) taken by a WTO member (which would include postal administrations that are government authorities) or by 'non-governmental bodies' (GATS Article I.3(a)) in the exercise of delegated governmental powers (which would include corporatized or privatized designated operators with delegated governmental powers); and that the terminal dues system applies as an obligation between, and is implemented by, UPU member governments (as opposed to their postal operators). The concept of 'measure' has been interpreted broadly in WTO disputes to date,[33] suggesting the scheme of terminal dues implemented may well be amenable to analysis as a 'measure', subject to GATS MFN requirements.

Second, on the issues of 'likeness' and less favourable treatment, we note that the treatment accorded clearly differs among categories of countries. Since the GATS MFN obligation is concerned with the non-discriminatory treatment of *both* services and service suppliers, and the services, at least, appear to be materially similar in virtually all respects, alarm bells should ring for postal regulators.

Concerns relating to the consistency of UPU rules with those of GATS are not limited to the terminal dues system. Other UPU rules on matters such as re-mail and extraterritorial offices of exchange have also come under particular scrutiny for their possible breaches of the MFN obligation (see e.g. TMC Asser Instituut 2004: 86–99; WTI 2007: 57–68).

[33] See e.g. Yanovich and Voon 2005: 117. The authors highlight that challenges have been directed to a 'diverse range of measures that may be adopted by other Members. These measures have included traditional legal documents, such as laws or regulations, as well as measures taking the form of practice or guidelines, and other actions' (*ibid.* 163).

6 Conclusion: regulatory lessons

This chapter highlights the radical changes in communications technology, significant evolution in the way in which the state takes part in the economy in many countries, and the resulting enhanced competitive environment in the postal sector. This dynamic situation, in which states continue to require USOs in a competitive environment, presents significant regulatory challenges. These in turn give rise to issues both of domestic regulatory policy and services trade policy.

While clearly not a comprehensive analysis, our review suggests at least six key lessons as take-home points for postal regulators.

First, clearly defining USOs is an absolute must. In a competitive environment, the scope of USOs and correlated calculations of their true cost are important determinants of how USOs are to be provided for and administered. That in turn has consequences for the structure of the postal market and, in particular, the contestability of its segments by domestic and foreign entrants. It also has consequences for what the appropriate focus of domestic competition laws as it relates to the postal sector should be.

Second, it would be prudent not to treat USOs as static parameters and to provide for regulatory processes that are quick to effect any USO changes needed to address market developments. The political obligation to provide USOs should not prevent them from adapting to new market realities, consumer needs and the digital revolution. Indeed, ever-evolving USOs might be a prerequisite to ensuring their sustainability and to avoiding any welfare losses arising out of the economic inefficiencies of badly designed static USOs.

Third, where reserved services are thought necessary, as part of delimiting their scope, it is appropriate to ensure that the USO-constrained operator does not abuse its monopoly position to gain an advantage in the competitive segments of the market. But in doing so, governments must be mindful not to exert a heavy hand on the operator. There is a clear risk of regulatory failure in relation to access regulation, which may not only be burdensome on USO-constrained operators, but, at worst, can kill incentives to invest in network infrastructure.

Fourth, there appear to be some under-explored issues relating to international price coordination in the postal sector and, in particular, the terminal dues system of the UPU. Such issues may merit further consideration and analysis.

Fifth, with the increasing prevalence of trade agreements providing for disciplines such as those of GATS, national postal regulations cannot be formulated in a domestic cocoon. The impacts of these trade disciplines on domestic postal policies and laws must be carefully assessed, and measures taken to effectively ring-fence USOs and, if applicable, the reserved services.

Sixth, trade agreements also have a significant bearing on the international rules governing the exchange of international mail. The potential rule conflicts that have been identified suggest the need for urgent and concerted policy action at an international level to mitigate the risk of such conflicts damaging the commercial and political relations of postal administrations.

References

ACCC (2011), *Australian Postal Corporation Price Notification for Bulk Letter Services: Decision*, Canberra: Australian Competition and Consumer Commission

Guide to Inquiries into Disputes about Bulk Interconnection Services, Draft August 2012, Canberra: Australian Competition and Consumer Commission

Adlung, R. (2006), 'Public Services and the GATS', *Journal of International Economic Law* 9(2): 455–85

Alverno, A. (2003), *A Brief Analysis of GATS and Its Implications for Measures Related to Extraterritorial Offices of Exchange*, Universal Postal Union

Ambrosini, X., Boldron, F. and Roy, B. (2006), 'Universal Service Obligations in the Postal Sector: Economic Learnings from Cross-Country Comparisons' in M.A. Crew and P.R. Kleindorfer (eds.), *Progress Toward Liberalization of the Postal and Delivery Sector*, New York: Springer

BCG (2011), *The Postman Always Brings Twice: Receiver-Driven Transformation of the Mail Business Model*, Boston Consulting Group

Cohen, R.H. and Chu, E.H. (1997), 'A Measure of Scale Economies for Postal Systems' in M.A. Crew and P.R. Kleindorfer (eds.), *Managing Change in the Postal Delivery Industries*, Boston: Kluwer Academic Publishers

Commission Decision (2001), Commission Decision of 20 March 2001 relating to a proceeding under Article 82 of the EC Treaty (Comp/35.141 – Deutsche Post AG) [2001] OJ L125/27, 5 May 2001

Commission Decision (2002), Commission Decision of 5 December 2001 relating to a proceeding under Article 82 of the EC Treaty (Comp/ 37.859 – De La Poste) [2002] OJ L61/32, 2 March 2002

Commission Decision (2004), Commission Decision of 23 October 2003 relating to a proceeding pursuant to Article 81 of the EC Treaty and Article 53 of the EEA Agreement, Case COMP/C/38.170 – REIMS II renotification [2004] OJ L56/76, 24 February 2004

Cremer, H., De Donder, P., Boldron, F., Joram, D. and Roy, B. (2008), 'Social Costs and Benefits of the Universal Service Obligation in the Postal Market' in M.A. Crew and P.R. Kleindorfer (eds.), *Competition and Regulation in the Postal and Delivery Sector*, Northampton: Edward Elgar

Crew, M.A. and Kleindorfer, P.R. (1998), 'Efficient Entry, Monopoly, and the Universal Service Obligations in Postal Services', *Journal of Regulatory Economics* 14(2): 103–25

Crew, M.A., Kleindorfer, P.R. and Campbell Jr, J.I. (eds.) (2009), *Handbook of Worldwide Postal Reform*, Northampton: Edward Elgar

EC Directive (2008), Directive 2008/6/EC of the European Parliament and the Council of the European Union [2008] OJ L52/3, 20 February 2008

Eccles, R. (2009), 'United Kingdom Postal Services Regulation' in M.A. Crew, P.R. Kleindorfer and J.I. Campbell Jr (eds.), *Handbook of Worldwide Postal Reform*, Northampton: Edward Elgar

Gallet, C. and Tolledano, J. (1997), 'The Cost of the Universal Postal Service in a Competitive Environment: Lessons from Telecommunications' in M.A. Crew and P.R. Kleindorfer (eds.), *Managing Change in the Postal Delivery Industries*, Boston: Kluwer Academic Publishers

IPC/BCG (2012), *Focus on the Future: Building a New Compelling Position for Posts*, International Postal Corporation/Boston Consulting Group

Leroux, E.H. (2006), 'What is a "Service Supplied in the Exercise of Governmental Authority" under Article I:3(b) and (c) of the General Agreement on Trade in Services?', *Journal of World Trade* 40(3) 345–85

Luff, D. (2002), 'International Regulation of Postal Services: UPU vs. WTO Rules' in D. Geradin (ed.), *The Liberalization of Postal Services in the European Union*, 34 European Monographs, Hague/London/New York: Kluwer Law International

Oates, S. (2012), 'Reforming UK Postal Regulation', *Regulatory Flash* 72 (October)

Okholm, H.B. and Winiarczyk, M. (2012), 'Regulatory Barriers to Innovation as Opportunities for Regulatory Management', *Regulatory Flash* 71(5)

TMC Asser Instituut (2004), *The Study of the Relationship Between the Constitution, Rules and Practice of the Universal Postal Union, the WTO Rules (in Particular the GATS), and the European Community Law: Final Report*, The Hague: TMC Asser Instituut

TNS BMRB (2012), *Universal Service Obligation: Postal User Needs 2012 – Quantitative Research Report*, London: TNS BMRB

USPRC (2011), *Advisory Opinion in Postal Regulatory Commission Docket No. N2010-1*, US Postal Regulatory Commission

USPS (2011), *Report of the United States Postal Service Regarding Advisory Opinion in Postal Regulatory Commission Docket No. N2010-1*, United States Postal Service

Walsh, T. (2002), 'Exit, Voice and Postal Performance in Developing Countries' in M.A. Crew and P.R. Kleindorfer (eds.), *Postal and Delivery Services: Delivering on Competition*, Boston: Kluwer Academic

WTI (2007), *Implications of the GATS and the Doha-Round Negotiations on the Provision of Postal Services*, Berne/Geneva: World Trade Institute

Yanovich, A. and Voon, T. (2005), 'What is the Measure at Issue?' in A. Mitchell (ed.), *Challenges and Prospects for the WTO*, London: Cameron May

Zhang, R. (2008), 'The Liberalization of Postal and Courier Services' in J.A. Marchetti and M. Roy (eds.), *Opening Markets for Trade in Services*, Cambridge: Cambridge University Press

12

Mobile money services provision in East Africa: the Ugandan experience

JOAN APECU, IRENE KAGGWA SEWANKAMBO AND YUSUF ATIKU ABDALLA

1 Introduction

Services constitute a major and growing sector of Uganda's economy in terms of its contribution to gross domestic product (GDP), exports and employment. Uganda's Service Sector Export Strategy of 2005 has also identified information and communications technology (ICT) services as a priority. Similar to the situation in many least developed countries (LDCs), Uganda's services sector is liberal. Specific General Agreement on Trade in Services (GATS) commitments have been undertaken on both telecommunications and financial services.[1] There is a high degree of foreign ownership in Uganda's financial and telecommunications sectors. In the financial sector, eighteen of the twenty-five commercial banks licensed in 2012 were foreign owned. In the telecommunications subsector, six of the seven operational mobile operators are foreign owned. In addition, this subsector has expanded rapidly in recent years with respect to domestic and foreign-owned mobile service providers (MSPs), the number of mobile subscriptions, and the emergence of non-voice services such as mobile money. Once established in Uganda, foreign and local suppliers of financial or telecommunications services are subject to the same regulatory and supervisory procedures.

East Africa has witnessed a rapid rise in money transfer services through leveraging mobile phone applications and use. First launched in Uganda in 2009, the concept and use of mobile money services provided by licensed telecommunications operators has been steadily growing, with the number of mobile money subscribers reaching about

[1] Although Uganda has signed the telecommunications Reference Paper (WTO Negotiating Group on Basic Telecommunications, Reference Paper, 24 April 1996), it is not a signatory of the WTO Information Technology Agreement.

11 million as of March 2013.[2] While the scope of the service is currently mainly confined to person to person sending and receiving money and the purchase of goods and services, with new technologies and increased competition, more products to further enhance mobile money use are being developed.[3]

While continued innovation and growth of mobile money services are contributing to the process of financial inclusion, its rapid development and evolution places regulators of financial and ICT services in relatively uncharted territory. Mobile financial services have blurred the clarity in distinction between financial and telecommunications services and with it created regulatory challenges. Although presently, regulators are accustomed to regulating areas under their separate mandates, the rapid expansion of mobile money services in Uganda will require a degree of regulatory convergence and development of a comprehensive regulatory framework. This could address the main financial risks of mobile money transactions and the protection of consumers, and ensure fair competition, while at the same time not curtailing innovation, growth and further liberalization of the sector. To ensure that conditions of competition and growth in this sector remain sustainable, and considering the cross-border nature of some transactions, regulatory convergence or harmonization and development of guidelines or best practices would also be required at the regional level within the East African Community (EAC), and multilaterally. This would require collaborative work with, among others, the International Monetary Fund (IMF), the International Telecommunication Union (ITU), the United Nations Conference on Trade and Development (UNCTAD), the World Bank and the World Trade Organization (WTO).

This chapter describes the operation of mobile money services in Uganda and highlights the regulatory challenges confronting the Uganda Communications Commission (UCC) and the Bank of Uganda in effectively regulating this fast growing and evolving market. Section 2 examines developments in the provision of mobile money services in East Africa and implications for the conduct of trade. Although some references are made to monetary and macroeconomic implications of the growth of mobile money financial services mainly in the context of financial sector regulatory considerations, the wider context is not

[2] Source: Bank of Uganda, data bank, www.bou.or.ug/bou/home.html.

[3] Other products could include payments, transfers, storage, savings, credit, insurance, pension, investment and international remittances.

addressed here. Section 3 assesses policy and regulatory frameworks for mobile money services in East Africa. Section 4 provides a case study on the development, evolution and regulation of mobile money financial services in Uganda. Insights about the way forward for the sector are provided in the concluding section.

2 Emergence and growth of mobile money services in Africa

2.1 Overview of mobile money services in Africa

Recent and evolving technological developments have spurred the rapid growth of mobile money services across Africa (Sey 2008). These, coupled with the need for banking services for the unbanked and the absence of electronic payment systems and facilities such as credit cards, have revolutionized the conduct of the provision of financial services that involve money transmissions and transfers, as well as the practice of payments for goods and services. It has also provided a platform for the extension of banking services, particularly among the lower income populations in remote areas that do not have adequate access to banking services. Mobile money services have therefore offered new frontiers and possibilities for financial services in a more inclusive manner in Africa.

With the rapid growth of mobile telephony in Africa, mobile money has emerged as one of the most used applications. Data from the GSM Association indicates that around 150 live mobile money services were deployed and implemented for the unbanked in seventy-two countries by the end of 2012.[4] Africa leads this trend with sixty systems applications.[5] This is a result of the heavy investment made by MSPs to develop networks and platforms that can penetrate deeper into remote areas in Africa, unlike conventional banking. These remote locations have historically been marginalized and unbanked. As the profitability of these investments began to wane over time, partly because of increased entry of new network service providers and as average revenues from traditional services declined, MSPs and their partners began to look at alternatives to diversify service provision, given that a reasonably large

[4] Penicard Claire, *GSMA: Mobile Money for the Unbanked: State of the Industry: Results from the 2012 Global Mobile Money Adoption Survey.*

[5] *Ibid.*

proportion of the population already owned and were familiar with the use of mobile telephony services.[6]

2.2 *Mobile money services in East Africa*

The experience of East Africa with mobile money services is an illustrative example of explosion of this service. Several individuals and small businesses have embraced mobile money services as a medium for transmissions of money.[7] East Africa is at the forefront of the mobile money revolution, where a number of schemes implemented so far have gained significant momentum. Table 12.1 provides an overview of the mobile money industry in East Africa.

Note: Data as of August 2011. Adapted from UNCTAD field interviews and EAC Communication regulators' websites.

Several providers are involved in the mobile money services ecosystem. Their roles differ. They derive a diversity of benefits from the mobile systems applications infrastructure (Jenkins 2008). They include (UNCTAD 2012):

- A mobile network operator that provides the infrastructure and a subscriber base that is active in using its communications services. The operator is obliged to ensure compliance with regulations and policy governing the provision and use of telecommunications services. In the EAC, many MSPs have a recognizable brand that has been cultivated through extensive marketing and service provision. MSPs potentially benefit from mobile money by increasing and maintaining the number of customers, reducing the cost of airtime distribution and by generating new revenue.
- A bank or any approved or licensed financial institution that facilitates the exchange of money between different parties. It may also provide

[6] The most common model in the mobile money market is where mobile operators partner with a bank or financial institution to provide services. However, an alternative model involving the provision of mobile financial services is being offered by banks and financial institutions over the networks of various mobile operators. The concern is whether the latter model is 'disadvantaged' by mobile operators already having mobile money products of their own.

[7] A distinction should be made between small businesses that work directly within the mobile services sector (small mobile sector enterprises) and those that are users (or potential users) of mobile money services in the day-to-day management of their businesses (small non-mobile sector enterprises). An example of the former is a mobile money agent, while a market vendor or individual is an example of the latter.

Table 12.1 *Mobile money industry in East Africa*

Category	*Burundi*	*Kenya*	*Rwanda*	*Tanzania*	*Uganda*
Population (in '000)	8,413	46,669	10,660	45,012	33,532
% of population 20 years and older	62.3	57.7	57.5	55.5	51.7
Mobile network operators	5	4	2	7	4
Mobile subscriptions (in millions)	1.076	24.96	3.73	21.20	16.02
Mobile money platforms	1	4	2	4	4
Mobile money subscriptions (in '000)	29.0	17,800	309.13	9,200	2,100
Ratio of mobile money subscriptions to mobile subscriptions	0.027	0.713	0.083	0.434	0.131

Sources: DESA 2011, the EAC and UNCTAD 2012.

oversight and compliance with financial regulations, while allowing correspondent banks to leverage their respective mobile money platforms in order to reach populations in traditionally unbanked areas at much lower banking services costs.

- Regulatory institutions across different sectors. In the EAC, the principal regulators are typically central banks (for regulating the financial sector) and telecommunications regulatory authorities (for regulating the communications sector).
- A network of agents[8] that are allowed to conduct cash-in (conversion of cash into mobile money) and cash-out (issuance of money on demand) transactions to effect convertibility between mobile money and cash. MSPs in the region have developed extensive agent networks to sell airtime and other products while those of the banks are rather limited to urban or highly populated areas. The agents earn commission on various types of transactions carried out by mobile money users. Over the years, MSPs have divested extensively into building networks of agents for purposes of selling telephone airtime and related products.

[8] These include individuals, automatic teller machines (ATMs) and communication services branches.

- Traders, merchants and retailers who accept payments for goods and services through mobile money payments, which in a sense assists in heightening and growing the demand for mobile money services.
- Business establishments that use mobile financial services to deliver their services.[9]
- Manufacturers and mobile platform providers which include an array of stakeholders such as mobile phone makers, network equipment vendors and providers of systems applications that together benefit from the increased sale of end-user mobile system devices, such as mobile phones, network equipment, fees and subscriptions.
- Mobile money service users, to whom benefits accrue on account of cheaper and more efficient means of money and payment transmissions to other economic and business agents and networks.

By the end of 2011, the number of mobile money platforms operated by different operators in East Africa had grown to fifteen. Table 12.2 shows the distribution of mobile network operators, their platforms and partnerships with banking and financial institutions.

Kenya, Tanzania and Uganda had each acquired four platforms by the end of 2011. Kenya accounted for 60.5 per cent of mobile money subscriptions in the region. At the national level, Kenya had 71.3 per cent of mobile money subscriptions. The M-PESA platform stood out prominently, with 15 million active customers engaged in transferring money using mobile phones up to an estimated 56 billion Kenya shillings (US$650 million) every month. It linked with over 37,000 mobile money agents and twenty-five banks. The service was also accessible through 700 ATMs (Business Daily 2012).

2.2.1 Structure and types of mobile money services

Mobile money services in East Africa have undergone substantial transformation to be able to deliver a range of mobile phone based services. These services have tended to impose a variety of charges on customers.[10] The services can be classified into three broad clusters:

- *mobile payment*: where a user of the service exchanges money for goods and services with another user;

[9] These include microfinance institutions and insurance companies.

[10] For a more comprehensive narrative and illustration of the types and characteristics of these mobile money services, see UNCTAD 2012.

Table 12.2 *Mobile network operators, platforms and bank partners*

Country	*Operator*	*Mobile money platform*	*Bank partners*
Burundi	Econet Wireless	EcoKash	National Post Office
	Africell	None	–
	Smart Mobile	None	–
	Onatel	None	–
	U-com	None	–
Kenya	Safaricom	M-PESA	Commercial Bank of Africa Standard Chartered Kenya CfC Stanbic Bank Equity Bank Kenya
	Airtel Kenya	Airtel Money	Citigroup
	Econet Wireless	Yu Cash	–
	Orange Kenya	Orange Money	Equity Bank Kenya
Rwanda	MTN Rwanda	MTN Mobile Money	Banque Commerciale du Rwanda
	Tigo Rwanda	Tigo Cash	Banque Commerciale du Rwanda
	Airtel Rwanda	None	–
Tanzania	Vodacom	M-PESA	National Bank of Commerce CRBD Bank National Microfinance Bank
	Airtel	Airtel Money	Citibank United Republic of Tanzania Postal Bank CRBD Bank
	Tigo	TigoPesa	National Bank of Commerce National Microfinance Bank
	Zantel	Z Pesa	–
	Smart Mobile	None	–
	Sasa Tel	None	–
	TTCL	None	–
Uganda	MTN Uganda	MTN Mobile Money	Stanbic Uganda
	Airtel Uganda	Airtel Money	Standard Chartered Bank
	Uganda Telecom	M Sente	DFCU Bank
	Orange Uganda	Orange Money	Pride Bank Post Bank
	Warid Telecom	Warid Pesa	Equity Bank

Source: Adapted from UNCTAD field interviews, see UNCTAD 2012.

- *mobile transfer*: where one user transfers money to another person without necessarily an accompanying exchange of goods and services (i.e. a person to person transfer);
- *mobile financial service*: where mobile money link to a bank account facilitates a subscriber to conduct a range of transactions (savings, debits and credits) that ordinarily would be conducted at a bank branch. A user can access a variety of financial services using the mobile phone.[11]

The full range and scope of mobile money services is usually offered to registered users of any MSP.[12] When conducting transactions, all MSPs are obliged to ensure that a registered user of the service first uploads money onto its mobile money account (or bank account) before performing any mobile money transaction. This entails regulatory control measures which require that all non-registered users can only be recipients of mobile money transfers either through the same MSP's network or platform or, in some cases, across all platforms. Hence, with the exception of only one platform in Kenya, no other mobile money platform can register and support users who may wish to access and manage their mobile money from competing MSP networks.

2.2.2 Types of mobile money service fees charged

Mobile money service agents are important partners within the mobile money service ecosystem. They provide the interface for users of the service in transmitting and converting cash into mobile money and mobile money into cash. All transactions used to attract fees which varied from time to time on account of competition and economies of scale. However, with further innovation most MSPs provide services at almost no cost to agents (Mas and Morawczynski 2009). This is partly driven by

[11] For instance, users can access their bank account and transfer money to another bank account holder without an accompanying exchange of goods or services (a form of a hybrid mobile money transaction that combines both mobile money transfers and mobile money financial services). Currently, the character of mobile money transactions in the region can be described as local (occurs within the jurisdiction of one country) or international (conducted across different national borders). International money transfers by Western Union or Money-gram services in partnership with MSPs could be an example of M-financial services.

[12] However, in some cases, particularly regarding mobile money transfers, non-registered users send money through mobile money agents without being registered. The challenge for the regulators is whether to strictly require registration of users (as is the norm) or to permit this flexibility that would promote increased use of the service and financial inclusion.

the fact that the scope and nature of transactions have grown substantially over the years, even though other forms of payments, particularly plastic debit and credit cards, still remain the preserve of banks and agents who hold such instruments of payment.

However, money transfers still constitute the most dominant of transactions for mobile money services and therefore attract charges at a premium. The implication is that, as a proportion of the transfer amount and for lack of alternative secure, reliable and speedy services, smaller amounts may attract relatively higher fees for both sending and receiving transfers.[13] Price discriminatory practices could be applied in respect of fees charged for providing the service to a non-registered user. The rationale is to encourage agents and individuals to register for and participate in the delivery of mobile money services using the various mobile money platforms. That is why service charges levied on registered users who use the service to transmit mobile money to a non-registered user are split between the registered user and the non-registered user. For non-registered users, the cost is borne entirely by the sender.

Mobile money payment services tend to attract lower fees compared to mobile money transfer services. This is probably because MSPs have to appear to be competitive in the exercise of collecting payments, just as banks do on the basis of nominal and flat fees. However, MSPs could still use their leverage of variable fee structures to encourage most registered users to use mobile money services instead of using banks to conduct payment transactions.[14] In response to the competitive designs of MSPs in delivering mobile money services, banks have recognized the need to offer similar services, often for free (e.g. payment of some bills and account management services for major customers).

Although the average value of mobile service transactions that are channelled by various platforms have increased progressively in recent years, mobile money payment services have not sufficiently caught the eye of many micro and small enterprises in East Africa that are yet to embrace this service. Ideally, it could be imagined that for a small enterprise, use of mobile money services to transmit funds could provide new cost-effective channels of conducting business with clients or customers. Overall, the flow of money through mobile money systems will continue to grow further provided certain improvements in

[13] For a comprehensive and detailed description of the range of service fees in the East African region, see UNCTAD 2012.
[14] UNCTAD 2012 field interviews in Uganda.

service delivery and costs are addressed. This is particularly important as mobile money services could potentially provide a platform for active innovation. This could be leveraged to provide other useful services for small enterprises, including access to capital or credit through microfinance institutions, insurance hedges against risks, and the development of optimal and more efficient business management opportunities.

2.2.3 Essential features and attributes of mobile money services in East Africa

The selected features below reflect structural characteristics of the industry, administrative arrangements, channels of delivery, consumer sentiments and awareness, and security considerations. The access channels of mobile money services in the region are organized through a menu item in a phone subscriber identity module (SIM) card. A potential user of the service can conduct all transactions, sending commands to the servers of the various platforms via a number of channels that include Short Message Service (SMS) and Unstructured Supplementary Service Data (USSD) commands, as well as SIM toolkits that provide a platform for itemizing transactions that aid the completion of the transaction.[15]

Security considerations are also important. A transaction may become vulnerable to interception if the required messages are not encrypted. In order to avert the risks, all systems rely on a protocol of a personal identification number (PIN) to facilitate the authentication of transactions. When conducting mobile money transactions by phone, all transactions have to be aligned to a SIM card and phone number, while observing security requirements for completing transactions.

Requirements for registration and transaction limits exist for use of mobile money services. Users are required to register for the service, presenting themselves in person in order to complete the necessary formalities, such as providing the necessary personal identification as appropriate. Once the user's registration is complete, a mobile money account is assigned and activated on the mobile money platform. With regard to transaction limits, certain thresholds apply but vary between different MSPs.[16] Normally, most transaction limits are

[15] This applies only to registered users and not services through agents.

[16] See www.centralbank.go.ke/index.php/legislation/29-payment-systems. In other jurisdictions, such as Sri Lanka, no pre-set limits exist, but each service limit must be approved by the central bank.

approved by a monetary authority or central bank. Agents often find the applicable thresholds and limits inadequate and restrictive, requiring regular reviews.[17]

Another important feature of the industry is the extensive nature of its networks that provide the interface for the functionality of the service (such as individuals, branches and ATMs). Hence, in most cases, extensive agency networks form an integral part of the network of mobile money services networks. Consumer awareness and support is another important feature of the industry, together with awareness and trust of the service providers, which are important for efficient service delivery. In that sense, mobile money support services have cultivated good support mechanisms for users of the service, thereby reducing the average incidence of common complaints, such as agency duress (including about cash availability); network downtime interruptions; incomplete, incorrect or failed transfers; and in some cases perceived or actual fraud (Ndiwalana *et al.* 2010).

3 Policy and the regulatory framework of mobile money services in East Africa

East Africa has witnessed a rapid rise in money transfer services through leverage on mobile phone applications and use, and the sector's tradable services are likely to transform well into second generation services, compared to the traditional person to person transfers. This proliferation of mobile money services into new and diverse forms raises new policy, regulatory and supervisory challenges.

On the one hand, whilst continuing innovation and growth of mobile money services might contribute to the process of financial inclusion, the challenge is managing growth of the sector in a manner that ensures orderliness without adverse and disruptive effects on the performance and stability of the financial system. The growth of mobile money financial services could require constant appraisal of its implications for key monetary aggregates that have far-reaching implications for the wider macroeconomy, particularly when these aggregates are susceptible to being driven by those financial services, and may in turn influence the conduct of monetary and macroeconomic policies. If mobile money services begin to affect key monetary aggregates, then it

[17] Thresholds are for consumers but advised to service providers by the central bank as the regulatory authority.

is incumbent upon a monetary authority to constantly assess and tailor policy actions in such a way as to strengthen and improve the conduct of monetary policy management.

Mobile money transactions could present regulatory challenges beyond what other normal financial services do mainly because of convergence with telecommunications services. In addition, these services are rather different from other more distinct services areas that have distinct regulations and are administered by specific regulatory bodies, such as telecommunications and information technology (IT) services. The regulation of mobile money services is therefore unique. In East Africa, mobile money services are still nascent and lack well-developed regulations or frameworks. Current legal and regulatory areas of relevance to the provision of mobile money services are derived from a set of complementary functions and regulations that govern exchange of different forms of money (i.e. petty cash), the storage of money in e-floats stored in mobile wallets, transfer of monies between different people and savings in the form of net balances from deposits less withdrawals. These component forms may attract different inherent risks that a typical regulator may wish to consider in designing an appropriate framework for regulating mobile money financial services.

The same kind of regulatory difficulties apply to the construction of regulatory norms for electronic commerce, which defines the purchase and sale of goods and services via electronic transactions and payments conducted on the Internet and mobile phones. In many ways, therefore, mobile money service transactions could be viewed in terms of the domain of applicable regulatory and legal frameworks that govern the conduct of electronic commerce (e.g. cyber laws). In addition, issues relating to consumer interest and protection under the domain of mobile money services might fall in different areas of regulations such as those relating to competition, telecommunications services, banking services and others that are often attuned to specific requirements, including protections against fraud and the principle of the free flow of information.

In light of the above regulatory challenges, the progress and evolution of mobile money services would require an acceptable form of convergence of different regulatory areas, particularly with respect to telecommunications and financial services which are by any measure now inextricably linked. East African countries have recognized the need to amalgamate the regulatory landscape so as to help mitigate complex issues. This would contribute to:

- correcting related issues that pertain to user security vulnerabilities;
- addressing questions about the extent and limits to the growth of MSPs, which could at any one time hold substantial net deposits of mobile money platforms with partner banks;
- the likely significant growth of cross-border transfers through mobile money remittances and leakages because of money transfers through informal systems;
- obligations dictated by the need to monitor foreign exchange flows and conversions to maintain the external stability of the financial system and that of the trading regime and the economy of East Africa.

In light of the increasing cross-border nature of mobile money services, it is equally important that the development of international or multilateral guidelines for regulating this services sector be considered by relevant bodies and stakeholders.

4 Uganda's experience

The drive towards financial inclusion has been a main motivation behind the growth of mobile money services in Uganda. Prior to 2009, many Ugandans were excluded from accessing financial services. Only 27 per cent of the population had access to formal financial institutions, while 34 per cent used informal means. About 40 per cent were completely excluded from the service, especially those in rural areas, notably women (Aomu 2012). Some of the barriers that hindered access to easy and affordable financial services included high bank charges, long distance to financial service points or bank branches, low financial literacy and lack of appropriate consumer protection regulations.

With the success of mobile money services in Kenya leveraging telecommunications platforms, many MSPs in Uganda began to invest in the provision of mobile money services driven by demand for affordable and fast financial services. As a result and over a modest period of time, mobile money services in Uganda have been diversified extensively beyond money transfers into other forms of financial service products. Through these mobile services, agents and consumers can settle payments for a variety of services and utilities, such as electricity, water, education and finance.

The rise of mobile money services in Uganda started when the central bank (Bank of Uganda), announced in 2009 the need to foster active financial inclusion among the population as a commitment to public interest. Even though MSPs sought for licences to launch and to operate mobile money services as early as 2009, the necessary deliberate effort towards achieving this commitment began in earnest in 2010. This was mainly a response to growing demand for financial innovations; the desire to close inherent gaps in financial literacy among the public; concern for consumer protection in the delivery of financial services; and emerging desires to improve access channels, quality and reliability of financial services within the economy.

In September 2009, the central bank launched the 'Financial Inclusion Project' along with a draft framework of implementation to cover three years, 2012 to 2014. In support of this scheme, four dedicated committees on financial inclusion were formed to spearhead the implementation of the agreed four pillars of the strategy at the national and official level. In parallel, MSPs had intensified their desires to operate mobile money networks. This was approved by the central bank in January 2010. With this decision, the Bank of Uganda offered 'no objection' to one prominent bank, Stanbic Bank Uganda, to partner the leading MSP in Uganda at the time, MTN Uganda, to provide mobile money financial services to the public. This led to the establishment of an escrow (trust) account with Stanbic Bank for which the bank would bear all prudential and supervisory responsibilities. It marked the beginning of the growth of the mobile money industry that was followed by quick successive issuance of 'no objection' to three other banks to facilitate their partnerships with three other MSPs to offer mobile money services. In addition, one more commercial bank was issued 'no objection' clearance to offer the service to customers on multiple-telephone networks, through a platform owned by a private IT software company.

In December 2011, the central bank refined its initial 'no objection' provisions in order to address emerging and escalating challenges and risks associated with mobile money transfer services. This resulted in the formation of a joint national working group between the telecommunications regulator, the UCC, and the central bank to formulate regulatory guidelines on mobile money services as a basis for the development of a durable regulatory regime.

4.1 Main industry providers

There are seven operational MSPs licensed by the UCC in Uganda (see Table 12.3). These are Airtel Uganda, MTN Uganda, Orange Uganda,

Table 12.3 *An overview of mobile money service providers in Uganda*

Service name	*Telecom operator*	*Lead financial institution*
MTN Mobile Money	MTN Uganda	Stanbic Bank Uganda
Airtel Money	Airtel	Standard Chartered Bank
M Sente	UTL	DFCU Bank
Warid Pesa	Warid Telecom	Equity Bank
M Cash	n/a	Housing Finance Bank
Orange Money	Orange	Pride Bank
		Post Bank

Table 12.4 *Mobile financial services statistics*

	2009	*2010*	*2011*	*2012**
Number of transactions (millions)	2.84	28.82	57.30	241.72*
Value of transactions (billion shillings.)	133	963	3.753	11.662*
Number of customers (cumulative)	552,047	1,683,713	2,879,968	8,870,873*
Year on year growth/ increase in the number of customers (%)	–	205	71	107*

Note: *Annualized projections for 2012 (see Aomu 2012)

Uganda Telecom Ltd, Warid Telecom, K2 Telecom and Smile Telecom. Of these, six have operational mobile money platforms.

4.2 *Quantitative indications of mobile money traffic in Uganda*

Indicative volumes and values of mobile money services transaction in Uganda can be presented in terms of the number of transactions, their value and the actors involved with the facilitation of the mobile money traffic. Table 12.4 provides a summary of statistics on the variables and their evolution since 2009. The indications show that over a period of three years, the year-on-year growth in mobile money services was phenomenal, averaging over 100 per cent.

Table 12.5 *Types of mobile money services in Uganda*

Types	*MTN Mobile Money*	*Airtel Money*	*UTL M-Sente*
M-transfers	- Domestic transfers up to maximum of 1,000,000 shillings for both unregistered (off-net) and registered (on-net) users.	- Domestic transfers up to a maximum of 35,000 shillings to unregistered (off-net) and 70,000 to registered (on-net) users. - Transfers from a user's phone to any bank.	- Domestic transfers up to a maximum of 35,000 shillings to both unregistered (off-net) and registered (on-net) users. - Only platform that registers users on other networks.
M-payments	- Buy airtime (on-network). - Pay, post-pay phone bills. - Educational institutions (school fees). - Multi-choice Uganda and Star TV (satellite TV bills). - National Water and Sewerage Corporation (water bills). - Online payments. - Financial institutions (loan disbursements and repayments). - Businesses (consumer to business payments). - Bulk payments (business to customer, i.e. salaries).	- Buy airtime (on-network). - Pay, post pay phone bills. - Multi-choice Uganda (satellite TV bills). - Businesses (customer to business payments). - Bulk payments (business to customers, i.e. salaries). - Online payments.	- Buy airtime (on-network). - Educational institutions (school fees). - National Water and Sewerage Corporation (water bills). - Online payments.
M-financial services	- Mobile banking services for customers of Post Bank Uganda.	ATM withdrawals by phone.	Transfer funds from and to a user's Equity bank account.

Source: UNCTAD field interviews, see UNCTAD 2012.

Taking the example of three of the six service providers, Table 12.5 highlights the different types of mobile money services in Uganda.

Mobile money service activities have not been free of challenges for regulators. The traditional risks include:

- fraud and money laundering despite prescribed transaction limits;
- liquidity risks;
- foreign exchange risks as a result of cross-border transfers of money;
- credit and operational risks because of agency mismanagement of escrow (trust) accounts and unforeseen interruptions and possible breakdowns of network systems;
- legal risks associated with existing gaps in governance structures of the market for mobile money services.

4.3 Regulatory regime affecting mobile money service provision

The regulatory regime affecting the provision of mobile money services is underpinned by a complex but interlinked set of financial legislation:

- Bank of Uganda Act (enacted 1969, amended in 2000);
- Financial Institutions Act (2004);
- Financial Institutions (Licensing) Regulations (2005);
- Micro Finance Deposit-Taking Institutions Act (2003);
- Micro Finance Deposit-Taking Institutions (Licensing) Regulations (2004);
- Foreign Exchange Act (2004);
- Foreign Exchange (Forex Bureaus and Money Remittance) Regulations (2006);
- Financial Institutions (Anti-Money Laundering) Regulations (2010);
- Anti-Terrorism Act (2002).

With the enactment of the Bank of Uganda Act, the Ugandan central bank was established. This Act, which was amended in 2000, defines the Bank's mandate. In its main capacity, the Bank of Uganda is the financial sector regulator. The scope of the regulatory framework for the financial sector in Uganda is contained in the Financial Institutions (Licensing) Regulations (2005) and other related regulations which guide the licensing and operation of accredited financial institutions.

There are two Acts which together regulate the provision of micro-finance services, and two for foreign exchanges. The Foreign Exchange Act (2004) defines rules for the exchange of foreign currencies, international payments and transfers of foreign exchange. The Foreign Exchange (Forex Bureaus and Money Remittance) Regulations (2006) guide and specify the licensing criteria and conditions and the activities of entities licensed as foreign exchange bureaus or those which are entitled to remit money.

With regard to criminal activities, both the Financial Institutions (Anti-Money Laundering) Regulations (2010) and the Anti-Terrorism Act (2002) are designed to regulate and criminalize the financing of terrorism and associated money laundering activities, while addressing anti-money laundering and counterfeit transaction incidences in Uganda.

Other legislation affecting the provision of mobile money services in Uganda includes:

- Uganda Communications Act (2013), which establishes and defines the mandate of the Uganda Communications Commission (UCC) (the regulator of the communications sector);
- Electronic Signatures Act (2010);
- Electronic Transactions Act (2010).

4.4 Challenges facing regulators of mobile money services in Uganda

The immediate challenges to regulators and the financial system, which emerged two years after the commencement of the trade, were weaknesses in transparency practices (full disclosure of all applicable fees and tariffs to customers) of individuals and agencies involved in the delivery of the services. Other challenges included: the inability of partner banks to independently access and evaluate information on mobile money users, particularly for those engaged in large value transactions; difficulties of ensuring consumer or user protection arising from settling associated transaction complaints in the event that the service provider or its banking partner or agents became insolvent or illiquid, especially in rural areas; and the risks of likely system breakdowns that could incapacitate users from accessing virtual money.

This multiplicity of potential risks led the central bank to pronounce additional new enhancement measures within the framework of its initial 'no objection' warrants for the industry to comply with, so as to mitigate these risks. Some of the proposals in the enhancement measures included:

- proposals for the automation of escrow (trust) accounts in order to separate balances of agents on a real time basis;

- requirements for partner banks to improve their systems to generate real time information;
- partner banks and the respective MSPs to establish and to observe transaction limits;
- in the event of system breakdowns, the immediate availability of necessary information to customers.

5 Conclusion: the way forward

The role of mobile money services in fostering financial sector inclusiveness has increasingly been recognized as its benefits continue to be better understood. Mobile money services are increasingly viewed as a stepping-stone for better access to banking and related financial services by the majority of the population, which previously lacked access to these services. However, a comprehensive regulatory framework is yet to be developed to address the main risks of mobile money transactions and to keep up with the much faster pace of technological innovation in this services sector. For instance, current regulation of the telecommunications sector addresses mainly basic telecommunications services and has not been transformed to take account of the explosion in use of mobile telephony for mobile money services. In addition, existing financial services regulations regulate traditional financial services and do not effectively regulate mobile financial services.

The regulations developed would have to address issues that confront the sector, such as protection of users of the service; transaction limits; user registration requirements; agency networks; and interoperability. Developing mobile money services regulations both at national and regional levels will be challenging considering that no prior global or regional regulatory regime exists that regulators could refer to for best practice. In order to develop effective regulations for this services sector at the national level that keep abreast of its rapid technological development, a high level of collaboration amongst all regulators involved will be paramount. This is particularly so for the financial services regulator (Bank of Uganda) and the telecommunications regulator (UCC). The regulatory roles and mandates of the two principal regulators will have to be clearly defined to ensure regulatory convergence.

Regulatory convergence in the mobile money services sector will also be necessary at the regional level. As the regional integration process in the EAC progresses, harmonization of policies in this crucial area will be important. Regional entities including the EAC Secretariat, the

East African Communications Organization and respective national regulators will need to collaborate closely to develop or harmonize existing laws and regulations governing mobile money services. In developing regulation for mobile money services, however, regulators at both the national and regional level need to ensure that the regulations developed do not muddle or curtail the pace of growth and technological innovation in this sector. In Uganda, the two principal regulators, the Bank of Uganda and the UCC, have recognized the necessity of regulatory convergence in this industry and have already begun to take steps to collaborate in developing regulations that would clearly demarcate respective roles in regulating mobile money services. In a rapidly evolving sector, this is not the last word. The evolution of the mobile money services sector, including the development and implementation of specific regulations, needs to be constantly studied and researched.

References

Aomu, M. (2012), 'Mobile Financial Services, Financial Inclusion and Potential for Poverty Alleviation', East Africa Workshop on Mobile Financial Services, Entebbe, Uganda, 27–29 June

Business Daily (2012), 'M-Pesa Drives Innovation Five Years After Launch', 22 March

DESA (2011), *World Population Prospects: The 2010 Revision*, CD-ROM edn, Department of Economic and Social Affairs

Jenkins, B. (2008), *Developing Mobile Money Ecosystems*, Washington, DC: International Finance Corporation/Harvard Kennedy School

Mas, I. and Morawczynski, O. (2009), 'Designing Mobile Money Services: Lessons from M-PESA', *Innovations: Technology, Governance, Globalization* 4(2): 77–91

Ndiwalana, A., Morawczynski, O. and Popov, O. (2010), *Mobile Money Use in Uganda: A Preliminary Study*, GSMA

Penicard Claire, GSMA: 'Mobile Money for the Unbanked: State of the Industry: Results from the 2012 Global Mobile Money Adoption Survey'

Sey, A. (2008), *Mobile Communication and Development: A Study of Mobile Phone Appropriation in Ghana*, Faculty of the Graduate School, University of Southern California

UNCTAD (2012), *Mobile Money for Business Development in the East African Community: A Comparative Study of Existing Platforms and Regulations*, Geneva: United Nations Conference on Trade and Development

13

Financial services liberalization and regulation in Japan: implications for future negotiation on market access and domestic regulations

MASAMICHI KONO, KOICHI IWAI AND YOSHITAKA SAKAI

1 Introduction

It appears that negotiations under the General Agreement on Trade in Services (GATS) to liberalize financial services trade are not proceeding smoothly. No major progress has been recorded since the Fifth Protocol to GATS came into effect in 1999. Under such circumstances, in order to promote a progressive liberalization of financial services, some insist that rationality, objectivity and transparency in domestic regulation should be achieved according to the principles of GATS Article VI. However, it is extremely difficult to form a consensus on domestic regulation under Article VI between developed and developing countries.[1] To complicate the issue even further, there appears to be no consensus or agreed definitions among World Trade Organization (WTO) members about the scope of application or the content of regulations subject to Article VI.

This chapter discusses various aspects of domestic regulation in light of Japanese experiences, examines the experience of financial system reform in Japan and draws lessons for advancing the GATS negotiations on financial services liberalization in the future. In order to maximize the benefits from liberalizing financial services, we argue that institutional frameworks to enhance the objectivity and transparency of investor protection laws and other domestic regulations should be put in place and enforced effectively, in addition to promoting the opening of markets

[1] Based on GATS Art. VI:4, the Working Party on Domestic Regulation began discussion on the discipline of domestic regulation, and at the Hong Kong WTO Ministerial Conference in 2005, it declared that such discipline would be developed prior to the conclusion of the Doha Round. However, at present, no remarkable achievements have materialized.

to foreign services providers. In our opinion, the recent global financial crisis strengthened the validity of such a view.

The rest of this chapter is structured as follows. We first study the recent history of financial system reforms in Japan, and confirm that the measures for financial services liberalization were implemented as part of the financial system reform packages. We point out that these packages in Japan consisted of several major pillars, including the liberalization of financial services, the development of laws and regulations for investor protection, and the rationalization of domestic regulations. We then discuss the effect of financial system reform on the Japanese financial market, paying attention to the investment management business which could be recognized as a typical example of the reform. We show that the reform with several pillars resulted in improvement of market access, market expansion and financial innovation in the investment management business. Finally, we conclude that the Japanese experience shows that it is essential to set an effective and appropriate regulatory environment for advancing further financial services liberalization in both advanced and developing countries. Throughout this chapter, the expression 'domestic regulation' has broader meanings than the usage under GATS Article VI, and includes all laws and regulations applicable to trade in financial services.

2 Financial system reforms in Japan

The Japanese economy was adversely affected by the collapse of the asset price bubble at the beginning of the 1990s, and was plunged into the deep and prolonged recession period, known as the 'lost decade'. The Japanese bank-centred financial system has been recognized as one of the main causes behind the formation and collapse of the asset bubble. This widely held view urged the Japanese government to undertake comprehensive financial reforms, ranging from restoring the banking industry to strengthening regulations related to capital markets (see Table 13.1).[2]

Note: Case numbers for administrative action show the number of orders relating to adverse dispositions, etc. issued and published by the FSA and Local Finance Bureaus (including business improvement orders, correction orders, warnings, orders to revise plans, business

[2] This chapter does not discuss countermeasures to the financial crisis following the collapse of the asset bubble, such as measures for dealing with bankrupt financial institutions. For a discussion on this point, see Nakaso 2001.

Table 13.1 *Recent history of financial system reforms in Japan*

Fiscal year	*Market-opening measures*	*Investor protection measures*	*Rationalization and transparency of domestic regulation*
1998	• Amendment of the Foreign Exchange and Foreign Trade Act (abolition of the system whereby only authorized banks can conduct foreign exchange transactions, complete liberalization of outward transactions). • Transition of the securities business from a licensing system to a registration system. • Transition of the investment trust management business from a licensing system to a permit system. • Introduction of private investment trusts and corporation-type investment trusts. • Lifting of the ban on over-the-counter sales of investment trusts at banks. • Lifting of the ban on outsourcing investment advice related to investment trusts. • Lifting of the ban on securities-related over-the-counter derivative transactions.	• Application of the disclosure system (Securities and Exchange Act) for domestic investment trusts. • Clarification of the obligation for separate management of customer assets. • Establishment of investor protection funds.	• Abolition of notices and office memos. • Cabinet decision for the 'Public Comment Procedure for Formulating, Amending or Repealing a Regulation'.

Table 13.1 (*cont.*)

Fiscal year	*Market-opening measures*	*Investor protection measures*	*Rationalization and transparency of domestic regulation*
1999	• Complete liberalization of brokerage commissions for stocks. • Abolition of restrictions on the scope of business conducted by securities subsidiaries, such as of banks.		
2000		• Passing of the Financial Products Sales Act (enforced in 2001).	• Cabinet decision to introduce the Prior Confirmation Procedures on the Application of Laws and Regulations (No Action Letter System).
2001	• Lifting of the ban on real estate investment trusts (J-REITs). • Listing of exchange trade funds (ETFs).	• Formulation and public release of the Securities Inspection Manual.	• Financial Services Agency (FSA): introduction of the No Action Letter System.
2002	• Lifting of the ban on banks and securities firms having joint branches.	• FSA: administrative actions (39 cases). • Formulation and public release of the Inspection Manual for Investment Trust Management and Investment Advisory Businesses.	
2003		• FSA: administrative actions (60 cases).	
2004		• FSA: administrative actions (69 cases).	

Table 13.1 (*cont.*)

Fiscal year	*Market-opening measures*	*Investor protection measures*	*Rationalization and transparency of domestic regulation*
2005		• FSA: administrative actions (156 cases).	• Legislation of the public comment system following the amendment to the Administrative Procedure Act. • FSA: formulation and public release of the 'Principles of Financial Supervision and Rules for Supervision Division Staff (Code of Conduct)' and the 'Financial Inspection Basic Guidelines'. • FSA: detailed procedural rules for the No Action Letter System translated into English and published. • FSA: clarification of the procedure for written inquiries regarding the general interpretation of laws and regulations. • FSA: release of details of administrative action cases to general public.

Table 13.1 (*cont.*)

Fiscal year	*Market-opening measures*	*Investor protection measures*	*Rationalization and transparency of domestic regulation*
2006		• FSA: administrative actions (119 cases).	• Institutionalization of *ex ante* evaluations – regulatory impact analysis (RIA) – and expansion of the policy assessment system.
2007	• Enforcement of the Financial Instruments and Exchange Act (FIEA): - considerable easing of subsidiary business regulations; - market entry regulations for the financial instruments business, in principle, standardized to a registration system; - easing of minimum capital requirements, etc.	• FIEA: - introduction of cross-sector investor protection laws; - clarification of conduct regulations (advertising regulations, obligation to issue documents, prohibition of unsolicited sales, principle of suitability, distinction between professional and amateur investors, etc.). • Application of FIEA user protection rules to financial instruments covered by the Banking Act and the Insurance Business Act. • FSA: administrative actions (65 cases).	• Enforcement of the FIEA. • FSA: Promotion of Better Regulation. • FSA: Revision of the No Action Letter System.
2008		• FSA: administrative actions (70 cases).	
2009		• Establishment of a system of designated dispute resolution institutions (alternative dispute resolution) following the amendment to the FIEA. • FSA: administrative actions (70 cases).	

Source: Prepared by authors.

improvement advisories, business suspension orders, cancellations of registration, cancellations of permit, recommendations and business abolition orders). Case numbers have been listed from fiscal year 2002.

In November 1996, the Hashimoto cabinet unveiled the Japanese Big Bang, a financial reform package based on free, fair and global principles, with reference to the UK Big Bang reform. The 'free' principle signified liberalized financial markets, specifically consisting of promoting mutual business entries among banking, securities and insurance sectors, expanding the products allowed to be handled by banks and securities firms, and liberalizing foreign currency transactions. The 'fair' principle meant a transparent and fair market. Under this notion, the principle of self-responsibility was promoted along with the improvement of information disclosure and clarification of rules, and regulators were expected to pursue rigorous enforcement against violations of rules. The 'global' principle signified creating an international marketplace through improvements of legal and accounting systems and establishment of international regulatory cooperation.

2.1 *Market opening measures*

Soon after the Big Bang proposal, specific reform plans were discussed by five government councils.[3] In June 1997, one of the councils, the Securities and Exchange Council, addressed the need to open up the capital market and recommended drastic deregulation of the securities market, investment products and market intermediaries. The arguments at the Council led to a series of amendments of laws, which came into effect in 1998 and were called collectively the 'Financial Reform Law'.[4]

The deregulation policies around this time provided the basis for subsequent financial reforms and characterized the current Japanese financial markets. Major deregulations included:

- liberalizing brokerage commissions;
- lowering the entry barriers for securities firms and investment management companies;

[3] Specifically, the Securities and Exchange Council, the Business Accounting Council, the Committee on Financial Systems Research, the Insurance Council and the Foreign Exchange Council.

[4] To be more precise, the Financial Reform Law is comprised of several amendments to laws, including the Securities and Exchange Act; Banking Act; Securities Investment Trust Act; Insurance Business Act; and Trust Business Act.

- abolishing major business restrictions for securities subsidiaries of banks;
- liberalizing the over-the-counter derivative markets and private offering by investment trusts.

These reforms expanded investment asset classes accessible for investors and enhanced competition between financial institutions. In addition, the Foreign Exchange and Foreign Trade Act was amended in 1998, and foreign currency transactions were completely liberalized.

In 2001, the Minister of State for Financial Services established a private consultation group, the Roundtable Committee on the Future Vision of the Japanese Financial System and Policies, in order to promote the structural reforms. The Committee strongly recommended the building of a two-track financial system comprised of the banking sector and the securities market, and insisted on further deregulation of the securities market and on the importance of transparency and fairness in financial markets. In response to this discussion, the Financial System Council submitted the *Medium-Term Vision Report for the Future of the Japanese Financial System* in 2002. This report was utilized for the subsequent institutional reforms, which included the removal of even more entry-barriers and the relaxation of restrictions on business scope for financial institutions.

Furthermore, the Financial Instruments and Exchange Act (FIEA), which was enacted in 2007, revolutionized the previous financial regulatory framework by integrating the dispersed regulations into a unified regulatory scheme. Before the FIEA was introduced, financial regulations had been established for each industry; for example, regulations for securities firms were independent of those for investment management. But under the FIEA, most financial institutions are recognized as institutions providing a 'financial instruments business' and are subject to unified regulation. Therefore, financial institutions covered by the FIEA need not, in principle, obtain additional approval from a regulator when they engage in subsidiary businesses under the FIEA, which promotes innovation in financial products and a degree of freedom in offering financial services. In addition, entry regulations, which had previously varied according to the business type, were integrated into a registration system and entry requirements were relaxed.[5]

[5] The minimum capital requirements were reduced dramatically to a low level where capital requirement could not be a major obstacle for new entrants.

In this way, the Japanese government adopted fundamental reforms in order to strengthen its financial system in response to the malfunctioning of financial intermediation after the collapse of the asset bubble. As a result of the liberalization measures during the second half of the 1990s, the degree of openness of Japan's financial system reached a high level, and it was recognized as more liberalized than other developed countries by the early 2000s. As we discuss in section 3, foreign financial institutions started to enter the Japanese financial market in accordance with the progress of fundamental reforms, and the Japanese economy benefited from the liberalization of financial markets.

2.2 *Investor protection measures*

Competition resulting from liberalization could increase bankruptcy risk for individual financial institutions. The greater diversity of investment products and the higher self-responsibility principle promote competition and improve efficiency in the securities market, but they could also increase the risks that individual investors assume. Accordingly, the Japanese financial authorities aimed not only to promote liberalization measures but also to strengthen investor protection as they promoted financial system reforms. Examples of investor protection measures at the time of the Financial Reform Law include the segregation duty of customer assets and the establishment of investor protection funds. The investor protection funds, which were established by the Securities and Exchange Act,[6] provide financial compensation for customers in the event of the collapse of a securities firm.

Even after that, there was a succession of important amendments of laws and regulations designed to improve investor protection. As diverse investment products were developed and became more accessible to individual investors, the number of troubles and disputes related to those newly introduced products increased, partly due to inadequate product explanations at the point of sale. To address this situation, the Financial Products Sales Act was passed in 2000 and came into effect the following year. The Act, focusing on civil liability, clarified what financial institutions ought to explain when they recommend and sell financial

[6] All securities firms were required to join an investor protection fund, and the law required all investor protection funds, when having received an application for membership, not to reject any application under unfair conditions. For example, the system has been designed so that foreign-owned financial institutions are not unfairly excluded.

products to their clients, such as specific risks and characteristics of each financial instrument. The Act also required financial institutions to consider the customer's knowledge, experience and financial conditions, and to provide appropriate explanations so that each investor would be able to understand the products. In addition, the FIEA also promoted investor protection by covering more diverse types of investment schemes than those protected by its antecedent, the Securities and Exchange Act. The FIEA also clarified various restrictions on business conduct – regulations on advertising; the obligation to issue documents; the prohibition of unsolicited sales; the principle of suitability; and the distinction between professional and amateur investors – and strengthened protection measures for retail investors. Furthermore, the same investor protection rules as in the FIEA were to be imposed on financial instruments covered by such laws as the Banking Act and the Insurance Business Act.

The system of dispute resolution was enhanced, too. Efforts were made to augment the alternative dispute resolution (ADR) system to promote mediation, brokerage and arbitration. ADR institutions were established following the 2009 amendment to the FIEA and other laws. With this amendment, the Financial Services Agency (FSA) was authorized to designate and supervise dispute settlement bodies, and secure the neutrality and impartiality of these bodies. Moreover, with the provision of the legal framework, disputes are now resolved swiftly and simply.

2.3 Measures to achieve rational and transparent domestic regulation

Because rational and transparent domestic regulation was recognized as an important issue for all administrative agencies in Japan, certain measures to rationalize the overall regulatory framework have been promoted. The 1993 enactment of the Administrative Procedure Act can be recognized as one of the most important developments which significantly improved the rationalization and transparency of Japan's administrative business.

As government-wide initiatives were promoted, the financial authority introduced changes to make the regulations and rules under its jurisdiction more rational and transparent. Specifically, one of the major objectives of the Big Bang reforms has been to increase the consistency and transparency of domestic regulations. First, the financial authorities have significantly changed their way of exercising and conducting administrative power. Before the Big Bang, the administrative style of the financial regulators, called the 'convoy system', placed importance on prior negotiations between the authorities and financial institutions. However, in June 1998, the supervisory notices and other official memos that had served as the basis of administrative guidance were, except for a small portion, essentially abolished in order to achieve more transparent administration. Furthermore, the financial authorities aimed to disseminate more information overseas from the mid-1990s using Internet technology and other media. A typical case can be found in the late 1990s, when they disclosed information in English on the progress and detailed discussions regarding the Financial Reform Law.

In the 2000s, the Japanese government adopted and implemented several institutional reforms with the intention of increasing the integrity and transparency of government businesses, and the FSA followed these developments. First, after the cabinet decided to adopt the No Action Letter System, the FSA also introduced this system in July 2001. The aim is to prevent impediments to financial innovation by clarifying in advance whether a new financial product or service would conflict with laws and regulations. The system allows private firms that are planning a new business to obtain confirmation in writing as to whether their new business violates laws and regulations. On receipt of an inquiry, the FSA responds in writing within thirty days, stating clearly its opinion and grounds in principle. The FSA also publishes the details of the inquiry and its response on its website within thirty days after issuing the response. The institutional arrangements and procedures of the FSA are fully consistent with the criteria contained in GATS Article VI. Furthermore, the Ministry of Internal Affairs and Communications, which is the government office responsible for the No Action Letter System, regularly investigates how the system is being used, and releases the results of its investigation to the general public.

Second, the Government Policy Evaluations Act was passed in 2001. It came into effect the following year, and a policy assessment system was introduced. The system is designed to help each government agency to ascertain, analyse and evaluate the effect of its own policies. It is expected that government agencies can use the lessons learned from the policy assessment system in planning and implementing new policies. An *ex ante* evaluation mechanism (called regulatory impact analysis, RIA) was also introduced in 2007. The FSA formulated the 'Basic Plan for Policy Evaluation at the Financial Services Agency', stipulating and publicly announcing the purpose, methods, procedures and other facets of policy assessments in financial administration. According to the plan, policy evaluations are to be applied both before and after a policy is implemented. It states that, when conducting a policy assessment, evaluations should be conducted from the three perspectives: necessity, efficiency and effectiveness.

Third, the Public Comment Procedure for Formulating, Amending or Repealing a Regulation was enacted following the June 2005 amendment of the Administrative Procedure Act. The public comment system introduced by this legislation has been put in place for administrative agencies to receive a variety of opinions and expertise from the public, and to ensure fairness and increase transparency in the process of formulating cabinet orders, ministerial ordinances and other regulatory actions.

Apart from these developments observed throughout government agencies, the FSA unveiled its own policy direction to improve the transparency and predictability of financial administration in the Financial Reform Program of 2004, and promoted a number of measures. First, the FSA formulated and publicly announced the 'Principles of Financial Supervision and Rules for Supervision Division Staff (Code of Conduct)'. This reaffirmed that there should be no discriminatory treatment between domestic and foreign-owned financial institutions in terms of administrative decisions. Second, the agency clarified the administrative procedure in the case where the public requires a general interpretation of financial regulations to improve the predictability of the application of laws and rules. Third, the FSA started to disclose all of the administrative disposals on its website in an effort to improve the convenience of users and to promote public awareness of the interpretation of laws and regulations.

A more recent measure has been the initiatives for better regulation. In 2007, the FSA adopted the slogan 'Achieving Better Regulation', focusing on improvements in transparency and predictability of regulation and supervision. In order to realize better regulation, the FSA presented a vision comprised of four pillars:

- the optimal combination of rule and principle-based regulatory supervision;
- early recognition and effective responses to high-priority issues (risk-focused, forward-looking approach);
- respecting the self-help efforts of financial institutions and placing greater emphasis on incentives for them;
- improving the transparency and predictability of administrative responses.

3 Effects of financial system reform

3.1 *Effects of financial reform: global experience and Japanese view*

At around the time when Japan was engaged in financial system reforms after the collapse of the asset bubble, financial sector reforms were also being advanced in other Asian countries that had experienced the Asian currency crisis. However, there were huge differences in their stance on financial services liberalization.

For example, the Republic of Korea adopted a variety of measures to promote liberalization of its financial market, partly due to demands from international organizations, while Association of Southeast Asian Nations (ASEAN) members, especially Malaysia and Indonesia, tended to adopt a relatively cautious approach to the liberalization of their financial markets – in particular to their GATS commitments.[7] In contrast, Japan's attitude on liberalization at the time was quite aggressive compared to those countries, as shown by its positive commitment to liberalization in the GATS Schedule and in its adoption of the Understanding on Commitments in Financial Services. Harms *et al.* (2003) confirm the fact that Japan's stance on liberalization was, on a global basis, at a notably high level – on par with New Zealand.

Up until the global financial crisis, a plethora of research suggested that active liberalization measures contributed to the stability and development of the financial system.[8] There was also the view that increasing competition between foreign-owned financial institutions and local financial institutions through liberalization measures had the effect of improving the efficiency of the financial market. The global financial crisis has forced us to rethink these views. In fact, as seen in the declarations by the Group of 20 (G20) leaders, the recognition that the liberalization and globalization of financial services destabilized financial systems has become widespread. Adverse effects in the wake of the financial crisis have, thus far, remained minor in Japan compared to developed countries in the West. Therefore, one could say that the benefits Japan has enjoyed from its financial system reforms since the 1990s seem to have surpassed the negative effects brought about by the recent global financial crisis.

[7] However, apart from GATS, ASEAN members had also expressed pledges for liberalization through the ASEAN Framework Agreement on Services (AFAS), and in general, the level of commitments to liberalization in the AFAS was higher than in GATS.

[8] For the following discussion, see e.g. Barth *et al.* 2001; 2004; and Kim 2002.

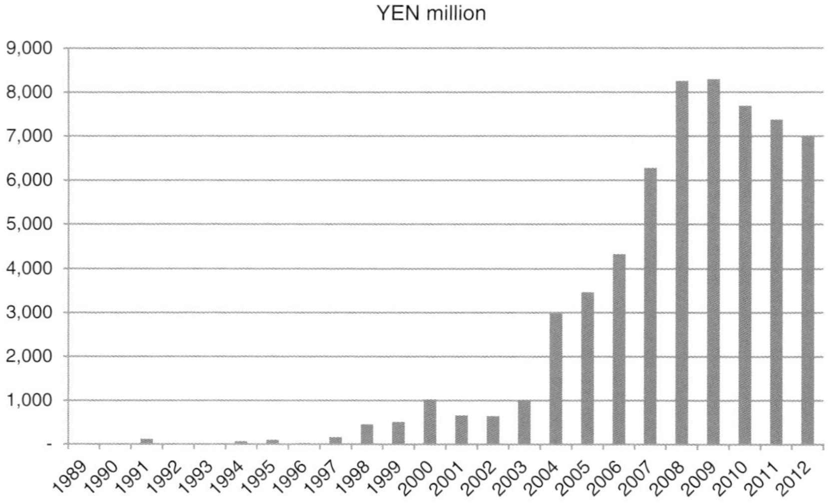

Figure 13.1 Inward securities investment (finance and insurance) (¥ billion)
Sources: Ministry of Finance and Bank of Japan

The notable feature of the Japanese experience is that, while the regulatory authorities promoted liberalization, rationalization and transparency of domestic regulation, they also enhanced investor protection. It is commonly thought that exhaustive implementation of investor protection contributes to delays in deregulation and restricts foreign-owned financial institutions from entering the market. However, Japan's experience shows that even if investor protection is implemented thoroughly, it does not necessarily lead directly to barriers to entry and financial innovation. Rather, implementing stronger investor protection in domestic markets will enhance investors' confidence in domestic markets and financial products, which could lead to more favourable business environments for both domestic and foreign financial institutions. Figure 13.1 shows the amounts of foreign direct investment into Japan by finance and insurance business operators located overseas. We can confirm that, since the turn of the century when the three measures of financial reforms – services liberalization, rationalization of domestic regulation and investor protection – were being simultaneously advanced, more and more foreign-owned financial institutions have entered the Japanese market. It would appear that the entry of foreign-owned financial institutions into the market stimulated competition with

Japanese-owned financial institutions, thereby contributing to greater efficiency in the financial market and to increasing financial innovation.

Note: Figures for 1989–2004 are for the end of each fiscal year, and figures for 2005–2010 are for the end of each year.

In the next subsection, by investigating experience in the investment management industry, we will argue that developing and enforcing effective regulations is essential for realizing financial innovation while containing the negative effects of financial services liberalization.

3.2 *Case study: Japanese investment management industry*

As stated earlier, during the reforms of Japan's financial system from the end of the 1990s, the establishment of a two-track financial system was recommended. The investment management industry was regarded as a base for developing large and diverse capital markets. Furthermore, fundamental institutional reforms related to this industry were thought imperative. Hence, all the reforms covering liberalization, investor protection and rationalization of domestic regulations have been pursued in this sector.

In terms of liberalization measures, entry regulations were eased from the permit system to the registration system as a result of the FIEA. The Prime Minister is required to approve the registration of an applicant unless there are facts that constitute a reason for refusal. Applicable reasons for refusal have been set forth in detail in laws and regulations, and regulators cannot discriminate against foreign applicants. In cases where the FSA refuses a registration, it is required to issue a notice of refusal of registration to the applicant, which clearly states the reasons for refusal, thereby ensuring impartiality and transparency in administrative decisions. This treatment by the FSA is considered to be consistent with the requirements described in GATS Article VI.

Contrary to the deregulation in entry requirements, it is also worthy to note that there is a requirement for investment trust companies to have a base established in Japan. Behind this requirement, there is a view that requiring a domestic base for investment managers can help regulatory bodies to conduct administrative supervision effectively, so that investor protection can be appropriately ensured. This view seems to have a feature in common with the Understanding on Commitments in Financial Services, where Mode 3 (provision of services through a business base) is actively promoted.

On the other hand, a variety of investor protection measures have been implemented in addition to the obligation to segregate customers' funds and the introduction of investor protection funds:

- the scope of investor protection has been expanded to include union-type funds;
- regulations on major shareholders have been introduced;
- the right for the authority to file a petition for commencement of bankruptcy proceedings has been implemented;
- the reasons for refusing a registration for the investment advisory business were expanded;
- in April 2002, the FSA formulated the *Inspection Manual for Investment Trust Management and Investment Advisory Businesses*, and has since conducted strict enforcement.

In this way, rapid liberalization, expanded investor protection and improved transparency of domestic regulation were promoted simultaneously in the Japanese investment management industry. Although deregulation sometimes led to the emergence of malicious business operators, the market size and product diversity of the industry has increased dramatically in the last twenty years. For example, while investment management business operators numbered 183 in 1998, this had increased to 320 by 2009. The ratio of foreign currency-denominated assets in publicly offered investment trusts increased from 12 per cent in 1998 to 47 per cent in 2009. Furthermore, the number of publicly offered stock investment trusts increased from 2,070 in 1998 to 3,075 in 2009. Compared to the time around the collapse of the asset bubble, Japan's financial market has continued to transform into a two-track financial system through expansion of the investment management business, overcoming various headwinds, including the global financial crisis.

4 Conclusion: suggestions for financial services liberalization

Japan's experience shows that there needs to be an appropriate progression of financial services liberalization, together with other policies, when a government wishes to build a resilient financial system and maximize the benefits to be derived from financial reforms. When Japan instituted financial services liberalization, it simultaneously pursued the reform of domestic regulation in increasing transparency and strengthening investor protection measures. Such a policy package could serve as a reference in the future for developing countries seeking to appropriately promote financial services liberalization.

Reflecting on the recent global financial crisis, we will increasingly need to turn our attention to the risks involved in undertaking financial services liberalization. Therefore, in future negotiations on this under GATS and in other forums, more attention than ever would need to be paid to developing an effective framework of domestic regulation that enhances investor protection and promotes financial stability. Specifically, the Japanese experience suggests that the following principles could be useful and effective in furthering the future negotiations for financial services liberalization:

- As is the case with the FIEA, the financial regulatory framework should cover the widest range of financial institutions and financial markets products and place them under consistent and effective rules.
- Those rules should be adjusted and modified in accordance with rapidly changing circumstances in financial markets and systems.
- Institutional mechanisms, such as the Japanese Administrative Procedure Act, the No Action Letter System and the policy evaluation systems, that enhance impartiality and transparency in administrative procedures and decision-making should be introduced as an important component of the financial regulatory framework.
- When implementing licensing and qualification requirements, regulators should ensure that the applicable standards do not distort competition by avoiding making them excessively burdensome or using them as *de facto* barriers to market access.
- Financial regulators must ensure the objectivity and transparency of investor protection laws and regulations, and conduct rigorous and effective enforcement, with a commitment to being accountable to the public.

Japanese authorities are currently pursuing further financial services liberalization where necessary and appropriate, even in the wake of the global financial crisis. For example, in discussions at the Roundtable Committee on Fundamental Issues of the Financial System Council, which was set up in July 2009, there was renewed recognition of the importance of building the two-track financial system, with deliberate containment of the possible side-effects of loose regulations. Based on this recognition, the FSA is proceeding with strengthening regulation for over-the-counter derivatives markets and prudential regulations on banks, while at the same time liberalizing regulations with respect to investment management business, for example, and reinforcing investor protection.

In developing countries, a balanced approach combining the development of effective domestic regulation and progressive liberalization would be appropriate, rather than back-pedalling on financial services liberalization in response to the global financial crisis. For countries, including some developed ones, that do not yet have a well-established system of investor protection laws and regulations, not only would they need to promote liberalization and improve the transparency of domestic regulation, they would also need to develop investor protection rules and ensure proper enforcement of those rules.

References

Barth, R.J., Caprio Jr, G. and Levine, R. (2001), *The Regulation and Supervision of Banks Around the World*, Policy Research Working Paper 2588, Washington, DC: World Bank

(2004), 'Bank Regulation and Supervision: What Works Best?', *Journal of Financial Intermediation* 13(2): 205–48

Harms, P., Mattoo, A. and Schuknecht, L. (2003), *Explaining Liberalization Commitments in Financial Services Trade*, Policy Research Working Paper 2999, Washington, DC: World Bank

Kim, Y.-H. (2002), *Financial Opening under the WTO Agreement in Selected Asian Countries: Progress and Issues*, ERD Working Paper Series No. 24, Manila: Asian Development Bank

Nakaso, H. (2001), *The Financial Crisis in Japan during the 1990s: How the Bank of Japan Responded and the Lessons Learnt*, BIS Papers No. 6, Basel: Bank for International Settlements

14

Domestic regulations in Malaysia's higher education sector

THAM SIEW YEAN AND NIK AHMAD KAMAL NIK MAHMOD

1 Introduction

The growth of private higher education institutions (PHEIs) in Malaysia is politically and economically motivated. Excess demand and the use of ethnic quotas in a limited number of public universities with the implementation of the New Economic Policy in 1970 had raised the potential for inter-ethnic conflicts in multi-ethnic Malaysia. The government therefore utilized private provision to supplement public supply, thereby increasing access and reducing the possibility of inter-ethnic conflicts due to limited access. Over time, the perennial deficit in services trade since independence in 1957 contributed to the idea of using private higher education to reduce student outflows and its negative impact on services trade and, instead, to increase export revenues through inflows of international students. This led to the aspiration to be a regional hub for higher education based on Malaysia's comparative advantage in terms of costs and language via the use of English in transnational programmes offered in PHEIs, with degrees awarded by parent institutions in developed countries such as Australia and the United Kingdom.

PHEIs grew rapidly with the formal opening up of the education sector in 1996[1] so that by 2012, there were twenty-nine private universities, twenty-one university colleges, five foreign university branch campuses, and 415 colleges.[2] Intense competition, due to the large number of private providers and a small domestic market, with a population of 28 million,

[1] This is considered to be a landmark year in the development of PHEIs in Malaysia because the Private Higher Educational Institutions Act was enacted in 1996. Prior to 1996, PHEIs were already operating in the country, but they were not allowed to confer degrees nor were there any regulations governing the sector then.

[2] Private universities and branch campuses are allowed to confer their own degrees while university colleges and colleges do not confer their own degrees and carry transnational or franchised programmes from local public universities.

has forced these institutions to look outwards for international students. These institutions are allowed to recruit up to 80 per cent of their enrolment from outside the country. By 2009, Malaysia had captured 2 per cent of the global market for international students and was the eleventh preferred study destination for higher education.[3] In 2010, 72 per cent of international students studying in Malaysia were enrolled in PHEIs, as public universities had capped their enrolment of international students at 5 per cent due to the continued excess demand from local students, as fees in public universities are highly subsidized.

Malaysia also has a well-established regulatory structure, including quality assurance overseeing the development of its higher education sector under the separate Ministry of Higher Education (MOHE), which was established in 2004. Given the importance of this sector to the country and Malaysia's potential in further developing its trade in higher education, the objectives of this chapter are to:

- explain the main provisions of the two main regulations governing the development of PHEIs;
- examine common regulatory practices;
- analyse the interface between trade liberalization and domestic regulations.

2 Key features of main Acts governing PHEIs

Two main Acts regulate and assure quality of PHEIs in Malaysia: the Private Higher Educational Institutions (PHEI) Act 1996 (Act 555) and the Malaysian Qualifications Agency (MQA) Act 2007 (Act 679).

2.1 Private Higher Educational Institutions (PHEI) Act 1996 (Act 555)

The long title of Act 555 states that it is '[a]n Act to provide for the establishment, registration, management and supervision of, and the control of the quality of education provided by, private higher educational institutions and for matters connected therewith'. Thus, Act 555 regulates the establishment and operation of all PHEIs, be they local or foreign. In other words, the Act is applied equally without any discrimination between local or foreign institutions. All PHEIs have to be registered under the Act and establishing a PHEI outside the Act is an offence

[3] 'Malaysia: The Preferred Destination for Higher Education', Education Malaysia, available at www.educationmalaysia.gov.my/about-us.

under section 76. PHEIs under the Act are divided into two types: those with the status of a university or college university or branch campus and those that are neither a university nor a college university. The former are regulated under section 22 and Part VI of the Act. Application under section 6 is made to the Registrar General (RG) of the MOHE, while section 22 is applicable only upon an invitation made by the Minister of Higher Education. Upon such invitation, the institution may apply for registration to be established as a PHEI with the status of a university/ university college/branch campus. This has raised the possibility of inequality of consideration and selective decision-making that may lead to the objection of unfair treatment among local and foreign educational institutions. However, as far as transparency is concerned, the establishment and registration processes are clear and unequivocal.

The Minister of Higher Education has the overall discretion to approve the registration of a PHEI but acts on the recommendation of the RG. Thus, the RG's role is significant, as section 9 states, among other things, that the RG may refuse to proceed with the application on technical grounds, such as incomplete information in the application, error or alteration in the application form or where it does not comply with requirements prescribed in section 9(c). Section 9 has to be read with paragraph 5 of the Private Higher Educational Institutions (Establishment) Regulations 1997,[4] as it includes basic criteria for approval, namely, the applicant has, for example, appropriate experience, the ability to provide qualified and experienced teachers, and strong financial provisions. The RG needs to supply notification of any unsuccessful applications under paragraph 6 of the Regulations. Once an establishment is approved, the PHEI must apply to the RG to register the institution. The RG issues a certificate of registration that is valid for five years. Despite the discretion given to the Minister, this is limited according to Malaysian law, as the applicants have recourse through the courts.

Upon approval for establishment, the PHEI is required to incorporate a company under the law with a paid-up capital of not less than RM 20 million for universities and RM 15 million for university colleges and colleges.[5] The Act further states that the equity participation and composition of the board of directors shall be as determined by the Minister.

[4] This is a subsidiary legislation passed by the Minister to provide procedures for processes such as establishment, registration and course of studies for PHEIs.

[5] Authors' interview with the Governance Division of Private Higher Education, MOHE, 20 December 2012.

There is, therefore, no stated limitation in terms of foreign equity ownership in the Act.

The general supervisory powers to ensure that a PHEI is maintaining its overall quality of services and products are provided as part of the Act's underlining goals and objectives. A PHEI must obtain the approval of its course of studies under section 38. The MOHE has the power to decide on the adequacy of educational facilities and determine the quality assurance of the course of studies (section 39), and it has the power to approve and to impose conditions for any course of studies (section 40). Control in certain aspects is quite intensive; for instance, the language of instruction is the national language, Bahasa Melayu, but leeway is given, with ministerial permission. It is to be noted here that the majority of PHEIs use English as the medium of instruction. Pursuing the national policy on the national language, section 42 makes it compulsory for the course on Bahasa Melayu to be taught to local students, and exemption is given to those who have achieved a certain level of proficiency. This, however, cannot be construed as a barrier to entry for foreign PHEIs, as international students are currently exempted from the requirement. Section 43 of the Act also states that PHEIs have to teach compulsory subjects, as determined by the RG, in addition to other subjects or courses of study taught. Malaysian citizens have to obtain a pass in these subjects before they can be awarded their certificate, degree or diploma. The compulsory subjects are Malaysian studies, Bahasa Melayu, and Islamic studies for Muslim students and moral education for non-Muslim students. These are mandatory for domestic students alone. Regulations on the discipline and conduct of students are covered in sections 46 to 49.

As for lecturers, the Permit to Teach (PT) provisions in sections 51 to 53 regulate the qualification and quality of teachers. Before a person is allowed to teach at a PHEI, he or she must obtain a PT. The RG has the power to issue such a permit. A PT specifies the subject taught and if the RG refuses to issue a PT, an appeal may be made to the Minister of Higher Education. Section 52 provides the basis to refuse a PT or grounds to revoke it if the person:

- has no qualification to teach;
- has made a false/misleading statement in the application;
- is not physically or mentally fit;
- has been convicted of an offence of fraud, dishonesty/moral turpitude, corruption, or any punishment of two years' imprisonment or more;
- has acted in a manner prejudicial/detrimental to the interests of Malaysia or the public.

The RG has a duty to give notice and to state reasons for refusal or revocation. The person aggrieved may appeal to the Minister within twenty-one days from the date of refusal or revocation. The main grievance has been that a similar requirement is not imposed on teachers in public universities, whilst the role and qualification is the same.

There are clear and objective requirements for issuance, revocation or refusal of a PT under the Act. The right to be heard is fairly comprehensive. The only concern is the additional reason to revoke on the ground of acting in a manner prejudicial or detrimental to Malaysia, which is considered wide and subjective and gives ample discretionary power to the RG. The Act also provides the power to inspect and to investigate in order to complement the whole process of monitoring. There are also appeal procedures against decisions made by the RG during the process of registration. All appeals are addressed to the Minister. However, there is no provision for an appeal against the Minister's decision during the application for establishment, although PHEIs may apply to challenge the decision in the High Court through a process of judicial review if they are not happy with the Minister's decision.

2.2 *Malaysian Qualifications Agency (MQA) Act 2007 (Act 679)*

By and large, the quality of study courses is not governed by Act 555 even though it does provide for evaluation, including of facilities and infrastructure during the process and renewal of registration. The quality of a course of study is instead regulated under the MQA Act 2007 (Act 679). The Act does not impose a mandatory requirement for a PHEI to apply for accreditation for its course of study. Nonetheless, when a PHEI is applying to renew its registration, a condition applies that its course of study is accredited before renewal is given by the RG. This indirectly makes accreditation an obligation on all PHEIs within the five-year cycle of their registration. There are four other advantages to accredited programmes:

- eligibility for students in accredited programmes to apply for loans from the National Higher Education Fund Corporation;[6]
- international students can only be recruited for accredited programmes;

[6] The fund was established in 1997 to provide subsidized loans to students studying in accredited programmes in public and private institutions of higher learning.

- credit transfer to some other higher education institutions at home and abroad;
- employment in the public sector, as the degrees awarded by accredited programmes are recognized by this sector.

All these advantages are important for attracting students to any given programme and provide strong incentives for PHEIs to seek accreditation.

Act 679 regulates accreditation of academic programmes at all levels offered by public and private higher education institutions in Malaysia. Section 37 states that no academic programme will be accredited if it does not fulfil Malaysian Qualifications Framework (MQF) requirements. All service providers that offer accredited programmes must follow MQF standards. The MQA has the power to grant accreditation (temporary or permanent), and a reason is given when accreditation is not granted. Before accreditation is given, an institutional audit is carried out. Accreditation may be revoked subject to the right to be heard and the right to request for new accreditation. Application for accreditation has clear procedures and requirements, including procedures on professional qualification, whereby a joint technical committee is established with the relevant professional body. The power and procedure to refuse, to revoke or to cancel an accreditation is also provided. Criteria for cancellation include failure to comply with the MQF or breach of an imposed condition. The procedure includes the issuance of notice and an opportunity to make representations within thirty days from the date of the notice. An institutional audit may be carried out for the purpose of accreditation, and a certificate of accreditation may be issued based on the results of the audit. The MQA may impose conditions on the certificate of accreditation, and the certificate may also be amended or revoked.

Procedures and requirements are similar to other accreditation procedures. Self-accreditation status requires the Minister to invite the higher education institution to apply for self-accreditation status, but the provision does not provide the criteria to be used by the Minister. An interview with the MQA reveals that the criteria used are the age of the establishment and its internal quality assurance standard, structure and mechanisms to undertake quality assurance evaluation.[7] The four oldest public universities in Malaysia with research university status were thus granted self-accreditation status in 2010.

[7] Authors' interview with the MQA, 19 December 2012.

Accreditation is not equivalent to recognition, as there is also an exclusion clause where no action lies against the MQA, the relevant professional body, the chief executive officer or officer of the MQA if the certificate issued is not accepted for the purpose of employment or for entry into further education. The two concepts differ, as accreditation is a process whereby the provider is accredited by the MQA as having met a minimum standard and is thus authorized to offer its educational programmes in that area,[8] while recognition of qualifications is for the purposes of employment. Although accredited programmes from the MQA are usually recognized for employment purposes, it is also possible for overseas qualifications that are not accredited by the MQA to be recognized for the same purpose. For foreign and overseas qualifications, accreditation from the MQA is needed as well. Procedures and requirements are similar to other accreditation procedures. Foreign branch campuses that have an established system of quality assurance in their home institution were awarded self-accreditation status in 2010.

Appeal can be made to the Minister within thirty days from the date of decisions that include decisions on provisional accreditation, accreditation and revocation of a certificate. The Minister may confirm, revoke or vary the decision. The Minister's decision is also final and conclusive. The finality of the decision means that appeal is not available. The only recourse is by way of judicial review, such as by bringing the case to the High Court to challenge the decision on administrative legal grounds.

3 Regulatory practices

Both the MOHE and the MQA have issued guidelines that can be downloaded from their websites to guide potential applicants on the process. *Guidebook: PHEI Management Sector*,[9] the guidelines from the MOHE, follows the Act in terms of the stages of approval for starting a PHEI in Malaysia. All charges or fees, application duration, validity period, as well as preconditions in terms of supporting documents and referred agencies, are clearly stated in the guidelines. The guidebook also states that application procedures are reviewed from time to time in line with amendments of the Act and regulations and to manage the quality of PHEIs in the country. However, the guidelines are silent on the criteria

[8] *Regulatory Issues in Sectors and Modes of Supply: Note by the Secretariat*, WTO doc. S/WPDR/W/48, 13 June 2012.

[9] Available at http://jpt.mohe.gov.my/IPT/guidebook%20IPTS.pdf.

used for inviting PHEIs to apply. These criteria are, however, in internal documents and circulars at the MOHE, although they are not made publicly available. Furthermore, the extent of foreign equity permitted is also not mentioned. Despite the lack of transparency, there are no recorded complaints related to the above matters.

Similarly, the MQA provides the MQF, as the framework for quality assurance, with supplementary guidelines, so that each institution can work on quality assurance and improvements in their standards based on the minimum standards provided by the MQA. The guidelines are the 'Code of Practice for Programme Accreditation' and the 'Code of Practice for Institutional Audit'. They provide the minimum and enhanced standards for assuring quality.

Institutions that have been conducting transnational programmes that were accredited in their home institutions did not understand why they had to undergo accreditation again with the MQA, thereby contributing to some of the dissatisfaction with the MQA requirements (Tham 2012). For example, many universities and colleges in the United Kingdom offer their higher education programmes in Malaysia. Their provision overseas is monitored and audited by the Quality Assurance Agency for Higher Education in the United Kingdom. It is in the interest of reputable parent institutions to ensure that the principle of offering the same degree as that offered in the parent institution is adhered to. Case studies investigating the export of twinning programmes and offshore degree programmes from Australia to Malaysia have shown that this happens in the case of accountancy education (Cooper and Adams 1997). This duplication has cost implications on providers because colleges usually offer several majors for each twinning programme and are charged for each major that is accredited (Tan 2002). In turn, this will affect the affordability of the programmes offered and the viability of PHEIs, as they are completely dependent on fees for their income.

Domestic capacity for forming review panels for quality assurance, with the requisite training and knowledge (especially for highly specialized courses), may not be readily available and this may lengthen the time needed to obtain the necessary accreditation. However, for PHEIs, a lengthy accreditation process constitutes a high opportunity cost, and this may deter them from offering highly specialized courses that may be needed to meet the human capital needs of the country (Bashir 2007; Tham and Kam 2007). Bottlenecks in the accreditation process are one of the five challenges identified in the Economic Transformation Plan (ETP) for this sector. Nevertheless, the processing time has improved significantly from the early days of accreditation under the National Accreditation Board (Lembaga Akreditasi Negara, LAN) that preceded the MQA, and it has been shortened from six to twelve months to about seven months.[10] All approved programmes are available online on the MQA website. As of 2009, there were a total of 7,074 programmes offered by PHEIs, of which 2,167 (31 per cent) had obtained full accreditation.

Due to the huge diversity in PHEIs in the country, different types have different supporting infrastructures, capacities and capabilities to meet the demands for assuring quality. For example, some PHEIs have well-developed internal quality assurance systems and a dedicated unit to meet the standards of the foreign partners of their transnational programmes and the requirements of the LAN. These institutions, therefore, have fewer problems with meeting the minimum standards of the MQA. Others, however, have to learn to do so and, hence, there are some complaints that new course approvals and accreditation processes remain cumbersome and expensive (Tham and Kam 2007; Nga 2009).

Since 2007, the MOHE has instituted two separate rating systems for teaching and learning at undergraduate level for universities, and university colleges and colleges, which is essentially based on their compliance with MQA requirements. The idea behind the rating is to encourage continual improvement, with specific incentives given to public and private institutions for achieving an excellent rating, such as entitlement to local and foreign government sponsored students, government research grants, enrolment of more postgraduate students, flexibility and exemptions in applying for teaching permits, and seeking approval for setting the salaries of foreign lecturers, as well as exemptions from obtaining approval for setting tuition fees and automatic enrolment of international students. In turn, these ratings are used as a marketing tool by PHEIs in their recruitment of both domestic and international students.

Accreditation does not imply recognition, especially outside Malaysia. However, the MQA has conducted benchmarking exercises with quality assurance bodies in Australia, India, the United Kingdom and many others to ensure that the minimum standards are comparable to world standards. The MQA is also a member of the International Network for Quality Assurance Agencies in Higher Education, the ASEAN Quality Assurance Network, the Asia-Pacific Quality Network and the

[10] Authors' interview with the MQA, 19 December 2012.

Association of Quality Assurance of the Islamic World. Although the membership rules do not include the right of accreditation by other members, the sharing of knowledge and information at the network meetings makes it easier for country members to persuade their government to accord recognition to the degrees accredited by the MQA. Hence, membership of these organizations facilitates the acceptance of MQA accreditation by other member countries.

Another way to achieve international recognition for accreditation activities is to sign Mutual Recognition Agreements (MRAs) with other countries for accreditation of academic programmes. This has been done with China (820 universities) and Chinese Taipei. Sources from the MQA have indicated that three countries have recognized accreditation issued by the MQA: Brunei Darussalam, Oman and Yemen. The government also plans to sign more MRAs in the future.

4 Interface between trade liberalization and domestic regulations

4.1 Summary of existing trade commitments

The private higher education sector was first offered under the ASEAN Framework of Services (AFAS) Package 5, which was signed during the Thirty-eighth ASEAN Economic Ministers Meeting, on 22 August 2006, in Kuala Lumpur. Malaysia has so far committed the higher education sector in the revised offers of the Doha Round of the World Trade Organization, the ASEAN AFAS, extra ASEAN agreements such as the ASEAN–China Agreement on Trade in Services (ACTIS), the ASEAN–Japan Comprehensive Economic Partnership (AJCEP), the ASEAN–Korea Free Trade Agreement (AKFTA) and the ASEAN–Australia–New Zealand Free Trade Agreement (AANZFTA), as well as the four bilateral agreements with Australia (Malaysia–Australia Free Trade Agreement, MAFTA), Japan (Malaysia–Japan Economic Partnership Agreement, MJEPA), New Zealand (Malaysia–New Zealand Free Trade Agreement, MNZFTA) and Pakistan (Malaysia–Pakistan Free Trade Agreement, MPFTA).

Overall, the commitments have not changed significantly since the revised offers were submitted to the General Agreement on Trade in Services (GATS) in December 2005 (Tham 2012). In Mode 1, it is unbound for both market access and national treatment. In the case of market access, two types of limitations are listed. The first limitation listed in the MJEPA and ACTIS are franchise and twinning arrangements between foreign-based institutions and Malaysian-based educational institutions, and the second in other agreements is the requirement of commercial presence.

For Mode 2, the earlier limitations inscribed in the GATS revised offers for market access have been removed in subsequent FTAs. For example, there are no limitations inscribed at all in the MNZFTA signed in October 2009.

In Mode 3, for market access, the main limitations are equity constraints, the economic needs test and specific types of courses preferred. Foreign equity is restricted to 49 per cent in all the agreements, except for the MPFTA, the AANZFTA, the MNZFTA and the MAFTA, with the highest foreign equity cap found in the MAFTA, as there are no limitations on foreign equity by 2015, with no economic needs test. However, more than 49 per cent of foreign equity is also listed as possible for specific courses in the revised offers for GATS, the MJEPA and ACTIS. In reality, the government has already allowed 100 per cent foreign equity ownership in the case of one of the branch campuses in the country. Hence, existing commitments fall short of current practices.

Commitments in Mode 4 are mainly unbound, except as indicated in the horizontal commitments for market access and national treatment, and in the case of the AKFTA, the AANZFTA, the MNZFTA and the MAFTA. The latter four agreements have a cap placed on the number of lecturers and experts who can be brought in.

4.2 *Interface with domestic regulations*

In Mode 1, imports of franchise and twinning programmes are governed by MQA accreditation and approval before the local franchise holder or college, including branch campuses, can be established and run the programme in Malaysia.

Programmes under the distance education mode are included under section 56 of the MQA Act. The MQA Act does not define 'distance education', but this is defined in Act 555 as:

> instruction or training on or teaching of higher education –
>
> (a) exclusively through the medium of electronics;
> (b) exclusively through correspondence;
> (c) partly through the medium of electronics and partly through correspondence and other methods of instruction, training or teaching; or
> (d) partly through the medium of electronics and partly through correspondence or other methods of instruction, training or teaching.

This implies that a PHEI has to apply for accreditation of a programme, irrespective of the mode of instruction. However, nothing in Act 555 imposes a mandatory requirement for a foreign PHEI that offers a distance education programme to apply to register its programme with the Malaysian authority. It is also to be noted that the Communications and Multimedia Act 1998 does not cover distance education programmes offered in the cyberworld. The Act covers four categories of licensable activities: network facilities providers, network services providers, applications service providers and content application service providers. A senior official of the MOHE confirmed that distance education over the Internet does not require a special licence for the services under the Act. Local law will only apply (the MQA Act and Act 555) upon application for accreditation or application to establish a PHEI. Hence, it is not possible to regulate distance education from outside the country without a local commercial presence. Degrees awarded by such distance education would not be recognized in Malaysia for employment purposes with the government.

There are no regulations currently covering outbound programmes. As more and more PHEIs are venturing offshore, there are increasing concerns and ongoing internal discussions regarding the regulation of offshore programmes in order to preserve the reputation of Malaysia's PHEIs.

For Mode 2, there are no regulations on outbound students. Degrees from outside Malaysia, especially from the developed world, are often perceived to be better in terms of training given to the students. In terms of public employment, the government has a list of universities that it recognizes, while professional bodies also have their respective list of overseas institutions that they recognize for the purposes of employment.

Inbound students require a student visa. Details of application for student visas are readily obtained from several websites, such as the MOHE's website or from http://studymalaysia.com. The issuance of visas requires coordination between the MOHE, the Ministry of Home Affairs, which licenses approved institutions to recruit international students, and the Immigration Department, which issues the visas. This can be cumbersome, as visas are given for each academic session rather than the whole duration of the programme. Increasing evidence of visa abuse from colleges with dubious international students engaged in drug trafficking and Internet scams[11] has led the government to impose additional

[11] 'Shady and Lucrative', *The Sun*, 17 December 2012.

requirements, such as the issuance of a No Objection Certificate as well as an offer letter before a visa and student pass can be issued.[12] It has also been announced recently that, as of 2013, international students will have to take two compulsory subjects: communicational Bahasa Melayu and Malaysian studies.[13]

In the case of Mode 3, although there is no stated equity limitation, the higher education sector was also subject to the guidelines provided by the Foreign Investment Committee (FIC) until it was repealed in 2009. Under the FIC, foreign equity ownership was capped at 30 per cent, although the higher education sector had allowed foreign equity of up to 49 per cent (Tham and Kam 2007). After the FIC ruling was abolished, the amount of foreign equity permitted for higher education was increased to 51 per cent from 31 December 2010 to 31 December 2012 (Tham 2012). Since then, foreign equity of up to 70 per cent has been permitted until 2015, after which 100 per cent foreign equity ownership will be allowed. This has been adjusted to allow for 100 per cent foreign equity ownership for foreign universities only (and not for university colleges or colleges) as of July 2012.[14] However, prior to 2012, foreign equity of up to 51 per cent could be considered, subject to an additional needs test which included, among other things, that the courses were deemed important to Malaysia attaining its educational objectives, and would result in the ability to generate export revenues. It is important to note that the government has the discretion to provide 100 per cent foreign equity ownership and has, in fact, practised this discretion to liberalize autonomously on a selective basis.

Besides the existing five branch campuses, there are many more reported to be in the pipeline, especially at the Educity in Iskandar Malaysia, in the southernmost tip of the country. Moreover, there are also private universities that have foreign equity which are not branch campuses, as these universities award their own degrees and not degrees from their foreign affiliated institution (Lane 2011), such as INTI International University and Manipal University. Some Malaysian universities have also established branch campuses or offices abroad, such as Limkokwing University and the Asia Pacific Institute of Information

[12] 'Entry into Higher Learning Institutions for Foreigners Tightened', *New Straits Times*, 19 July 2012.

[13] See www.mysinchew.com.

[14] Authors' interview with the Governance Division of Private Higher Education, MOHE, 20 December 2012.

Technology, and there is increasing concern about the governance of exported Malaysian programmes.

As for Mode 4, although it is unbound, the application for a PT, which has a validity of two years for foreign staff and five years for local staff, is taking its toll on PHEIs. There are suggestions that a PT should be given for life and to the actual holder and not based on the institution at which the teacher is employed. Lecturers may take the PT wherever they go. This requirement and the requirement of an invitation from the Minister before an application can be made have been considered to be burdensome enough for the Malaysian Association of Private Colleges and Universities to appeal to the Performance Management and Delivery Unit[15] to review Act 555 in 2011. Consequently, the MOHE has convened a group of local consultants to review the Act, in consultation with associations representing the different providers in the country. The review is expected to be finalized in 2013.

5 Conclusion

Private higher education has evolved and grown tremendously since the enactment of the PHEI Act 1996. Trade in higher education services has also grown in tandem with the development of PHEIs to the extent that Malaysia is not just a sending country but it is also increasing in its importance as a receiving country for international students from the developing world. Despite this, Malaysia is generally cautious about making irreversible commitments in its service sector, including the higher education sector. Since private higher education is a relatively mature and open sector, making binding markets will offer greater predictability that could attract more investors and students.

While the industry has well-established regulatory structures and procedures to safeguard students' interests, enforcing and monitoring compliance can be difficult given the large number of providers, while the MOHE has limited human resources (Tham 2010). This has given rise to the presence of delinquent institutions and visa abuse by dubious students, despite increasing efforts to enforce and monitor compliance leading to a drastic drop in the number of institutions from over 700 to over 400 in the last decade (Tham 2012). The government will, therefore, have to accelerate its efforts to weed out dubious institutions

[15] This is a special unit established in the Prime Minister's department in 2010 to oversee the ETP that was formulated to propel Malaysia to a high-income economy by 2020.

and international students to further rationalize the industry and strengthen the quality of private higher education in the country.

In view of Malaysia's experience in regulating the development of private and public higher institutions, additional international disciplines on domestic regulations that can assist trade in this sector have to facilitate quality assurance, accreditation and recognition. In the case of quality assurance and accreditation, regularly published self-reviews of a country's practices, benchmarked against best practices, will help policy-makers, providers and students to better understand the practices. It will also enhance transparency in these issues. Regulatory cooperation in recognition will also help providers and consumers to have cross-border learning experiences and their credits transferred.

References

Bashir, S. (2007), *Trends in International Trade in Higher Education: Implications and Options for Developing Countries*, Education Working Paper Series, Washington, DC: World Bank

Cooper, B.J. and Adams, K. (1997), 'The Export of Accountancy Education to Malaysia and Singapore: An Australian Experience', *Asian Review of Accounting* 5(2): 109–23

Lane, J.E. (2011), 'Importing Private Higher Education: International Branch Campuses', *Journal of Comparative Policy Analysis: Research and Practice* 13(4): 367–81

MOHE (2009), *Private Higher Educational Institutions Act 1996*, Putrajaya: Ministry of Higher Education

MQA (2007), *Malaysian Qualifications Agency Act 2007*, Kuala Lumpur: Malaysian Qualifications Agency

Nga, J.C.L. (2009), *The Internationalization of Malaysian Private Higher Education Institutions for Increasing Higher Education Exports*, DBA thesis, Southern Cross University, Lismore, Australia

Tan, A.M. (2002), *Malaysian Private Higher Education: Globalisation, Privatisation, Transformation and Marketplaces*, London: ASEAN Academic Press

Tham, S.Y. (2010), 'Trade in Higher Education Services in Malaysia: Key Policy Challenges', *Higher Education Policy* 23(1): 99–22

(2012), 'Malaysia's Trade and Regulations in Tertiary Education', paper presented at the ADBI–OECD Conference on International Trade in Services, New Delhi, 18–19 January 2012

Tham, S.Y. and Kam, J.Y.A. (2007), 'Trade and Investment Linkages in Higher Education Services in Malaysia' in *Towards Coherent Policy Framework: Understanding Trade and Investment Linkages*, Studies in Trade and Investment 62, New York: Economic and Social Commission for Asia and the Pacific

15

Domestic regulations and India's trade in health services: a study of hospital and telemedicine services

RUPA CHANDA AND PRALOK GUPTA

1 Introduction

Estimated at US$36 billion and employing over four million people, the Indian health care sector is one of the largest service sectors in the economy today. With a compound annual growth rate (CAGR) of 15 per cent, the Indian health care sector is expected to reach US$280 billion by 2020.[1] A 2003 report titled *India's New Opportunity: 2020*, prepared jointly by the All India Management Association, Boston Consulting Group and the Confederation of Indian Industries, predicts that over 40 million new jobs and US$200 billion increased revenues are expected to be generated by the Indian services sector by 2020, and the health care sector will play an important role in generating these jobs and revenues (AIMA/BCG 2003). Hence, this sector is predicted to grow rapidly and is seen to have considerable potential due to the growing demand for health care services in India. The reasons are many, including rising incomes, a growing propensity to spend on health care, an emergence of lifestyle-related diseases, and demographics.

Given the growing demand, the emergence of reputable private operators, and the vast investment needs in this sector, there has been growing interest among foreign investors and non-resident Indians to enter the Indian health care market to explore investment opportunities in areas such as drugs and pharmaceuticals, medical devices and hospitals. In the hospitals and medical devices sector alone, at least twenty international groups are competing to have a share in the Indian health care market. These investors enter mainly through joint ventures with

[1] Health care sector information available at www.ibef.org/artdisplay.aspx?cat_id=60&art_id=29869

Indian companies but also through technology and training collaborations (Chanda 2010). Another emerging field is telemedicine, which is about providing health care at a distance, either online or over the phone. In this sector, India has the potential to provide state-of-the-art services at cost-effective rates.

Paradoxically, India's health care is both over- and under-regulated, that is, some aspects of health services are subject to many regulations which adversely affect the availability of them, and some others are either poorly regulated or not at all, so that there is an adverse effect on the quality of these services in India.[2] Areas of regulation that are pertinent to trade include standards for medical establishments, accreditation of medical professionals and foreign direct investment (FDI). Regulations in some of these areas are still evolving, but there has been considerable streamlining in recent years to establish and improve standards and ensure governance in various segments of the Indian health care sector. It is to be noted that, though the growing potential in this sector is highlighted in reports by industry associations and consulting firms, very little has been discussed regarding domestic regulations.

This chapter examines the prevailing regulatory environment in two important segments of the Indian health care sector – hospital and telemedicine services – and discusses how domestic regulations affect India's imports and exports of these two segments, respectively. Section 2 examines the key areas of domestic regulation affecting trade in hospital services in the form of FDI or Mode 3 of the General Agreement on Trade in Services (GATS).[3] Section 2 also provides a quantitative index for these regulations to highlight their incidence, as well as the trends in liberalizing FDI in India's hospital services. Section 3 discusses domestic regulations affecting India's exports of telemedicine services through cross-border supply or GATS Mode 1. The analysis is mainly based on

[2] For example, there are many regulations on the setting up of medical educational establishments in terms of size and acreage, requirements which affect the supply of such institutions. On the other hand, there is wide variation in the standard of medical education and training across the country due to lack of stringent regulations on the certification of such establishments, resulting in a wide variation in the quality of medical manpower produced in the country.

[3] GATS distinguishes between four modes of supplying services: Mode 1 (cross-border trade); Mode 2 (consumption abroad); Mode 3 (commercial presence); and Mode 4 (presence of natural persons). Mode 1 is defined as services flowing from the territory of one member into the territory of another. Mode 3 occurs when a service supplier of one member establishes a territorial presence, including through investment, ownership or lease of premises, in another member's territory to provide a service.

discussions and interviews with various stakeholders in the Indian health care sector, conducted by one of the authors, in two separate studies: a 2007 study for the World Health Organization (WHO) and the Indian Ministry of Health on FDI in Indian hospitals; and a 2008–2009 study for the Ministry of Commerce on India's exports of health services, including telemedicine exports.[4] Section 4 concludes by summarizing the commonalities across both these sectors and provides some policy prescriptions to facilitate imports of hospital services through GATS Mode 3 and exports of telemedicine services through GATS Mode 1.

2 Hospital services imports through FDI

In India, FDI in hospitals can take place either through the automatic route or after receiving Foreign Investment Promotion Board (FIPB) approval. Since January 2000, up to 100 per cent of FDI in hospitals is allowed under the automatic route system. Thus, FIPB approval is not required as long as the Indian company correctly files documentation with the regional office of the Reserve Bank of India, India's central bank, within thirty days of receipt of inward remittances and submits the required documents along with form FC-GPR (Foreign Collaboration – General Permission Route) to the regional office within thirty days of issue of shares to the non-resident investors. A controlling stake in hospitals is also permitted for foreign investors. FIPB approval is currently only required for foreign investors with prior technical collaboration, but up to 100 per cent investment is permitted (Chanda 2010).

Some other forms of capital mobilization are also permitted and treated as FDI by current regulations in India. For instance, Indian companies can raise foreign currency resources abroad through the issue of American Depositary Receipts or Global Depositary Receipts, in accordance with the Issue of Foreign Currency Convertible Bonds and Ordinary Shares (Through Depository Receipt Mechanism) Scheme, 1993 and guidelines issued periodically by the Indian government.[5] Such investments are also treated as FDI.[6]

[4] See Chanda 2007 and Chanda 2011 for details on the survey methodology, coverage and discussion of results.

[5] More information on this scheme is available from www.moneycontrol.com/mccode/news/lp_news_detail.php?autono=2659.

[6] Reserve Bank of India, *Master Circular on Foreign Investment in India*, Master Circular No. 13/2010–11, 1 July 2010.

However, the government has laid down associated terms and conditions that any foreign investment in hospital services must follow (Government of India 2012):

> (5) The project shall conform to the norms and standards, including land use requirements and provision of community amenities and common facilities, as laid down in the applicable building control regulations, bye-laws, rules, and other regulations of the State Government/Municipal/Local Body concerned.
>
> (6) The investor/investee company shall be responsible for obtaining all necessary approvals, including those of the building/layout plans, developing internal and peripheral areas and other infrastructure facilities, payment of development, external development and other charges and compliance with all other requirements as prescribed under applicable rules/bye-laws/regulations of the State Government/Municipal/Local Body concerned.
>
> (7) The State Government/Municipal/Local Body concerned, which approves the building/development plans, would monitor compliance of the above conditions by the developer.

2.1 Domestic regulations and FDI in hospital services

The following discussion highlights the regulatory constraints restricting FDI in India's hospital services, based on the interviews carried out with practitioners, management, officials, industry associations and academics for the Chanda (2007) study. The discussions indicated that the regulations make it difficult to invest in India's hospital segment, by raising the costs of establishment as well as the costs of supplying hospital services. The latter, in turn, adversely affects the profitability of hospital services but also reduces its attractiveness for foreign investment. Two points are worth noting. First, many of these regulatory issues are constraints not only for foreign investors, but also for domestic investors. Second, many of these regulations are in areas such as education, insurance and technology, which are related to, but do not directly fall within, the hospital segment.

2.1.1 Medical equipment and technology

One of the regulatory constraints cited by several stakeholders pertains to the procurement of medical devices and technologies. The latter constitutes around 30 per cent of all fixed assets of hospitals (Chanda 2007). Seventy per cent or more of medical devices are imported, often at high cost due to relatively high import duties. Respondents noted problems arising from regulatory formalities such as end-use requirements and paperwork associated with the import of such equipment. High import duties and regulatory requirements raise the overall procurement and operating costs of hospitals, which decreases the profitability of investing. Respondents called for further rationalization of import duties on medical equipment and technologies, and the introduction of flat, uniform rates for a wide range of medical devices, simplification of associated bureaucracy and the removal of conditions on end-use and performance requirements.

2.1.2 Manpower availability and quality issues

FDI (as well as domestic private investment) in hospital services is also affected by the availability, cost and quality of human resources at all levels (i.e. doctors, nurses, paramedics, support staff, managers and administrators). Respondents primarily attributed the existing shortage of quality human resources in India's health care sector to a set of arcane regulations which impede the establishment of medical training institutions, thus creating a bottleneck in the supply of doctors and nurses. Some respondents specifically cited the guidelines laid down by the Medical Council of India (MCI) regarding the setting up of medical schools and training facilities, which permit only government or trust hospitals to set up education facilities. Moreover, there are conditions on the amount of land required, and the number of classrooms and their size. For instance, hospitals are required to be 500-bed units in order to obtain permission for establishing training colleges. The health care education facility is required to be at least a ten-acre campus. This requirement is also applicable to education facilities set up by private hospitals. The entire regulatory approach for establishing medical education facilities is based on infrastructure and volume rather than focusing on quality and functional excellence. Ironically, while the MCI has not permitted corporate hospitals to set up training facilities because of failing to meet regulatory requirements, it has permitted a plethora of substandard, private medical colleges, which have political patronage and make money through huge capitation fees.[7] Many of these private institutes lack basic faculty equipment and infrastructure and are unable to provide relevant and high-quality training.

[7] Capitation fee refers to the collection of payment, not advertised in the prospectus of the institution, by educational bodies, usually in exchange for admission to the institution.

Similarly, the Nursing Council does not allow private operators to enter into nursing education unless they form trusts. Hospitals need to tie up with another organization in order to grant a postgraduate diploma in hospital administration. Again, the institutions are required to have a 500-seat auditorium and twenty-five acres of contiguous land – conditions which are often difficult to fulfil in large Indian cities – and not necessarily an imperative for turning out a large number of quality professionals.

The fallout from these inappropriate regulations on the establishment of medical education and training facilities is that the supply of doctors and nurses is indirectly restricted. This leads to higher manpower costs for both foreign investors and domestically owned hospitals. Management at leading hospitals noted that the shortage of high-quality personnel has caused the cost of the most-talented to rise by around 20 per cent per year and by around 50 to 60 per cent for junior and middle level health personnel (Chanda 2007). Hospitals are coping with the manpower constraint in different ways. Some share resources across different centres or call in additional manpower from other locations for critical treatments and emergencies. Some plan for up to 30 per cent overcapacity to ensure consistent service-quality delivery, incurring additional costs. Hospitals are also encouraging existing technicians to upgrade through training. Some private hospitals operate in partnership with overseas institutions, such as medical schools in the United Arab Emirates, for staff training. Since employee development is important, the initial period often consists of extensive training programmes, which can be expensive and are a major deterrent for many entrepreneurs, both foreign and domestic.

2.1.3 Health insurance

FDI in hospitals is also constrained by regulations affecting the health insurance sector and the low level of insurance penetration in India. The current policy permits only 26 per cent FDI participation through joint ventures in the insurance sector, along with minimum capital requirements (Government of India 2012). Several respondents noted that limited insurance penetration in India effectively reduces the size of the market which can be served by FDI-based hospitals, thereby affecting the attractiveness of the hospital services segment to foreign investors. Moreover, the absence of adequate regulations with regard to classification of procedures, standardization of guidelines, malpractice and fraudulent claims, inhibits the expansion of the insurance sector and the entry of foreign providers. Hence, there is clearly a synergistic relationship between the expansion of health insurance and the growth of corporate hospitals (domestic or foreign) in India.

2.1.4 Other regulations

Another regulatory issue is that of standards, accreditation and registration guidelines for setting up hospitals and nursing homes. The respondents pointed out that the Indian government does not have a proper framework to guide the establishment of new hospitals and nursing homes. It does not set benchmarks for service delivery, nor does it demand that stakeholders comply with basic norms. It also does not carry out any kind of local or zone-based needs assessment before allowing new facilities to register. Furthermore, the absence of a disclosure policy and sharing of information by hospitals has impeded the development of a mature health care delivery system.

Lack of supportive and transparent regulations concerning the procurement of land, as well as delays in obtaining regulatory clearances for setting up supporting infrastructure (such as water supply and electricity), cumbersome regulatory requirements and corruption were all cited as constraints to both foreign and domestic investor-owned hospitals.[8]

Overall, discussions with stakeholders revealed a lack of transparency and predictability in the policy environment with adverse effects on the interests of foreign investors, undermining the otherwise liberal FDI regulations in India's hospital services segment.

2.2 Quantifying domestic regulations affecting FDI in hospital services

An attempt is made to quantify the prevailing regulations affecting FDI in hospital services in India and related trends to assess the extent and nature of liberalization.

The regulatory barriers are classified into two categories: at the border (AtB) barriers; and behind the border (BtB) barriers. AtB barriers are

[8] Project costs, land and construction of buildings constitute around 40 per cent to 50 per cent of total project costs, with medical equipment accounting for around 40 per cent and the remaining 10 to 20 per cent for operational expenses and human resources. If a hospital spends a higher share of the investment cost on procuring land, this will affect the pricing of services which, along with other operational, maintenance and technology upgrading costs, puts pressure on margins and increases service costs and ultimately the level of healthcare affordability (see Chanda 2007).

barriers affecting the entry decisions of a foreign firm, such as FDI limits and form of entity. BtB barriers are those which affect operations of a foreign firm, such as licensing and authorization requirements, and taxation. Both the AtB and BtB regimes must be liberalized for full liberalization of a service sector, otherwise easier market-entry conditions (liberal AtB regime) may be nullified by restrictive BtB conditions. This study quantifies both AtB and BtB barriers for GATS Mode 3 in hospital services for India by creating a Trade Restrictiveness Index (TRI) for selected years during 1996–2011.[9]

The trends in the indices, presented in Figure 15.1, indicate a significant degree of liberalization in AtB regulations over the years. The value of the AtB TRI in 2011 is close to zero, showing almost complete openness of the sector to the entry of foreign stakeholders in India's hospital services, as up to 100 per cent of FDI has been allowed through the automatic route since 2000. Earlier, it was only partially allowed and through government approval only. The market structure has also become more competitive over time, with the emergence of private operators. The BtB indices trends, however, indicate that there has been relatively less liberalization in BtB regulations compared to AtB regulations. As seen earlier, the main BtB restrictions relate to regulations concerning medical education, insurance, standards and setting up of establishments. The continued presence of BtB regulatory barriers possibly explains the limited FDI realized thus far in India's hospital services sector, notwithstanding the liberal FDI policies in existence since 2000. According to data from the Department of Industrial Policy and Promotion, FDI equity inflows in hospital and diagnostic centres for April 2000–October 2012 period, amounted to only US$1.48 billion, or 0.80 per cent of total FDI equity inflows (US$185 billion) in India (DIPP 2012). Although there have been many proposals for foreign investment in hospital services in India, actual investment has been far

[9] The TRI is calculated by dividing various regulatory barriers into AtB and BtB categories and defining degrees of restrictiveness and assigning scores to each type of regulatory barrier based on the intensity of restriction. Scores range from 0 for the least restrictive to 1 for the most restrictive. For example, for the 'FDI approval process' barrier, 'no automatic approval is allowed' is given a score of 1, as it is the most restrictive, 'FDI is allowed partially through automatic route and beyond a limit through government approval' is given a score of 0.5 due to its moderate intensity and 'FDI is allowed through automatic route' is given a score of 0, as it is the most liberal. The TRI is the sum of the score for each regulation normalized to 1.

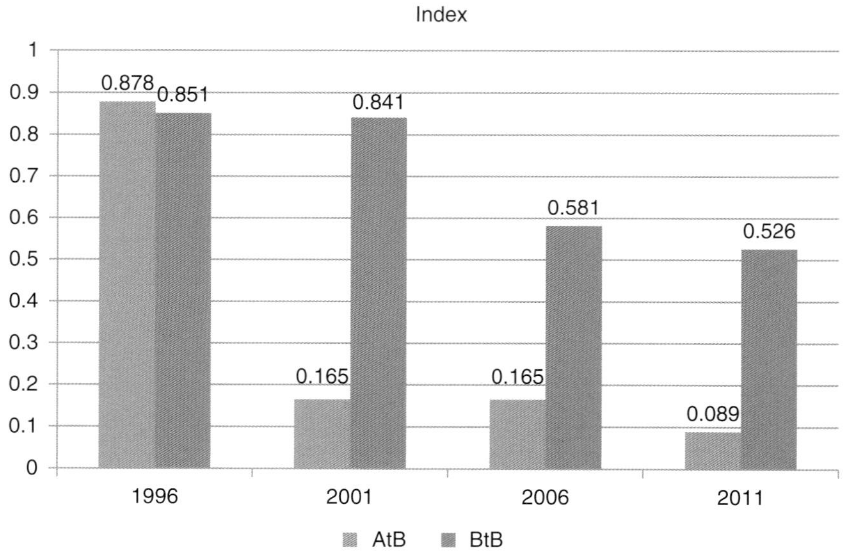

Figure 15.1 TRI for hospital services, selected years
Source: Authors' calculations based on information retrieved from the FDI policies of the Indian government.

lower than approved. Thus, BtB regulations appear to be playing an important role in determining the amount of FDI.

3 Telemedicine services exports

The telemedicine market in India is estimated to be US$7.5 million and is predicted to grow at a CAGR of around 20 per cent over the next five years (Business Standard 2012). Growth in telemedicine in India has been supported by the Indian Space Research Organisation (ISRO), which has provided very small aperture terminal (VSAT) connectivity, hardware and software to various organizations as part of the Indian government's efforts to improve health care access in remote parts of the country. Private partners along with ISRO also provide telemedicine services to neighbouring countries, such as Bhutan, Myanmar and Sri Lanka.

The main telemedicine services offered by Indian providers include teleradiology and telepathology services. At present, India's telemedicine exports are mainly to Singapore and the United States, with the client base expanding to over fifty hospitals in a few years (Economic Times

2006). The National Healthcare Group in Singapore has linked up with telemedicine institutions in India to provide teleradiology services to designated hospitals in Singapore. Contracts have also been signed between telemedicine establishments in India and hospitals in Dubai and Malaysia.

3.1 Domestic regulations affecting India's telemedicine exports

Discussions with leading telemedicine providers as part of the 2008–2009 study on India's exports of health services in Chanda (2011) reveal that, although India's telemedicine exports have been growing rapidly and prospects are bright, a variety of domestic regulations currently affect the realization of the actual potential. These regulations pertain to manpower and training, legal frameworks, standards and data protection.

3.1.1 Manpower

Telemedicine services in India are subject to severe manpower constraints, particularly for teleradiology services. The supply constraints are due to the limited number of training facilities set up. Although telemedicine establishments are interested in training employees in areas such as teleradiology, they are not permitted to do so, as regulations require a medical training institution to have an affiliated 100-bed hospital in order to receive certification for training radiologists. Experts note that, while this requirement is appropriate for general training of radiologists in order to ensure sufficient clinical practice, it is inappropriate in the case of teleradiology, as the latter does not involve in-patient care.

One leading Indian telemedicine firm, which exports teleradiology services to Malaysia, Singapore, the United States and some African countries, reported that it had applied to the national board for permission to provide training but had not been permitted to do so or to award diplomas, as it did not meet the requirement of being affiliated to a 100-bed hospital. It pointed out that it is possible to carry out over 2,000 scans in a telemedicine establishment without having a large number of beds. Moreover, given the possibility for continuing education through e-classes, training websites and investments in software platforms, a telemedicine firm such as theirs has the capability to provide quality training like any traditional medical training institution. The respondent noted that the growing demand–supply imbalance for radiologists, including teleradiologists, is leading to higher costs for Indian telemedicine providers, thus undermining their competitiveness and even forcing them to outsource part of their work to other developing countries, such as the Philippines, in order to contain costs and retain competitive margins.

3.1.2 Malpractice liability

Another concern raised by the respondents was the inadequate regulations concerning malpractice. Respondents noted that existing regulations are ambiguous about liability and jurisdiction in the event of any malpractice. They do not explicitly specify who is liable for any wrong diagnosis with telemedicine services. At present, Indian provider companies purchase malpractice policies in the client country's market and buy separate policies for each contract. As malpractice regulations and the limits of coverage vary across countries, this poses practical difficulties for Indian telemedicine establishments. One respondent noted that breach of contract and jurisdictional issues are likely to pose difficulties in entering into contracts with developed countries, such as EU Member States, where liability regulations are very stringent.

3.1.3 Standards, accreditation of establishments and recognition

Establishment of standards for telemedicine providers and accreditation of telemedicine firms can play an important role in signalling quality and can enable these firms to secure more and higher value contracts from overseas hospitals. Although the introduction of the National Accreditation Board for Hospitals and Healthcare Providers and the National Accreditation Board for Testing and Calibration Laboratories has been a welcome step, at the ground level, quality assurance is still lacking for health care establishments in India. According to respondents, much more needs to be done to improve perceptions regarding India's ability to deliver high-quality health-care services, including telemedicine services, to other markets. Individual telemedicine companies presently receive accreditation from the health ministries of other states, such as Singapore, in order to export telemedicine services to them. Similarly, in the absence of mutual recognition of qualifications, Indian teleradiologists cannot officially validate their readings. This affects the value of the contracts Indian health care providers can secure and also the scope of their work. Lack of mutual recognition of qualifications also has a bearing on the supply of health care personnel in India, as overseas trained radiologists cannot practise in India since their credentials are not currently recognized by the MCI.

3.1.4 Data protection

Absence of data protection legislation is also perceived to be a major regulatory constraint to telemedicine services exports from India. Respondents noted that several overseas authorities, such as those in the European Union, do not deem India to be data secure and thus prohibit outsourcing patient data for telemedicine purposes to Indian providers. Several respondents noted that protection of patient data which is outsourced to telemedicine firms in India is not guaranteed by any national legislation. Rather, the individual firms have to demonstrate their compliance with internationally recognized data protection norms, such as the US law, Health Insurance Portability and Accountability Act of 1996, and BS7799.[10] Discussions indicated that the introduction of a national data protection Act would not only help signal to overseas authorities that data is safe in India, but would also help provide clear and uniform guidelines to Indian telemedicine providers regarding what they can and cannot do and reduce the costs of compliance.

3.1.5 Medical equipment

High costs for procuring medical equipment pose a competitive challenge for Indian telemedicine exporters. Most of this equipment is imported and is subject to relatively high import duties. One exporting firm indicated that Indian telemedicine providers cannot completely pass on the high cost of medical equipment to the final consumer, as they must ensure the affordability of their services to domestic consumers, which in turn affects their margins. Further, costly medical equipment imports also threaten to undermine their cost advantage in the international market. The lack of lower cost, indigenously manufactured equipment required by these firms and, more importantly, the lack of regulations to ensure standardization of quality in the medical equipment industry, affect the competitiveness of telemedicine exporting firms in India.

[10] BS7799, developed by British Standards, has since been adopted as an international standard, ISO 27001.

4 Conclusion: summary and policy implications

This chapter has examined domestic regulations affecting FDI prospects in India's hospitals and telemedicine services exports. One of the main findings is that a variety of domestic regulations within the health care sector, as well as in related areas, constrain the realization of India's trade prospects in these segments. These regulatory constraints arise due to both under- and over-regulation. Although regulation in social-service sectors such as health care or education is justified on public policy grounds, discussions with stakeholders in both the hospital and telemedicine segments indicate that many of the regulatory constraints they face do not serve any public policy objectives. The regulation is either not required given the current realities (such as those pertaining to medical education and training), or these regulations are inadequate or completely absent (such as those pertaining to standards and intellectual property rights). Often, domestic regulations outside the sector (such as in health insurance) also indirectly affect the prospects for trade in health services. Hence, there is a clear need for reforms in terms of strengthening certain regulations as well as liberalizing or removing others. In addition, supportive policies and regulatory frameworks are needed in some areas to facilitate trade in health services and to make it more viable.

Perhaps the single most important area which is over-regulated and where negative disciplines on domestic regulation could be helpful concerns medical education and training. The required regulatory reforms in this regard include the expansion of medical training facilities at all levels and, in particular, the removal of regulations which currently impede the provision of training and awarding of diplomas and degrees by telemedicine firms and corporate hospitals. Aligning the curriculum to international standards and modifying research and training to meet the needs of sectors is also required. Inappropriate regulatory restrictions about who can instruct medical education need to be relaxed, and the focus of medical training needs to shift away from a checklist of meeting physical infrastructural requirements towards quality assurance. Freeing up the provision of medical education by permitting bona fide and reputable private hospitals and telemedicine firms to provide medical education and training, while subjecting them and all other medical training providers to strict quality controls, would help expand the supply of quality medical personnel at all levels and contain rising costs, which otherwise threaten to undermine India's cost advantage in health services trade.

Related to regulatory reforms to ensure adequate supply and quality of human resources is the need to move towards mutual recognition of qualifications in health care, with selected countries having the potential for cross-border engagement in health services. Mutual recognition of qualifications and tiering of medical training institutions would not only facilitate outsourcing of work to India and thus telemedicine exports, but would also benefit other areas of health services trade, such as medical value travel[11] as well as partnerships with overseas institutions and personnel. Agreement on qualifications and standards would also enable India to draw on medical personnel who are trained in other countries, such as EU Member States, particularly the United Kingdom, for work in India, thereby adding to the pool of human resources for both the Indian and overseas markets. The discussions also revealed the need to stipulate minimum standards for establishments in the health care sector, while ensuring that these standards are comprehensive and up-to-date, effectively and regularly monitored, and attuned to ground realities. International best practices need to be followed by initially granting licences based on some form of external evaluation and compliance with minimum standards, followed by frequent audits and disclosure of information for effective quality assurance.[12]

In several areas, domestic regulatory frameworks need to be introduced, improved and made transparent, with many potential spill-over benefits for health services trade and for the health care sector at large. In these areas, positive disciplines on domestic regulation could be helpful. For instance, standardization and classification issues need to be addressed in the area of health insurance to improve penetration. Opening up the insurance sector would facilitate the entry of foreign insurance companies and tie-ups with local insurance companies, thus enabling telemedicine firms engaged in teleradiology exports or corporate hospitals engaged in

[11] 'Medical value travel' is a synonym used for 'medical tourism' implying the practice of travelling across national borders to obtain health care.

[12] Medical establishments which wish to signal their superior quality and standards obtain international accreditation, such as the Joint Commission International and the Joint Commission on the Accreditation of Hospital Organizations. In addition, many countries adopt national standards for their establishments. In India, organizations such as the Quality Council of India and its National Accreditation Board for Hospitals and Health-care Providers set benchmarks for quality and standards and provide a mechanism for quality assurance through a rigorous review process. Around the world, developed and developing countries have instituted national quality assurance and accreditation programmes in their health sectors, with national bodies that are affiliated to the International Society for Quality in Healthcare (see WHO 2003).

medical tourism exports to obtain malpractice insurance with global coverage but at lower cost in India. A national data protection act needs to be introduced to signal that India is a data secure destination for outsourcing health care information.

In some areas, more supportive, transparent and streamlined domestic regulations are required to help health care providers. Measures are needed to facilitate the acquisition of land and other assets and to expedite regulatory clearances and approvals associated with establishing hospitals. Regulations which lower the cost of importing medical equipment and technologies and which incentivize their domestic production and standardization would facilitate technology transfer and help contain these input costs. Such steps would facilitate foreign-investor hospitals, as well as Indian health care providers more generally, to deliver international quality service at affordable prices and to retain their cost advantage in the global market.

Overall, there is a need to recognize the direct and indirect effects of domestic regulations on prospects for exports and imports of health services. There is a synergy across different segments and GATS modes of health services trade between different service subsectors and between goods and services trade. For instance, domestic regulations related to the recognition of qualifications may affect the movement of health professionals between countries. Similarly, conditions on insurance availability for foreign medical treatment may affect medical tourism. The cost and availability of medical equipment may, in turn, affect the supply of health services in a country. Given such synergies, the negotiations and disciplines on domestic regulations should adopt a cross-sectoral or cluster-wise focus (within services and across services and goods) rather than adopting a narrow sectoral approach or an all-inclusive horizontal approach. Such an approach would require domestic regulations to take into account cross-sectoral linkages and implications, without becoming unduly burdensome. They should meet sectoral, subsectoral and cross-sectoral requirements, and should also be flexible enough to adapt to technological and other developments in the concerned, as well as in other related sectors (e.g. insurance). Needless to say, this approach is not limited to health services. It must be kept in mind more generally when designing and implementing domestic regulations in any sector.

References

AIMA/BCG (2003), *India's New Opportunity: 2020*, New Delhi: All India Management Association/Boston Consulting Group

Business Standard (2012), 'KIT: Telemedicine Market in India: Strategic Tools for the Practising Manager', 9 April 2012

Chanda, R. (2007), *Foreign Investment in Hospitals in India: Status and Implications*, Indian Institute of Management Bangalore, in collaboration with WHO Country Office, New Delhi and WTO Cell, Ministry of Health and Family Welfare, Government of India

(2010), 'Constraints to Foreign Direct Investment in Indian Hospitals', *Journal of International Commerce, Economics and Policy* 1(1): 121–43

(2011), 'India–EU Relations in Health Services: Prospects and Challenges', *Globalization and Health* 7(1): 1–13

DIPP (2012), *Fact Sheet on Foreign Direct Investment (FDI): From April 2000 to October 2012*, Department of Industrial Policy and Promotion: Government of India

Economic Times (2006), 'Break a Bone in NY, see X-Ray in B'lore', 3 August

Government of India (2012), *Consolidated FDI Policy*, D/o IPP F. No. 5(2)/2012-FC-I, Ministry of Commerce and Industry: Department of Industrial Policy and Promotion

WHO (2003), *Quality and Accreditation in Health Care Services: A Global Review*, Geneva: World Health Organization

16

Operating integrated logistics services in a fragmented regulatory environment: what is the cost?

RUOSI ZHANG

1 Introduction

The importance of logistics services in both the national and global economy is widely recognized and increasingly more apparent. From the trade perspective, the role of logistics services is twofold: it facilitates the international flow of goods and thus provides key support to trade in goods and global supply chains; and, at the same time, it generates trade flow in its own right and constitutes an important industry in many economies. The significance of logistics services has also been underlined in trade negotiations. In 2004, for the first time in trade negotiations, a group of World Trade Organization (WTO) members advocated considering logistics services as a distinct sector. They defined logistics services as dealing 'with the supply chain process that plans, implements, and controls the efficient and effective point-to-point flow and storage of goods, services and related information, throughout the production, distribution and delivery stages, from the initial suppliers of inputs to final customers of products'.[1] Without ambition to change the current General Agreement on Trade in Services (GATS) classification system, which does not contain a separate category for logistics services, this group of WTO members take a pragmatic checklist approach, encouraging trading partners to undertake commercially meaningful liberalization commitments on all logistics-related sectors. The proposed checklist is very broad, containing about twenty services subsectors which are regrouped into three blocks: core freight logistics; related freight logistics;

[1] *Communication from Australia; Hong Kong, China; Liechtenstein; Mauritius; New Zealand; Nicaragua; Switzerland; and the Separate Customs Territory of Taiwan, Penghu, Kinmen and Matsu: Logistics Services*, WTO doc. TN/S/W/20, 25 June 2004.

and non-core freight logistics. Identified core freight logistics services include cargo handling, storage and warehousing, transport agency and other auxiliary services to transport.

Together with its increased visibility in trade, logistics services have evolved significantly in coverage and complexity.[2] At the same time, more trade is taking place in the sector than before, as more and more logistics services have become tradable thanks to outsourcing and other emerging business models as well as information technologies. With economies closely interconnected through supply chains, an economy's overall competitiveness is now positively correlated with its ability to participate in global supply chains, and its logistics performance plays a crucial role in this respect. To improve logistics performance has become one of the priority economic policies for most countries, especially developing countries whose logistics industry is much less advanced. Foreign investment is widely accepted as an important means to enhance logistics capacity. While adequate infrastructure (e.g. such as highways, railways, ports and airports) is essential for an efficient and reliable logistics services, it has been recognized that good logistics performance also requires that a supportive regulatory environment be put in place.

This chapter examines the regulatory factor in logistics services against the backdrop of the integration trend in the sector. In particular, a case study is undertaken to see how China's regulatory framework affects its logistics performance. From the example of China and studies elsewhere, this chapter attempts to draw some general observations.

2 Integration as both a market trend and a regulatory challenge

Logistics functions used to be carried out by in-house departments in enterprises. As outsourcing has become a trend in business since 1990s,

[2] There is no uniform definition of logistics. In the business world, the concept of logistics has been evolving over decades. It is believed to be inspired by the military operations dealing with the procurement, distribution, maintenance and replacement of military materiel and personnel. In the early stages, in the 1960s and 1970s, logistics mainly meant managing a set of freight transport-related activities to ensure the efficient delivery of finished goods to customers. In the 1980s and 1990s, logistics was viewed as an integrated process combining internal material management with the outbound distribution of finished goods. Since 2000, logistics has been associated with supply chain management, which is not only about coordinating logistics activities, but also integrating logistics activities with other functions, including production planning and scheduling, sourcing and procurement, manufacturing, marketing, financing, and managing information flow.

with a view to reducing costs and increasing efficiency, more and more enterprises contract specialized firms to operate logistics activities for them. A recent logistics survey shows that the predominant direction among shippers is to move toward increased use of outsourced logistics services (Langley 2012). To meet customers' needs and requirements as well as to explore new business space, traditional freight forwarders, couriers and transportation companies have engaged in broader and more complex logistics operations. For example: in a warehouse, in addition to warehousing services, providers now also supply packaging, labelling, cargo consolidation, even repair services; in transportation, service suppliers provide transportation management solutions that manage and distribute information to their customers over global networks. A term, 'third party logistics (3PL) provider', is now widely used to refer to a company providing multiple logistics services to their customers.[3]

The strongest driving force behind logistics outsourcing is probably the delocalization of production at the global level. A manufacturing company requires logistics support in production planning, material procurement, production assembly and delivery of the finished product. As production is fragmented and delocalized globally and new technologies are used to shorten product development cycles and respond more quickly to customers, efficient logistics has become a crucial competitive edge, especially for companies that are expanding in global markets. In this context, operating logistics has become more challenging than ever. Not only has the logistics chain extended geographically, but also more activities and business processes need to be coordinated among players up and down the supply chain. More than transporting goods from one point to another, logistics is today closely connected to organizing and monitoring the entire supply chain. With logistics tasks becoming increasingly complex, it has been widely recognized that they are better assumed by specialized companies (i.e. logistics services providers). The latter identify and grasp the opportunities to become involved in the whole process, from raw materials to work-in-process

[3] 'The functional as well as the geographic purview of third party logistics management services have expanded over time. Third party services providers offer their clients a constantly increasing variety of options ranging from narrow ones, for example, ones limited to managing various aspects of physical distribution, to broad ones, including ones which involve them actively managing various aspects of clients' supply chains, providing them with customer service support, such as equipment installation, recycling and product re-use and re-manufacture' (Kopicki 2009: 18).

inventory to finished goods. Dramatic advances in information technology (IT) have enabled and accelerated such evolution.[4]

Integration has probably been the most remarkable trend in logistics evolution over the past two decades. One can say that today's logistics is all about integration. From the supply chain perspective, to provide logistics services is to integrate logistics into the supply chain management.[5] This is demand-driven and becomes more challenging than before, but it also offers more business opportunities. Those companies that are sourcing and distributing globally often prefer to deal with a single party for their logistics support in order to ensure the connectivity of their supply chains. They also increasingly look to form strategic partnership with their logistics suppliers in order to take advantage of the latter's widespread knowledge and networks. Logistics services providers, especially globally networked multinationals, respond by providing integrated logistics solutions to meet their customers' demands.[6] With the reach of logistics services expanding globally, trade flow in logistics services has also increased significantly.

Efficiency and reliability are usually the main indicators to assess logistics performance. Good policies or regulations appear to be those that may help increase competition, lower costs, expedite delivery, and reduce uncertainty and risks.[7] As logistics services tend to be provided in an integrated manner and are associated with supply chains, the potential impact on supply chains can also be an important parameter to judge policies and regulations affecting logistics. The understanding is that the supply-chain connectivity should be ensured and the integrated process

[4] Logistics is one of the most important commercial areas of IT application. For example, thanks to barcodes and radio frequency identification technology, real-time information can be stored and transmitted using such tags on pallets, containers and parcels to efficiently manage flows of goods. Internal warehouse management systems and IT systems, such as track and trade systems, are often components of modern logistics.

[5] Within a company, activities such as warehousing and transport do not exist as separate operations. Logistics is viewed as an integrated process and the entire logistics chain is managed as a single entity.

[6] 'If the original justification for engaging the services of third party logistics service providers was to reduce transport and inventory costs and to release capital for more product use, more recent justifications relate to accelerating market growth, engaging new sources of supply and improving services to new categories of customers. These new justifications . . . imply longer-term relationships and more reciprocity between industrial buyers and integrated logistics service providers' (Kopicki 2009: 19).

[7] From macroeconomic and social perspectives, logistics efficiency should also take into consideration external costs (e.g. safety hazards and pollution), energy conservation and optimal utilization of resources.

should not be fragmented or disrupted. This requirement may pose regulatory challenges because components of logistics services (such as freight forwarding, cargo handling, storage and warehousing, and transportation) are usually subject to a variety of governmental departments and agencies with separate jurisdiction. The existing regulatory framework in many countries may not measure up to business realities in logistics.

According to the World Bank Logistics Performance Index (LPI),[8] while improving country connectivity to global networks requires improving infrastructure such as ports, airports and highways, it also requires improving the domestic regulatory environment, with attention to competition, to entry barriers, and to policies that increase the costs of trade (Arvis *et al.* 2012: 16). For example, in countries with high logistics performance, logistics operators typically deal with much fewer government agencies than do those in countries with low logistics performance. In interpreting the LPI, the World Bank has concluded that there are two main causes of logistics inefficiency in developing countries: the fragmentation of services and the small size of local markets; and the policy of separating functions, which works against the integration of global supply chains (Arvis *et al.* 2012: 29).

In the Asia-Pacific Economic Cooperation (APEC) Supply-Chain Connectivity Framework, eight logistics chokepoints are identified as impeding trade flow in the Asia-Pacific region, and APEC countries are encouraged to make progress in these areas:

- *Chokepoint 1*: Lack of awareness and coordination among government agencies on policies affecting the logistics sector; absence of single contact point or champion agency on logistics matters;
- *Chokepoint 2*: Inefficient or inadequate transport infrastructure; lack of cross-border physical linkages (e.g. roads and bridges);

[8] The LPI is widely accepted as an important indicator to assess the level of an economy's logistics industry, in particular trade logistics. It analyses countries in six components: the efficiency of customs and border management clearance; the quality of trade and transport infrastructure; the ease of arranging competitively priced shipments; the competence and quality of logistics services; the ability to track and trace consignments; and the frequency with which shipments reach consignees within scheduled or expected delivery times. The components were chosen based on theoretical and empirical research as well as on the practical experience of logistics professionals involved in international freight forwarding. The LPI suggests that domestic regulations relating to trade and transport infrastructure, customs and the supply of logistics services are the most relevant for logistics performance outcome.

- *Chokepoint 3*: Lack of capacity of local and regional logistics sub-providers;
- *Chokepoint 4*: Inefficient clearance of goods at customs; lack of coordination among border agencies, especially relating to clearance of regulated goods 'at the border';
- *Chokepoint 5*: Burdensome customs documentation and other procedures (including for preferential trade);
- *Chokepoint 6*: Underdeveloped, multimodal transport capabilities; inefficient air, land and multimodal connectivity;
- *Chokepoint 7*: Variations in cross-border standards and regulations for movement of goods, services and business travellers;
- *Chokepoint 8*: Lack of regional cross-border customs-transit arrangements.

Among these chokepoints, while some arise from inadequate infrastructure and transport capabilities, most of them are regulatory problems ranging from a lack of coordination among government agencies to burdensome border procedures. The chokepoints also suggest that, as supply chains are often cross-border, national policies of one state may raise business costs in others.

The following section examines China in order to take an in-depth view of the regulatory challenges in logistics services.

3 Operating logistics in a fragmented regulatory environment: the case of China

3.1 New policies on logistics: what is the message?

In the context of China's rapid growth 'miracle', it is not surprising that the value added of logistics has grown annually by 14 per cent since 2000, and reached over US$432 billion in 2010, accounting for about 16 per cent of the total value added of China's tertiary industry and 6.9 per cent of gross domestic product (GDP). Increased demand from China's huge manufacturing sector and ever-expanding merchandise trade is the driving force behind the rapid development of the logistics industry in the country.

While China's logistics' spending decreased from 19.4 per cent of GDP in 2000 to 17.8 per cent in 2010, its logistics performance remains much lower than the average level of that in developed countries, where the logistics spending normally accounts for 10 per cent of GDP. China's total logistics cost is even higher than that of major developing countries.[9] China, the world's second largest economy, ranked only twenty-sixth out of 155 countries (Arvis *et al.* 2012). Among the six indicators for logistics performance, China ranked slightly better in infrastructure and international shipments, but less well in customs, cargo tracking and tracing, timeliness, and logistics quality and competency. There is much room for improvement in logistics management systems, the application of IT and the regulatory framework.

Recognizing the need to improve logistics performance, the Chinese government has made large investments in infrastructure, building modern highways, railways, ports and airports, as well as numerous logistics hubs.[10] At the same time, a series of important policies have been instituted to provide guidance for the development of the logistics sector.[11] These policies consistently stress the urgency for logistics regulatory reform and coordination between various departments, promote integration of logistics operations and the breaking down of barriers between industries and regions, and encourage consolidation of logistics resources and further market opening to foreign investment and domestic private capital. These policies partly represent the Chinese government's attempt to provide an official definition of the logistics industry and the logistics enterprise, which underlines the integration trend in modern logistics.[12]

[9] For example, Brazil's total cost of logistics is around 11.6 per cent, India's 13.0 per cent and Mexico's 14.9 per cent.

[10] According to the China Federation of Logistics and Purchasing, China's fixed asset investment in the logistics industry was ¥3.07 trillion in 2010, of which 75.7 per cent (¥2.3 trillion) was in transport and 7.2 per cent (¥223.8 billion) in warehousing and the postal industry. From 2000 to 2010, the fixed asset investment in this industry increased by 24.1 per cent annually.

[11] For example, in 2004, nine governmental departments jointly issued the *Opinions on Promoting a Modern Logistics Industry* which were addressed to relevant government departments and governments at provincial level. As one of the measures to respond to the financial crisis, the Chinese government issued the *Restructuring and Revitalization Plan for the Logistics Industry* in 2009 to further promote the development of logistics in China. As another attempt to boost the logistics sector, China's State Council issued *Guidelines to Promote the Healthy Development of Logistics Industry* in 2011. The new document reiterated the previous policies, with more specific guidance for implementation.

[12] The *Restructuring and Revitalization Plan for the Logistics Industry* defines the logistics industry as 'a compound service industry integrating transport, warehousing, freight forwarding and information technology'. The *Opinions on Promoting a Modern Logistics Industry* define a logistics enterprise as an economic entity that possesses or rents transport and storage facilities, engages in more than two types of transport (or transport agencies) and warehousing businesses, is able to provide services integrating transport,

It appears that these policies are intended to tackle thorny problems that hinder the development of the logistics industry and undermine logistics efficiency in China. So, what are those problems?

These policies acknowledge that both logistics demand and supply are largely suppressed in China for institutional reasons, and that the enormous logistics market potential has yet to be realized. They therefore require that logistics resources be reallocated or consolidated.

The concept of 3PL is relatively new to China and the 3PL market remains at its early stages. Most domestic enterprises continue to operate their own logistics as an in-house business. State-owned enterprises (SOEs) are the least likely to outsource 3PL services, as they have the in-house assets and people to handle logistics and usually do not follow logistics tracks. In other words, SOEs are insensitive to higher-value logistics services. The majority of multinational corporations use 3PL in China; only 15 per cent of domestic companies use outside logistics firms. 3PL's share of China's logistics market is estimated to be around 20 per cent, which is considered low when compared with 35 per cent in the European Union, 57 per cent in the United States and 80 per cent in Japan (KPMG 2008).

Logistics operators competing in China's market consist of foreign-invested and domestic enterprises. Most large domestic logistics operators are state-owned or controlled, and have developed from traditional state-owned transport or warehousing enterprises. Some are subsidiaries of SOEs in other industries (e.g. chemical, electronics or mineral industries). State-owned or controlled enterprises hold over 50 per cent of China's logistics market, and many of them are monopoly or duopoly operators in certain important segments of logistics services.[13] The majority of domestic logistics companies are private small and medium-sized enterprises (SMEs), and often operate only local businesses and are involved in a single service (e.g. such as trucking, warehousing, express delivery or freight forwarding).

agency, warehousing, loading and unloading, processing, distribution and delivery, and is equipped with appropriate information management systems.

13 China Ocean Shipping (Group) Company (COSCO) is the largest domestic logistics enterprise, with revenue of ¥181.3 billion in 2012. Other top domestic logistics enterprises include China Shipping (Group) Company; China National Foreign Trade Transportation (Group) Corporation (SINOTRANS); China National Material Storage and Transportation Corporation (CMST); China Railway Express Co. Ltd (CRE); and China Post. The CRE has the largest service network throughout China, while COSCO's network mainly covers the coastal areas.

With its accession to the WTO, China opened important segments of its logistics market to foreign investment. For example, foreign investors may now establish fully-owned subsidiaries to provide storage and warehousing services, freight forwarding agency services, and freight transport services by rail and road, and express delivery; foreign investors may also engage in a number of logistics services related to maritime freight transport through establishing joint ventures (e.g. maritime cargo handling services, container station and depot services, and customs clearance services for maritime transport). Over twenty of the world's largest logistics operators are present in China. Foreign-invested logistics enterprises mainly serve multinational manufacturers and retailers with limited penetration into the domestic market. They typically enter China with their customers in an effort to service those customers' global needs. One study indicated that services provided by foreign-invested logistics enterprises represent about 22 per cent of China's logistics market, less than half the market share of state-owned or controlled logistics enterprises (Mei and Liu 2010).

Another important feature of China's logistics industry is that the market is highly fragmented, with a large number of small-scale, local enterprises. Even the largest enterprise in this industry has a market share of less than 2 per cent. The number of registered logistics enterprises in China exceeds 700,000, but less than 1 per cent of them are truly integrated logistics providers capable of providing single-party, one-way bill, door-to-door logistics services. The latter are mainly foreign-invested enterprises.

Despite large amounts of government investment in improving the logistics infrastructure, a nationwide transport network has yet to be established. Multimodal transport, which is crucial for integrated logistics services, is underdeveloped in China, and one of the reasons for that is probably the lack of, or imperfect, connectivity between regional transport facilities and between different means of transport. While numerous logistics hubs have been established or planned in recent years, most of them are concentrated on the eastern sea coast – the logistics infrastructure in the west lags far behind. With the government promoting economic development in the interior provinces and moving lots of manufacturing bases from east to west, high logistics costs of transporting goods from inland to the coast are one of the important bottlenecks to overcome.

In addition, these policies draw attention to the necessity and urgency to address fragmented regulation affecting logistics services and the lack of coordination between relevant government departments. So, how does the existing regulatory framework affect logistics services in China?

3.2 A closer look at the regulatory framework

As logistics remains a nascent industry, it appears normal that there is no single competent authority overseeing it in China. Components of logistics are subject to various ministries, bureaux or commissions. More than a dozen government departments actually have partial jurisdiction over logistics. Logistics-related laws, regulations or rules are scattered in various sectoral instruments. For instance, there are numerous regulations governing transport, including freight transport and auxiliary services (e.g. such as cargo handling and warehousing), which have significant effects on the supply of logistics services, as these services are major logistics components.[14] The allocation of authority among Chinese government departments can sometimes be confusing and difficult to understand for foreigners. For example, maritime, inland waterway and road transport are within the competence of the Ministry of Communication. At the same time, there are two other separate departments responsible for air and rail transport respectively: the Civil Aviation Administration and the Ministry of Railways. The latest reform is to abolish the Ministry of Railways and merge its authority into the Ministry of Communication. Freight forwarding, another important component of logistics services, is within the jurisdiction of the Ministry of Commerce, which has introduced several specific regulations governing this service.[15] Express delivery is increasingly integrated into logistics services, but the newly amended Postal Law places it under the authority of the Postal Administration, which is in charge of issuing express delivery licences.[16] There are other government organs, in

[14] There are numerous laws and regulations governing transport. To name only a few: Maritime Law (1992); Regulation on International Maritime Transport (2002); Administrative Measures on Foreign Investment in International Maritime Transport (2004); Regulation on Road Transport (2004); Administrative Measures on International Road Transport (2005); Administrative Regulation on Waterways Transport (2009); Measures on Foreign Investment in Civil Air Transport (2001); among others.

[15] Administrative Regulation on International Forwarding Agency Services and its Implementation Rules (2004); Administrative Measures on International Forwarding Agency Enterprises with Foreign Investment (2005); and Interim Measures for the Filing of International Freight Forwarders (2005).

[16] The Postal Authority adopted the Administrative Measures on Operation Licence of Express Delivery Services (2009).

particular those responsible for customs, inspection and quarantine, and insurance, which also have partial jurisdiction over logistics services, as they are all mandated to monitor the implementation of a number of logistics-related regulations within their respective authority.[17]

While several government departments and agencies are responsible for regulating various segments of logistics services, their mandates are not necessarily coordinated in the interests of the coherence and consistency of the logistics industry development. Regulations are usually drawn up to meet the regulatory needs of a particular sector, while logistics cuts across a number of sectors and goes beyond the competence sphere of a single regulatory body. Moreover, reflecting one of 'China's characteristics', among these sectors some are considered to be of strategic importance and continue to be subject to tight state control, while others are open to fierce competition with a low market access threshold. As a result, some segments of logistics services are highly regulated or even under a monopoly, while other segments show signs of excessive competition. As logistics services evolve toward an integrated process, the gap between the regulatory framework and business reality is becoming more and more visible.

Fragmented regulation and the lack of coordination among government agencies lead to compounded, sometimes even conflicting, regulations which have important repercussions on market entry. For logistics services providers, one consequence is that they have to comply with burdensome licensing and qualification requirements. For example, 3PL providers who normally operate multiple services (usually including, among other things, multimodal transport, freight forwarding, cargo handling and warehousing services) need to apply for several licences or register with a number of authorities, and thus bear much higher regulatory compliance costs. To some extent, burdensome licensing and qualification requirements may be one of the reasons why the majority of logistics enterprises in China provide a single service, and only very few companies are truly integrated service providers.

For example, according to the regulations governing international freight forwarding, a company registered as an international freight forwarder is allowed to supply a wider range of services, including booking (leasing of ships, chartering of airplanes and shipping space); warehousing; cargo handling (supervising loading and unloading,

[17] Administrative Rules on the Registration of Customs Declaration Enterprises (2005); and Administrative Rules on Entry and Exit Inspection and Quarantine Agencies (2002).

container grouping and unpacking); customs clearance; customs examination and inspection; insurance; filling out relevant documentation, multimodal transport and container transport; international express delivery; and other international freight forwarding agency businesses. In practice, an international freight forwarder wants to offer as broad a service as possible. For this purpose, in addition to registration with the authority responsible for commerce, it needs to:

- apply for licences or receive approval from the Ministry of Communication for various businesses, including non-vessel operating common carrier, shipping agency services, storage and warehousing, and road transport;
- obtain qualification approval from the civil aviation administration for air freight forwarding agency services;
- obtain a licence for express delivery from the postal administration;
- fulfil requirements for registration or qualification approval at the customs administration for customs clearance services, at the inspection authority for customs inspection services, and at the insurance regulator for insurance agency services.

Another consequence of subjecting logistics services to a fragmented regulatory framework is excessive red tape, which increases logistics costs and leads to inefficiency. As many as 100 documents are required to meet port, railway, highway, customs, quarantine and insurance requirements to move international containerized cargo in China. These documents are designed by different authorities, often asking for the same information, with little regard for the burden they place on trade. The lack of data and document harmonization, as well as complex multimodal transport paperwork requirements, cause long container dwell time in ports (ADB 2012: 31).

The lack of technical standards, or the existence of inconsistent sectoral standards, is another aspect of China's fragmented regulatory framework for logistics services. For example, a large variety of vehicles, with different dimensions, designs and construction, operate on the highways, making vehicle interchange (necessary for drop-and-pull operations) difficult. An absence of standardization of inland waterway vessels affects port handling efficiency and the throughput of locks. Old, low-performance and low-safety vessels also slow down the development of inland waterway transport. Railway containers are subject to different standards from that of international maritime containers. As a result, more than 80 per cent of imported goods moving in container trains must be unloaded from inbound international shipping containers and then transferred to railway containers (ADB 2012: 31).

The fragmentation of the regulatory framework is also embodied in insufficient coordination between central and local government and between local governments in adopting policies affecting logistics. It has been indicated that there is no coordination in the planning and construction of logistics parks and transport networks (ADB 2012: 33).[18] Logistics parks are generally not connected to multimodal transport hubs; most of these parks are connected to only one transport network. Most seaports and river ports are only connected to road networks, but not to rail. The eighteen major railway container logistics centres are not synchronized with the road network, and the planning and construction of rail freight stations and logistics parks are carried out separately, without coordination (Mei and Liu 2010: 305–6). As a result, logistics parks in China serve only limited functions,[19] and multimodal transport is inefficient and costly. Another example is that local governments across the country impose excessive highway tolls despite the central government's policies aimed at reducing logistics costs, which have long been viewed as a severe problem facing logistics operators in China. Many local governments also create specific requirements (e.g. permits for in-town trucking transport) which make cross-region logistics operations costly and inefficient.[20]

[18] According to a 2012 survey carried out by the China Federation of Logistics and Purchasing, until 2012, there were 754 logistics parks in China, increasing 58.7 per cent from 475 in 2008; 46 per cent of the logistics parks were in operation; more than half of these logistics parks were located in coastal regions and the region of Yangzi River. In terms of size and function, these logistics parks are very diverse, ranging from small spots with a few warehouses or distribution centres, to large, comprehensive industrial zones grouping various logistics enterprises. Some logistics parks were built and operated by local governments as supporting services provided to business. The report also points out various problems in logistics parks.

[19] It is recently reported that on average 60 per cent of space in logistics parks remains vacant. See the website of the China Federation of Logistics and Purchasing, www.chinawuliu.com.cn/zixun/201307/29/243548.shtml.

[20] Probably to address urban congestion or to protect local trucking companies, many municipal governments have taken a number of measures, such as permits for in-town truck transport, limitation on truck operation hours and limited access to certain urban roads. These measures significantly affect logistics services. Logistics operators who fail to obtain trucking permits may either pay higher costs to hire trucking firms with permits to transport the goods, or operate without a permit with the risk of being fined (Li and Fung Research Centre 2012: 21).

As mentioned above, the operation of certain segments of logistics services is not open to competition but remains under state monopoly or duopoly, operated by one or two SOEs. Although maintained for various policy considerations (e.g. such as national strategy, public security and social benefits), a monopoly generates market distortion effects and usually nurtures and protects vested interest. As far as logistics is concerned, a monopoly also affects efficiency, and sometimes disrupts the connectivity of supply chains. For example, the rail freight transport market is dominated by two state-owned carriers, both of which have a close relationship with the Ministry of Railways, the owner of the railway infrastructure and the policy-maker of rail transport. In particular, railway container transport, which is critical to multimodal transport, continues to be operated under a monopoly. Rail freight transport rates and capacity allocation are not subject to market competition, but are, to a great extent, under government control. The inefficiency of rail freight transport is such that most international containers cannot be moved inland by rail in China. The throughput of sea-to-rail container transport represents only 1.6 per cent of the total throughput of China's seaports.

As indicated in the above-mentioned policies, measures have been taken, or at least designed, to tackle the problem of regulatory fragmentation. A National Inter-Ministerial Joint Meeting on Modern Logistics was set up at the central government level in 2005. This new institution, with the National Development and Reform Commission of the State Council taking the lead, involves fifteen ministries and agencies, which meet once or twice a year to coordinate logistics-related policies and measures.[21] The government is also promoting the application of uniform logistics-related technical standards across the country as part of its efforts to integrate the logistics industry. A subcommission on logistics technical standardization was established under the State Standardization Commission in 2003. The latter, together with other ministries and agencies, issued the National Specific Programme for Logistics Standardization in 2010, which identified standardization tasks

[21] The fifteen departments and agencies include: Ministry of Commerce; Ministry of Railways; Ministry of Transport; Ministry of Industry and Information Technology; Civil Aviation Administration; Ministry of Finance; Ministry of Public Security; General Administration of Customs; State Administration of Taxation; State Administration for Industry and Commerce; General Administration of Quality Supervision, Inspection and Quarantine; State Standardization Commission; China Federation of Logistics and Purchasing; and China Transport Association.

related to logistics in thirteen areas, including transport, storage and warehousing, freight forwarding, some special products-related logistics (such as grains, cold chain, pharmaceutics and car parts), and postal and express delivery. By the end of 2010, twenty-two national logistics standards and more than twenty logistics industrial standards had been issued. More recently, again, the central government urged that the reform of the logistics regulatory framework be accelerated, that compounded administrative examination and approval requirements for logistics enterprises be reduced, and that blockades and barriers between regions and departments on logistics operations be eliminated.[22] Nevertheless, it remains to be seen to what extent the problems could be addressed, as it all depends on whether good policies will be faithfully implemented.

4 Conclusion: general observations

Some studies have been undertaken to look into factors that affect logistics services and supply chains.[23] Various business surveys also provide insight in this regard (e.g. Langley 2012). Based on the case study of China and studies elsewhere, we may draw some general observations with respect to the regulatory factor in logistics services.

Logistics services involve a wide range of activities in various sectors, and inevitably fall under the jurisdiction of multiple governmental departments and agencies. The main lesson from the case of China is that the lack of coordination and coherence across these government agencies has repercussions for logistics services. Multiple licensing and registration requirements raise transaction costs, in particular for integrated logistics service providers because they either have to choose the time-consuming and costly process of applying for all required licences or subcontract domestic suppliers to deliver services. As logistics services are increasingly customized to meet the needs of the client, integrated operators often need to directly engage in a wide range of services or control the entire logistics chain in order to guarantee high service quality and, in the case of subcontracting, domestic suppliers may not possess the expertise necessary to deliver goods at the right

[22] *Guidelines to Promote the Healthy Development of Logistics Industry*, issued in August 2011 by China's State Council.

[23] For example, see USITC 2005; De Sousa and Findlay 2006; OECD/ITF 2010; WEF 2012; 2013.

place, at the right time, for the right price and quality. Sometimes licensing requirements are difficult to be justified as necessary.[24] Burdensome licensing and registration requirements are often compounded by a lack of transparency. This is why it has been suggested in trade negotiations that service suppliers be allowed to supply, in combination, the services in the logistics chain – from cargo handling, warehousing and freight forwarding, to transport, distribution and delivery.[25] It has also been suggested that the government should create a high-level body to oversee all regulation directly affecting the supply chain, and establish effective coordination mechanisms linking the various regulatory and control bodies that set and enforce regulations affecting the supply chain (WEF 2013: 26). Some studies show that this suggestion is workable and, indeed, produces positive effects on logistics services.[26]

Another lesson from the case of China is that competition may be an issue in logistics services, especially when logistics infrastructure owners (e.g. such as railways and ports) are directly or indirectly engaged in logistics services. The existence of monopolies in certain segments of logistics services not only distorts the market, but it may also disrupt the connectivity of supply chains. Other studies suggest that, even if there is formal accounting separation between the rail infrastructure business and train operations, it is difficult to guarantee the absence of discrimination between the rail owner and competitors in the allocation and pricing of track access and ancillary services (OECD/ITF 2010: 23). It has been suggested that full separation would be a better guarantee of neutrality and of ensuring that infrastructure public funding would not leak into indirect support for other activities (*ibid.*). In China, as in some other countries, as the incumbent postal operator has expanded their businesses into logistics services, competition concerns have also been raised due to the possibility of cross-subsidization by the incumbent postal operator through its businesses in the reserved area.

[24] An example is that companies must obtain a licence for a warehouse to ship to customers, and then goods can only flow from that warehouse (see Langley 2012).

[25] *Communication from Australia; Hong Kong, China; Liechtenstein; Mauritius; New Zealand; Nicaragua; Switzerland; and the Separate Customs Territory of Taiwan, Penghu, Kinmen and Matsu: Logistics Services*, WTO doc. TN/S/W/20, 25 June 2004.

[26] De Sousa and Findlay 2006 indicate that the success of the export of tuna from South Australia to Japan is partly attributable to initiatives taken by government bodies in Australia and Japan. In Australia, air, sea and land freight councils have been established to address issues such as process and control concerning the logistics supply chain.

The case of China shows that the domination of SOEs in certain segments of logistics services – and in particular their close relationship with responsible government agencies – may raise competition concerns, especially to the detriment of SMEs. As integration has become a trend of structural change in the logistics industry as a way to enhance competitiveness (e.g. a shipping line integrates into its business the functions of shipping agents, cargo handling companies, freight forwarders and inland transport providers), abuse of market power may also arise from excessive market concentration which may eliminate or discriminate against competitors or raise entry barriers or create price cartels.[27]

The case of China further tells us that excessive documentation requirements significantly affect the efficiency of logistics services and, at the same time, increase logistics costs. This is confirmed by other studies. According to USITC 2005, border clearance procedures, including customs and inspection, constitute the greatest impediment to the supply of global logistics services. In the survey undertaken by the World Bank, efficiency of the customs clearance process is one of the six indicators to assess the logistics performance of an economy (Arvis *et al.* 2012). Excessive documentation for customs clearance, limited hours of operation at customs facilities, preferred treatment for domestic carriers, and security-related delays in inspection are cited as factors that make it more difficult for logistics suppliers to make timely deliveries. Positive examples presented in some studies illustrate that minimal documentation requirements can be reconciled with rigorous quality standards without imposing unduly onerous obligations on exporters, and that computerized single windows at customs in both exporting and importing countries can minimize trade barriers (De Sousa and Findlay 2006). It has been proposed in the WTO Doha Round negotiations and negotiations on preferential trade agreements (PTAs) that various procedures and formalities such as documentation requirements, customs clearance, customs inspection and

[27] In the past few years, coordinated antitrust investigations against major freight forwarding companies have been launched in several jurisdictions, including Brazil, the European Union, Switzerland and the United States. In March 2012, the European Commission imposed fines totalling €169 million on fourteen international freight forwarders for operating four price-fixing cartels between 2002 and 2007. Four international freight forwarders were fined US$6.75 million by Switzerland's Competition Commission for price fixing. The freight forwarders were alleged to have agreed to fees and surcharges between 2003 and 2007.

electronic processing should not be unnecessarily burdensome. One specific suggestion is for WTO members to accept electronic trade administration documents.[28] In some PTAs, states have made certain regulatory commitments to facilitate customs clearance and inspection procedures.

There is no doubt that a state's regulatory environment matters for its logistics performance. It should be further recognized that logistics services that are constantly evolving may also pose challenges to the existing regulatory framework and thus require necessary regulatory responses.

References

ADB (2012), *Transport Efficiency Through Logistics Development: Policy Study*, Philippines: Asian Development Bank

Arvis, J.-F., Mustra, M.A., Ojala, L., Shepherd, B. and Saslavsky, D. (2012), *Connecting to Compete 2012: Trade Logistics in the Global Economy – The Logistics Performance Index and Its Indicators*, Washington, DC: International Bank for Reconstruction and Development/World Bank

De Sousa, D. and Findlay, C. (2006), *The Relationship Between Liberalization in the Logistics Sector and Trade Facilitation*, Asia-Pacific Research and Training Network on Trade, Working Paper No. 16

Kopicki, R. (2009), *Freight Transport for Development Toolkit: Integrated Logistics Services*, Washington, DC: International Bank for Reconstruction and Development/World Bank

KPMG (2008), *Logistics in China: Property and Infrastructure*, Hong Kong, China: KPMG

Langley Jr, C.J. (2012), *2012 Third-Party Logistics Study: The State of Logistics Outsourcing*, Atlanta: Capgemini

Li and Fung Research Centre (2012), *China's Logistics Industry Update 2012*, Hong Kong, China: Li and Fung Research Centre

Mei, Z. and Liu, J. (eds.) (2010), *Report on China's International Freight Forwarding Development*, Beijing: China Materials Press

OECD/ITF (2010), *Integration and Competition Between Transport and Logistics Businesses*, Paris: Organisation for Economic Co-operation and Development/International Transport Forum

[28] *Communication from Australia; Hong Kong, China; Liechtenstein; Mauritius; New Zealand; Nicaragua; Switzerland; and the Separate Customs Territory of Taiwan, Penghu, Kinmen and Matsu: Logistics Services*, WTO doc. TN/S/W/20, 25 June 2004.

USITC (2005), *Logistics Services: An Overview of the Global Market and Potential Effects of Removing Trade Impediments*, Washington, DC: United States International Trade Commission

WEF (2012), *Outlook on the Logistics and Supply Chain Industry 2012: Global Agenda Council on Logistics and Supply Chains 2011–2012*, Geneva: World Economic Forum

(2013), *Enabling Trade: Valuing Growth Opportunities*, Geneva: World Economic Forum

17

Domestic regulation of retail food distribution services in Israel: the missing link between food prices and social protest

TOMER BROUDE AND LIOR HERMAN

1 Introduction

This chapter provides a case study tracing the impact of domestic regulation on market structure in the retail distribution services sector and its ultimate effects on consumer food prices. Taking Israel, a small and relatively liberalized Organisation for Economic Co-operation and Development (OECD) economy, as an example, our research investigates whether market concentration and the absence of international competition can be attributed to domestic regulation. We place this discussion in the context of recent consumer-led social protest against the rising cost of food in Israel.

Distribution services in general, and retail distribution in particular, is at the nexus of economic activity, connecting producers, wholesale traders and importers of goods, on one hand, with end-consumers, on the other. By some accounts, retail distribution services constitute one-third of global consumer services (Nordås *et al.* 2008: 8), with retail food services comprising a significant part of it. This is a field in which a wide range of measures that could be considered as domestic regulation in the terms of General Agreement on Trade in Services (GATS) Article VI may apply as a matter of course, such as business opening hours and zoning requirements (Pilat 1997; Boylaud and Nicoletti 2001). Thus, even in instances where specific market access and national treatment commitments or general transparency and most favoured nation (MFN) obligations are not violated, domestic regulation may have adverse effects on international and local competition and optimal trade patterns, making it an especially interesting services sector.

Moreover, in practical terms 'distribution services' are rarely regulated as such, and hardly ever as a unitary sector. Rather, they are usually governed indirectly or tangentially through the regulation of the production and sale of the particular goods being distributed, or through cross-cutting commercial activity requirements. For example, where specific retail distribution licences (as opposed to general commercial activity licences) are required, they normally relate to the distribution of specific sectors of products, with the primary goal of regulating the product market, rather than the market for distribution services. This phenomenon – the unique and almost inextricable linkage of services with tangible goods sectors – is well reflected in the Central Product Classification for distribution services,[1] which distinguishes between distribution services not only by their particular business model (e.g. franchises or commission agents) and economic level (wholesale or retail), but also by their subjects in a wide range of products (e.g. such as food or non-food, fish, pharmaceutical or footwear).

The chapter proceeds as follows. Section 2 presents consumer remonstration about the rising costs of food products as a backdrop for examining the relatively concentrated market structure of retail food distribution services in Israel. In section 3, we discuss several types of domestic regulation which, in our analysis, may constitute impediments to entry of foreign enterprises to the Israeli market, thus contributing to domestic market concentration in retail food distribution services, as well as to wider effects on trade in goods and food prices. Prior to concluding, section 4 examines the government response to recent consumer protest and the reform measures in the domestic regulation of food retail services.

2 Retail food distribution in Israel and discontentment

Retail food prices have attracted considerable public attention in Israel in recent years. Like many OECD countries, Israel experienced significant social protest in 2011, directed primarily at reforming national

[1] Distribution services include five main subcategories: wholesale services, retail services, franchising, commission agents' services and other distribution services. This categorization corresponds to section 4 of *Services Sectoral Classification List: Note by the Secretariat*, WTO doc. MTN.GNS/W/120, 10 July 1991, with some categories matched by specific categories. For a review of several issues related to classification of distribution services subsectors, see *Distribution Services: Background Note by the Secretariat*, WTO doc. S/C/W/326, 29 October 2010. For exact sector and subsector definitions, see the Provisional Central Product Classification explanatory notes at http://unstats.un.org/unsd/cr/registry/regcst.asp?Cl=9&Lg=1. In this chapter, we will focus on retail distribution.

governmental policies affecting the economic situation of the 'middle class' (Broude 2013). Epitomized by an improvised mass tent encampment on Rothschild Boulevard, at the heart of Tel Aviv's financial district, Israel's social protest brought together hundreds of thousands of Israelis in mass street demonstrations. Rising costs of living, notably food, housing and child care, sparked this unprecedented protest, which at the time shook the political system.

Retail food costs played a major part in the protest (as well as in its aftermath, discussed in section 4). Indeed, the first manifestation of the protest was directly related to the production and distribution of food staples. The so-called 'Cottage Cheese Protest' of June 2011 was aimed against a sharp rise in food prices, entailing a social network-led consumer boycott of certain brands of the popular cottage cheese product, whose prices had risen by at least 40 per cent within only three years (Levin 2012). In the cottage cheese product segment, three local producers dominate the Israeli market, one of which holds an effective monopoly of 70 per cent market share. Although this particular market concentration exists at the producer/wholesale level of trade, it is both symptomatic of, and instrumental in, the perpetuation of a broader phenomenon of domestic market concentration within Israel's retail food sector. After all, food retailers were not the ones complaining against the rise in prices, simply passing it on to end-consumers and, in many cases, actively contributing to it. Indeed, much of the public acrimony during the Israeli summer of 2011 and ever since was directed at the owners of the large retail food distribution chains, especially Mr Nochi Dankner, whose indirect holdings include the largest retail food distribution chain in Israel, Shufersal.

Retail services link producers of goods and services with final consumers.[2] This intermediary role serves several goals, which mostly stem from the characteristics of consumers. One such characteristic relates to consumers' relative small size as purchasing units, as well as expenditure capacity. Since retailers can exploit economies of scale advantages and other bargaining power resources vis-à-vis producers and wholesale distributors of goods and services, they facilitate lower trade costs and greater availability of goods, which cannot be achieved by individual consumers on their own. Furthermore, retail services provision in

[2] Corporate and business consumers are usually included in wholesale rather than retail services. This private–business separation also includes business activities whereby purchases are aimed at final consumption. See *Distribution Services: Background Note by the Secretariat*, WTO doc. S/C/W/326, 29 October 2010.

proximity to customers can reduce high transaction, uncertainty and information costs associated with the need to identify the availability and range of producers and products, their prices, quality and reliability, as well as considerable transportation, storage, time and post-sale costs (London Economics 1997).[3] Thus, in theory, retail distribution plays an important role in lowering costs to end-consumers. In practice, however, in the absence of sufficient competition at both national and local levels, retail distributors may actually contribute to higher prices. Market concentration in retail food distribution has been identified as one contributing factor in this respect (Dobson and Waterson 1999).

Indeed, food distribution services are a significant share of retail services concerns. Retailers in this sector range from small grocers, greengrocers, butchers' shops and convenience stores to open-air markets, supermarkets and hypermarkets.[4] The importance of food retail services is well exemplified in the case of Israel. Food retail services are some 70 per cent of Israel's food market, which account for 90 billion shekels (US$23.6 billion) a year,[5] equivalent to approximately 10 per cent of Israel's gross domestic product. Ownership in the sector is mixed in character, with smaller retailers mostly privately owned, and larger retailers being either privately owned, public trade corporations or cooperatives.[6]

Israeli consumers purchase most of their food in retail chains, accounting for almost 60 per cent of all food purchases. Of lesser significance are grocers, which account for 16 per cent of purchases and markets, greengrocers and butchers' shops, where 17 per cent of total food purchases are conducted.[7] Figure 17.1 provides a detailed

[3] *Ibid.*

[4] From a definitional point of view, food distribution to end-consumers may also include restaurants, food served in hotels and certain catering services. Nevertheless, these somewhat different activities would be classified as different forms of services (e.g. tourism services) and are also subject to significantly different types of domestic regulation, and so for coherence purposes are not covered in this chapter.

[5] Private consumption of food, beverages and tobacco figures for 2011 (Central Bureau of Statistics).

[6] Notable examples of the latter include Co-Op Blue Square (Ribua Cahol), which operated as a cooperative until the mid-2000s, and Co-Op Israel (Co-Op Shop).

[7] Specific figures for 2010 are chain stores (58.3 per cent), grocers (16.3 per cent), butchers' shops (8.0 per cent), specialty shops (8.1 per cent), markets (4.8 per cent), greengrocers (4.3 per cent) and others (0.4 per cent). Specialty shops include such establishments as bakeries and spice shops. Data reported relates to 'expenditure on food' (excluding meals away from home) by type of shop (Central Bureau of Statistics, available at www.cbs.gov.il/webpub/pub/text_page_eng.html?publ=25&CYear=2010&CMonth=1). It should also be noted that differences in purchasing patterns exist between the Jewish and Arab

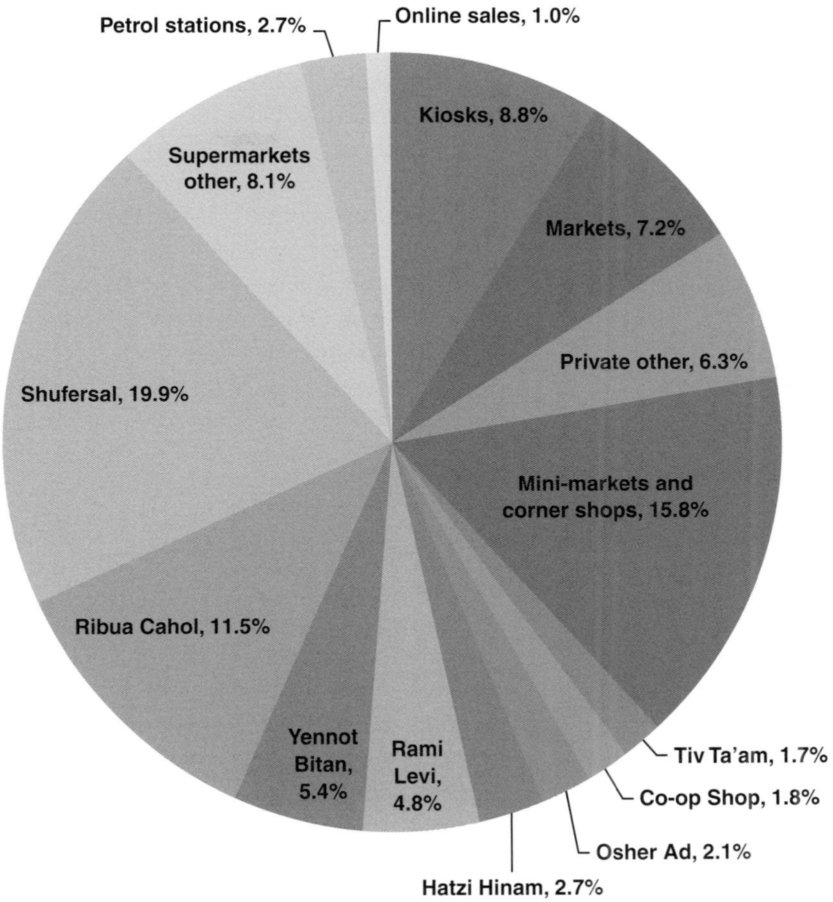

Figure 17.1 Israel's food retail services market structure
Source: *The Marker*, 10 October 2012, p. 8 (based on Czamanski Ben Shahar and Co. figures) available at www.czamanski.com/Czamanski/SendFile.asp?DBID=1&LNGID=2&GID=808.

breakdown of the Israeli food retail services sector, identifying the key actors. Notably, Shufersal, Israel's biggest food chain retailer, holds at least one-fifth of the overall market. Other chains, such as Ribua Cahol, Yennot Bitan and Rami Levi have large, though much smaller, individual market shares. After them are smaller discount chains, such as Hatzi

populations of Israel and the latter's propensity of buying at retail chains is lower than that of the Jewish population (Bar-Tzuri 2007).

Hinam and Osher Ad. The combined market share at the national level of the top four retailers is 41.6 per cent. This would appear to be consistent with levels of concentration at national level in European markets, though significantly higher than in the United States (Richards and Pofahl 2010). However, alternative figures suggest an even higher degree of concentration.[8]

One aspect of the domestic market concentration in Israel is striking, and that is the virtual absence of international food retailers in Israel operating in any form of commercial presence, whether through 'greenfield' establishment of foreign-branded supermarket chains or through direct investment in (and acquisition of) local chains. This is despite general OECD analysis that demonstrates the existence of a global trend towards transnational expansion of global retail food chains (Wrigley and Lowe 2010). In the absence of global food retailers' commercial decision-making data, it remains unclear why these global chains have so far refrained from entering the Israeli food market. Nevertheless, there is evidence that several global retailers, such as Walmart in 2010, have considered market entry.[9]

While regular media coverage suggests that strong competition between the chains prevails, there is considerable evidence that this competition is, in fact, limited. Hence, competition is confined to relatively small geographic areas, rather than taking place on a national scale. Evidence for the importance of location as a determining factor for competition is supported by the low numbers of consumers travelling for food purchases to relatively distant discount shops, despite price differences. Moreover, retail chains' high profitability and continual rapid growth rates suggest that once location is obtained by a supermarket, price competition becomes marginal and restricted to a limited geographical area. Chains and other food retailers, as well as consumers, compare prices within a limited range, often restricting competition to specific local sales area. Nevertheless, when regulation and other factors limit the number of retailers in local sales areas, competition can be highly suppressed (Slater 2011).

The role played by location in restricting competition suggests that domestic regulation may have a restrictive impact on foreign

[8] See www.calcalist.co.il/marketing/articles/1,7340,L-3577094,00.html, which reports that Shufersal holds 36.2 per cent of the retail food market and that the top four retailers hold an extremely high market share of over 70 per cent.

[9] See www.themarker.com/misc/article-print-page/1.580901.

participation and overall competition in Israel's food retail services sector. The total absence of foreign actors, such as any of the twenty largest global food retailers, is highly visible in this sector. This foreign absence is notable also given market penetration opportunities indicated by high growth rates of domestic retail chains, which have grown at an average pace of over 6 per cent in the last decade.

The lack of competition in retail food distribution services is also evident in high food prices in Israel, which have been rising in both real and nominal terms over the past years, at a faster rate than the average trend of inflation reflected in the general consumer price index (CPI).[10] From 2005 and until May 2011, food prices nominally increased by 31.6 per cent compared to the CPI increase of only 18 per cent. This increase contrasts OECD trends, whereby food prices in real terms in the same period rose by only 12.7 per cent for all OECD countries as a group, with much lower increases in specific countries, such as the European Union (3.6 per cent), the United States (1.3 per cent), and a decrease in Switzerland (-4.7 per cent) (Agmon and Tzadik 2011). Furthermore, and perhaps most importantly, analysis of output prices indicates that food retailers increased prices at a much higher rate on average than the increase in wholesale food prices (*ibid.*). This suggests that food retailers have successfully leveraged their market power vis-à-vis consumers.

With this backdrop, we now turn to discuss domestic regulation of retail food distribution services in Israel. Has domestic regulation in this services sector contributed to the absence of international competition, in turn promoting local (and localized) market concentration and market power, leading to higher food prices that have been the source of social protest?

3 Domestic regulation of retail food distribution in Israel: restrictive dimensions

Israel joined the General Agreement on Tariffs and Trade (GATT) in 1962 and acceded to the World Trade Organization (WTO) in 1995. In its GATS schedule[11] and in subsequent supplements (from 1997 and

[10] As reported in 'Consumer Price Index by Industry' (Central Bureau of Statistics), available at www.cbs.gov.il.

[11] *Israel: Schedule of Specific Commitments*, WTO doc. GATS/SC/44, 15 April 1994 (amended by subsequent supplements).

1998), Israel did not make any specific commitments on market access or national treatment in retail distribution services. It has not tendered any offers in this sector in the context of the Doha Round,[12] nor (to the best of our knowledge) in negotiations on bilateral trade agreements. However, this avoidance of explicit market liberalization commitments does not appear to stem from any preferential or discriminatory policy in favour of local retail distributors. Indeed, in our analysis, no significant measures exist in Israel that are clearly identifiable as market access or national treatment restrictions in retail food distribution.[13] This suggests that the domestic bias in market concentration in retail food distribution services can be attributed at least partially to prevailing domestic regulation, although other causes may be present (such as the relatively small market, or linguistic, cultural and political reasons).

Retail food services in Israel are regulated neither as a single sector nor within a coherent distribution services framework. Instead, the regulation of the sector is diffuse and carried out across different product market and legislative areas, as well as at different governmental levels, from nationwide statutes, to municipal by-laws. In goods sectors in which distribution is regulated directly or indirectly, authority may be dispersed among several government ministries (such as health, agriculture, industry, trade and labour), and/or by statutory trade councils (such as milk, vegetables and peanuts). This legal and regulatory pluralism (and even incoherence) is typical of distribution services worldwide, resulting in many product-specific rules and regulations, as well as in cross-cutting legislation that indirectly affects distribution, such as business licensing, labelling and competition laws. From a WTO law perspective, these regulations cannot generally be classified as either market access restrictions (i.e. regulations that conform to the exhaustive list of regulations listed in GATS Article XVI), or as national treatment restrictions under GATS Article XVII. Nevertheless, they can result in market restrictiveness, as demonstrated by restrictiveness indicators.

[12] *Communication from Israel: Initial Offer*, WTO doc. TN/S/O/ISR, 17 April 2003.

[13] Although distinctions between national treatment, market access and domestic regulation can be difficult (see Pauwelyn 2005). In fact, our impression from discussions with Israeli negotiators is that market access and national treatment commitments in retail distribution were not made in the 1990s because the regulation of the field was perceived to be too complicated for analysis, suggesting that regulatory complexity reduced the effectiveness of formal liberalization.

Table 17.1 *Regulatory restrictiveness index*[a]

	Israel	*OECD*[b]	*Emerging economies*[c]
Registration in commercial register	0.0	1.6	2.5
Licences or permits needed to engage in commercial activity	4.0	3.2	3.2
Specific regulation of large outlet	3.0	2.1	0.8
Protection of existing firms	3.0	2.6	1.0
Regulation of shop opening hours	4.0	3.4	3.3
Price controls	3.0	1.7	2.5
Barriers to entry	2.3	2.3	2.8
Operational restrictions	2.8	2.7	2.7
Retail (Overall indicator)	**2.7**	**2.3**	**2.8**

Source: OECD International Regulation Database.
Notes:
[a]Data for 2008. Historical scores are not available for Israel and emerging economies group.
[b]Unweighted average for the OECD grouping.
[c]Unweighted average for Brazil, China, India, Indonesia, the Russian Federation and South Africa.

The OECD International Regulation Database provides cross-country indicators on domestic regulation curbing market competition.[14] Anti-competitive regulation is covered in the database with respect to both entry and conduct regulations. Entry regulations cover provisions which create explicit barriers or raise market access costs. Conduct regulations include rules and procedures affecting business decisions concerning inputs, supply or pricing (Conway and Nicoletti 2006). Table 17.1 shows that, compared with the OECD group and with a group of six key emerging economies, retail regulation in Israel is almost always more restrictive than the average scores for the other two groups.

[14] Indicators in the database focus on regulation types which adversely impact competition rather than on regulation having lesser or no effect and that serves a variety of market-correcting or non-economic purposes. The index varies from 0 to 6, whereby the higher the score, the greater the trade restrictiveness reflected by regulation. For an earlier index of trade restrictiveness in regulation distribution services (comparing thirty-eight economies, but not including Israel) (see Kalirajan 2000).

The following is a brief survey of some salient dimensions of domestic regulation that contribute to this restrictiveness.

3.1 Registration and licensing

While there is no need to register new food outlets in a special commercial register, retailers are required under Israeli corporate law (as in all sectors) to incorporate as an Israeli company (holding a domestic business office); as a foreign incorporated company registered in Israel; or as an Israeli-registered foreign partnership. There are no statutory nationality requirements with respect to ownership of distribution service providers as such.

However, distribution services and their physical facilities are subject to the general framework of business licensing in Israel, which imposes numerous substantive conditions and considerable bureaucratic burdens. Licensing is required essentially for all retail food distribution outlets, such as supermarkets, kiosks, grocers, greengrocers, butchers' shops, as well as any other type of food retailing business. These licences are granted in accordance with public health and safety requirements, sanitary and environmental considerations, parking and accessibility requirements, and additional regulatory public purposes. While general licensing requirements are legislated at the national statutory level, licences are granted by local authorities and municipalities, who also establish specific requirements in by-laws which may vary from municipality to municipality both in content and in strictness of enforcement. By law, business licensing must be withheld where permits are required under any other legislation, until such permits are procured. There are also product-specific licensing requirements for the sale of tobacco goods, alcoholic beverages, meat, poultry, fish and eggs. Consequently, new retail distribution outlets will normally need to receive the approval of numerous authorities (such as the fire department, veterinary services and experts on accessibility for people with disabilities), which are not always well-coordinated, before receiving a business licence. Licensing decisions are subject to the standard judicial review that applies to administrative determinations in Israel.[15]

Moreover, legislation on the supervision of goods and services requires food producers, wholesalers, stockpilers or agents to receive a licence

[15] Licence applicants, including foreign entrants established in Israel, may challenge any decision made by local authorities and municipalities in Israeli district courts sitting as Courts for Administrative Affairs.

from relevant authorities, including district offices of the Ministry of Industry, Trade and Labour. This requirement is not stipulated as applying specifically to retail distributors, but would inevitably apply to retailers with food storage facilities.

3.2 *Zoning*

As a small country with very concentrated urban and suburban population areas, land for retail outlets is scarce and expensive. This is compounded by municipal zoning plans, which may distinguish between areas for wholesale activity and areas for retail activity. Municipal zoning rules may include specific regulations regarding the location of retail distribution outlets. In addition, zoning plans may limit the size of individual buildings and outlets. These circumstances may constitute barriers to entry for new (domestic and foreign) retail food chains.

3.3 *Shop opening hours*

Business hours are regulated through a combination of national labour laws (among others, specifying Saturday as a mandatory day of rest for Jewish employees, and either Friday, Saturday or Sunday as a mandatory day of rest for non-Jewish employees according to preference) and local business licensing and general by-laws. This is a source of significant controversy in Israel, and has implications beyond formal regulation: for example, businesses with branches open on Saturday may not receive certificates from the rabbinical authorities relating to Kashrut, or may be boycotted by religious private consumers.

3.4 *Specific food product regulation*

Under general legislation on the supervision of goods and services, the government is granted broad authority to declare certain goods and services as subject to supervision and regulation. This is a central statutory basis for various standards, price controls and licensing arrangements, all of which may directly or indirectly impact upon retail food distribution. Depending on the product sector, domestic regulation (in combination with protection from imports) may make entry to the retail food market extremely difficult. Two product sectors are of particular importance to retail food distribution: dairy products, and fruit and vegetables.

3.4.1 Milk and dairy products

This is, of course, the product sector in which the original 'cottage cheese protest' occurred. Dairy products are fundamental to any retail food distributor. The retail distribution of milk and dairy products does not require special licensing in Israel. However, the milk market is highly regulated in ways that impact upon access to the milk distribution market. Dairy products enjoy high tariff protection from imports as well as price controls, whereas milk production quotas are administered and allocated to producers on an annual basis, through a combination of laws, regulations and orders, and the administrative practices of the Israeli Dairy Council, a company established by the Israeli government, which has served as a board for coordinating market supervision between the government, producers, farmers and dairy enterprises since the 1960s. In practice, the outcome of this system has been that wholesale distribution of dairy products is limited to a small number of incumbent market actors, reducing the scope for price competition in the retail food sector, consequently raising a significant entry barrier to new entrants. The milk sector was the subject of new legislation from 2011 and was scrutinized in depth following the social protest of the same year.

3.4.2 Fruit and vegetables

Wholesale marketers of most types of fruit and vegetables require a licence from the Plant Council, a statutory trade board established by the Plant Law, which has been amended several times over the last few years, in effect amalgamating a number of agricultural boards that were abrogated at the time. The Plant Council now covers vegetables, fruit, citrus products and olives. Licensing requirements may have indirect effects on the retail market, although to a lesser extent than in dairy products.

4 Response to social protest: Trajtenberg Committee and Kedmi Committee

The magnitude and persistence of the 2011 social protest led the Israeli government to appoint two committees to explore comprehensive solutions to the rise in living costs: the Committee for Economic and Social Change (Trajtenberg Committee) and the Committee to Examine Competitiveness and Prices in the Food and Consumer Goods

Market (Kedmi Committee).[16] Both committees addressed restrictive domestic regulation, lack of exposure to foreign competition and market concentration in several sectors as having significantly influenced the rising cost of living in Israel (Kedmi 2011; 2012; Trajtenberg 2011). Many of the findings affect foreign service suppliers' market access and ability to compete effectively in the food retail market.

4.1 *Problems identified*

The committee reports indicate that market entry, as well as the ability to exploit scale advantages (which are of importance to retail food distribution chains), is hindered by excessive bureaucracy. Regulatory and administrative requirements do not discriminate between foreign and domestic suppliers, but they do create challenges for foreign market entrants. Examples are slow licensing processes for new retail food shops,[17] which also include disproportional requirements when compared with other markets. Competition is *de facto* restricted as a consequence of urban planning and zoning regimes in many municipalities. Scarcity of retail-designated land prevents the entry of new market actors and benefits domestic incumbents. Moreover, there is evidence that competition is restricted in many commercial areas through collusion restricting land use (sale, lease or rental) by competitors of existing food retailers (Kedmi 2011).

In several respects, product-related restrictions have contributed to barriers to entry and reduced competition in retail food distribution. Foreign competitors find differentiated product standardization in Israel to be a major barrier in their ability to exploit global value chain advantages, restricting self-importation of products for marketing (including private labels). Furthermore, import licensing procedures create barriers for parallel importing of food products, and limit the scope for price competition between retail suppliers. These regulatory barriers adversely impact competition because many imported food products are protected by exclusivity agreements between domestic

[16] In addition, the protest movement created its own public committee for social and economic change, as an alternative to the official Trajtenberg Committee's report. A third governmental committee, the Committee for Competitiveness Enhancement in the Market (known as the Concentration Committee) had already been established in October 2010 to investigate economy-wide market concentration.

[17] Licensing times vary between municipalities but are no less than several months, usually between six months and a year.

importers, retailers and foreign producers. Evidence indicates that, where parallel imports succeed, significant price reductions ensue (Monitor Company Group 2012). These procedures severely affect foreign competitors' access into the retail food market, and make them dependent upon existing concentrated distribution networks.

Another relevant aspect of domestic regulation is antitrust law. Agriculture is exempted from the prohibition of collusive behaviour in Israel's antitrust law.[18] This broad exemption applies to fruit, vegetables, milk, eggs, honey, beef, goat, poultry, fish, and more. As we have seen, production and marketing in several of these key product sectors is regulated in ways that reduce competition. This directly causes higher consumer prices and also affects retail competition. In practice, many agricultural products are priced very highly by wholesale distributors, often several times the price paid to farmers (Deshe 2001). Collusion, as well as mergers and acquisitions in the wholesale distribution segment of the value chain, impose high costs on food retailers, restrain their ability to exploit scale advantages, and affect their internal operations, such as decision-making over shelf space allocation and arrangement, as well as inability to purchase directly from farmers (Kedmi 2012). Accusations by retailers concerning the effects of such anti-competitive practices by major wholesale distributors recently triggered a formal investigation by the antitrust authority against Tnuva, a dominant wholesaler and a monopoly in many agricultural products.[19] Another example of anti-competitive behaviour was the decision to fine Strauss-Elite, Israel's chocolate monopoly controlling some 70 per cent of Israel's 1 billion shekel chocolate market, for abuse of dominant position and collusion. In this case, Strauss-Elite used its market power in relation

[18] The agriculture sector enjoyed a unique status in the early days of the establishment of the state of Israel, extending beyond traditional and general arguments concerning it being a special economic sector, different to other sectors (e.g. non-flexibility of demand and the necessity to maintain price stability and reduce volatility of supply). Agriculture symbolized the return and resettlement of the Jews in the Land of Israel (*geulat ha'aretz, ha'chalutzim*). This ethos was an important factor in the Knesset's willingness to exempt the sector from the antitrust law, as reflected in the words of Levi Eshkol, (the then Minister of Finance and later Prime Minister): 'we should see these men labouring the land as men and farms worthy of special treatment. Therefore, when they come together to organize production and distribution to protect their interests, we should view it favourably, encourage them and help them' (Knesset Protocol, 13 January 1958, quoted in Deshe 2001).

[19] See www.globes.co.il/news/article.aspx?did=1000657946; see also www.themarker.com/law/1.1777313#.

to food retailers to restrict Cadbury from successfully penetrating the Israeli market, a practice that resulted in a consent order by the Israeli Antitrust Authority in 2007.[20]

4.2 *Possible remedies*

The Trajtenberg and Kedmi reports recommended numerous reforms aimed at enhancing competition and lowering living costs. Some of them relate to regulatory problems hindering foreign retailers from entering the market and competing with domestic incumbents. The implementation of these recommendations is uncertain at the time of writing.[21]

In order to address the geographical dimension of competition inherent in the food retail market, it was recommended that food retailers with a substantial market share in specific geographical zones be granted approval for further expansion subject to competition impact assessment. This would consider demand and competition criteria, such as the distance of shops from consumers, travel time, geographical market share, number of competitors, and more. In certain cases, dominant retailers may be requested to sell or close down part of their business.[22] Dominant retailers engaged in restricting competitors from purchasing or renting real estate in the same geographical area will be prosecuted under antitrust law.

One recommendation is to align Israeli food standards with international standards within a period of two years, permitting Israeli standards only where no international standards are available. Given wide disagreement on the adoption of these reform measures, including within the Ministry of Trade, Industry and Labour, which is in charge of product standards, it is uncertain that reform will take place in the near future. This disagreement relates mainly to domestic incumbents' fear of competition.

20 See www.themarker.com/advertising/1.243491; see also www.antitrust.gov.il/files/9275/02-2007.pdf.

21 The Trajtenberg Committee submitted its report in September 2011. Despite an initial attempt to approve the report in one piece, political differences led to a gradual piecemeal approach, which resulted in substantial changes in many reform measures suggested, as well as to a slow implementation process. The Kedmi Committee submitted its report in July 2012, and its recommendations were approved with various changes in September that year.

22 For example, in the case of a dominant retailer holding three shops and 50 per cent of total revenue in a specified geographical zone.

Another reform suggested by the committees, as well as by the Israeli State Comptroller, was to extend price controls for food products (State Comptroller 2012). This recommendation, which has yet to be adopted, suggests applying price ceilings for a maximum period of two years for some food products where wholesale distribution is highly concentrated. It should be noted that, while this recommendation serves a legitimate socially desirable goal intended at food price reduction, it can also have an undesired effect on competition. Foreign retailers seeking to compete with domestic retailers by importing products subjected to maximum pricing, yet of higher quality, may be forced to lose the quality competitive edge due to profitability considerations. Another reform measure of similar effect that had already entered into force is an obligation for food retailers to allocate sufficient and visible shelf space for products under price control, and to distinguish them from products under no price regulation. Past experience with comparable measures has not yielded positive results.

Finally, a key reform proposal has been to limit the agriculture exemption from the antitrust law to curtail the ability of agricultural producers and wholesalers to manipulate the market and adversely affect retailers' operations, as well as prevent collusion from moving upward in the value chain.

5 Conclusion

Retail distribution is a Janus-faced services sector. Retailers provide a distribution service to producers and wholesale traders, but their actual customers are end-consumers shopping for goods. As we have seen in this case study, domestic regulation can significantly impact the market structure of retail distribution service providers, creating and preserving anti-competitive trends that harm consumers. In Israel, this has resulted in disproportionate increases in food prices that have justifiably led to social protest.

However, most of the regulatory problems in this sector are not at all directly related to retail distribution services. Anti-competitive bottlenecks in other sectors, such as in agricultural production, wholesale distribution and real estate, prevent competition in the retail sector, restricting entry by transnational retail chains that could reduce food prices. Indeed, it is one of the paradoxes of the 2011 social protest in Israel, often depicted as aimed against neo-liberal economic policies, that in one of its core grudges (high food prices) it ultimately calls for greater liberalization and market oriented 'trust-busting'; but again, this liberalization is needed primarily in upstream market sectors.

For this reason, and as a final comment in this respect, it is likely that for WTO disciplines on domestic regulation (GATS Article VI) to have any effect on the Israeli market for retail food distribution services, they should be applied to related non-retail food distribution services, in addition to being linked with measures on trade in goods. Thus, regardless of specific commitments to be made in food retail services, we conclude with a list of examples of possible disciplines to be instituted:

- adoption of international standards for food products, where such standards are available, as well as simplification of standardization processes and ensuring that domestic standards are not more burdensome than necessary;
- provision of exemptions from competition law and policy only when such exemptions are transparent, impartial and justified by public policy reasons;
- simplification of import procedures, particularly for parallel importing, and ensuring that parallel importing procedures consider economic efficiency, are impartial and no more burdensome than necessary, as well as do not in themselves restrict trade and supply of services;
- simplification of new retail food services licensing procedures on the basis of necessity, transparency and non-trade restrictiveness.

References

Agmon, T. and Tzadik, A. (2011), *Rise in Food Prices in Israel,* paper submitted to the Knesset Economy Department, Jerusalem: Knesset Centre for Research and Information

Bar-Tzuri, R. (2007), *Food Retail Chains in Israel: Sales Share, Consumers Portfolio and International Comparison,* Jerusalem: Israeli Ministry of Trade, Industry and Labour

Boylaud, O. and Nicoletti, G. (2001), *Regulatory Reform in Retail Distribution,* OECD Economic Studies No. 32, Paris: Organisation for Economic Co-operation and Development

Broude, T. (2013), 'From Seattle to "Occupy": Trade, Human Rights and the Shifting Focus of Social Protest' in D. Drache and L. Jacobs (eds.), *Linking Global Trade and Human Rights: New Policy Space in Hard Economic Times* (forthcoming)

Conway, P. and Nicoletti, G. (2006), *Product Market Regulation in the Non-Manufacturing Sectors of OECD Countries: Measurements and Highlights,*

Economics Department Working Paper No. 530, Paris: Organisation for Economic Co-operation and Development

Deshe, V. (2001), 'The Agriculture Exemption in the Competition Law: Comparative Research and Thoughts Concerning the Extent of its Application', *Hapraklit* 51(1): 349–403

Dobson, P. and Waterson, M. (1999), 'Retailer Power: Recent Developments and Policy Implications', *Economic Policy* 14(28): 135–64

Kalirajan, K. (2000), *Restrictions on Trade in Distribution Services*, Productivity Commission Staff Research Paper, Canberra: AusInfo

Kedmi, S. (2011), *Interim Report of the Committee for Examining Competitiveness and Prices in the Food and Consumption Market*, Jerusalem: Ministry of Trade, Industry and Labour

(2012), *Final Report: The Committee for Examining Competitiveness and Prices in the Food and Consumption Market*, Jerusalem: Ministry of Trade, Industry and Labour

Levin, D. (2012), 'The Cottage Cheese Boycott: The Conjunction Between News Construction and Social Protest on Facebook', *JOMEC Journal: Journalism, Media and Cultural Studies* 1: 2–16

London Economics (1997), *Competition in Retailing, Research Paper 13*, London: Office of Fair Trading

Monitor Company Group (2012), *Examination of Competition Level and Prices in the Food Products and FMCG Market in Israel*, Jerusalem: Ministry of Trade, Industry and Labour

Nordås, H.K., Geloso Grosso, M. and Pinali, E. (2008), *Market Structure in the Distribution Sector and Merchandise Trade*, OECD Trade Policy Working Paper No. 68, Paris: Organisation for Economic Co-operation and Development

Pauwelyn, J. (2005), 'Rien ne Va Plus? Distinguishing Domestic Regulation from Market Access in GATT and GATS', *World Trade Review* 4(2): 131–70

Pilat, D. (1997), *Regulation and Performance in the Distribution Sector*, Economics Department Working Paper No. 180, Paris: Organisation for Economic Co-operation and Development

Richards, T.J. and Pofahl, G. (2010), 'Pricing Power by Supermarket Retailers: A Ghost in the Machine?', *Choices* 25(2): 1–11

Slater, M. (2011), *Food Retail*, Tel Aviv: Dash Investment House

State Comptroller (2012), *Opinion: Supervision of Food Prices and Supervision of Dairy Products*, Jerusalem: State Comptroller of the State of Israel

Trajtenberg, M. (2011), *Report of the Committee for Economic and Social Change*, Jerusalem: State of Israel

Wrigley, N. and Lowe, M. (2010), *The Globalization of Trade in Retail Services: Report Commissioned by the OECD Trade Policy Linkages and Services Division for the OECD Experts Meeting on Distribution Services, Paris 17 November 2010*, Paris: Organisation for Economic Co-operation and Development

18

Regulatory impact analysis: addressing the trade and regulatory nexus

DARRELL PORTER AND LAUREN WIGHT

1 Introduction

The potential for productivity growth to generate higher incomes makes it a natural and important consideration for decision-makers. Productivity is the only driver of income growth that is unlimited, as opposed to resource exploitation or increases in population and labour force participation, each of which faces natural limits. The continuing need to stimulate productivity growth rightly remains at the forefront of government policy, and is a key priority of the Australian government.

Almost all regulations have the potential to impact on productivity, either through the incentives which they provide to businesses to change operating and investment decisions, or more directly through their impacts on compliance costs. It is inconceivable to think of a modern economy functioning without regulation. However, the challenge for government is to deliver effective and efficient regulation. Good quality regulation is critical to a well-functioning economy, while poor regulation can cause frustration and unintended consequences, or simply add red tape that adds nothing useful to the economy.

To improve the efficiency and effectiveness of regulation the Australian government introduced the regulatory impact analysis (RIA) requirements. These requirements are designed to improve the quality of regulations by ensuring that the key principles of efficiency, transparency, accountability, adaptability and coherence are embedded into the policy development process.

In order to reap the benefits and respond to the challenges of ongoing globalization, an economy needs to be as efficient, flexible and responsive as possible. Rather than providing specific industry support, it is more effective to ensure that general microeconomic settings are in place to allow industries with the best prospects to compete, so that the most productive industries will expand.

2 Regulatory governance

Across Organisation for Economic Co-operation and Development (OECD) countries, the nature of regulatory management and reform has changed over recent decades (OECD 2002: 16). What began in the 1980s and 1990s as 'deregulation' evolved into a focus on regulatory reform, encompassing a mixture of deregulation, re-regulation and initiatives to improve the effectiveness of regulatory instruments (see Box 18.1). These approaches to improve the effectiveness of regulations have, in turn, evolved into the wider notion of 'regulatory governance'. Regulatory governance embraces the wider issues of transparency (through the openness of consultation and the decision-making process); accountability (of regulators and appeal mechanisms); efficiency (maximizing the benefits to the whole community, taking into account the costs); adaptability (flexibility over time); and coherence (across government and between governments).

BOX 18.1 REGULATION REFORMS IN AUSTRALIA

Over recent decades, substantial regulation reforms have occurred in Australia. Many of the reforms made Australia an outward looking, dynamic economy by integrating with the global economy. Some of the major reforms are outlined below:

- *Trade liberalization* involved reductions in tariff assistance (beginning in 1973) and the abolition of quantitative import controls. These reforms gathered pace in the 1980s. The effective rate of assistance to manufacturing (the most protected sector) fell from around 35 per cent in the early 1970s to 5 per cent by 2000.
- *In capital markets*, the Australian dollar was floated in March 1983, foreign exchange controls and capital rationing (through interest rate controls) were removed progressively from the early 1980s and foreign-owned banks were allowed to compete initially for corporate customers and then, in the 1990s, to act as deposit-taking institutions.
- *National Competition Policy* reforms commenced in 1995 and have continued under all Australian governments. The reforms involved a coordinated national programme of broad-ranging reforms and included reforms to essential services (such as energy and road transport), government businesses and a wide range of anti-competitive regulations.
- *Seamless National Economy* is a current programme aimed at improving the national 'coherence' of regulation and reducing its costs, while maintaining or enhancing effectiveness. It covers thirty-six areas of reform, including twenty-seven deregulation priorities, eight competition reform areas and ongoing reforms to improve processes for regulation-making and review.

Source: Productivity Commission 2011.

3 OECD guiding principles

The OECD contends that a coherent, whole-of-government approach is needed to create a regulatory environment favourable to the creation and growth of businesses, productivity gains, competition, investment and international trade (OECD 2005: 1). The OECD *Guiding Principles for Regulatory Quality and Performance* capture the dynamic, whole-of-government approach to implementing regulatory policy:

- Adopt, at the political level, broad programmes of regulatory reform that establish clear objectives and frameworks for implementation.
- Assess impacts and review regulations systematically to ensure that they meet their intended objectives efficiently and effectively in a changing and complex economic and social environment.
- Ensure that regulations, regulatory institutions charged with implementation, and regulatory processes are transparent and non-discriminatory.
- Review and strengthen where necessary the scope, effectiveness and enforcement of competition policy.
- Design economic regulations in all sectors to stimulate competition and efficiency, and eliminate them except where clear evidence demonstrates that they are the best way to serve broad public interests.
- Eliminate unnecessary regulatory barriers to trade and investment through continued liberalization and enhance the consideration and better integration of market openness throughout the regulatory process, thus strengthening economic efficiency and competitiveness.
- Identify important linkages with other policy objectives and development policies to achieve those objectives in ways that support reform.

RIA is a common tool across the OECD used to incorporate these principles into government decision-making processes.

4 Australian model

The OECD guiding principles have been endorsed by the Australian government and serve to provide broad guidance on its regulatory governance arrangements. In Australia, consistency with these principles is achieved through RIA and specifically the best practice regulation requirements.

The government has adopted the term 'best practice regulation requirements' to signal to officials developing regulatory proposals that this is the process that should be used to ensure high quality regulation. This is not to say that it is the 'best' worldwide. In an international context, the different institutional arrangements in different countries or jurisdictions mean that there will be variations, but the main features will remain the same to achieve good policy development.

Within the RIA process, preparing a regulation impact statement (RIS) is a practical way of embedding good policy development processes across Australian government departments and agencies. The RIS codifies good policy development. With the level of analysis commensurate with the impacts of the regulatory proposal, it targets effort in providing the best package of information to the decision-maker, including the Cabinet, the Prime Minister or individual Ministers.

4.1 Regulation impact statements

An RIS is required to be prepared when a proposal is likely to have a regulatory impact on business or the not-for-profit sector, unless that impact is of a minor or machinery nature. The RIS requirements apply to all regulatory activity not just regulatory proposals impacting on a particular industry. Despite adopting a broad definition of regulation, only a small proportion of Australian government regulatory proposals require an RIS each year.

In Australia, the Office of Best Practice Regulation (OBPR) is an independent body responsible for assessing RISs against the government's best practice regulation requirements and for assisting an agency in preparing an RIS. However, the responsibility for preparing the RIS lies with the agency and Minister.

Once the OBPR has assessed the RIS as adequate, the agency provides it to the decision-maker. When the decision is announced, the RIS is made public as soon as practicable. It is a requirement to publish the RIS on the OBPR website[1] and, to inform Parliament, the RIS is included in the explanatory material for the regulation which is tabled in Parliament.

The RIS consists of seven elements which are essential to good regulation-making processes. The elements include the problem, objectives, options, impact analysis, a consultation statement, conclusion, and implementation and review. An overview of the elements is provided below and further details are in the *Best Practice Regulation Handbook*

[1] Further details are available at www.ris.finance.gov.au.

(Australian Government 2010). Note that for each element, the level of detail and depth of analysis should be commensurate with the magnitude of the problem and the size of the potential impacts of the proposal. Consequently, effort is being targeted to where it matters most.

4.1.1 Problem identification

The first section of the RIS should specify the perceived problem or issue that has prompted a consideration of government action. Information should be provided on the nature and magnitude of the problem and identify what government actions (if any) have been taken in the past to address the problem. Any underlying market failure (such as the presence of externalities), regulatory failure (e.g. unintended consequences or ineffective existing regulation), or risk, should also be identified.

A description of why the government's involvement is required to deal with the identified problem should be included in the RIS. As government action is not costless, the significance of the problem needs to be considered.

Clearly identifying the problem, its significance and a case for government intervention is crucial in the policy development process and preparing a good quality RIS. To provide guidance regarding the clear identification of problems and consequences of no action, Australian officials are required to address a series of points when considering proposals for new or amended regulation (see Box 18.2).

4.1.2 Objectives

The second section of the RIS should clearly explain the objectives, outcomes, goals or targets that are sought in relation to the identified problem. It should not prejustify a preferred solution, but should be specified broadly enough to allow consideration of all relevant alternative solutions. However, it should not be so broad or general that the range of alternatives becomes too large to assess, or the extent to which the objectives have been met becomes too hard to establish.

4.1.3 Options

To help decision-makers select the most effective and efficient approach, the RIS should test the effectiveness and appropriateness of alternative (regulatory and non-regulatory) options for achieving the stated objectives. This section of the RIS should describe each alternative option and explain how the option, if implemented, would achieve the desired result.

If any options involve establishing or amending standards in areas where international standards apply, the RIS should indicate whether the

BOX 18.2 IDENTIFYING A PROBLEM

The RIS needs to clearly define the problem associated with the proposal. The problem identified should be associated with the following:

- *Market failure*: such as a lack of or misleading information, presence of externalities or public goods, or use of excessive market power.

An externality occurs when one party imposes on others benefits that are not paid for or costs that are not compensated through market prices. For example, individuals may choose to drive on congested roads, increasing congestion and imposing costs on other road users.

- *Regulatory failure*: such as a government imposed restriction on competition that is not in the public interest.
- *Unacceptable hazard or risk*: such as human health and safety standards, or threats of damage to the physical environment.
- *Social goals/equity issues*: such as individuals or groups being unable to access available market information, goods or services.

– How significant is the problem? What is its magnitude? In the case of risk, what is the likelihood of the adverse event occurring? What evidence is there to support this initial assessment?
– What is the nature of the problem? What is the loss, harm or other adverse consequence that is being experienced, and by whom?
– How is the problem currently regulated? Are there deficiencies in the existing regulatory system that might fix the problem if corrected?
– Is there a case for government intervention or is the problem of purely private interest? Why does current regulation not properly address the identified problem?
– What are the consequences of not taking action? Could relying on the market in conjunction with the general application of existing laws and regulations solve the problem? If not, why not?
– Will the problem self-correct within a reasonable timeframe?

Source: Australian Government 2010.

standards under consideration deviate from the relevant international standards. A ‘do nothing’ option should always be included in the analysis. This is the base case against which alternatives will be compared. Different types of regulation include:

- *self-regulation*: characterized by industry formulating rules or codes of conduct, with industry solely responsible for enforcement;

- *quasi-regulation*: includes a wide range of rules or arrangements where governments influence businesses to comply, but which do not form part of explicit government regulation;
- *co-regulation*: this typically refers to the situation where industry develops and administers its own arrangements, but government provides legislative backing to enable the arrangements to be enforced;
- *explicit government regulation*: sometimes referred to as black-letter law, it comprises primary and subordinate legislation. It is the most commonly used form of regulation.

As outlined above, there is a spectrum of the types of options that can be tested, ranging from non-regulatory (such as information and education campaigns) through to black-letter law. Officials are encouraged to examine 'light-handed' regulation in the RIS.

4.1.4 Impact analysis: costs, benefits and risks

The next step in drafting the RIS is to conduct a comprehensive assessment of the expected impacts (costs and benefits) of each feasible option. The objective is to inform decision-makers on the likely merits of available options, and thereby assist their decision.

When analysing each option, consideration should be given to who would be affected if the option were implemented, what costs, benefits and, where relevant, levels of risk would result, and how significant they would be. Where possible the impacts should be quantified. At a minimum, the analysis should attempt to quantify all highly significant costs and benefits. All assessments of costs and benefits, whether quantitative or qualitative, should be based on evidence, with data sources and assumptions clearly identified.

A start is to identify all the groups affected by the problem and its proposed solution, whether directly or indirectly affected. In addition, Australian officials are required to assess the effects on the community as a whole, such as environmental and social impacts. Groups should generally be distinguished as consumers, business and government. Depending on the nature of the proposal these groups may be further subdivided.

Costs and benefits are terms used to describe the positive and negative effects of a proposal. A cost is any item that makes someone worse off or reduces a person's well-being. Cost items may include 'opportunities forgone' because a particular proposal has been adopted. A benefit includes any item that makes any person better off, regardless of whether it can be easily measured or quantified. Once the costs and benefits to each of the affected parties are identified, an assessment is made about the net impact of each option on the community as a whole.

Some existing and proposed regulations restrict competition. Such regulations can restrict consumer choice, raise prices and reduce overall economic productivity by denying the economy the efficiency gains competition provides. Significant restrictions on competition range from legislated monopolies that block competition in entire sectors, to a host of less visible restrictions on starting up and operating businesses, such as quotas on business licences.

In Australia, where a particular proposal restricts competition, the RIS must demonstrate that it will deliver benefits to the community that outweigh its costs, and that there are no alternative means of achieving the same objective without restricting competition. This is a requirement to meet the government's commitments under the intergovernmental Competition Principles Agreement, which is designed to promote competition in the economy and the benefits that it can bring to the community.

4.1.5 Consultation

In general, any policy development process, including proposed new regulation or changes to regulation, will involve consultation with relevant stakeholders. This will include the main parties affected by the proposal such as businesses, the community, regulators and other government agencies. Consultation helps to ensure that the full range of impacts are taken into account when assessing how best to solve a problem and the transparency it fosters helps build trust in the policy process.

It is important that consultation be conducted with the attitude that the stakeholders' views will be listened to and taken seriously. When developing the RIS, the official needs to outline the process and outcomes from consultation undertaken during the policy development process. Relevant information includes:

- the main views of the stakeholders;
- areas of agreement as well as areas of difference;
- information on intergovernmental consultation;
- how the proposal has been modified to take account of stakeholders' views. If the proposal has not been modified, the RIS should explain why dissenting views have not been accepted.

This process ensures transparency in the consideration of all stakeholder views received during consultation, which reduces the risk of particular stakeholders dominating the consultation process.

The government has developed a set of best practice regulation principles which should be followed by all agencies developing regulation. These principles are:

- *continuity*: consultation should be continual, and start early in the policy development process;
- *targeting*: consultation should be widely based to ensure it captures the diversity of stakeholders affected by the proposed changes. This includes other levels of government and other relevant agencies;
- *timeliness*: consultation should start when policy objectives and options are being identified. Throughout the consultation process, stakeholders should be given sufficient time to provide considered responses;
- *accessibility*: stakeholder groups should be informed of proposed consultation and be provided with information about proposals through a range of means appropriate to these groups. Agencies should be aware of the opportunities to consult jointly with other agencies to minimize the burden on stakeholders;
- *transparency*: policy agencies need to explain clearly the objectives of the consultation process and the regulation policy framework within which consultations will take place, and provide feedback on how they have taken consultation responses into consideration;
- *consistency and flexibility*: consistent consultation procedures can make it easier for stakeholders to participate. However, this must be balanced with the need for consultation arrangements to be designed to suit the circumstances of the particular proposal under consideration;
- *evaluation and review*: agencies should evaluate consultation processes and continue to examine ways of making them more effective.

In order to fulfil the requirement to undertake targeted consultation with those affected by a proposal, consultation should be undertaken with international as well as domestic stakeholders. Broad consultation will enhance the analysis of the costs and benefits to all stakeholder groups.

As part of the government's best practice regulation process, agencies responsible for regulatory changes that may have a significant impact on business are required to prepare and publish an annual regulatory plan at the beginning of the financial year, and update it as appropriate. The plans provide business and the community with information about planned changes to government regulation, and make it easier for business to take part in the development of regulation that is likely to affect them. The plans contain information about proposed regulatory activity, including a description of the issue, information about the consultation strategy and an expected timetable. Annual regulatory plans are published on the website of each agency.

4.1.6 RIS conclusion

The RIS conclusion should provide a clear statement identifying the preferred option, indicating the costs and benefits of this option for the range of groups that are affected, and highlighting any areas of uncertainty. The conclusion should be supported by the preceding analysis.

4.1.7 Implementation and review

Having identified the preferred option to meet the objectives stated at the beginning of the RIS, it is necessary to consider how the option will be implemented and enforced, and to establish a review strategy that will allow the option to be evaluated after it has been in place for some time.

It is important to consider some practical implementation issues (if they have not yet been considered) before the option is adopted. These include minimizing compliance costs, considering transitional arrangements (including industry adjustment programmes) and enforcement.

5 Addressing the challenges posed by the trade and regulatory nexus

At times, decision-makers can face a tension between domestic regulation and international trade. As mentioned earlier, rather than providing specific industry support, it is more effective to ensure that general microeconomic settings are in place to allow industries with the best prospects to compete, so that the most productive industries will expand. Nonetheless, it is the decision-maker who is responsible for making that choice.

The RIA process provides a systematic, objective way to bring all the relevant information to the decision-maker. The key steps involve:

- problem identification and justification for government intervention;
- identifying a range of feasible options (including 'light-handed' regulation);

- analysing the impacts (costs, benefits and risks) on stakeholder groups;
- taking into account the views of stakeholders (including dissenting views);
- reaching a logical conclusion that benefits the community.

The RIA process ensures that short-term interests do not override the long-term perspective. This is important, since once poor regulation is in place it can be difficult to change. The objective process is also useful where a small but vocal group of self-interested stakeholders (e.g. an existing industry group) push for a specific regulatory approach at the expense of others (e.g. consumers) particularly when the likely costs are spread widely. To appropriately inform the decision-maker, the RIS must consider the impacts on all relevant stakeholders as well as the distributional impacts of the proposal by each stakeholder group. So, if a proposal is expected to benefit a particular group of stakeholders with the majority of costs felt by a different group of stakeholders, this must be transparent in the RIS.

As mentioned earlier, the RIA process also includes a further, more stringent test if a proposal is likely to restrict competition. For example, if regulations were proposed that restricted the use of medical professionals, accountants or architects from other countries (restricted access to services), the proposal would be required to pass the further competition test, since it distorts the market for these services. If a restriction on competition is identified, the RIS would need to demonstrate that the proposal will deliver benefits to the community that outweigh its costs and that there are no alternative means of achieving the same objectives without restricting competition. This allows an assessment of whether or not the proposed regulation is the most effective option for all stakeholders.

Also under the government's best practice regulation process, where a proposed regulation has a direct bearing on trade performance, a trade impact assessment should be incorporated into the RIS. This assessment should summarize the impact of regulatory options and proposals on exporters and importers, and assess the overall impact on Australia's international trade.

An Australian example of how the RIA process can be used to inform decision-makers is in the RIS for the Seasonal Worker Program. This programme provides access to low-skilled seasonal employment opportunities in Australia. It delivers financial gains and employment experience to seasonal workers and helps employers to accommodate unmet demand for seasonal labour. Some of the key points for each element of the RIS are provided in Box 18.3.

BOX 18.3 SEASONAL WORKER PROGRAM

Problem

Employment opportunities in Pacific Island countries and East Timor are low, and Australian employers still experience difficulties in filling vacancies with suitable local labour.

Objective

- Contribute to economic development in the Pacific and East Timor.
- Provide employment opportunities for workers from Pacific Island countries and East Timor while maintaining the integrity of Australian employment conditions.
- Assist employers in agricultural and horticultural industries to fill their seasonal low-skilled vacancies.

Options

- Option 1: 'no change' – discontinue the current pilot scheme.
- Option 2: regulated ongoing labour mobility programme.
- Option 3: self-regulation – an industry driven and regulated programme.

Impact Analysis

Option 1

- Costs: if the programme does not continue, there would be productivity losses for participating employers, with reduced access to a reliable and proven labour force.
- Benefits: there would be more work opportunities for working holiday-makers and other itinerant workers.

Option 2

- Costs: for the Australian government, costs were estimated at AU$20 million over four years. For participating countries, it would mean a loss of labour resources. For seasonal workers, they will incur a visa application charge (AU$305) and other costs, such as part of their airfare. For employers, there are a number of steps involved, including demonstrating their commitment to employing Australian workers.
- Benefits: the programme is a cost-effective way for the government to assist Pacific Islands and East Timor. It also enhances the employment opportunities for unemployed low-skilled workers from these regions, as well as satisfying demand in the horticulture and tourism industry for low-paid seasonal workers.

BOX 18.3 (*cont.*)

Option 3

- Costs: for the Australian government, costs would be less than for Option 2. There would also be similar costs for seasonal workers as in Option 2. High risk to Australian job seekers being displaced and workers could be exploited.
- Benefits: a low-cost way of achieving Option 2.

Consultation

Consultation was undertaken with domestic and international stakeholders, this included participating countries, growers and seasonal workers.

Conclusion

After the costs and benefits discussed in the impact analysis were considered, the preferred option recommended was the regulated labour mobility programme for Pacific Island countries and East Timor.

Implementation and review

An overarching implementation, risk management, stakeholder management, communication and evaluation plan was to be developed. The programme will be reviewed on an ongoing basis.

Source: DEEWR 2012.

6 Key concerns with the implementation of the RIA requirements

Some form of RIA process has been adopted by the Australian government and for each state and territory government. In its country reviews of regulatory reform, the OECD found that Australia is one of the front-running countries in the OECD in terms of its regulatory reform practices (OECD 2010: 15). However, these processes are still evolving. In a recent report by the Productivity Commission, *Regulatory Impact Analysis: Benchmarking* (Productivity Commission 2012), it concluded that there is considerable scope to improve the way that regulations are developed and scrutinized.

The Productivity Commission noted that, while RIA processes are reasonably well designed and supported in all jurisdictions, there are some shortcomings and a significant gap between agreed and actual practice that must be addressed. It identified a number of leading practices in RIA that, if more widely adopted, would improve the efficacy of policy development processes, including:

- publication of all RISs and compliance assessments by oversight bodies;
- the use of a two-stage impact analysis process, with stakeholders being able to comment on all draft RISs;
- reducing the opportunities to avoid assessment;
- more effective targeting of RIA resources.

The Productivity Commission stated that more widespread and consistent adoption of the leading practices it identified, particularly in relation to transparency and accountability, would create stronger incentives for governments to demand and officials to deliver policies that are well considered and supported by rigorous analysis of different options and their impacts. This should increase the commitment to the best practice regulation process by Ministers and agencies.

Agencies need to develop capabilities to undertake RIA. Some officials may prepare RISs on a regular basis, while others may only be required to prepare a RIS once every few years. Consequently, the OBPR provides advice and assistance through the *Best Practice Regulation Handbook*, a website and various training packages. The OBPR also provides advice (written or through meetings) on draft RISs to help the agency improve the quality of the RIS to achieve the government's adequacy standard.

The OBPR has provided training to Asia-Pacific Economic Cooperation (APEC) economies to help in building high quality regulatory environments, in order to assist in promoting free and open trade and investment in the region. APEC leaders have agreed to strengthen a programme on good regulatory practices to reduce the negative impact of regulatory divergences on trade and investment (APEC 2011). During 2012, Australia, in collaboration with Mexico and New Zealand, developed a major capacity-building project to conduct a series of RIA training courses for interested APEC economies. Through APEC and other initiatives, the OBPR has provided RIA training to China; Hong Kong, China; Indonesia; Malaysia; Mexico; the Philippines; the Russian Federation; Chinese Taipei; and Vietnam.

Some observers question whether the RIA process provides a net benefit to the community. From Australia's experience, there are examples where the process has stopped poor proposals progressing or where a better option has been pursued. A recent example can illustrate this: an agency was required to undertake consultation as part of the RIA process. As a result of the consultation process, the agency became aware of the difficulty of requiring businesses to implement the proposed regulatory changes within a fixed two-year period. Based on submissions received, the preferred option was modified to extend the transitional period to five years. Another example of a situation where a better regulatory outcome was achieved was a proposal that was modified to capture additional sections of the market in order to enhance the reform. This change was based on comments received from the consultation process, which was required as part of the RIA process. However, since the primary purpose of the RIA process is to document policy development processes, it is difficult to know what might have happened if the RIA process was not followed.

Also, the Victorian Competition and Efficiency Commission found that the RIA requirements led to significant savings in the costs imposed by Victorian regulations, relative to a situation with no RIA process (Abusah and Pingiaro 2011: 15). Their key finding was that in the periods 2005–2006 and 2009–2010, the RIA process achieved estimated gross savings (i.e. a reduction in regulatory costs) of AU$902 million (present value) over the ten-year life of the regulations. In terms of cost-effectiveness, for every dollar incurred by the key parties involved in the RIA process, gross savings of between AU$28 and AU$56 million were identified. These results show the value of the RIA process in policy development.

7 Conclusion

Different countries have different processes in place for achieving good policy development. The Australian model described in this chapter is one example of implementing a RIA process. The RIA process (including the preparation of the RIS) is a practical way of embedding the key principles of efficiency, transparency, accountability, adaptability and coherence into the policy development process. It can assist in addressing some of the challenges posed by the trade and regulatory nexus. The systematic process helps reduce the level of unnecessary or poorly designed regulation, which can reduce the adverse effects on the economy and external trade. However, there are still challenges in implementing the RIA process.

References

Abusah, S. and Pingiaro, C. (2011), *Cost-Effectiveness of Regulatory Impact Assessment in Victoria*, Staff Working Paper, Victorian Competition and Efficiency Commission

APEC (2011), 'Leaders' Declaration: Annex D – Strengthening Implementation of Good Regulatory Practices', Honolulu, Hawaii, United States, 13 November

Australian Government (2010), *Best Practice Regulation Handbook*, Canberra: Commonwealth of Australia

DEEWR (2012), *Regulation Impact Statement: Seasonal Labour Mobility Initiative with Pacific Island Countries and East Timor for Development Purposes*, Canberra: Department of Education, Employment and Workplace Relations

OECD (2002), *Regulatory Policies in OECD Countries: From Intervention to Regulatory Governance*, OECD Reviews of Regulatory Reform, Paris: Organisation for Economic Co-operation and Development

(2005), *Guiding Principles on Regulatory Quality and Performance*, Paris: Organisation for Economic Co-operation and Development

(2010), *Australia: Towards a Seamless National Economy*, OECD Reviews of Regulatory Reform, Paris: Organisation for Economic Co-operation and Development

Productivity Commission (2011), *Identifying and Evaluating Regulation Reforms*, Research Report, Canberra: Commonwealth of Australia

(2012), *Regulatory Impact Analysis: Benchmarking*, Research Report, Canberra: Commonwealth of Australia

PART IV

Concluding remarks

19

Services liberalization, negotiations and regulation: some lessons from the GATS experience

HAMID MAMDOUH

1 Introduction

The services economy has been undergoing a major transformation over the last three decades, moving away from the old model, where services were more often than not government functions provided by public utility entities, towards a new paradigm of private, sector-led, competitive markets, where services are exchanged on a commercial basis. Accordingly, the role of governments has fundamentally changed in many activities from being the provider of the service into that of the supervisor or regulator in pursuit of public interests. Increasingly, services markets continue to be liberalized, motivated by the usual gains from competition (better quality, lower prices, wider choices, expanding markets and more job creation).

The General Agreement on Trade in Services (GATS) is the international community's response to the transformation (or paradigm shift) in the services sector. It provides a legal framework that institutionalizes concepts for a new form of international trade, through the four modes of supply. Rather than triggering the process of liberalization, it was seen as a rules-based framework for international cooperation in the field of trade in services, consolidating liberalizing steps, and as a multilateral antidote to backsliding in national policies (the role of policy commitments).

In pursuing the further liberalization of trade in services towards achieving desired benefits, it would be useful to look briefly at how the process has advanced over the last few decades, at the role of trade negotiations and, more importantly, at the role of regulation.

2 Most liberalization has been autonomous

The liberalization of services markets has been driven, to a large extent, by national self-interest. It has been fuelled by technological progress, innovation and new business models, as well as the continuous liberalization and facilitation of cross-border movements of goods, capital, information and people. In other words, it is an organic process, driven by natural forces. One of the most active ingredients in the process is increasing competition resulting from technical innovation and attendant regulatory evolution. The autonomous nature of services liberalization has led to a situation where existing regulatory regimes are more liberal than what is being reflected by way of commitments in trade agreements. In the case of GATS, the gap is particularly vast.

GATS provides a legal framework for negotiating and binding the liberalization of trade in services. So far, with the exception of countries that have recently acceded to the World Trade Organization (WTO), it has not been used by members as a driving force for services liberalization and reform. At the same time, the potential of liberalizing services through negotiations in the WTO must not be underestimated. Indeed, under the right conditions, negotiations under GATS can produce impressive results (e.g. post-Uruguay Round negotiations on basic telecommunications and financial services). Negotiations under GATS, however, have their peculiarities.

First, unlike negotiations on merchandise trade, with negotiations on services, WTO members are often not motivated by the reciprocal exchange of concessions opening up new export opportunities, but are mostly driven in their reforms by the pursuit of national self-interest.

Second, there is the risk of hostage-taking in the framework of negotiations being a single undertaking. Progress in services could be held back in return for progress elsewhere. Nevertheless, the conference on services in July 2008 was a good example that positive linkages can also be established.

Third, the institutional structure in states for policy-making and regulation on services involves a wide range of ministries and agencies (including non-governmental organizations). This represents a considerable challenge in coordinating the national positions to be represented by the negotiating ministry.

Fourth, the involvement of higher levels of political leadership might therefore be necessary, particularly where new liberalizing steps are being negotiated, in order to access a multitude of policy areas. This is borne out by the examples of members that have recently negotiated accession to the WTO.

Fifth, apart from coordinating national positions, the actual negotiating process often requires the active participation of sectoral experts and regulators, especially in negotiating new liberalization, which might not be easily available in the Geneva process.

Sixth, certain policy and regulatory issues in negotiations on services could be of particular sensitivity to national governments. A good example, but not the only one, is Mode 4. Unfortunately, such sensitivity has been translated into a reluctance to engage. In a way, this perpetuates ambiguities and misperceptions regarding the actual scope of negotiations and the implications for domestic policies.

Seventh, traditionally negotiations have focused on the removal of measures constituting trade barriers. In services, it is normally the removal of market access and national treatment limitations. Having said that, trade restriction in services is sometimes a result of the absence of regulation. In other words, a barrier to services trade sometimes lies not in the existence of a measure but in the absence of, for example, transparent and objective rules for licensing. These situations sometimes lead to the worst of regulatory instruments: discretionary authority.

These peculiarities of negotiations on services do not mean that the liberalization objective of WTO members cannot be achieved. They only mean that the negotiations would have to take into account these points and develop an effective approach to deal with them. The following are some considerations:

- Given the negotiating realities of the single undertaking, overall momentum in the Doha Round negotiations is a prerequisite for progress to be made in services.
- The process of plurilateral request-and-offer negotiations already undertaken under the framework of the GATS has usefully identified sectors of negotiating interest and specific barriers to be negotiated in each; and between co-sponsors and recipients, the critical mass of WTO members from whom priority commitments are expected.
- Given the vast gap between current commitments in schedules and existing levels of liberalization, and in view of the pace of liberalization over the past ten years, the value of underpinning existing liberalization should not be underestimated. This should not be to the exclusion of negotiating new market opening. After all, the objective of the negotiations according to GATS, the negotiating guidelines and the Hong Kong Ministerial Declaration, is to achieve 'progressively higher levels of liberalization', not just higher levels of commitments.
- Intensive engagement in the request-and-offer negotiations needs to be focused and pointed towards specific priorities that are essential for

the end-game phase. It needs to be at the appropriate level, involving the relevant institutions and the required expertise.

- Sensitive issues requiring clarification and further technical work must be addressed directly. To use the example of Mode 4, which is certainly not the only one, the following might be considered. First, regulators need to understand the specific scope of this mode. It is important for them to distinguish the scope of Mode 4 from immigration policy. Furthermore, it is not a North–South issue. All WTO members, including Mode 4 *demandeurs*, are particularly restrictive in this area. There is a need to move away from the purely defensive mind-set regarding this mode and consider own-offensive interests in this area. The private sector could play an important role in identifying such interests. Second, there is a need to start thinking creatively in the negotiations about possible arrangements for regulatory collaboration between sending and receiving countries. Sending countries could contemplate undertaking obligations, such as establishing pre-screening arrangements, providing guarantees for return of citizens to ensure temporariness of stay, as well as assuming other responsibilities (including social security arrangements) vis-à-vis Mode 4 citizens residing in 'export' markets. The scope of this effort can extend to many concerns raised by receiving countries. Such arrangements could go a long way in facilitating more Mode 4 commitments. A useful example of cooperation in such areas is the APEC Business Traveller Card scheme.

It is not sufficient to address services liberalization through market access negotiations. Regulatory issues need to be addressed as a supplement to market access and national treatment commitments, where the absence of domestic regulation leads to the restriction of services trade. Negotiations on domestic regulation disciplines which apply to all services sectors are expected to address these types of issues. At the same time, there is room for negotiating sector-specific or mode-specific provisions as additional commitments. These may also include any forms of regulatory cooperation designed to promote services trade.

3 The regulatory challenge

The greatest challenge that governments and policy-makers face in the transformation of the services sector is the regulatory challenge. One of the most important conceptual bases to GATS is the distinction between liberalization and (de)regulation. From a legal perspective, liberalization under GATS, in sectors where commitments are made, means granting market access (GATS Article XVI) and national treatment (GATS Article XVII). These provisions have a defined legal scope that applies only to six types of market access restrictions and any form of discrimination. Apart from that, governments and regulators are free to decide the shape and content of the remaining regulatory framework. While GATS does not interfere with the regulatory agenda, by the same token it does not provide much guidance either on how to pursue a sound regulatory approach.

3.1 *Guidelines for regulatory principles?*

While each services sector has its specificities and technical complexities, some general guiding principles might be identified to assist policy-makers and regulators in taking the 'right path'. Such principles could be identified at a general level that might be applicable across various sectors and, at the same time, leave appropriate space for sovereign and societal policy choices. They could even be envisaged as a set of initial general questions for 'regulatory audit' type of analysis. Based on practical experience drawn from GATS, the following elements were identified and may be worth considering for further elaboration.

An effective approach to sound regulation normally emanates from a clear policy vision for the services sector concerned, its role in the economy, its contribution to society and the direction that the process of reform needs to take. At the end of the day, the regulatory challenge may involve two important aspects: rules and institutions.

3.2 *Rules*

Rules relating to the supply of services need to contain four characteristics outlined below: content, design, scope-jurisdiction and transparency.

- *Content*: The rules relating to the supply of the service need to be clearly stated and drafted, based on objective criteria and coherent. They should also, to the maximum extent possible, reduce the scope for discretionary decision-making.
- *Design*: The choice of which rules may be contained in general legislation and which may be left to other forms of regulation, decrees or administrative guidelines, is important. It should be made in a manner that facilitates effective application. At the same time, the design should

take into account the need for possible future flexibility to adjust in the light of market developments.

- *Scope-jurisdiction*: The interface between central and sub-central government levels is important to take into account. Both levels must act in a coherent and complementary way. The same goes for the interface between sector-specific and cross-cutting types of rules (e.g. telecommunications and competition policy).
- *Transparency*: Rules must be transparent, including their underlying rationale. They should be easily accessible. Furthermore, the regulatory process itself needs to be transparent, allowing different stakeholders to observe and, where appropriate, take part.

3.3 *Institutions*

When establishing the framework for regulatory institutions, policy-makers need to take into account the following:

- *Mandate*: The institutional framework for the development and implementation of regulation is key. The mandate of a regulatory institution must be carefully drawn to reflect its objectives, functions and modus operandi. Often mandates need to be reviewed (sometimes completely changed) to reflect the change of policy direction, for example, from a government-controlled to a competitive market structure.
- *Independence*: The independence of regulatory institutions needs to be ensured. A regulator must be independent from any market commercial interest as well as from political influence. The risk of falling captive to vested interests must be avoided.
- *Interface*: The institutional structure should provide for an effective interface between different governmental institutions dealing with different regulatory frameworks of mutual relevance. The interface with private-sector institutions, think-tanks and civil-society organizations should also be encouraged and facilitated.
- *Accountability*: A regulatory body must be accountable for its decisions and the achievement of its objectives in a manner that does not compromise its independence. The authority to whom a regulator is accountable and the terms of such accountability must be drawn carefully.
- *Human resources*: Institutions must be equipped with the required expertise in sufficient capacity. A sound human resource base is key

to the sound functioning of regulators. In view of technological developments and the dynamic and innovative nature of competitive markets, this particular aspect should be a priority.

4 Conclusion

International cooperation on services regulatory matters is expanding with important organizations, such as the World Bank, playing an increasing role. Research efforts and empirical analyses often focus on sectoral perspectives. This sectoral focus is well justified in view of the specificities of services sectors and the peculiarity of regulatory issues arising in each.

Having said that, it might be worthwhile to develop a set of 'guidelines for regulatory principles' – ones that could serve as an introductory step towards best practices. Such guidelines need not be negotiated as legally binding principles, but as recommendations based on informed work carried out by international organizations in the field, such as the World Bank, the WTO, and others. Any such guidelines would never be enough to fulfil all needs for regulatory guidance. Not all liberalization efforts have been successful, in spite of the best intentions of policy-makers and regulators. Developing recommendations along these lines, however, based on wider consultations, could be extremely helpful, not least in various activities aimed at building capacity.

20

Addressing the domestic regulation and services trade interface: reflections on the way ahead

AIK HOE LIM AND BART DE MEESTER

1 Introduction

The contributions in this book have been wide-ranging. Parts I and II combined economic and legal perspectives on the purpose of regulation, its potential impact on trade and the relevance of existing World Trade Organization (WTO) principles in addressing trade effects that may arise from domestic regulation. Part III supplemented this discussion with country and sector-specific case studies illustrating a particular regulatory experience or challenge. While these case studies cannot be considered to be exhaustive, they do provide some insight into the problems of the type discussed in the WTO negotiations on domestic regulation disciplines. In particular, the case studies raise a number of recurring issues. These, when considered against the discussion of WTO principles in Part II, provide a form of 'reality check' on how the unfinished business of developing domestic regulation disciplines have been addressed and whether there are other approaches or issues that should be considered.

2 Themes emerging from the case studies and essays

A basic purpose of this book has been to improve understanding of the regulatory issues faced in services sectors as well as their potential impact on trade. In doing this, we have sought to document significant experiences or accounts of how governments and regulatory and supervisory authorities have dealt with services liberalization and regulation as a practical challenge. We have not sought to distil 'best practices' out of the essays and case studies collected in this book, as there is still much to be learnt about the trade and regulation interface. However, we did find that while many of the concerns and regulatory practices are specific to the context of the individual case study, the issues raised appear to have wider significance either for all services sectors or for certain subsectors.

These recurring issues illustrate well the challenges of managing services liberalization and domestic regulation, and can be grouped under the following themes:

- liberalization needs re-regulation and not deregulation;
- market access and national treatment commitments are not sufficient to address regulatory impediments to trade;
- development of new services is challenged by fragmented regulation and supervision;
- recognition and the role of international standards;
- importance of transparent, reasonable, objective and impartial rule-making and supervision;
- ensuring that regulatory requirements are relevant to the objective and not more burdensome than necessary.

2.1 Liberalization needs re-regulation

Tinne Heremans explains that governments consider regulation to be essential for their service sectors, given the 'corrective' (addressing market failures such as abuse of market power, information asymmetry and negative externalities) and 'redistributive' (redistribution to serve public or private interests) functions of regulation. For this reason, some WTO members have been hesitant to commit to 'disciplines' because they perceive these only as a *limitation* on their right to achieve certain policy objectives (such as universal service supply at a reasonable cost or quality protection). In other words, any WTO trade disciplines, which inevitably constrain government action, are misperceived as *deregulatory tools.*

On the other hand, the General Agreement on Trade in Services (GATS) negotiating mandate for domestic regulation could also provide a basis for re-regulation, as WTO disciplines are based upon commonly shared principles of non-discrimination, transparency, impartiality and certainty. Faced with fast-developing services sectors that are increasingly subject to international competition and growing consumer demand, it is not uncommon for regulators to utilize trade liberalization as a strategy for anchoring regulatory reform. In the telecommunications sector, for example, it was the decision by many developed and developing countries to liberalize the market, which resulted in the introduction of new legislation that promoted consumer interests through disciplines on interconnection, transparent licensing procedures, independent regulators, non-discriminatory universal service obligations, and so on. There can thus be strong synergies between trade and regulatory instruments. The Reference Paper on telecommunications, which was developed by WTO members as a set of pro-competitive regulatory principles to accompany market access commitments, is an interesting example of liberalization and re-regulation. These principles, when undertaken as additional commitments, strengthened the hand of regulators to control the dominant incumbent service supplier from engaging in an anti-competitive manner. They also assured new entrants to the market that they would be treated in an impartial manner by the regulatory body.

The fact that re-regulation is a precondition for opening up to international competition, rather than an obstacle to such competition, and that the instruments designed to accompany services liberalization can also serve the objectives of regulators, were stressed in several case studies. For instance, Henry Gao notes that sectors, such as the telecommunications sector in China, that have been characterized for years by state monopolies did not need specific regulations for reconciling public interest objectives with efficient market competition. However, once competition was introduced, the regulatory framework needed to be strengthened rather than dismantled. The same conclusion is reached by Masamichi Kono, Koichi Iwai and Yoshitaka Sakai, who note that promoting competition in the financial services market could create risks for individual investors. Therefore, the Japanese authorities decided to promote liberalization measures and also to strengthen investor protection as they promoted financial system reforms.

Krishna Oolun described the relationship between liberalization and re-regulation as a dynamic process. In his 'adaptive regulatory model', he outlines a continuum with four stages:

- the WTO commitment undertaken to introduce competition in telecommunications;
- reforming the legislative framework to provide the necessary legislative instruments to legally allow the changes;
- liberalization;
- the introduction of full competition.

It is interesting that he sees a distinction between 'liberalization' and 'competition'. The former is viewed as the opening of the market to new entrants, which is a policy decision that is confirmed by legislation, while the latter is a more complex process requiring the establishment, and continual evolution, of the regulatory framework. The distinction between 'liberalization' and 're-regulation' as separate but interdependent processes resurfaces in the overview by Hamid Mamdouh on the regulatory challenge of services liberalization. The point that comes through from these, and other case studies and essays, is that both consumer and producer interests in a liberalized services market are best advanced through a transparent, objective and impartial regulatory environment. Tham Siew Yean and Nik Kamal Nik Mahmod, in particular, document how liberalization of private higher education, and development of the market for education services, was complemented by continuous evolution of the regulatory structure and establishment of new institutions responsible for quality assurance.

2.2 Need for broadened disciplines on domestic regulation that go beyond market access and national treatment

The essays on the principles, as well as the practical case studies in this book, challenge the legal distinctions drawn in GATS between market access and national treatment, on the one hand, and domestic regulation, on the other.

Indeed, Hildegunn Kyvik Nordås concludes that differences in regulation may be a considerable barrier to international trade in its own right. She refers to non-discriminatory regulation that may *de facto* impose higher costs on foreign than local service suppliers. This is because foreign suppliers must learn how to deal with an unfamiliar regulatory environment, and compliance costs are often at least partly duplicated in each market a firm enters. Service suppliers may need to redesign their product or to restructure their business model to meet the host country requirements. Without the addition of disciplines on non-discriminatory minimum requirements that service providers are required to meet, the benefits of international competition may not be sufficiently realized.

Henry Gao makes the same point, noting that measures that do not violate the market access or national treatment commitments may nevertheless still have significant effects on the willingness and ability of foreign suppliers to provide the service. In his view, without proper domestic regulation, the process of trade liberalization could well be delayed or even stalled. Disciplines on domestic regulation are thus currently the 'missing link' in GATS.

This is exactly the reason why GATS Article VI:4 includes a mandate for negotiating disciplines '[w]ith a view to ensuring that measures relating to qualification requirements and procedures, technical standards and licensing requirements do not constitute unnecessary barriers to trade in services'. Although not completed, the exercise of negotiating horizontal disciplines on qualification requirements and procedures, technical standards and licensing requirements has arguably developed negotiators' understanding of what is necessary to avoid domestic regulation constituting an unnecessary barrier to trade in services. Given that the negotiations on horizontal disciplines focused on a broader range of services sectors than the professional services sector (for which the Article VI:4-mandate was initially developed), new regulatory issues emerged in discussions that are not necessarily typical for professional services.

Indeed, the traditional conception of domestic regulation, as specified in the mandate for negotiations in GATS Article VI:4, seems overtaken by current fast-developing services sectors.

For example, competition disciplines appear to be an essential component of such disciplines. Government regulation can only partly address barriers to trade and competition. Even if market access and national treatment commitments are respected, and regulations comply with disciplines on domestic regulation, private conduct may still seek to lessen competition.

This was illustrated by Tomer Broude and Lior Herman when discussing retail food distribution in Israel. They explain that high food costs in retail shops are partly caused by collusion between large wholesale distributors and mergers and acquisitions among them. They note that such distributors are able to extract high costs from food retailers, restrain their ability to exploit scale advantages, and affect their internal operations, such as decision-making over shelf space allocation and arrangement, as well as inability to purchase directly from farmers. The fact that agriculture is exempted from the antitrust law in Israel hampers action against such problems.

Siva Somasundram and Iain Sandford highlight that also in postal markets that are, or are being, liberalized, there is a range of competition issues that need to be addressed. First, it is sometimes the case that government measures create legal barriers to entry on the basis that restricting competition is judged beneficial. Second, even in cases where formal legal or regulatory barriers are not imposed, barriers to market entry may exist in the form of a dominant firm's ability to affect entry conditions to keep out potential competition. Third, in other cases, a firm's power to affect conditions of entry to one market can arise through its dominance in another market. A fourth situation can arise where a firm has market power through its control of the infrastructure necessary for the delivery of a service, since the need to access or recreate such infrastructure is itself a barrier to the entry of competitors. The first issue could arguably be a market access concern under GATS Article XVI, but not the other three issues cited by Somasundram and Sandford.

Competition issues are already addressed to a certain extent in GATS Article VIII (on monopolies and exclusive service suppliers) and GATS Article IX (on restrictive business practices). However, these are limited in scope and depth. Therefore, it would be an important contribution of the disciplines on domestic regulation to find alternative instruments to build on these principles, in parallel with the Article VI:4 negotiations.

Further, as Hamid Mamdouh explains, negotiations on domestic regulation need to focus on developing guidance on how to pursue a sound regulatory approach, and should not be perceived as a deregulatory tool. Such guidelines could offer to regulators and policy-makers in WTO members indications on how they could design their rules and institutions to make sure the adopted domestic regulation facilitates trade rather than hampers it. Hence, such a broader interpretation of the mandate in Article VI:4 is desirable. In Hamid Mamdouh's view, 'guidelines for regulatory principles' could serve as an introductory step towards best practices. Such guidelines need not be negotiated as legally binding principles, but as recommendations based on informed work carried out by international organizations in the field, such as the World Bank, the WTO, and others.

2.3 Development of new services is challenged by fragmented regulation and supervision

A significant recurring issue in the case studies is the fact that, as markets develop and new types of service provision occur, regulatory structures need to follow. However, such new services may not easily be classified within one single service sector or one regulatory area.

For instance, the case study on mobile money services in Uganda illustrates the regulatory challenges encountered. Joan Apecu, Irene Kaggwa Sewankambo and Yusuf Atiku Abdalla note that these services 'present regulatory challenges beyond what other normal financial services could do because of [their] convergence with telecommunication services'. For these services, relevant regulation includes existing rules on e-commerce, consumer protection, telecommunications services and banking services. Logically, while these different regulatory areas and services sectors are traditionally supervised by different authorities, they also require enhanced coordination between these authorities or designation of one single responsible authority.

The case study on logistics services in China also illustrates the challenge of fragmented regulation and supervision in light of fast-developing services sectors. Ruosi Zhang notes that 'logistics remains a nascent industry' and that there is no single competent authority overseeing it in China. Different types of transport (maritime, inland waterway, road, air and rail) fall under the competence of different authorities and require application for separate licences. Furthermore, related services such as cargo handling and warehousing could be provided by the same integrated service provider, creating further challenges for obtaining the correct licences and complying with the correct regulations.

Another case in point is the example of India's telemedicine services. Rupa Chanda and Pralok Gupta note that 'a variety of domestic regulations currently affect the realization of the actual potential' of India's telemedicine exports. It concerns in particular regulations on medical training that make it difficult for telemedicine providers to recruit the required manpower. Further, inadequate regulations concerning malpractice (not specifying precisely who is liable in case of wrong diagnosis) would limit the possibility of providing these services in countries where stringent regulations prevail. Also, the absence of data protection legislation and high import duties for the required telemedicine equipment affect the development of telemedicine services. Chanda and Gupta also point to the fact that many of the regulatory issues constraining foreign direct investment in health services are in areas such as education, insurance and technology, which are related to, but do not directly fall within, the hospital segment.

Another feature of fragmentation which comes up clearly in the case study of US legal services by Erica Moeser and Laurel Terry is that of separate jurisdictions within a single territory, with no overarching federal regulatory body. Because the practice of law is regulated by each of the fifty US states, the District of Columbia (Washington, DC) and US territories, formal permission is required on a jurisdiction-by-jurisdiction basis. While not a 'new service', the fragmented regulatory landscape they describe highlights the lack of inter-jurisdictional mobility as an issue not just for foreign but also for domestic lawyers. How such fragmentation can be accommodated in trade disciplines which assume the existence of a single regulatory framework for each territory is far from obvious. The authors of this case study do not see any likelihood of changing the constitutionally derived prerogatives of each state to regulate its legal profession. However, they suggest alternative ways to facilitate the mobility of lawyers, including through the transparency of requirements and procedures and the creation of a unified bar exam. While the case study is specific to the United States, the issues which are raised by separate jurisdictions are not uncommon in other countries.

These case studies show two problems of regulatory fragmentation. First, different regulators may be competent to regulate and to supervise one and the same service activity. This requires better cooperation and coordination across sectors, as well between jurisdictions in a 'federal–state' regulatory structure. Second, it may be difficult to classify a new service within a specific service sector. This problem of regulatory fragmentation has consequences for any disciplines on domestic regulation. Even if it would be agreed that sector-specific negotiations should be started to address the specific problems that occur in specific sectors, such negotiations cannot take place without regard to overlapping regulatory issues for other sectors.

2.4 *Recognition and the role of international standards*

When services are provided in different countries, with diverse regulatory regimes, this creates questions of equivalence of these regulatory regimes. Indeed, ensuring compliance with different regulatory regimes at the same time and obtaining the required authorizations in different countries constitutes a significant cost for service providers. However, national regulators may be hesitant to accept that another country's regulatory regime equally achieves the policy objectives they seek to achieve in their own national context.

Disciplines on domestic regulation could encourage recognition of equivalence of regulations. However, this would very likely require an agreement on some minimum standards that all countries involved consider essential for achieving their policy objectives. International standards, negotiated in appropriate multilateral or regional forums, may constitute an important basis for such mutual recognition.

Yet, as new forms of service provision are created, new international standards will be required. Joan Apecu, Irene Kaggwa Sewankambo and Yusuf Atiku Abdalla consider that, for mobile money services, no prior global or regional regulatory regime exists that regulators can refer to as a best practice. Hence, even if disciplines on domestic regulation encouraged recognition of equivalence, based on international standards, international or regional initiatives on developing minimum standards would need to be able to follow the developments in the services sectors quickly enough.

The case study on the Malaysian higher education system by Tham Siew Yean and Nik Kamal Nik Mahmod also illustrates the importance of recognition of equivalence and the development of international standards. Accreditation and recognition of equivalence would guarantee the quality of the higher education services provided. Based on Malaysia's experience of regulating private higher education, they conclude that additional international disciplines on domestic regulation can facilitate quality assurance, accreditation and recognition, and enhance transparency.

Further, Rupa Chanda and Pralok Gupta note that the lack of recognition of the quality standards of India's telemedicine services hampers trade in such services from India. They note that, in the absence of mutual recognition of qualifications, Indian teleradiologists cannot officially validate their readings. This affects the value of the contracts Indian health care providers can secure and also the scope of their work. Lack of mutual recognition of qualifications also has a bearing on the supply of health care personnel in India, as foreign-trained radiologists cannot practise in India.

Joel Trachtman has considered the question whether and how the WTO can address impediments created by domestic regulation through the harmonization of regulation or recognition of the equivalence of regulations. He considers that it is unlikely that the WTO will engage in harmonization – which is most often a precondition for recognition – but that it may rely on harmonized rules developed by functionally specialized international agencies, such as the Basel Committee or the International Accounting Standards Board. He also explains that any recognition arrangement should be open, rather than closed. This means that any WTO member should be permitted to demonstrate that its regulatory regime should also benefit from the recognition accorded.

He nevertheless warns that such combination of essential harmonization and recognition may exclude WTO members with limited regulatory capacity and limited possibilities for actively participating in the functionally specialized international agencies – in particular, developing countries. He therefore calls for technical assistance to enable developing countries to participate in, and qualify for, harmonization and recognition processes. Thanks to such technical assistance, a system of 'open recognition', whereby other WTO members would always be permitted to submit their own regulatory regimes for review to benefit from the recognition arrangement, would be sensitive to developing countries' particularities.

GATS Article VII:1 indeed already provides for the possibility of recognition of 'education or experience obtained, requirements met, or licenses or certifications granted in a particular country'. Article VII:2 specifies that WTO members party to a recognition agreement or arrangement 'shall afford adequate opportunity for other interested Members to negotiate their accession to such agreement or arrangement or to negotiate comparable ones with it'. GATS thus already expresses the importance of open recognition and stresses that a member shall not accord recognition 'in a manner which would constitute a means of discrimination between countries in the application of its standards or criteria for the authorization, licensing or certification of services suppliers, or a disguised restriction on trade in services' (GATS Article VII:3). Article VII:5 finally adds that '[w]herever appropriate, recognition should be based on multilaterally agreed criteria'. Hence, GATS already provides important tools facilitating recognition arrangements based on essential harmonization.

Also within the discussions of the Working Party on Domestic Regulation, some WTO members made the proposal to note explicitly the role which mutual recognition agreements can play in facilitating the process of verification of qualifications or in establishing equivalence of education. Raising awareness of the interplay between international standards and recognition is arguably an important element of the negotiations.

2.5 *Transparent, reasonable, objective and impartial rule-making and supervision*

Given the extensive domestic regulation that exists for services sectors, the risk may exist that, in designing regulations, policy-makers insufficiently take into account the interests of all stakeholders, including foreign service providers that want to provide services into a host country – or already do so. Regulations that are blind to these interests may hamper competition in the market. Moreover, supervision of compliance with the existing domestic regulations (for instance, in order to obtain the authorization to provide the service) may also insufficiently take into account the specificities and difficulties encountered by foreign service providers.

Andrew Mitchell and Tania Voon discuss how GATS Article VI:1 may provide a useful tool to guarantee due process in the administration of measures of general application. This provision could indeed be an important safeguard against administrative decisions and procedures that are not reasonable, objective nor impartial. However, given the vagueness of these concepts, it seems essential that a WTO member challenging administrative decisions provides the necessary evidence to establish a violation. Moreover, one may wonder whether a member would bring a challenge against an administrative decision where, for instance, a specific service provider is denied the authorization to provide a service. Rather, it seems more likely that such a challenge will be brought only when *several* such decisions exist that allegedly fail to be reasonable, objective or impartial.

It therefore would appear important to create procedures that contribute to ensuring a reasonable, objective and impartial outcome of decisions. In this respect, Masamichi Kono, Koichi Iwai and Yoshitaka Sakai describe how Japan created a regulatory system that requires the regulators to analyse and to evaluate the impact of policies, including an *ex ante* evaluation mechanism ('regulatory impact analysis'). Further, when policies are formulated, amended or repealed, administrative agencies are *required to seek opinions and expertise from the public*. In respect of the granting or refusal of authorizations to provide a financial service, Japan provides that the financial services authority is required to approve the registration of an applicant, *unless there are reasons for a refusal*. Such reasons are set out in laws and regulations and the specific reasons for the refusal of a specific application must be explained in a notice to the applicant. This provides a good example of mechanisms that seek to ensure that rule-making and supervision is transparent, reasonable, objective and impartial.

In addition, the case study on Malaysia's higher education discusses how the reasons for refusal of a 'permit to teach' are set out in law, and indicates that a possibility of appeal exists. However, the authors of the case study note that certain ground for refusal could benefit from further clarification. This illustrates how including into disciplines on domestic regulation a requirement to set out clearly conditions and reasons for refusal of authorization would greatly help to avoid decisions that lack reasonableness, objectivity or impartiality (or that at least give such impression).

A necessary complement to objective and impartial rule-making and supervision are clear, transparent and predictable regulations. While arguing for legal certainty, Markus Krajewski points out the necessary balance between transparency and flexibility. In his view, disciplines seeking to guarantee legal certainty should not impede regulatory flexibility. These concepts seem not in contradiction, as long as legal certainty and transparency are interpreted as the possibility for service suppliers to know, in an easily understandable language, what rules are or will be applicable to them. This general principle is, in our view, already enshrined in GATS, in particular in Article III, and can be further elaborated through the Article VI:4 mandate. Krajewski cautions against rules that could be interpreted to limit regulatory flexibility, in particular the pre-establishment condition in paragraph 11 of the Chair's March 2009 text.[1] It seems therefore desirable to make explicit that, once regulations are amended, applicants for licences would be permitted to adjust and be provided with necessary time to obtain the regulation. Making such nuances explicit in any eventual disciplines on domestic regulation seems desirable from the perspective of Krajewski.

In some ways, the case study on Australia's regulatory impact analysis, by Darrell Porter and Lauren Wight, provides a detailed example of procedural safeguards to ensure transparent, reasonable and objective rule-making can become part of the domestic regulatory process. These authors describe how, starting from the Organisation for Economic Co-operation and Development (OECD) guiding principles for Regulatory Quality and Performance, Australia has introduced a 'regulatory impact analysis' (RIA) scheme. They discuss the different steps through which regulation is formulated, including formulating the problem, setting objectives and options (including whether or not deviating from international standards), assessing costs, benefits and risks, consultation with interested stakeholders and specifically considering the trade and regulatory nexus. They immediately warn that the Australian 'best practice' may not be the most appropriate worldwide, given that many variations may need to be made to take account of national specificities.

[1] Paragraph 11 of the Chair's text reads: 'Measures relating to licensing requirements and procedures, qualification requirements and procedures, and technical standards shall be pre-established, based on objective and transparent criteria and relevant to the supply of the services to which they apply'. The Chair's March 2009 text is contained in *Disciplines on Domestic Regulation Pursuant to GATS Article VI:4: Chairman's Progress Report*, WTO doc. S/WPDR/W/45, 14 April 2011.

If horizontal disciplines on domestic regulation would see the light of day within the WTO, these could provide examples of good practices for developing regulation which takes trade concerns into account. However, given the WTO's wide and diverse membership, these good practices would have to be sufficiently attentive to developing countries' concerns and different legislative traditions.

2.6 Necessity

The creation of a so-called 'necessity-test' as part of the horizontal disciplines on domestic regulation has been a contentious issue in the negotiations. As noted by Panagiotis Delimatsis, 'necessity has been traditionally considered as the prevailing proxy for the identification and discipline of protectionist or unduly burdensome regulatory behaviour'. He argues that the mandate in Article VI:4, and in particular the envisaged discipline that qualification requirements and procedures, technical standards and licensing requirements must not be 'more burdensome than necessary', aims to facilitate drawing the line of equilibrium between the multilateral interest in progressive liberalization of trade in services and each WTO member's interest in preserving its regulatory autonomy. It is indeed this tension between each individual member's right to regulate, on the one hand, and the objective of realizing the benefits of liberalization of trade in services, on the other hand, that has made the negotiations on a 'necessity test' in the horizontal disciplines so difficult.

Nonetheless, the concern that measures pursuing perfectly legitimate policy objectives nevertheless impose a burden on foreign service suppliers to provide their services in a host country emerges inevitably in one form or another in discussions on regulation of services sectors.

The importance of balancing the objective of realizing the benefits of liberalization of trade in services with other public policy objectives indeed emerges from several case studies in this book. For example, Joan Apecu, Irene Kaggwa Sewankambo and Yusuf Atiku Abdalla stress that the continuing innovations and growth of mobile money services may contribute to the process of financial inclusion; the challenge is managing the growth of the sector in a manner that ensures orderliness without adverse and disruptive effects on the performance and stability of the financial system.

Also Masamichi Kono, Koichi Iwai and Yoshitaka Sakai note that 'promot[ing] competition through liberalization measures could increase bankruptcy risk for individual financial institutions' and that the Japanese authorities aim not only to promote liberalization measures but also to strengthen investor protection as they promoted financial system reforms. In this respect, they stress that regulators should ensure that the applicable standards do not distort competition by making them excessively burdensome or using them as *de facto* barriers to market access.

Siva Somasundram and Iain Sandford make the point that, in the postal services sector, measures reserving the provision of services subject to a universal service obligation should not go further than is necessary to ensure the provision of the universal service. They note that there 'is a clear risk of regulatory failure in relation to access regulation which can not only be burdensome on [universal service obligation]-constrained operators, but, at worst, can kill incentives to invest in network infrastructure'.

A concrete concern about burdensome regulations that pursue perfectly legitimate policy objectives is expressed by Ruosi Zhang, who considers that 'excessive documentation requirements significantly affect the efficiency of logistics services and, at the same time, increase logistics cost'. The degree to which a requirement is excessive would likely need to be examined in light of the objective that is pursued by the documentary requirement.

In dispute settlement cases relating to GATS, panels and the Appellate Body may be pressured by litigants to develop some balancing test to respond to the tension between the objective to pursue legitimate non-trade policy objectives and the objective of trade liberalization. Panagiotis Delimatsis even goes as far as suggesting that the failure to incorporate a necessity test in the disciplines developed on the basis of GATS Article VI:4 would 'go against the letter and spirit of Members' legal mandate'. Be this as it may, it is quite likely that, when service suppliers are faced with burdens created through regulation that are not of the type tackled through the market access and national treatment obligations in, respectively, GATS Articles XVI and XVII, potential litigants will explore the language in future disciplines to challenge such measures.

Many proposals have been made in the course of the negotiations on domestic regulation.[2] Each of the proposals met with opposition from

[2] In particular, see the overview of proposals in Annex I to *Negotiations on Trade in Services: Report by the Chairman, Ambassador Fernando de Mateo, to the Trade Negotiations Committee*, WTO doc. TN/S/36, 21 April 2011.

several WTO members, for diverse reasons. Nevertheless, as Panagiotis Delimatsis points out, members may want to take the current opportunity to design such a test themselves, rather than allow WTO jurisprudence to design such a test in the context of a concrete dispute. We also note that in the absence of disciplines under GATS Article VI:4, the provisions of Article VI:5 apply. This provision already includes the criteria that requirements should be 'not more burdensome than necessary to ensure the quality of the service'. However, it does not provide any further guidance on how to evaluate the 'burdensomeness' of the requirements. Through negotiations, members could deal with this ambiguity by specifying explicitly the criteria for and limits of such a necessity test.

3 Conclusion: reflections on the way ahead

3.1 Revisiting the scope of GATS VI:4

How best to strengthen trade disciplines in services without unduly curtailing national regulatory freedoms has been a central question which has not been fully resolved in the domestic regulation negotiations. The GATS framework has focused primarily on the negotiation of market-opening commitments, leaving other aspects of domestic regulation and practice largely untouched. Yet, since the establishment of the WTO in 1995, WTO members have grappled with the question of what additional disciplines are required on licensing, qualification and technical standards to ensure that they are not more burdensome than necessary to achieve legitimate policy objectives. The case studies in this book have illustrated the pervasiveness of regulations in services sectors. They have also shown that, in many situations, regulatory objectives are pursued through the use of instruments which essentially seek to promote transparency, impartiality, certainty and necessity of regulatory intervention. These values are also found and promoted in trade agreements.

Despite these synergies, why has it been so difficult to conclude domestic regulation disciplines? One reason often given is that in seeking to develop 'horizontal' disciplines, which would apply to all services sectors without exception, the negotiations have been too ambitious. WTO members in favour of such an approach have argued that a single set of disciplines would be the most efficient way to address trade concerns since the rationale for regulation is similar across sectors. Other members have, on the other hand, highlighted that sector-specific disciplines could potentially be a more practical route to pursue, as the disciplines could be shaped in accordance with the particularities of that sector.

A deeper consideration of this issue would tend to suggest that discussions on 'horizontal' versus 'sectoral' approaches hide a more fundamental tension, namely, the principal concern that trade disciplines on domestic regulation might result in a loss of regulatory freedom to pursue non-trade objectives. However, this is an issue which exists not only in services trade, but also in goods trade. Nonetheless, WTO members were able to agree to technical barriers to trade (TBT) and sanitary and phytosanitary (SPS) disciplines to ensure that technical regulations, standards and procedures on goods do not create unnecessary obstacles to international trade, as well as ensuring that import licensing procedures are no more burdensome than necessary to administer the relevant measure. Thus, while we see the choice of negotiating approach to be fundamentally important, it is not sufficient to explain why progress on a broadly similar set of issues in services trade has been much harder to achieve.

The crux of the problem is that services trade, which involves four modes of supply, is much broader in scope than goods trade. Thus, unlike traditional trade in goods agreements, services trade agreements are primarily concerned with how an economy is regulated. Such regulation may be of a general nature, in the sense that it affects all economic activity, or it may be specific to a particular sector, type of transaction or even geographical area. What matters in services trade is often the overall level of contestability of the market, and not just its openness to participation by foreign service suppliers. Thus, at first sight, disciplines on domestic regulation may be perceived to extend quite far beyond the traditional trade concern of non-discrimination to the fundamental societal question of the balance between regulation and market freedom.

A closer reading of the Article VI:4 mandate and the subsequent Decision on Domestic Regulation would, however, reveal that the intent of WTO members was much more modest. The scope of Article VI:4 does not cover all domestic regulation but only measures relating to licensing and qualification requirements and procedures, and technical standards. It does not suggest that the underlying policy objectives for which such requirements and standards have been established are to be disciplined, but that when these are used they should be based on objective and transparent criteria, and not more burdensome than necessary to ensure the quality of the service.

3.2 *Unresolved question of a 'necessity test'*

Yet, in practice, the negotiations have stumbled on what would be the appropriate benchmark upon which these criteria should be evaluated. Focusing on the heavily contested issue of the desirability and feasibility of a 'necessity test', it is worth recalling that the WTO 1998 Disciplines on Domestic Regulation in the Accountancy Sector ('Accountancy Disciplines') already contain a 'necessity test', similar to that in the TBT and SPS Agreements, which requires WTO members to ensure that 'measures are not more trade restrictive than necessary to achieve a legitimate objective'. The test provides an illustrative list of objectives. Such a test was designed to leave the choice of objectives to members, with the focus of the discipline on the necessity of the *measure* used to achieve its avowed purpose, rather than on the necessity of the *objective pursued.* However, it should be kept in mind that unlike in the case of TBT and SPS measures, there is no tangible 'product' in services which can be sampled, tested and inspected based on scientific methods. Thus, reaching agreement on what would be the appropriate criteria for determining and evaluating necessity could be inherently more difficult.

Should a 'necessity test' of the type already found in the TBT or SPS Agreements, or a variation of it, be used in domestic regulation disciplines? The negotiations, so far, have found no common view on this issue. Yet, a recurring principle in trade agreements is the requirement that the measure used to achieve a certain legitimate objective should be the 'least/less trade restrictive option reasonably available'. Uncertainty remains among certain regulators as to whether their autonomy to regulate would be excessively restricted by a necessity test. On the other hand, proponents of the principle of necessity have argued that a test can be designed that does not question the necessity of the policy objectives chosen, but solely the necessity of the measure used. Many questions have arisen in the negotiations. These relate, for example, to the factors to be considered in determining what is 'necessary' and what is not, and whether the implementation of a necessity test should also require consideration of whether the policy objective is legitimate or not.

3.3 *Negotiations may want to consider how disciplines will be integrated into GATS*

The challenge of developing domestic regulation disciplines cannot be reduced only to the question of the 'necessity test'. There is also the question of whether other approaches should be considered to increase the willingness to establish disciplines on domestic regulation. In the negotiations on domestic regulation disciplines, there has been little discussion on how any eventual results might be captured. While this might seem to be an issue that is best left till the end of the negotiations, clarity on the options available could well have an impact on the substance of the disciplines and the willingness to proceed with negotiations. Although not formally agreed upon, there is an unspoken working assumption that any eventual disciplines would be integrated into GATS as an Annex. Such an approach would have the advantage of uniform application of the disciplines across the entire WTO membership. However, it also has the disadvantage of being relatively inflexible as the obligations would have to be taken at the same level of ambition without exception. Any flexibility would have to be inscribed into the obligation itself, which runs the risk of members negotiating towards the lowest common denominator. An Annex would also require an amendment to GATS, following the procedure of Article X:5 of the Agreement Establishing the World Trade Organization. This procedure and the eventual entry into force, in light of recent experience with other agreements, could take a very long time.

Another option, which has been somewhat under-explored, is to use GATS Article XVIII, which allows WTO members to schedule additional commitments on any regulatory matter that concerns measures not covered by market access and national treatment. The procedure depends solely on the acceptance by each individual member to incorporate the disciplines into its schedule. Such acceptance can be done unilaterally, in which case it is not dependent upon actions by other members, or as a collective act by means of a Protocol. Since members decide individually to undertake additional commitments, there is considerable flexibility both in terms of application across the membership, as well as the obligations undertaken. An obvious example of a successful implementation of such an approach was the Reference Paper on regulatory principles for basic telecommunications. This was developed by a group of members as a full set of principles that would be committed to on an individual basis. On the other hand, the flexibility of the additional commitments route could also be viewed as a disadvantage, as it would provide less certainty as to whether the disciplines would be fully applied by all members, as compared to the adoption of an Annex.

It is beyond the scope of this book to prescribe one approach over another, but it seems that after some fifteen years of negotiations, there is merit in reconsidering how existing instruments in the GATS toolkit, which already allow for differentiated obligations, might be more effectively used to overcome fundamental stumbling blocks on the ambition and scope of domestic regulation disciplines. The case studies have also revealed that there might be merit in considering instruments and approaches that allow for greater flexibility to deal specifically with the key trade concern in a sector, or to cater for differences in regulatory traditions.

Whilst WTO members have yet to conclude their negotiations on horizontal disciplines applicable to all services sectors, it is important not to lose sight that there are two other elements under the domestic regulation mandate, namely, the consideration of sector-specific disciplines and continued work on professional services. Experience with horizontal disciplines has highlighted the tendency to negotiate towards the lowest common denominator so as to accommodate the particularities and sensitivities of each sector. This begs the question of whether concerns in respect of regulatory autonomy might after all be more efficiently handled at the sectoral level, where solutions can be addressed without spillover effects to other sectors.

The two instances where WTO members were able to conclude regulatory disciplines have been with regard to specific sectors, the Accountancy Disciplines, and outside the context of GATS Article VI:4, the Reference Paper on telecommunications. Could such a model of variable geometry, which uses the additional commitments provision of GATS, provide a sound avenue to pursue domestic regulation disciplines?

3.4 Initiatives outside the WTO may facilitate WTO negotiations on disciplines on domestic regulation

Apart from what can be negotiated in the WTO, there is the question of what more can be done elsewhere to improve cooperation and awareness among regulators, policy-makers and trade negotiators of the links between regulatory issues and trade principles. There are also problems of capacity which have made it difficult for negotiators to engage on issues that are not within the traditional realm of trade policy. Regulatory capacity-building, in terms of the ability of authorities to formulate and enforce rules appropriate to services trade opening, may not be a new challenge, but it is certainly one which has yet to be addressed in a systematic and meaningful way by the multilateral trade community.

There also remains the challenge of advancing harmonization and mutual recognition. An obvious link exists between multilateral rules on domestic regulation and efforts to harmonize and recognize standards, qualifications, requirements and procedures. The need for disciplines to curb unnecessarily burdensome domestic regulation would clearly be diminished if jurisdictions were to move towards common regulatory practices or develop more arrangements for mutual recognition. These considerations raise the question whether international standards could be used to a greater extent in services. Common international standards would need to be set at a level and in a manner that does not favour those with the greatest capacity to influence the process and outcomes. For the most part, this work would have to be undertaken outside the WTO, which is not a forum for setting standards.

Finally, capacity-building is a vital element, given the defining role of regulation in services sectors, and could do much to facilitate further market opening. There is a need to strengthen the ability of regulators to identify, design and implement policies that address market failures, undertake regulatory impact assessments and share knowledge on good practices. While not directly addressed in this book, initiatives such as 'Aid for Trade' could make a substantial contribution to assisting regulators to meet the challenge of regulatory reforms. So far, this has been an under-utilized resource. There are currently very few initiatives that are aimed at specifically addressing capacity constraints in the development of services-related regulatory and institutional frameworks. Similarly, there is relatively little on how service suppliers in developing countries can be facilitated to meet requirements and procedures in export markets. Finding ways to support regulatory capacity-building and cooperation so as to complement services policy reform and minimize the effects of regulatory diversity across jurisdictions could do much to foster trade and development. This could in turn help raise confidence and capacity to negotiate domestic regulation disciplines.

INDEX